Saint Gregory of Nazianzus

Selected Works

Printed in the United States of America

ISBN:9781631740817

Table of Contents:

On Easter and His Reluctance

I. It is the Day of the Resurrection, and my Beginning has good auspices. Let us then keep the Festival with splendor, and let us embrace one another. Let us say Brethren, even to those who hate us; much more to those who have done or suffered aught out of love for us. Let us forgive all offenses for the Resurrection's sake: let us give one another pardon, I for the noble tyranny, which I have suffered (for I can now call it noble); and you who exercised it, if you had cause to blame my tardiness; for perhaps this tardiness may be more precious in God's sight than the haste of others. For it is a good thing even to hold back from God for a little while, as did the great Moses of old, and Jeremiah later on; and then to run readily to Him when He calls, as did Aaron and Isaiah, so only both be done in a dutiful spirit; — the former because of his own want of strength; the latter because of the Might of Him That calleth.

II. A Mystery anointed me; I withdrew a little while at a Mystery, as much as was needful to examine myself; now I come in with a Mystery, bringing with me the Day as a good defender of my cowardice and weakness; that He Who today rose again from the dead may renew me also by His Spirit; and, clothing me with the new Man, may give me to His New Creation, to those who are begotten after God, as a good modeller and teacher for Christ, willingly both dying with Him and rising again with Him.

III. Yesterday the Lamb was slain and the door-posts were anointed, and Egypt bewailed her Firstborn, and the Destroyer passed us over, and the Seal was dreadful and reverend, and we were walled in with the Precious Blood. To-day we have clean escaped from Egypt and from Pharaoh; and there is none to hinder us from keeping a Feast to the Lord our God — the Feast of our Departure; or from celebrating that Feast, not in the old leaven of malice and wickedness, but in the unleavened bread of sincerity and truth, carrying with us nothing of ungodly and Egyptian leaven.

IV. Yesterday I was crucified with Him; today I am glorified with Him; yesterday I died with Him; today I am quickened with Him; yesterday I was buried with Him; today I rise with Him. But let us offer to Him Who suffered and rose again for us — you will think perhaps that I am going to say gold, or silver, or woven work or transparent and costly stones, the mere passing material of earth, that remains here below, and is for the most part always possessed by bad men, slaves of the world and of the Prince of the world. Let us offer ourselves, the possession most precious to God, and most fitting; let us give back to the Image what is made after the Image. Let us recognize our Dignity; let us honor our Archetype; let us know the power of the Mystery, and for what Christ died.

V. Let us become like Christ, since Christ became like us. Let us become God's for His sake, since He for ours became Man. He assumed the worse that He might give us the better; He became poor that we through His poverty might be rich; He took upon Him the form of a servant that we might receive back our liberty; He came down that we might be exalted; He was tempted that we might conquer; He was dishonored that He might glorify us; He died that He might save us; He ascended that He might draw to Himself us, who were lying low in the Fall of sin. Let us give all, offer all, to Him Who gave Himself a Ransom and a Reconciliation for us. But one can give nothing like oneself, understanding the Mystery, and becoming for His sake all that He became for ours.

VI. As you see, He offers you a Shepherd; for this is what your Good Shepherd, who lays down his life for his sheep, is hoping and praying for, and he asks from you his subjects; and he gives you himself double instead of single, and makes the staff of his old age a staff for your spirit. And he adds to the inanimate temple a living one; to that exceedingly beautiful and heavenly shrine, this poor and small one, yet to him of great value, and built too with much sweat and many labors. Would that I could say it is worthy of his labors. And he places at your disposal all that belongs to him (O great generosity! — or it would be truer to say, O fatherly love!) his hoar hairs, his youth, the temple, the high priest, the testator, the heir, the discourses which you were longing for; and of these not such as are vain and poured out into the air, and which reach no further than the outward ear; but those which the Spirit writes and engraves on tables of stone, or of flesh, not merely superficially graven, nor easily to be rubbed off, but marked very deep, not with ink, but with grace.

VII. These are the gifts given you by this august Abraham, this honorable and reverend Head, this Patriarch, this Restingplace of all good, this Standard of virtue, this Perfection of the Priesthood, who today is bringing to the Lord his willing Sacrifice, his only Son, him of the promise. Do you on your side offer to God and to us obedience to your Pastors, dwelling in a place of herbage, and being fed by water of refreshment; knowing your Shepherd well, and being known by him; and following when he calls you as a Shepherd frankly through the door; but not following a stranger climbing up into the fold like a robber and a traitor; nor listening to a strange voice when such would take you away by stealth and scatter you from the truth on mountains, and in deserts, and pitfalls, and places which the Lord does not visit; and would lead you away from the sound Faith in the Father, the Son, and the Holy Ghost, the One Power and Godhead, Whose Voice my sheep always heard (and may they always hear it), but with deceitful and corrupt words would tear them from their true Shepherd. From which may we all be kept, Shepherd and flock, as from a poisoned and deadly pasture; guiding and being guided far away from it, that we may all be one in Christ Jesus our Lord, now and unto the heavenly rest. To Whom be the glory and the might for ever and ever. Amen.

2

In defense of his flight to Pontos, and his return, after his ordination to the Priesthood, with an exposition of the character of the priestly office.

1. I have been defeated, and own my defeat. I subjected myself to the Lord, and prayed unto Him. Let the most blessed David supply my exordium, or rather let Him Who spoke in David, and even now yet speaks through him. For indeed the very best order of beginning every speech and action, is to begin from God, and to end in God. As to the cause, either of my original revolt and cowardice, in which I got me away far off, and remained away from you for a time, which perhaps seemed long to those who missed me; or of the present gentleness and change of mind, in which I have given myself up again to you, men may think and speak in different ways, according to the hatred or love they bear me, on the one side refusing to acquit me of the charges alleged, on the other giving me a hearty welcome. For nothing is so pleasant to men as talking of other people's business, especially under the influence of affection or hatred, which often almost entirely blinds us to the truth. I will, however, myself, unabashed, set forth the truth, and arbitrate with justice between the two parties, which accuse or gallantly defend us, by, on the one side, accusing myself, on the other, undertaking my own defense.

2. Accordingly, that my speech may proceed in due order, I apply myself to the question which arose first, that of cowardice. For I cannot endure that any of those who watch with interest the success, or the contrary, of my efforts, should be put to confusion on my account, since it has pleased God that our affairs should be of some consequence to Christians, so I will by my defense relieve, if there be any such, those who have already suffered; for it is well, as far us possible, and as reason allows, to shrink from causing, through our sin or suspicion, any offense or stumbling-block to the community: inasmuch as we know how inevitably even those who offend one of the little ones will incur the severest punishment at the hands of Him who cannot lie.

3. For my present position is due, my good people, not to inexperience and ignorance, nay indeed, that I may boast myself a little, neither is it due to contempt for the divine laws and ordinances. Now, just as in the body there is one member which rules and, so to say, presides, while another is ruled over and subject; so too in the churches, God has ordained, according either to a law of equality, which admits of an order of merit, or to one of providence, by which He has knit all together, that those for whom such treatment is beneficial, should be subject to pastoral care and rule, and be guided by word and deed in the path of duty; while others should be pastors and teachers, for the perfecting of the church, those, I mean, who surpass the majority in virtue and nearness to God, performing the functions of the soul in the body, and of the intellect in the soul; in order that both may be so united and compacted together, that, although one is lacking and another is pre-eminent, they may, like the members of our bodies, be so combined

3

and knit together by the harmony of the Spirit, as to form one perfect body, really worthy of Christ Himself, our Head.

4. I am aware then that anarchy and disorder cannot be more advantageous than order and rule, either to other creatures or to men; nay, this is true of men in the highest possible degree, because the interests at stake in their case are greater; since it is a great thing for them, even if they fail of their highest purpose — to be free from sin — to attain at least to that which is second best, restoration from sin. Since this seems right and just, it is, I take it, equally wrong and disorderly that all should wish to rule, and that no one should accept it. For if all men were to shirk this office, whether it must be called a ministry or a leadership, the fair fullness of the Church would be halting in the highest degree, and in fact cease to be fair. And further, where, and by whom would God be worshipped among us in those mystic and elevating rites which are our greatest and most precious privilege, if there were neither king, nor governor, nor priesthood, nor sacrifice, nor all those highest offices to the loss of which, for their great sins, men were of old condemned in consequence of their disobedience?

5. Nor indeed is it strange or inconsistent for the majority of those who are devoted to the study of divine things, to ascend to rule from being ruled, nor does it overstep the limits laid down by philosophy, or involve disgrace; any more than for an excellent sailor to become a lookout-man, and for a lookout-man, who has successfully kept watch over the winds, to be entrusted with the helm; or, if you will, for a brave soldier to be made a captain, and a good captain to become a general, and have committed to him the conduct of the whole campaign. Nor again, as perhaps some of those absurd and tiresome people may suppose, who judge of others' feelings by their own, was I ashamed of the rank of this grade from my desire for a higher. I was not so ignorant either of its divine greatness or human low estate, as to think it no great thing for a created nature, to approach in however slight degree to God, Who alone is most glorious and illustrious, and surpasses in purity every nature, material and immaterial alike.

6. What then were my feelings, and what was the reason of my disobedience? For to most men I did not at the time seem consistent with myself, or to be such as they had known me, but to have undergone some deterioration, and to exhibit greater resistance and self-will than was right. And the causes of this you have long been desirous to hear. First, and most important, I was astounded at the unexpectedness of what had occurred, as people are terrified by sudden noises; and, losing the control of my reasoning faculties, my self-respect, which had hitherto controlled me, gave way. In the next place, there came over me an eager longing for the blessings of calm and retirement, of which I had from the first been enamored to a higher degree, I imagine, than any other student of letters, and which amidst the greatest and most threatening dangers I had promised to God, and of which I had also had so much experience, that I was then upon its threshold, my longing having

4

in consequence been greatly kindled, so that I could not submit to be thrust into the midst of a life of turmoil by an arbitrary act of oppression, and to be torn away by force from the holy sanctuary of such a life as this.

7. For nothing seemed to me so desirable as to close the doors of my senses, and, escaping from the flesh and the world, collected within myself, having no further connection than was absolutely necessary with human affairs, and speaking to myself and to God to live superior to visible things, ever preserving in myself the divine impressions pure and unmixed with the erring tokens of this lower world, and both being, and constantly growing more and more to be, a real unspotted mirror of God and divine things, as light is added to light, and what was still dark grew clearer, enjoying already by hope the blessings of the world to come, roaming about with the angels, even now being above the earth by having forsaken it, and stationed on high by the Spirit. If any of you has been possessed by this longing, he knows what I mean and will sympathize with my feelings at that time. For, perhaps, I ought not to expect to persuade most people by what I say, since they are unhappily disposed to laugh at such things, either from their own thoughtlessness, or from the influence of men unworthy of the promise, who have bestowed upon that which is good an evil name, calling philosophy nonsense, aided by envy and the evil tendencies of the mob, who are ever inclined to grow worse: so that they are constantly occupied with one of two sins, either the commission of evil, or the discrediting of good.

8. I was influenced besides by another feeling, whether base or noble I do not know, but I will speak out to you all my secrets. I was ashamed of all those others, who, without being better than ordinary people, nay, it is a great thing if they be not worse, with unwashen hands, as the saying rims, and uninitiated souls, intrude into the most sacred offices; and, before becoming worthy to approach the temples, they lay claim to the sanctuary, and they push and thrust around the holy table, as if they thought this order to be a means of livelihood, instead of a pattern of virtue, or an absolute authority, instead of a ministry of which we must give account. In fact they are almost more in number than those whom they govern; pitiable as regards piety, and unfortunate in their dignity; so that, it seems to me, they will not, as time and this evil alike progress, have any one left to rule, when all are teachers, instead of, as the promise says, taught of God, and all prophesy, so that even "Saul is among the prophets," according to the ancient history and proverb. For at no time, either now or in former days, amid the rise and fall of various developments, has there ever been such an abundance, as now exists among Christians, of disgrace and abuses of this kind. And, if to stay this current is beyond our powers, at any rate it is not the least important duty of religion to testify the hatred and shame we feel for it.

9. Lastly, there is a matter more serious than any which I have mentioned, for I am now coming to the finale of the question: and I will not deceive you; for that would

not be lawful in regard to topics of such moment. I did not, nor do I now, think myself qualified to rule a flock or herd, or to have authority over the souls of men. For in their case it is sufficient to render the herd or flock as stout and fat as possible; and with this object the neatherd and shepherd will look for well watered and rich pastures, and will drive his charge from pasture to pasture, and allow them to rest, or arouse, or recall them, sometimes with his staff, most often with his pipe; and with the exception of occasional struggles with wolves, or attention to the sickly, most of his time will be devoted to the oak and the shade and his pipes, while he reclines on the beautiful grass, and beside the cool water, and shakes down his couch in a breezy spot, and ever and anon sings a love ditty, with his cup by his side, and talks to his bullocks or his flock, the fattest of which supply his banquets or his pay. But no one ever has thought of the virtue of flocks or herds; for indeed of what virtue are they capable? Or who has regarded their advantage as more important than his own pleasure?

10. But in the case of man, hard as it is for him to learn how to submit to rule, it seems far harder to know how to rule over men, and hardest of all, with this rifle of ours, which leads them by the divine law, and to God, for its risk is, in the eyes of a thoughtful man, proportionate to its height and dignity. For, first of all, he must, like silver or gold, though in general circulation in all kinds of seasons and affairs, never ring false or alloyed, or give token of any inferior matter, needing further refinement in the fire; or else, the wider his rule, the greater evil he will be. Since the injury which extends to many is greater than that which is confined to a single individual.

11. For it is not so easy to dye deeply a piece of cloth, or to impregnate with odors, foul or the reverse, whatever comes near to them; nor is it so easy for the fatal vapor, which is rightly called a pestilence, to infect the air, and through the air to gain access to living being, as it is for the vice of a superior to take most speedy possession of his subjects, and that with far greater facility than virtue its opposite. For it is in this that wickedness especially has the advantage over goodness, and most distressing it is to me to perceive it, that vice is something attractive and ready at hand, and that nothing is so easy as to become evil, even without any one to lead us on to it; while the attainment of virtue is rare and difficult, even where there is much to attract and encourage us. And it is this, I think, which the most blessed Haggai had before his eyes, in his wonderful and most true figure: — "Ask the priests concerning the law, saying: If holy flesh borne in a garment touch meat or drink or vessel, will it sanctify what is in contact with it? And when they said No; ask again if any of these things touch what is unclean, does it not at once partake of the pollution? For they will surely tell you that it does partake of it, and does not continue clean in spite of the contact."

12. What does he mean by this? As I take it, that goodness can with difficulty gain a hold upon human nature, like fire upon green wood; while most men are ready and

disposed to join in evil, like stubble, I mean, ready for a spark and a wind, which is easily kindled and consumed from its dryness. For more quickly would any one take part in evil with slight inducement to its full extent, than in good which is fully set before him to a slight degree. For indeed a little wormwood most quickly imparts its bitterness to honey; while not even double the quantity of honey can impart its sweetness to wormwood: and the withdrawal of a small pebble would draw headlong a whole river, though it would be difficult for the strongest dam to restrain or stay its course.

13. This then is the first point in what we have said, which it is right for us to guard against, viz.: being found to be bad painters of the charms of virtue, and still more, if not, perhaps, models for poor painters, poor models for the people, or barely escaping the proverb, that we undertake to heal others while ourselves are full of sores.

14. In the second place, although a man has kept himself pure from sin, even in a very high degree; I do not know that even this is sufficient for one who is to instruct others in virtue. For he who has received this charge, not only needs to be free from evil, for evil is, in the eyes of most of those under his care, most disgraceful, but also to be eminent in good, according to the command, "Depart from evil and do good." And he must not only wipe out the traces of vice from his soul, but also inscribe better ones, so as to outstrip men further in virtue than he is superior to them in dignity. He should know no limits in goodness or spiritual progress, and should dwell upon the loss of what is still beyond him, rather than the gain of what he has attained, and consider that which is beneath his feet a step to that which comes next: and not think it a great gain to excel ordinary people, but a loss to fall short of what we ought to be: and to measure his success by the commandment and not by his neighbors, whether they be evil, or to some extent proficient in virtue: and to weigh virtue in no small scales, inasmuch as it is due to the Most High, "from Whom are all things, and to Whom are all things."

15. Nor must he suppose that the same things are suitable to all, just as all have not the same stature, nor are the features of the face, nor the nature of animals, nor the qualities of soil, nor the beauty and size of the stars, in all cases the same: but he must consider base conduct a fault in a private individual, and deserving of chastisement under the hard rule of the law; while in the case of a ruler or leader it is a fault not to attain to the highest possible excellence, and always make progress in goodness, if indeed he is, by his high degree of virtue, to draw his people to an ordinary degree, not by the force of authority, but by the influence of persuasion. For what is involuntary apart from its being the result of oppression, is neither meritorious nor durable. For what is forced, like a plant violently drawn aside by our hands, when set free, returns to what it was before, but that which is the result of choice is both most legitimate and enduring, for it is preserved by the bond of

good will. And so our law and our lawgiver enjoin upon us most strictly that we should "tend the flock not by constraint but willingly."

16. But granted that a man is free from vice, and has reached the greatest heights of virtue: I do not see what knowledge or power would justify him in venturing upon this office. For the guiding of man, the most variable and manifold of creatures, seems to me in very deed to be the art of arts and science of sciences. Any one may recognize this, by comparing the work of the physician of souls with the treatment of the body; and noticing that, laborious as the latter is, ours is more laborious, and of more consequence, from the nature of its subject matter, the power of its science, and the object of its exercise. The one labors about bodies, and perishable failing matter, which absolutely must be dissolved and undergo its fate, even if upon this occasion by the aid of art it can surmount the disturbance within itself, being dissolved by disease or time in submission to the law of nature, since it cannot rise above its own limitations.

17. The other is concerned with the soul, which comes from God and is divine, and partakes of the heavenly nobility, and presses on to it, even if it be bound to an inferior nature. Perhaps indeed there are other reasons also for this, which only God, Who bound them together, and those who are instructed by God in such mysteries, can know, but as far as I, and men like myself can perceive, there are two: one, that it may inherit the glory above by means of a struggle and wrestling with things below, being tried as gold in the fire by things here, and gain the objects of our hope as a prize of virtue, and not merely as the gift of God. This, indeed, was the will of Supreme Goodness, to make the good even our own, not only because sown in our nature, but because cultivated by our own choice, and by the motions of our will, free to act in either direction. The second reason is, that it may draw to itself and raise to heaven the lower nature, by gradually freeing it from its grossness, in order that the soul may be to the body what God is to the soul, itself leading on the matter which ministers to it, and uniting it, as its fellow-servant, to God.

18. Place and time and age and season and the like are the subjects of a physician's scrutiny; he will prescribe medicines and diet, and guard against things injurious, that the desires of the sick may not be a hindrance to his art. Sometimes, and in certain cases, he will make use of the cautery or the knife or the severer remedies; but none of these, laborious and hard as they may seem, is so difficult as the diagnosis and cure of our habits, passions, lives, wills, and whatever else is within us, by banishing from our compound nature everything brutal and fierce, and introducing and establishing in their stead what is gentle and dear to God, and arbitrating fairly between soul and body; not allowing the superior to be overpowered by the inferior, which would be the greatest injustice; but subjecting to the ruling and leading power that which naturally takes the second place: as indeed the divine law enjoins, which is most excellently imposed on His whole creation, whether visible or beyond our ken.

8

19. This further point does not escape me, that the nature of all these objects of the watch-fullness of the physician remains the same, and does not evolve out of itself any crafty opposition, or contrivance hostile to the appliances of his art, nay, it is rather the treatment which modifies its subject matter, except where some slight insubordination occurs on the part of the patient, which it is not difficult to prevent or restrain. But in our case, human prudence and selfishness, and the want of training and inclination to yield ready submission are a very great obstacle to advance in virtue, amounting almost to an armed resistance to those who are wishful to help us. And the very eagerness with which we should lay bare our sickness to oar spiritual physicians, we employ in avoiding this treatment, and shew our bravery by struggling against what is for our own interest, our skill in shunning what is for our health.

20. For we either hide away our sin, cloaking it over in the depth of our soul, like some festering and malignant disease, as if by escaping the notice of men we could escape the mighty eye of God and justice. Or else we allege excuses in our sins, by devising pleas in defense of our falls, or tightly closing our ears, like the deaf adder that stoppeth her ears, we are obstinate in refusing to hear the voice of the charmer, and be treated with the medicines of wisdom? by which spiritual sickness is healed. Or, lastly, those of us who are most daring and self-willed shamelessly brazen out our sin before those who would heal it, marching with bared head, as the saying is, into all kinds of transgression. O what madness, if there be no term more fitting for this state of mind! Those whom we ought to love as our benefactors we keep off, as if they were our enemies, hating those who reprove in the gates, and abhorring the righteous word; and we think that we shall succeed in the war that we are waging against those who are well disposed to us by doing ourselves all the harm we can, like men who imagine they are consuming the flesh of others when they are really fastening upon their own.

21. For these reasons I allege that our office as physicians far exceeds in toilsomeness, and consequently in worth, that which is confined to the body; and further, because the latter is mainly concerned with the surface, and only in a slight degree investigates the causes which are deeply hidden. But the whole of our treatment and exertion is concerned with the hidden man of the heart, and our warfare is directed against that adversary and foe within us, who uses ourselves as his weapons against ourselves, and, most fearful of all, hands us over to the death of sin. In opposition then, to these foes we are in need of great and perfect faith, and of still greater co-operation on the part of God, and, as I am persuaded, of no slight countermaneuvring on our own part, which mast manifest itself both in word and deed, if ourselves, the most precious possession we have, are to be duly tended and cleansed and made as deserving as possible.

22. To turn however to the ends in view in each of these forms of healing, for this point is still left to be considered, the one preserves, if it already exists, the health

and good habit of the flesh, or if absent, recalls it; though it is not yet clear whether or not these will be for the advantage of those who possess them, since their opposites very often confer a greater benefit on those who have them, just as poverty and wealth, renown or disgrace, a low or brilliant position, and all other circumstances, which are naturally indifferent, and do not incline in one direction more than in another, produce a good or bad effect according to the will of, and the manner in which they are used by the persons who experience them. But the scope of our art is to provide the soul with wings, to rescue it from the world and give it to God, and to watch over that which is in His image, if it abides, to take it by the hand, if it is in danger, or restore it, if ruined, to make Christ to dwell in the heart by the Spirit: and, in short, to deify, and bestow heavenly bliss upon, one who belongs to the heavenly host.

23. This is the wish of our schoolmaster the law, of the prophets who intervened between Christ and the law, of Christ who is the fulfiller and end of the spiritual law; of the emptied Godhead, of the assumed flesh, of the novel union between God and man, one consisting of two, and both in one. This is why God was united to the flesh by means of the soul, and natures so separate were knit together by the affinity to each of the element which mediated between them: so all became one for the sake of all, and for the sake of one, our progenitor, the soul because of the soul which was disobedient, the flesh because of the flesh which co-operated with it and shared in its condemnation, Christ, Who was superior to, and beyond the reach of, sin, because of Adam, who became subject to sin.

24. This is why the new was substituted for the old, why He Who suffered was for suffering recalled to life, why each property of His, Who was above us, was interchanged with each of ours, why the new mystery took place of the dispensation, due to loving kindness which deals with him who fell through disobedience. This is the reason for the generation and the virgin, for the manger and Bethlehem; the generation on behalf of the creation, the virgin on behalf of the woman, Bethlehem because of Eden, the manger because of the garden, small and visible things on behalf of great and hidden things. This is why the angels glorified first the heavenly, then the earthly, why the shepherds saw the glory over the Lamb and the Shepherd, why the star led the Magi to worship and offer gifts, in order that idolatry might be destroyed. This is why Jesus was baptized, and received testimony from above, and fasted, and was tempted, and overcame him who had overcome. This is why devils were cast out, and diseases healed, and the mighty preaching was entrusted to, and successfully proclaimed by men of low estate.

25. This is why the heathen rage and the peoples imagine vain things; why tree is set over against tree, hands against hand, the one stretched out in self indulgence, the others in generosity; the one unrestrained, the others fixed by nails, the one expelling Adam, the other reconciling the ends of the earth. This is the reason of the lifting up to atone for the fall, and of the gall for the tasting, and of the thorny

crown for the dominion of evil, and of death for death, and of darkness for the sake of light, and of burial for the return to the ground, and of resurrection for the sake of resurrection. All these are a training from God for us, and a healing for our weakness, restoring the old Adam to the place whence he fell, and conducting us to the tree of life, from which the tree of knowledge estranged us, when partaken of unseasonably, and improperly.

26. Of this healing we, who are set over others, are the ministers and fellow-laborers; for whom it is a great thing to recognize and heal their own passions and sicknesses: or rather, not really a great thing, only the viciousness of most of those who belong to this order has made me say so: but a much greater thing is the power to heal and skillfully cleanse those of others, to the advantage both of those who are in want of healing and of those whose charge it is to heal.

27. Again, the healers of our bodies will have their labors and vigils and cares, of which we are aware; and will reap a harvest of pain for themselves from the distresses of others, as one of their wise men said; and will provide for the use of those who need them, both the results of their own labors and investigations, and what they have been able to borrow from others: and they consider none, even of the minutest details, which they discover, or which elude their search, as having other than an important influence upon health or danger. And what is the object of all this? That a man may live some days longer on the earth, though he is possibly not a good man, but one of the most depraved, for whom it had perhaps been better, because of his badness, to have died long ago, in order to be set free from vice, the most serious of sicknesses. But, suppose he is a good man, how long will he be able to live? Forever? Or what will he gain from life here, from which it is the greatest of blessings, if a man be sane and sensible, to seek to be set free?

28. But we, upon whose efforts is staked the salvation of a soul, a being blessed and immortal, and destined for undying chastisement or praise, for its vice or virtue, — what a struggle ought ours to be, and how great skill do we require to treat, or get men treated properly, and to change their life, and give up the clay to the spirit. For men and women, young and old, rich and poor, the sanguine and despondent, the sick and whole, rulers and ruled, the wise and ignorant, the cowardly and courageous, the wrathful and meek, the successful and failing, do not require the same instruction and encouragement.

29. And if you examine more closely, how great is the distinction between the married and the unmarried, and among the latter between hermits and those who live together in community, between those who are proficient and advanced in contemplation and those who barely hold on the straight course, between townsfolk again and rustics, between the simple and the designing, between men of business and men of leisure, between those who have met with reverses and those who are prosperous and ignorant of misfortune. For these classes differ sometimes more

11

widely from each other in their desires and passion than in their physical characteristics; or, if you will, in the mixtures and blendings of the elements of which we are composed, and, therefore, to regulate them is no easy task.

30. As then the same medicine and the same food are not in every case administered to men's bodies, but a difference is made according to their degree of health or infirmity; so also are souls treated with varying instruction and guidance. To this treatment witness is borne by those who have had experience of it. Some are led by doctrine, others trained by example; some need the spur, others the curb; some are sluggish and hard to rouse to the good, and must be stirred up by being smitten with the word; others are immoderately fervent in spirit, with impulses difficult to restrain, like thoroughbred colts, who run wide of the turning post, and to improve them the word must have a restraining and checking influence.

31. Some are benefited by praise, others by blame, both being applied in season; while if out of season, or unreasonable, they are injurious; some are set right by encouragement, others by rebuke; some, when taken to task in public, others, when privately corrected. For some are wont to despise private admonitions, but are recalled to their senses by the condemnation of a number of people, while others, who would grow reckless under reproof openly given, accept rebuke because it is in secret, and yield obedience in return for sympathy.

32. Upon some it is needful to keep a close watch, even in the minutest details, because if they think they are unperceived (as they would contrive to be), they are puffed up with the idea of their own wisdom: Of others it is better to take no notice, but seeing not to see, and hearing not to hear them, according to the proverb, that we may not drive them to despair, under the depressing influence of repeated reproofs, and at last to utter recklessness, when they have lost the sense of self-respect, the source of persuasiveness. In some cases we must even be angry, without feeling angry, or treat them with a disdain we do not feel, or manifest despair, though we do not really despair of them, according to the needs of their nature. Others again we must treat with condescension and lowliness, aiding them readily to conceive a hope of better things. Some it is often more advantageous to conquer — by others to be overcome, and to praise or deprecate, in one case wealth and power, in another poverty and failure.

33. For our treatment does not correspond with virtue and vice, one of which is most excellent and beneficial at all times and in all cases, and the other most evil and harmful; and, instead of one and the same of our medicines invariably proving either most wholesome or most dangerous in the same cases — be it severity or gentleness, or any of the others which we have enumerated — in some cases it proves good and useful, in others again it has the contrary effect, according, I suppose, as time and circumstance and the disposition of the patient admit. Now to set before you the distinction between all these things, and give you a perfectly

exact view of them, so that you may in brief comprehend the medical art, is quite impossible, even for one in the highest degree qualified by care and skill: but actual experience and practice are requisite to form a medical system and a medical man.

34. This, however, I take to be generally admitted — that just as it is not safe for those who walk on a lofty tight rope to lean to either side, for even though the inclination seems slight, it has no slight consequences, but their safety depends upon their perfect balance: so in be case of one of us, if he leans to either side, whether from vice or ignorance, no slight danger of a fail into sin is incurred, both for himself and those who are led by him. But we must really walk in the King's highway, and take care not to turn aside from it either to the right hand or to the left, as the Proverbs say. For such is the case with our passions, and such in this matter is the task of the good shepherd, if he is to know properly the souls of his flock, and to guide them according to the methods of a pastoral care which is fight and just, and worthy of our true Shepherd.

35. In regard to the distribution of the word, to mention last the first of our duties, of that divine and exalted word, which everyone now is ready to discourse upon; if anyone else boldly undertakes it and supposes it within the power of every man's intellect, I am amazed at his intelligence, not to say his folly. To me indeed it seems no slight task, and one requiring no little spiritual power, to give in due season to each his portion of the word, and to regulate with judgment the truth of our opinions, which are concerned with such subjects as the world or worlds, matter, soul, mind, intelligent natures, better or worse, providence which holds together and guides the universe, and seems in our experience of it to be governed according to some principle, but one which is at variance with those of earth and of men.

36. Again, they are concerned with our original constitution, and final restoration, the types of the truth, the covenants, the first and second coming of Christ, His incarnation, sufferings and dissolution, with the resurrection, the last day, the judgment and recompense, whether sad or glorious; I, to crown all, with what we are to think of the original and blessed Trinity. Now this involves a very great risk to those who are charged with the illumination of others, if they are to avoid contracting their doctrine to a single Person, from fear of polytheism, and so leave us empty terms, if we suppose the Father and the Son and the Holy Spirit to be one and the same Person only: or, on the other hand, severing It into three, either foreign and diverse, or disordered and unprincipled, and, so to say, opposed divinities, thus falling from the opposite side into an equally dangerous error: like some distorted plant if bent far back in the opposite direction.

37. For, amid the three infirmities in regard to theology, atheism, Judaism, and polytheism, one of which is patronized by Sabellius the Libyan, another by Arius of Alexandria, and the third by some of the ultra-orthodox among us, what is my position, can I avoid whatever in these three is noxious, and remain within the

limits of piety; neither being led astray by the new analysis and synthesis into the atheism of Sabellius, to assert not so much that all are one as that each is nothing, for things which are transferred and pass into each other cease to be that which each one of them is, of that we have an unnaturally compound deity, like those mythical creatures, the subject of a picturesque imagination: nor again, by alleging a plurality of severed natures, according to the well named madness of Arius, becoming involved in a Jewish poverty, and introducing envy into the divine nature, by limiting the Godhead to the Unbegotten One alone, as if afraid that our God would perish, if He were the Father of a real God of equal nature: nor again, by arraying three principles in opposition to, or in alliance with, each other, introducing the Gentile plurality of principles from which we have escaped?

38. It is necessary neither to be so devoted to the Father, as to rob Him of His Fatherhood, for whose Father would He be, if the Son were separated and estranged from Him, by being ranked with the creation, (for an alien being, or one which is combined and confounded with his father, and, for the sense is the same, throws him into confusion, is not a son); nor to be so devoted to Christ, as to neglect to preserve both His Sonship, (for whose son would He be, if His origin were not referred to the Father?) and the rank of the Father as origin, inasmuch as He is the Father and Generator; for He would be the origin of petty and Unworthy beings, or rather the term would be used in a petty and unworthy sense, if He were not the origin of Godhead and goodness, which are contemplated in the Son and the Spirit: the former being the Son and the Word, the latter the proceeding and indissoluble Spirit. For both the Unity of the Godhead must be preserved, and the Trinity of Persons confessed, each with His own property.

39. A suitable and worthy comprehension and exposition of this subject demands a discussion of greater length than the present occasion, or even our life, as I suppose, allows, and, what is more, both now and at all times, the aid of the Spirit, by Whom alone we are able to perceive, to expound, or to embrace, the truth in regard to God. For the pure alone can grasp. Him Who is pure and of the same disposition as himself; and I have now briefly dwelt upon the subject, to show how difficult it is to discuss such important questions, especially before a large audience, composed of every age and condition, and needing like an instrument of many strings, to be played upon in various ways; or to find any form of words able to edify them all, and illuminate them with the light of knowledge. For it is not only that there are three sources from which danger springs, understanding, speech, and hearing, so that failure in one, if not in all, is infallibly certain; for either the mind is not illuminated, or the language is feeble, or the hearing, not having been cleansed, fails to comprehend, and accordingly, in one or all respects, the truth must be maimed: but further, what makes the instruction of those who profess to teach any other subject so easy and acceptable — viz. the piety of the audience — on this subject involves difficulty and danger.

40. For having undertaken to contend on behalf of God, the Supreme Being, and of salvation, and of the primary hope of us all, the more fervent they are in the faith, the more hostile are they to what is said, supposing that a submissive spirit indicates, not piety, but treason to the truth, and therefore they would sacrifice anything rather than their private convictions, and the accustomed doctrines in which they have been educated. I am now referring to those who are moderate and not utterly depraved in disposition, who, if they have erred in regard to the truth, have erred from piety, who have zeal, though not according to knowledge, who will possibly be of the number of those not excessively condemned, and not beaten with many stripes, because it is not through vice or depravity that they have failed to do the will of their Lord; and these perchance would be persuaded and forsake the pious opinion which is the cause of their hostility, if some reason either from their own minds, or from others, were to take hold of them, and at a critical moment, like iron from flint, strike fire from a mind which is pregnant and worthy of the light, for thus a little spark would quickly kindle the torch of truth within it.

41. But what is to be said of those who, from vain glory or arrogance, speak unrighteousness against the most High, arming themselves with the insolence of Jannes and Jambres, not against Moses, but against the truth, and rising in opposition to sound doctrine? Or of the third class, who through ignorance and, its consequence, temerity, rush headlong against every form of doctrine in swinish fashion, and trample under foot the fair pearls of the truth?

42. What again of those who come with no private idea, or form of words, better or worse, in regard to God, but listen to all kinds of doctrines and teachers, with the intention of selecting from all what is best and safest, in reliance upon no better judges of the truth than themselves? They are, in consequence, borne and turned about hither and thither by one plausible idea after another, and, after being deluged and trodden down by all kinds of doctrine, and having rung the changes on a long succession of teachers and formula, which they throw to the winds as readily as dust, their ears and minds at last are wearied out, and, O what folly! they become equally disgusted with all forms of doctrine, and assume the wretched character of deriding and despising our faith as unstable and unsound; passing in their ignorance from the teachers to the doctrine: as if anyone whose eyes were diseased, or whose ears had been injured, were to complain of the sun for being dim and not shining, or of sounds for being inharmonious and feeble.

43. Accordingly, to impress the truth upon a soul when it is still fresh, like wax not yet subjected to the seal, is an easier task than inscribing pious doctrine on the top of inscriptions — I mean wrong doctrines and dogmas — with the result that the former are confused and thrown into disorder by the latter. It is better indeed to tread a road which is smooth and well trodden than one which is untrodden and rough, or to plough land which has often been cleft and broken up by the plough: but a soul to be written upon should be free from the inscription of harmful

15

doctrines, or the deeply cut marks of vice: otherwise the pious inscriber would have a twofold task, the erasure of the former impressions and the substitution of others which are more excellent, and more worthy to abide. So numerous are they whose wickedness is shown, not only by yielding to their passions, but even by their utterances, and so numerous the forms and characters of wickedness, and so considerable the task of one who has been intrusted with this office of educating and taking charge of souls. Indeed I have omitted the majority of the details, lest my speech should be unnecessarily burdensome.

44. If anyone were to undertake to tame and train an animal of many forms and shapes, compounded of many animals of various sizes and degrees of tameness and wildness, his principal task, involving a considerable struggle, would be the government of so extraordinary and heterogeneous a nature, since each of the animals of which it is compounded would, according to its nature or habit, be differently affected with joy, pleasure or dislike, by the same words, or food, or stroking with the hand, or whistling, or other modes of treatment. And what must the master of such an animal do, but show himself manifold and various in his knowledge, and apply to each a treatment suitable for it, so as successfully to lead and preserve the beast? And since the common body of the church is composed of many different characters and minds, like a single animal compounded of discordant parts, it is absolutely necessary that its ruler should be at once simple in his uprightness in all respects, and as far as possible manifold and varied in his treatment of individuals, and in dealing with all in an appropriate and suitable manner.

45. For some need to be fed with the milk of the most simple and elementary doctrines, viz., those who are in habit babes and, so to say, new-made, and unable to bear the manly food of the word: nay, if it were presented to them beyond their strength, they would probably be overwhelmed and oppressed, owing to the inability of their mind, as is the case with our material bodies, to digest and appropriate what is offered to it, and so would lose even their original power. Others require the wisdom which is spoken among the perfect, and the higher and more solid food, since their senses have been sufficiently exercised to discern truth and falsehood, and if they were made to drink milk, and fed on the vegetable diet of invalids, they would be annoyed. And with good reason, for they would not be strengthened according to Christ, nor make that laudable increase, which the Word produces in one who is rightly feel, by making him a perfect man, and bringing him to the measure of spiritual stature.

46. And who is sufficient for these things? For we are not as the many, able to corrupt the word of truth, and mix the wine, which maketh glad the heart of man, with water, mix, that is, our doctrine with what is common and cheap, and debased, and stale, and tasteless, in order to turn the adulteration to our profit, and accommodate ourselves to those who meet us, and curry favor with everyone,

becoming ventriloquists and chatterers, who serve their own pleasures by words uttered from the earth, and sinking into the earth, and, to gain the special good will of the multitude, injuring in the highest degree, nay, ruining ourselves, and shedding the innocent blood of simpler souls, which will be required at our hands.

47. Besides, we are aware that it is better to offer our own reins to others more skillful than ourselves, than, while inexperienced, to guide the course of others, and rather to give a kindly hearing than stir an untrained tongue; and after a discussion of these points with advisers who are, I fancy, of no mean worth, and, at any rate, wish us well, we preferred to learn those canons of speech and action which we did not know, rather than undertake to teach them in our ignorance. For it is delightful to have the reasoning of the aged come to one even until the depth of old age, able, as it is, to aid a soul new to piety. Accordingly, to undertake the training of others before being sufficiently trained oneself, and to learn, as men say, the potter' s art on a wine-jar, that is, to practice ourselves in piety at the expense of others' souls seems to me to be excessive folly or excessive rashness — folly, if we are not even aware of our own ignorance; rashness, if in spite of this knowledge we venture on the task.

48. Nay, the wiser of the Hebrews tell us that there was of old among the Hebrews a most excellent and praiseworthy law, that every age was not entrusted with the whole of Scripture, inasmuch as this would not be the more profitable course, since the whole of it is not at once intelligible to everyone, and its more recondite parts would, by their apparent meaning, do a very great injury to most people. Some portions therefore, whose exterior is unexceptionable, are from the first permitted and common to all; while others are only en-trusted to those who have attained their twenty-fifth year, viz., such as hide their mystical beauty under a mean-looking cloak, to be the reward of diligence and an illustrious life; flashing forth and presenting itself only to those whose mind has been purified, on the ground that this age alone can be superior to the body, and properly rise from the letter to the spirit.

49. Among us, however, there is no boundary line between giving and receiving instruction, like the stones of old between the tribes within and beyond the Jordan: nor is a certain part entrusted to some, another to others; nor any rule for degrees of experience; but the matter has been so disturbed and thrown into confusion, that most of us, not to say all, almost before we have lost our childish curls and lisp, before we have entered the house of God, before we know even the names of the Sacred Books, before we have learnt the character and authors of the Old and New Testaments: (for my present point is not our want of cleansing from the mire and marks of spiritual shame which our viciousness has contracted) if, I say, we have furnished ourselves with two or three expressions of pious authors, and that by hearsay, not by study; if we have had a brief experience of David, or clad ourselves properly in a cloaklet, or are wearing at least a philosopher' s girdle, or have girt

about us some form and appearance of piety — phew! how we take the chair and show our spirit! Samuel was holy even in his swaddling-clothes: we are at once wise teachers, of high estimation in Divine things, the first of scribes and lawyers; we ordain ourselves men of heaven and seek to be called Rabbi by men; the letter is nowhere, everything is to be understood spiritually, and our dreams are utter drivel, and we should be annoyed if we were not lauded to excess. This is the case with the better and more simple of us: what of those who are more spiritual and noble? After frequently condemning us, as men of no account, they have forsaken us, and abhor fellowship with impious people such as we are.

50. Now, if we were to speak gently to one of them, advancing, as follows, step by step in argument: "Tell me, my good sir, do you call dancing anything, and flute - playing?" "Certainly," they would say. "What then of wisdom and being wise, which we venture to define as a knowledge of things divine and human?" This also they will admit. "Are then these accomplishments better than and superior to wisdom, or wisdom by far better than these?" "Better even than all things," I know well that they will say. Up to this point they are judicious. "Well, dancing and flute-playing require to be taught and learnt, a process which takes time, and much toil in the sweat of the brow, and sometimes the payment of fees, and entreaties for initiation, and long absence from home, and all else which must be done and borne for the acquisition of experience: but as for wisdom, which is chief of all things, and holds in her embrace everything which is good, so that even God himself prefers this title to all the names which He is called; are we to suppose that it is a matter of such slight consequence, and so accessible, that we need but wish, and we would be wise?" "It would be utter folly to do so." If we, or any learned and prudent man, were to say this to them, and try by degrees to cleanse them from their error, it would be sowing upon rocks, and speaking to ears of men who will not hear: so far are they from being even wise enough to perceive their own ignorance. And we may rightly, in my opinion, apply to them the saying of Solomon: There is an evil which I have seen under the sun, a man wise in his own conceit; and a still greater evil is to charge with the instruction of others a man who is not even aware of his own ignorance.

51. This is a state of mind which demands, in special degree, our tears and groans, and has often stirred my pity, from the conviction that imagination robs us in great measure of reality, and that vain glory is a great hindrance to men's attainment of virtue. To heal and stay this disease needs a Peter or Paul, those great disciples of Christ, who in addition to guidance in word and deed, received their grace, and became all things to all men, that they might gain all. But for other men like ourselves, it is a great thing to be rightly guided and led by those who have been charged with the correction and setting right of things such as these.

52. Since, however, I have mentioned Paul, and men like him, I will, with your permission, pass by all others who have been foremost as lawgivers, prophets, or

leaders, or in any similar office — for instance, Moses, Aaron, Joshua, Elijah, Elisha, the Judges, Samuel, David, the company of Prophets, John, the Twelve Apostles, and their successors, who with many toils and labors exercised their authority, each in his own time; all these I pass by, to set forth Paul as the witness to my assertions, and for us to consider by his example how important a matter is the care of souls, and whether it requires slight attention and little judgment. But that we may recognize and perceive this, let us hear what Paul himself says of Paul.

53. I say nothing of his labors, his watchings, his sufferings in hunger and thirst, in cold and nakedness, his assailants from without, his adversaries within. I pass over the persecutions, councils, prisons, bonds, accusers, tribunals, the daily and hourly deaths, the basket, the stonings, beatings with rods, the traveling about, the perils by land and sea, the deep, the shipwrecks, the perils of rivers, perils of robbers, perils from his countrymen, perils among false brethren, the living by his own hands, the gospel without charge, the being a spectacle to both angels and men, set in the midst between God and men to champion His cause, and to unite them to Him, and make them His own peculiar people, beside those things that are without. For who could worthily detail these matters, the daily pressure, the individual solicitude, the care of all the churches, the universal sympathy, and brotherly love? Did anyone stumble, Paul also was weak; did another suffer scandal, it was Paul who was on fire.

54. What of the laboriousness of his teaching? The manifold character of his ministry? His loving kindness? And on the other hand his strictness? And the combination and blending of the two; in such wise that his gentleness should not enervate, nor his severity exasperate? He gives laws for slaves and masters, rulers and ruled, husbands and wives, parents and children, marriage and celibacy, self-discipline and indulgence, wisdom and ignorance, circumcision and uncircumcision, Christ and the world, the flesh and the spirit. On behalf of some he gives thanks, others he upbraids. Some he names his joy and crown, others he charges with folly. Some who hold a straight course he accompanies, sharing in their zeal; others he checks, who are going wrong. At one time he excommunicates, at another he confirms his love; at one time he grieves, at another rejoices; at one time he feeds with milk, at another he handles mysteries; at one time he condescends, at another he raises to his own level; at one time he threatens a rod, at another he offers the spirit of meekness; at one time he is haughty toward the lofty, at another lowly toward the lowly. Now he is least of the apostles, now he offers a proof of Christ speaking in him; now he longs for departure and is being poured forth as a libation, now he thinks it more necessary for their sakes to abide in the flesh. For he seeks not his own interests, but those of his children, whom he has begotten in Christ by the gospel. This is the aim of all his spiritual authority, in everything to neglect his own in comparison with the advantage of others.

55. He glories in his infirmities and distresses. He takes pleasure in the dying of Jesus, as if it were a kind of ornament. He is lofty in carnal things, he rejoices in things spiritual; he is not rude in knowledge, and claims to see in a mirror, darkly. He is bold in spirit, and buffets his body, throwing it as an antagonist. What is the lesson and instruction he would thus impress upon us? Not to be proud of earthly things, or puffed up by knowledge, or excite the flesh against the spirit. He fights for all, prays for all, is jealous for all, is kindled on behalf of all, whether without law, or under the law; a preacher of the Gentiles, a patron of the Jews. He even was exceedingly bold on behalf of his brethren according to the flesh, if I may myself be bold enough to say so, in his loving prayer that they might in his stead be brought to Christ. What magnanimity! what fervor of spirit! He imitates Christ, who became a curse for us, who took our infirmities and bore our sicknesses; or, to use more measured terms, he is ready, next to Christ, to suffer anything, even as one of the ungodly, for them, if only they be saved.

56. Why should I enter into detail? He lived not to himself, but to Christ and his preaching. He crucified the world to himself, and being crucified to the world and the things which are seen, he thought all things little, and too small to be desired; even though from Jerusalem and round about unto Illyricum he had fully preached the Gospel, even though he had been prematurely caught up to the third heaven, and had a vision of Paradise, and had heard unspeakable words. Such was Paul, and everyone of like spirit with him. But we fear that, in comparison with them, we may be foolish princes of Zoan, or extortioners, who exact the fruits of the ground, or falsely bless the people: and further make themselves happy, and confuse the way of your feet, or mockers ruling over you, or children in authority, immature in mind, not even having bread and clothing enough to be rulers over any; or prophets teaching lies, or rebellious princes, deserving to share the reproach of their elders for the straitness of the famine, or priests very far from speaking comfortably to Jerusalem, according to the reproaches and protests urged by Isaiah, who was purged by the Seraphim with a live coal.

57. Is the undertaking then so serious and laborious to a sensitive and sad heart — a very rottenness to the bones o of a sensible man: while the danger is slight, and a fall not worth consideration? Nay the blessed Hosea inspires me with serious alarm, where he says that to us priests and rulers pertaineth the judgment, because we have been a snare to the watchtower; and as a net spread upon Tabor, which has been firmly fixed by the hunters of men's souls, and he threatens to cut off the wicked prophets, and devour their judges with fire, and to cease for a while from anointing a king and princes, because they ruled for themselves, and not by Him.

58. Hence again the divine Micah, unable to brook the building of Zion with blood, however you interpret the phrase, and of Jerusalem with iniquity, while the heads thereof judge for reward, and the priests teach for hire, and the prophets divine for money — what does he say will be the result of this? Zion shall be

plowed as a field, and Jerusalem be as a lodge in a garden, and the mountain of the house be reckoned as a glade in a thicket. He bewails also the scarcity of the upright, there being scarcely a stalk or a gleaning grape left, since both the prince asketh, and the judge curries favor, so that his language is almost the same as the mighty David's: Save me, O Lord, for the godly man ceaseth: and says that therefore their blessings shall fail them, as if wasted by the moth.

59. Joel again summons us to wailing, and will have the ministers of the altar lament under the presence of famine: so far is he from allowing us to revel in the misfortunes of others: and, after sanctifying a fast, calling a solemn assembly, and gathering the old men, the children, and those of tender age, we ourselves must further haunt the temple in sackcloth and ashes, prostrated right humbly on the ground, because the field is wasted, and the meat-offering and the drink-offering is cut off from the house of the Lord, till we draw down mercy by our humiliation.

60. What of Habakkuk? He utters more heated words, and is impatient with God Himself, and cries down, as it were our good Lord, because of the injustice of the judges. O Lord, how long shall I cry and Thou wilt not hear? Shall I cry out unto Thee of violence, and Thou wilt not save? Why dost Thou show me toil and labor, causing me to look upon perverseness and impiety? Judgment has been given against me, and the judge is a spoiler. Therefore the law is slacked, and judgment doth never go forth. Then comes the denunciation, and what follows upon it. Behold, ye despisers, and regard, and wonder marvelously, and vanish away, for I work a work. But why need I quote the whole of the denunciation? A little further on, however, for I think it best to add this to what has been said, after upbraiding and lamenting many of those who are in some respect unjust or depraved, he upbraids the leaders and teachers of wickedness, stigmatizing vice as a foul disorder, and an intoxication and aberration of mind; charging them with giving their neighbors drink in order to look upon the darkness of their soul, and the dens of creeping things and wild beasts, viz.: the dwelling places of wicked thoughts. Such indeed they are, and such teachings do they discuss with us.

61. How can it be right to pass by Malachi, who at one time brings bitter charges against the priests, and reproaches them with despising the name of the Lord, and explains wherein they did this, by offering polluted bread upon the altar, and meat which is not firstfruits, which they would not have offered to one of their governors, or, if they had offered it, they would have been dishonored; yet offering these in fulfillment of a vow to the King of the universe, to wit, the lame and the sick, and the deformed, which are utterly profane and loathsome. Again he reminds them of the covenant of God, a covenant of life and peace, with the sons of Levi, and that they should serve Him in fear, and stand in awe of the manifestation of His Name. The law of truth, he says, was in his mouth, and unrighteousness was not found in his lips; he walked with me uprightly in peace, and turned away many from iniquity: for the priest's lips shall keep knowledge, and they shall seek the law

at his mouth. And how honorable and at the same time how fearful is the cause! for he is the messenger of the Lord Almighty. Although I pass over the following imprecations, as strongly worded, yet I am afraid of their truth. This however may be cited without offense, to our profit. Is it right, he says, to regard your sacrifice, and receive it with good will at your hands, as if he were most highly incensed, and rejecting their ministrations owing to their wickedness.

62. Whenever I remember Zechariah, I shudder at the reaping-hook, and likewise at his testimony against the priests, his hints in reference to the celebrated Joshua, the high priest, whom he represents as stripped of filthy and unbecoming garments and then clothed in rich priestly apparel. As for the words and charges to Joshua which he puts into the angel's mouth, let them be treated with silent respect, as referring perhaps to a greater and higher object than those who are many priests: but even at his right hand stood the devil, to resist him. A fact, in my eyes, of no slight significance, and demanding no slight fear and watchfulness.

63. Who is so bold and adamantine of soul as not to tremble and be abashed at the charges and reproaches deliberately urged against the rest of the shepherds. A voice, he says, of the howling of the shepherds, for their glory is spoiled. A voice of the roaring of lions, for this hath befallen them. Does he not all but hear the wailing as if close at hand, and himself wail with the afflicted. A little further is a more striking and impassioned strain. Feed, he says, the flock of slaughter, whose possessors slay them without repentance, and they that sell them say, "Blessed be the Lord, for we are rich:" and their own shepherds are without feeling for them. Therefore, I will no more pity the inhabitants of the land, saith the Lord Almighty. And again: Awake, O sword, against the shepherds, and smite the shepherds, and scatter the sheep, and I will turn My Hand upon the shepherds; and, Mine anger is kindled against the shepherds, and I will visit the lambs: adding to the threat those who rule over the people. So industriously does he apply himself to his task that he cannot easily free himself from denunciations, and I am afraid that, did I refer to the whole series, I should exhaust your patience. This must then suffice for Zechariah.

64. Passing by the elders in the book of Daniel; for it is better to pass them by, together with the Lord's righteous sentence and declaration concerning them, that wickedness came from Babylon from ancient judges, who seemed to govern the people; how are we affected by Ezekiel, the beholder and expositor of the mighty mysteries and visions? By his injunction to the watchmen not to keep silence concerning vice and the sword impending over it, a course which would profit neither themselves nor the sinners; but rather to keep watch and forewarn, and thus benefit, at any rate those who gave warning, if not both those who spoke and those who heard?

65. What of his further invective against the shepherds, Woe shall come upon woe, and rumor upon rumor, then shall they seek a vision of the prophet, but the law shall perish from the priest, and counsel from the ancients, and again, in these terms, Son of man, say unto her, thou art a land that is not watered, nor hath rain come upon thee in the day of indignation: whose princes in the midst of her are like roaring lions, ravening the prey, devouring souls in their might. And a little further on: Her priests have violated My laws and profaned My holy things, they have put no difference between the holy and profane, but all things were alike to them, and they hid their eyes from My Sabbaths, and I was profaned among them. He threatens that He will consume both the wall and them that daubed it, that is, those who sin and those who throw a cloak over them; as the evil rulers and priests have done, who caused the house of Israel to err according to their own hearts which are estranged in their lusts.

66. I also refrain from entering into his discussion of those who feed themselves, devour the milk, clothe themselves with the wool, kill them that are fat, but feed not the flock, strengthen not the diseased, nor bind up that which is broken, nor bring again that which is driven away, nor seek that which is lost, nor keep watch over that which is strong, but oppress them with rigor, and destroy them with their pressure; so that, because there was no shepherd, the sheep were scattered over every plain and mountain, and became meat for all the fowls and beasts, because there was no one to seek for them and bring them back. What is the consequence? As I live, saith the Lord, because these things are so, and My flock became a prey, behold I am against the shepherds, and I will require My flock at their hands, and will gather them and make them My own: but the shepherds shall suffer such and such things, as bad shepherds ought.

67. However, to avoid unreasonably prolonging my discourse, by an enumeration of all the prophets, and of the words of them all, I will mention but one more, who was known before he was formed, and sanctified from the womb, Jeremiah: and will pass over the rest. He longs for water over his head, and a fountain of tears for his eyes, that he may adequately weep for Israel; and no less does he bewail the depravity of its rulers.

68. God speaks to him in reproof of the priests: The priests said not, Where is the Lord, and they that handled the law knew Me not; the pastors also transgressed against Me. Again He says to him: The pastors are become brutish, and have not sought the Lord, and therefore all their flock did not understand, and was scattered. Again, Many pastors have destroyed My vineyard, and have polluted My pleasant portion, till it was reduced to a trackless wilderness. He further inveighs against the pastors again: Woe be to the pastors that destroy and scatter the sheep of My pasture! Therefore thus saith the Lord against them that feed My people: Ye have scattered My flock, and driven them away, and have not visited them: behold I will visit upon you the evil of your doings. Moreover he bids the shepherds to howl, and

23

the rams of the flock to lament, because the days of their slaughter are accomplished.

69. Why need I speak of the things of ancient days? Who can test himself by the rules and standards which Paul laid down for bishops and presbyters, that they are to be temperate, soberminded, not given to wine, no strikers, apt to teach, blameless in all things, and beyond the reach of the wicked, without finding considerable deflection from the straight line of the rules? What of the regulations of Jesus for his disciples, when He sends them to preach? The main object of these is — not to enter into particulars — that they should be of such virtue, so simple and modest, and in a word, so heavenly, that the gospel should make its way, no less by their character than by their preaching.

70. I am alarmed by the reproaches of the Pharisees, the conviction of the Scribes. For it is disgraceful for us, who ought greatly surpass them, as we are bidden, if we desire the kingdom of heaven, to be found more deeply sunk in vice: so that we deserve to be called serpents, a generation of vipers, and blind guides, who strain out a gnat and swallow a camel, or sepulchers foul within, in spite of our external comeliness, or platters outwardly clean, and everything else, which they are, or which is laid to their charge.

71. With these thoughts I am occupied night and day: they waste my marrow, and feed upon my flesh, and will not allow me to be confident or to look up. They depress my soul, and abase my mind, and fetter my tongue, and make me consider, not the position of a prelate, or the guidance and direction of others, which is far beyond my powers; but how I myself am to escape the wrath to come, and to scrape off from myself somewhat of the rust of vice. A man must himself be cleansed, before cleansing others: himself become wise, that he may make others wise; become light, and then give light: draw near to God, and so bring others near; be hallowed, then hallow them; be possessed of hands to lead others by the hand, of wisdom to give advice.

72. When will this be, say they who are swift but not sure in every thing, readily building up, readily throwing down. When will the lamp be upon its stand, and where is the talent? For so they call the grace. Those who speak thus are more fervent in friendship than in reverence. You ask me, you men of exceeding courage, when these things shall be, and what account I give of them? Not even extreme old age would be too long a limit to assign. For hoary hairs combined with prudence are better than inexperienced youth, well-reasoned hesitation than inconsiderate haste, and a brief reign than a long tyranny: just as a small portion honorably won is better than considerable possessions which are dishonorable and uncertain, a little gold than a great weight of lead, a little light than much darkness.

73. But this speed, in its untrustworthiness and excessive haste, is in danger of being like the seeds which fell upon the rock, and, because they had no depth of earth, sprang up at once, but could not bear even the first heat of the sun; or like the foundation laid upon the sand, which could not even make a slight resistance to the rain and the winds. Woe to thee, O city, whose king is a child, says Solomon. Be not hasty of speech, says Solomon again, asserting that hastiness of speech is less serious than heated action. And who, in spite of all this, demands haste rather than security and utility? Who can mold, as clay-figures are modeled in a single day, the defender of the truth, who is to take his stand with Angels, and give glory with Archangels, and cause the sacrifice to ascend to the altar on high, and share the priesthood of Christ, and renew the creature, and set forth the image, and create inhabitants for the world above, aye and, greatest of all, be God, and make others to be God?

74. I know Whose ministers we are, and where we are placed, and whither we are guides. I know the height of God, and the weakness of man, and, on the contrary, his power. Heaven is high, and the earth deep; and who of those who have been cast down by sin shall ascend? Who that is as yet surrounded by the gloom here below, and by the grossness of the flesh can purely gaze with his whole mind upon that whole mind, and amid unstable and visible things hold intercourse with the stable and invisible? For hardly may one of those who have been most specially purged, behold here even an image of the Good, as men see the sun in the water. Who hath measured the water with his hand, and the heaven with a span, and the whole earth in a measure? Who hath weighed the mountains in scales, and the hills in a balance? What is the place of his rest? and to whom shall he be likened?

75. Who is it, Who made all things by His Word, and formed man by His Wisdom, and gathered into one things scattered abroad, and mingled dust with spirit, and compounded an animal visible and invisible, temporal and immortal, earthly and heavenly, able to attain to God but not to comprehend Him, drawing near and yet afar off. I said, I will be wise, says Solomon, but she (i.e. Wisdom) was far from me beyond what is: and, Verily, he that increaseth knowledge increaseth sorrow. For the joy of what we have discovered is no greater than the pain of what escapes us; a pain, I imagine, like that felt by those who are dragged, while yet thirsty, from the water, or are unable to retain what they think they hold, or are suddenly left in the dark by a flash of lightning.

76. This depressed and kept me humble, and persuaded me that it was better to hear the voice of praise than to be an expounder of truths beyond my power; the majesty, and the height, and the dignity, and the pure natures scarce able to contain the brightness of God, Whom the deep covers, Whose secret place is darkness, since He is the purest light, which most men cannot approach unto; Who is in all this universe, and again is beyond the universe; Who is all goodness, and beyond all goodness; Who enlightens the mind, and escapes the quickness and height of the

mind, ever retiring as much as He is apprehended, and by His flight and stealing away when grasped, withdrawing to the things above one who is enamored of Him.

77. Such and so great is the object of our longing zeal, and such a man should he be, who prepares and conducts souls to their espousals. For myself, I feared to be cast, bound hand and foot, from the bride-chamber, for not having on a wedding-garment, and for having rashly intruded among those who there sit at meat. And yet I had been invited from my youth, if I may speak of what most men know not, and had been cast upon Him from the womb, and presented by the promise of my mother, afterwards confirmed in the hour of danger: and my longing grew up with it, and my reason agreed to it, and I gave as an offering my all to Him Who had won me and saved me, my property, my fame, my health, my very words, from which I only gained the advantage of being able to despise them, and of having something in comparison of which I preferred Christ. And the words of God were made sweet as honeycombs to me, and I cried after knowledge and lifted up my voice for wisdom. There was moreover the moderation of anger, the curbing of the tongue, the restraint of the eyes, the discipline of the belly, and the trampling under foot of the glory which clings to the earth. I speak foolishly, but it shall be said, in these pursuits I was perhaps not inferior to many.

78. One branch of philosophy is, however, too high for me, the commission to guide and govern souls — and before I have rightly learned to submit to a shepherd, or have had my soul duly cleansed, the charge of caring for a flock: especially in times like these, when a man, seeing everyone else rushing hither and thither in confusion, is content to flee from the malice and escape, in sheltered retirement, from the storm and gloom of the wicked one: when the members are at war with one another, and the slight remains of love, which once existed, have departed, and priest is a mere empty name, since, as it is said, contempt has been poured upon princes.

79. Would that it were merely empty! And now may their blasphemy fall upon the head of the ungodly! All fear has been banished from souls, shamelessness has taken its place, and knowledge and the deep things of the Spirit are at the disposal of anyone who will; and we all become pious by simply condemning the impiety of others; and we claim the services of ungodly judges, and fling that which is holy to the dogs, and cast pearls before swine, by publishing divine things in the hearing of profane souls, and, wretches that we are, carefully fulfill the prayers of our enemies, and are not ashamed to go a whoring with our own inventions. Moabites and Ammonites, who were not permitted even to enter the Church of the Lord, frequent our most holy rites. We have opened to all not the gates of righteousness, but, doors of railing and partisan arrogance; and the first place among us is given, not to one who in the fear of God refrains from even an idle word, but to him who can revile his neighbor most fluently, whether explicitly, or by covert allusion; who

rolls beneath his tongue mischief and iniquity, or to speak more accurately, the poison of asps.

80. We observe each other's sins, not to bewail them, but to make them subjects of reproach, not to heal them, but to aggravate them, and excuse our own evil deeds by the wounds of our neighbors. Bad and good men are distinguished not according to personal character, but by their disagreement or friendship with ourselves. We praise one day what we revile the next, denunciation at the hands of others is a passport to our admiration; so magnanimous are we in our viciousness, that everything is frankly forgiven to impiety.

81. Everything has reverted to the original state of things before the world, with its present fair order and form, came into being. The general confusion and irregularity cry for some organizing hand and power. Or, if you will, it is like a battle at night by the faint light of the moon, when none can discern the faces of friends or foes; or like a sea fight on the surge, with the driving winds, and boiling foam, and dashing waves, and crashing vessels, with the thrusts of poles, the pipes of boatswains, the groans of the fallen, while we make our voices heard above the din, and not knowing what to do, and having, alas! no opportunity for showing our valor, assail one another, and fall by one another's hands.

82. Nor indeed is there any distinction between the state of the people and that of the priesthood: but it seems to me to be a simple fulfillment of the ancient curse, "As with the people so with the priest." Nor again are the great and eminent men affected otherwise than the majority; nay, they are openly at war with the priests, and their piety is an aid to their powers of persuasion. And indeed, provided that it be on behalf of the faith, and of the highest and most important questions, let them be thus disposed, and I blame them not; nay, to say the truth, I go so far as to praise and congratulate them. Yea! would that I were one of those who contend and incur hatred for the truth's sake: or rather, I can boast of being one of them. For better is a laudable war than a peace which severs a man from God: and therefore it is that the Spirit arms the gentle warrior, as one who is able to wage war in a good cause.

83. But at the present time there are some who go to war even about small matters and to no purpose, and, with great ignorance and audacity, accept, as an associate in their ill-doing, anyone whoever he may be. Then everyone makes the faith his pretext, and this venerable name is dragged into their private quarrels. Consequently, as was probable, we are hated, even among the Gentiles, and, what is harder still, we cannot say that this is without just cause. Nay, even the best of our own people are scandalized, while this result is not surprising in the case of the multitude, who are ill-disposed to accept anything that is good.

84. Sinners are planning upon our backs; and what we devise against each other, they turn against us all: and we have become a new spectacle, not to angels and men, as says Paul, that bravest of athletes, in his contest with principalities and powers, but to almost all wicked men, and at every time and place, in the public squares, at carousals, at festivities, and times of sorrow. Nay, we have already — I can scarcely speak of it without tears — been represented on the stage, amid the laughter of the most licentious, and the most popular of all dialogues and scenes is the caricature of a Christian.

85. These are the results of our intestine warfare, and our extreme readiness to strive about goodness and gentleness, and our inexpedient excess of love for God. Wrestling, or any other athletic contest, is only permitted according to fixed laws, and the man will be shouted down and disgraced, and lose the victory, who breaks the laws of wrestling, or acts unfairly in any other contest, contrary to the rules laid down for the contest, however able and skillful he may be; and shall anyone contend for Christ in an unchristlike manner, and yet be pleasing to peace for having fought unlawfully in her name.

86. Yea, even now, when Christ is invoked, the devils tremble, and not even by our ill-doing has the power of this Name been extinguished, while we are not ashamed to insult a cause and name so venerable; shouting it, and having it shouted in return, almost in public, and every day; for My Name is blasphemed among the Gentiles because of you.

87. Of external warfare I am not afraid, nor of that wild beast, and fullness of evil, who has now arisen against the churches, though he may threaten fire, sword, wild beasts, precipices, chasms; though he may show himself more inhuman than all previous madmen, and discover fresh tortures of greater severity. I have one remedy for them all, one road to victory; I will glory in Christ namely, death for Christ's sake.

88. For my own warfare, however, I am at a loss what course to pursue, what alliance, what word of wisdom, what grace to devise, with what panoply to arm myself, against the wiles of the wicked one. What Moses is to conquer him by stretching out his hands upon the mount, in order that the cross, thus typified and prefigured, may prevail? What Joshua, as his successor, arrayed alongside the Captain of the Lord's hosts? What David, either by harping, or fighting with his sling, and girded by God with strength unto the battle, and with his fingers trained to war? What Samuel, praying and sacrificing for the people, and anointing as king one who can gain the victory? What Jeremiah, by writing lamentations for Israel, is fitly to lament these things?

89. Who will cry aloud, Spare Thy People, O Lord, and give not Thine heritage to reproach, that the nations should rule over them? What Noah, and Job, and Daniel, who are reckoned together as men of prayer, will pray for us, that we may have a slight respite from warfare, and recover ourselves, and recognize one another for a while, and no longer, instead of united Israel, be Judah and Israel, Rehoboam and Jeroboam, Jerusalem and Samaria, in turn delivered up because of our sins, and in turn lamented.

90. For I own that I am too weak for this warfare, and therefore turned my back, hiding my face in the rout, and sat solitary, because I was filled with bitterness and sought to be silent, understanding that it is an evil time, that the beloved had kicked, that we were become backsliding children, who are the luxuriant vine, the true vine, all fruitful, all beautiful, springing up splendidly with showers from on high. For the diadem of beauty, the signet of glory, the crown of magnificence has been changed for me into shame; and if anyone, in face of these things, is daring and courageous, he has my blessing on his daring and courage.

91. I have said nothing yet of the internal warfare within ourselves, and in our passions, in which we are engaged night and day against the body of our humiliation, either secretly or openly, and against the tide which tosses and whirls us hither and thither, by the aid of our senses and other sources of the pleasures of this life; and against the miry clay in which we have been fixed; and against the law of sin, which wars against the law of the spirit, and strives to destroy the royal image in us, and all the divine emanation which has been bestowed upon us; so that it is difficult for anyone, either by a long course of philosophic training, and gradual separation of the noble and enlightened part of the soul from that which is debased and yoked with darkness, or by the mercy of God, or by both together, and by a constant practice of looking upward, to overcome the depressing power of matter. And before a man has, as far as possible, gained this superiority, and sufficiently purified his mind, and far surpassed his fellows in nearness to God, I do not think it safe for him to be entrusted with the rule over souls, or the office of mediator (for such, I take it, a priest is) between God and man.

92. What is it that has induced this fear in me, that, instead of supposing me to be needlessly afraid, you may highly commend my foresight? I hear from Moses himself, when God spake to him, that, although many were bidden to come to the mount, one of whom was even Aaron, with his two sons who were priests, and seventy elders of the senate, the rest were ordered to worship afar off, and Moses alone to draw near, and the people were not to go up with him. For it is not everyone who may draw near to God, but only one who, like Moses, can bear the glory of God. Moreover, before this, when the law was first given, the trumpet-blasts, and lightnings, and thunders, and darkness, and the smoke of the whole mountain, and the terrible threats that if even a beast touched the mountain it should be stoned, and other like alarms, kept back the rest of the people, for whom

29

it was a great privilege, after careful purification, merely to hear the voice of God. But Moses actually went up and entered into the cloud, and was charged with the law, and received the tables, which belong, for the multitude, to the letter, but, for those who are above the multitude, to the spirit.

93. I hear again that Nadab and Abihu, for having merely offered incense with strange fire, were with strange fire destroyed, the instrument of their impiety being used for their punishment, and their destruction following at the very time and place of their sacrilege; and not even their father Aaron, who was next to Moses in the favor of God, could save them. I know also of Eli the priest, and a little later of Uzzah, the former made to pay the penalty for his sons' transgression, in daring to violate the sacrifices by an untimely exaction of the first fruits of the cauldrons, although he did not condone their impiety, but frequently rebuked them; the other, because he only touched the ark, which was being thrown off the cart by the ox, and though he saved it, was himself destroyed, in God's jealousy for the reverence due to the ark.

94. I know also that not even bodily blemishes in either priests or victims passed without notice, but that it was required by the law that perfect sacrifices must be offered by perfect men — a symbol, I take it, of integrity of soul. It was not lawful for everyone to touch the priestly vesture, or any of the holy vessels; nor might the sacrifices themselves be consumed except by the proper persons, and at the proper time and place; nor might the anointing oil nor the compounded incense be imitated; nor might anyone enter the temple who was not in the most minute particular pure in both soul and body; so far was the Holy of holies removed from presumptuous access, that it might be entered by one man only once a year; so far were the veil, and the mercy-seat, and the ark, and the Cherubim, from the general gaze and touch.

95. Since then I knew these things, and that no one is worthy of the mightiness of God, and the sacrifice, and priesthood, who has not first presented himself to God, a living, holy sacrifice, and set forth the reasonable, well-pleasing service, and sacrificed to God the sacrifice of praise and the contrite spirit, which is the only sacrifice required of us by the Giver of all; how could I dare to offer to Him the external sacrifice, the antitype of the great mysteries, or clothe myself with the garb and name of priest, before my hands had been consecrated by holy works; before my eyes had been accustomed to gaze safely upon created things, with wonder only for the Creator, and without injury to the creature; before my ear had been sufficiently opened to the instruction of the Lord, and He had opened mine ear to hear without heaviness, and had set a golden earring with precious sardius, that is, a wise man's word in an obedient ear; before my mouth had been opened to draw in the Spirit, and opened wide to be filled with the spirit of speaking mysteries and doctrines; and my lips bound, to use the words of wisdom, by divine knowledge, and, as I would add, loosed in due season: before my tongue had been filled with

exultation, and become an instrument of Divine melody, awaking with glory, awaking right early, and laboring till it cleave to my jaws: before my feet had been set upon the rock, made like hart's feet, and my footsteps directed in a godly fashion so that they should not well-nigh slip, nor slip at all; before all my members had become instruments of righteousness, and all mortality had been put off, and swallowed up of life, and had yielded to the Spirit?

96. Who is the man, whose heart has never been made to burn, as the Scriptures have been opened to him, with the pure words of God which have been tried in a furnace; who has not, by a triple inscription of them upon the breadth of his heart, attained the mind of Christ; nor been admitted to the treasures which to most men remain hidden, secret, and dark, to gaze upon the riches therein? and become able to enrich others, comparing spiritual things with spiritual.

97. Who is the man who has never beheld, as our duty is to behold it, the fair beauty of the Lord, nor has visited His temple, or rather, become the temple of God, and the habitation of Christ in the Spirit? Who is the man who has never recognized the correlation and distinction between figures and the truth, so that by withdrawing from the former and cleaving to the latter, and by thus escaping from the oldness of the letter and serving the newness of the spirit, he may clean pass over to grace from the law, which finds its spiritual fulfillment in the dissolution of the body.

98. Who is the man who has never, by experience and contemplation, traversed the entire series of the titles and powers of Christ, both those more lofty ones which originally were His, and those more lowly ones which He later assumed for our sake — viz.: God, the Son, the Image, the Word, the Wisdom, the Truth, the Light, the Life, the Power, the Vapor, the Emanation, the Effulgence, the Maker, the King, the Head, the Law, the Way, the Door, the Foundation, the Rock, the Pearl, the Peace, the Righteousness, the Sanctification, the Redemption, the Man, the Servant, the Shepherd, the Lamb, the High Priest, the Victim, the Firstborn before creation, the Firstborn from the dead, the Resurrection: who is the man who hearkens, but pays no heed, to these names so pregnant with reality, and has never yet held communion with, nor been made partaker of, the Word, in any of the real relations signified by each of these names which He bears?

99. Who, in fine, is the man who, although he has never applied himself to, nor learnt to speak, the hidden wisdom of God in a mystery, although he is still a babe, still fed with milk, still of those who are not numbered in Israel, nor enrolled in the army of God, although he is not yet able to take up the Cross of Christ like a man, although he is possibly not yet one of the more honorable members, yet will joyfully and eagerly accept his appointment as head of the fullness of Christ? No one, if he will listen to my judgment and accept my advice! This is of all things

most to be feared, this is the extremest of dangers in the eyes of everyone who understands the magnitude of success, the utter ruin of failure.

100. Let others sail for merchandise, I used to say, and cross the wide oceans, and constantly contend with winds and waves, to gain great wealth, if so it should chance, and run great risks in their eagerness for sailing and merchandise; but, for my part, I greatly prefer to stay ashore and plough a short but pleasant furrow, saluting at a respectful distance the sea and its gains, to live as best I can upon a poor and scanty store of barley-bread, and drag my life along in safety and calm, rather than expose myself to so long and great a risk for the sake of great gains.

101. For one in high estate, if he fail to make further progress and to disseminate virtue still more widely, and contents himself with slight results, incurs punishment, as having spent a great light upon the illumination of a little house, or girt round the limbs of a boy the full armor of a man. On the contrary, a man of low estate may with safety assume a light burden, and escape the risk of the ridicule and increased danger which would attend him if he attempted a task beyond his powers. For, as we have heard, it is not seemly for a man to build a tower, unless he has sufficient to finish it.

102. Such is the defense which I have been able to make, perhaps at immoderate length, for my flight. Such are the reasons which, to my pain and possibly to yours, carried me away from you, my friends and brothers; yet, as it seemed to me at the time, with irresistible force. My longing after you, and the sense of your longing for me, have, more than anything else, led to my return, for nothing inclines us so strongly to love as mutual affection.

103. In the next place there was my care, my duty, the hoar hairs and weakness of my holy parents, who were more greatly distressed on my account than by their advanced age — of this Patriarch Abraham whose person is honored by me, and numbered among the angels, and of Sarah, who travailed in my spiritual birth by instructing me in the truth. Now, I had specially pledged myself to become the stay of their old age and the support of their weakness, a pledge which, to the best of my power, I have fulfilled, even at the expense of philosophy itself, the most precious of possessions and titles to me; or, to speak more truly, although I made it the first object of my philosophy to appear to be no philosopher, I could not bear that my labor in consequence of a single purpose should be wasted, nor yet that blessing should be lost, which one of the saints of old is said to have stolen from his father, whom he deceived by the food which he offered to him, and the hairy appearance he assumed, thus attaining a good object by disgraceful trickery. These are the two causes of my submission and tractability. Nor is it, perchance, unreasonable that my arguments should yield and submit to them both, for there is a time to be conquered, as I also think there is for every purpose, and it is better to be honorably overcome than to win a dangerous and lawless victory.

104. There is a third reason of the highest importance which I will further mention, and then dismiss the rest. I remembered the days of old, and, recurring to one of the ancient histories, drew counsel for myself therefrom as to my present conduct; for let us not suppose these events to have been recorded without a purpose, nor that they are a mere assemblage of words and deeds gathered together for the pastime of those who listen to them, as a kind of bait for the ears, for the sole purpose of giving pleasure. Let us leave such jesting to the legends and the Greeks, who think but little of the truth, and enchant ear and mind by the charm of their fictions and the daintiness of their style.

105. We however, who extend the accuracy of the Spirit to the merest stroke and tittle, will never admit the impious assertion that even the smallest matters were dealt with haphazard by those who have recorded them, and have thus been borne in mind down to the present day: on the contrary, their purpose has been to supply memorials and instructions for our consideration under similar circumstances, should such befall us, and that the examples of the past might serve as rules and models, for our warning and imitation.

106. What then is the story, and wherein lies its application? For, perhaps, it would not be amiss to relate it, for the general security. Jonah also was fleeing from the face of God, or rather, thought that he was fleeing: but he was overtaken by the sea, and the storm, and the lot, and the whale's belly, and the three days' entombment, the type of a greater mystery. He fled from having to announce the dread and awful message to the Ninevites, and from being subsequently, if the city was saved by repentance, convicted of falsehood: not that he was displeased at the salvation of the wicked, but he was ashamed of being made an instrument of falsehood, and exceedingly zealous for the credit of prophecy, which was in danger of being destroyed in his person, since most men are unable to penetrate the depth of the Divine dispensation in such cases.

107. But, as I have learned from a man skilled in these subjects, and able to grasp the depth of the prophet, by means of a reasonable explanation of what seems unreasonable in the history, it was not this which caused Jonah to flee, and carried him to Joppa and again from Joppa to Tarshish, when he entrusted his stolen self to the sea: for it was not likely that such a prophet should be ignorant of the design of God, viz., to bring about, by means of the threat, the escape of the Ninevites from the threatened doom, according to His great wisdom, and unsearchable judgments, and according to His ways which are beyond our tracing and finding out; nor that, if he knew this he would refuse to co-operate with God in the use of the means which He designed for their salvation. Besides, to imagine that Jonah hoped to hide himself at sea, and escape by his flight the great eye of God, is surely utterly absurd and stupid, and unworthy of credit, not only in the case of a prophet, but even in the case of any sensible man, who has only a slight perception of God, Whose power is over all.

108. On the contrary, as my instructor said, and as I am myself convinced, Jonah knew better than any one the purpose of his message to the Ninevites, and that, in planning his flight, although he changed his place, he did not escape from God. Nor is this possible for any one else, either by concealing himself in the bosom of the earth, or in the depths of the sea, or by soaring on wings, if there be any means of doing so, and rising into the air, or by abiding in the lowest depths of hell, or by enveloping himself in a thick cloud, or by any other of the many devices for ensuring escape. For God alone of all things cannot be escaped from or contended with; if He wills to seize and bring them under His hand, He outstrips the swift, He outwits the wise, He overthrows the strong, He abases the lofty, He subdues rashness, He represses power.

109. Jonah then was not ignorant of the mighty hand of God, with which he threatened other men, nor did he imagine that he could utterly escape the Divine power; this we are not to believe: but when he saw the falling away of Israel, and perceived the passing over of the grace of prophecy to the Gentiles — this was the cause of his retirement from preaching and of his delay in fulfilling the command; accordingly he left the watchtower of joy, for this is the meaning of Joppa in Hebrew, I mean his former dignity and reputation, and flung himself into the deep of sorrow: and hence he is tempest-tossed, and falls asleep, and is wrecked, and aroused from sleep, and taken by lot, and confesses his flight, and is cast into sea, and swallowed, but not destroyed, by the whale; but there he calls upon God, and, marvelous as it is, on the third day he, like Christ, is delivered: but my treatment of this topic must stand over, and shall shortly, if God permit, be more deliberately worked out.

110. Now however, to return to my original point, the thought and question occurred to me, that although he might possibly meet with some indulgence, if reluctant to prophesy, for the cause which I mentioned — yet, in my own case, what could be said, what defense could be made, if I longer remained restive, and rejected the yoke of ministry, which, though I know not whether to call it light or heavy, had at any rate been laid upon me.

111. For if it be granted, and this alone can be strongly asserted in such matters, that we are far too low to perform the priest' s office before God, and that we can only be worthy of the sanctuary after we have become worthy of the Church, and worthy of the post of president, after being worthy of the sanctuary, yet some one else may perhaps refuse to acquit us on the charge of disobedience. Now terrible are the threatenings against disobedience, and terrible are the penalties which ensue upon it; as indeed are those on the other side, if, instead of being reluctant, and shrinking back, and concealing ourselves as Saul did among his father's stuff — although called to rule but for a short time — if, I say, we come forward readily, as though to a slight and most easy task, whereas it is not safe even to resign it, nor to amend by second thoughts our first.

34

112. On this account I had much toilsome consideration to discover my duty, being set in the midst betwixt two fears, of which the one held me back, the other urged me on. For a long while I was at a loss between them, and after wavering from side to side, and, like a current driven by inconstant winds, inclining first in this direction, then in that, I at last yielded to the stronger, and the fear of disobedience overcame me, and has carried me off. Pray, mark how accurately and justly I hold the balance between the fears, neither desiring an office not given to me, nor rejecting it when given. The one course marks the rash, the other the disobedient, both the undisciplined. My position lies between those who are too bold, or too timid; more timid than those who rush at every position, more bold than those who avoid them all. This is my judgment on the matter.

113. Moreover, to distinguish still more clearly between them, we have, against the fear of office, a possible help in the law of obedience, inasmuch as God in His goodness rewards our faith, and makes a perfect ruler of the man who has confidence in Him, and places all his hopes in Him; but against the danger of disobedience I know of nothing which can help us, and of no ground to encourage our confidence. For it is to be feared that we shall have to hear these words concerning those who have been entrusted to us: I will require their souls at your hands; and, Because ye have rejected me, and not been leaders and rulers of my people, I also will reject you, that I should not be king over you; and, As ye refused to hearken to My voice, and turned a stubborn back, and were disobedient, so shall it be when ye call upon Me, and I will not regard nor give ear to your prayer. God forbid that these words should come to us from the just Judge, for when we sing of His mercy we must also by all means sing of His judgment.

114. I resort once again to history, and on considering the men of best repute in ancient days, who were ever preferred by grace to the office of ruler or prophet, I discover that some readily complied with the call, others deprecated the gift, and that neither those who drew back were blamed for timidity, nor those who came forward for eagerness. The former stood in awe of the greatness of the ministry, the latter trustfully obeyed Him Who called them. Aaron was eager, but Moses resisted, Isaiah readily submitted, but Jeremiah was afraid of his youth, and did not venture to prophesy until he had received from God a promise and power beyond his years.

115. By these arguments I charmed myself, and by degrees my soul relaxed and became ductile, like iron, and time came to the aid of my arguments, and the testimonies of God, to which I had entrusted my whole life, were my counselors. Therefore I was not rebellious, neither turned away back, saith my Lord, when, instead of being called to rule, He was led, as a sheep to the slaughter; but I fell down and humbled myself under the mighty hand of God, and asked pardon for my former idleness and disobedience, if this is at all laid to my charge. I held my peace, but I will not hold my peace for ever: I withdrew for a little while, till I had considered myself and consoled my grief: but now I am commissioned to exalt Him

in the congregation of the people, and praise Him in the seat of the elders. If my former conduct deserved blame, my present action merits pardon.

116. What further need is there of words. Here am I, my pastors and fellow-pastors, here am I, thou holy flock, worthy of Christ, the Chief Shepherd, here am I, my father, utterly vanquished, and your subject according to the laws of Christ rather than according to those of the land: here is my obedience, reward it with your blessing. Lead me with your prayers, guide me with your words, establish me with your spirit. The blessing of the father establisheth the houses of children, and would that both I and this spiritual house may be established, the house which I have longed for, which I pray may be my rest for ever, when I have been passed on from the church here to the church yonder, the general assembly of the firstborn, who are written in heaven.

117. Such is my defense: its reasonableness I have set forth: and may the God of peace, Who made both one, and has restored us to each other, Who setteth kings upon thrones, and raiseth up the poor out of the dust and lifteth up the beggar from the dunghill, Who chose David His servant and took him away from the sheepfolds, though he was the least and youngest of the sons of Jesse, Who gave the word to those who preach the gospel with great power for the perfection of the gospel, — may He Himself hold me by my right hand, and guide me with His counsel, and receive me with glory, Who is a Shepherd to shepherds and a Guide to guides: that we may feed His flock with knowledge, not with the instruments of a foolish shepherd, according to the blessing, and not according to the curse pronounced against the men of former days: may He give strength and power unto his people, and Himself present to Himself His flock resplendent and spotless and worthy of the fold on high, in the habitation of them that rejoice, in the splendor of the saints, so that in His temple everyone, both flock and shepherds together may say, Glory, in Christ Jesus our Lord, to Whom be all glory for ever and ever. Amen.

To those who had invited him, and not come to receive him (About Easter A.D. 362.)

I. How slow you are, my friends and brethren, to come to listen to my words, though you were so swift in tyrannizing over me, and tearing me from my Citadel Solitude, which I had embraced in preference to everything else, and as coadjutress and mother of the divine ascent, and as deifying man, I had especially admired, and had set before me as the guide of my whole life. How is it that, now you have got it, you thus despise what you so greatly desired to obtain, and seem to be better able to desire the absent than to enjoy the present; as though you preferred to possess my teaching rather than to profitby it? Yes, I may even say this to you: "I became a surfeit unto you before you tasted of me, or gave me a trial" — which is most strange.

II. And neither did you entertain me as a guest, nor, if I may make a remark of a more compassionate kind, did you allow yourselves to be entertained by me, reverencing this command if nothing else; nor did you take me by the hand, as beginning a new task; nor encourage me in my timidity, nor console me for the violence I had suffered; but — I shrink from saying it, though say it I must — you made my festival no festival, and received me with no happy introduction; and you mingled the solemn festival with sorrow, because it lacked that which most of all would have contributed to its happiness, the presence of you my conquerors, for it would not be true to call you people who love me. So easily is anything despised which is easily conquered, and the proud receives attention, while he who is humble before God is slighted.

III. What will ye? Shall I be judged by you, or shall I be your judge? Shall I pass a verdict, or receive one, for I hope to be acquitted if I be judged, and if I give sentence, to give it against you justly? The charge against you is that you do not answer my love with equal measure, nor do you repay my obedience with honor, nor do you pledge the future to me by your present alacrity — though even if you had, I could hardly have believed it. But each of you has something which he prefers to both the old and the new Pastor, neither reverencing the gray hairs of the one, nor calling out the youthful spirit of the other.

IV. There is a Banquet in the Gospels, and a hospitable Host and friends; and the Banquet is most pleasant, for it is the marriage of His Son. He calleth them, but they come not: He is angry, and — I pass over the interval for fear of bad omen — but, to speak gently, He filleth the Banquet with others. God forbid that this should be your case; but yet you have treated me (how shall I put it gently?) with as much haughtiness or boldness as they who after being called to a feast rise up against it, and insult their host; for you, though you are not of the number of those who are without, or are invited to the marriage, but are yourselves those who invited me, and bound me to the Holy Table, and shewed me the glory of the

Bridal Chamber, then deserted me (this is the most splendid thing about you) —
one to his field, another to his newly bought yoke of oxen, another to his just-
married wife, another to some other trifling matter; you were all scattered and
dispersed, caring little for the Bridechamber and the Bridegroom.

V. On this account I was filled with despondency and perplexity — for I will not
keep silence about what I have suffered — and I was very near withholding the
discourse which I was minded to bestow as a Marriage-gift, the most beautiful and
precious of all I had; and I very nearly let it loose upon you, whom, now that the
violence had once been done to me, I greatly longed for: for I thought I could get
from this a splendid theme, and because my love sharpened my tongue — love
which is very hot and ready for accusation when it is stirred to jealousy by grief
which it conceives from some unexpected neglect. If any of you has been pierced
with love's sting, and has felt himself neglected, he knows the feeling, and will
pardon one who so suffers, because he himself has been near the same frenzy.

VI. But it is not permitted to me at the present time to say to you anything
upbraiding; and God forbid I ever should. And even now perhaps I have
reproached you more than in due measure, the Sacred Flock, the praise-worthy
nurslings of Christ, the Divine inheritance; by which, O God, Thou art rich, even
wert Thou poor in all other respects. To Thee, I think, are fitting those words,
"The lot is fallen unto Thee in a fair ground: yea Thou hast the goodliest heritage."
Nor will I allow that the most populous cities or the broadest flocks have any
advantage over us, the little ones of the smallest of all the tribes of Israel, of the least
of the thousands of Judah, of the little Bethlehem among cities, where Christ was
born and is from the beginning well-known and worshipped; amongst those whom
the Father is exalted, and the Son is held to be equal to Him, and the Holy Ghost is
glorified with Them: we who are of one soul, who mind the same thing, who in
nothing injure the Trinity, neither by preferring One Person above another, nor by
cutting off any: as those bad umpires and measurers of the Godhead do, who by
magnifying One Person more than is fit, diminish and insult the whole.

VII. But do ye also, if you bear me any good will — ye who are my husbandry, my
vineyard, my own bowels, or rather His Who is our common Father, for in Christ
he hath begotten you through the Gospels — shew to us also some respect. It is
only fair, since we have honored you above all else: ye are my witnesses, ye, and
they who have placed in our hands this — shall I say Authority, or Service! And if
to him that loveth most is due, how shall I measure the love, for which I have made
you my debtors by my own love? Rather, shew respect for yourselves, and the
Image committed to your care, and Him Who committed it, and the Sufferings of
Christ, and your hopes therefrom, holding fast the faith which ye have received,
and in which ye were brought up, by which also ye are being saved, and trust to
save others (for not many, be well assured, can boast of what you can), and
reckoning piety to consist, not in often speaking about God, but in silence for the

most part, for the tongue is a dangerous thing to men, if it be not governed by reason. Believe that listening is always less dangerous than talking, just as learning about God is more pleasant than teaching. Leave the more accurate search into these questions to those who are the Stewards of the Word; and for yourselves, worship a little in words, but more by your actions, and rather by keeping the Law than by admiring the Lawgiver; shew your love for Him by fleeing from wickedness, pursuing after virtue, living in the Spirit, walking in the Spirit, drawing your knowledge from Him, building upon the foundation of the faith, not wood or hay or stubble, weak materials and easily spent when the fire shall try our works or destroy them; but gold, silver, precious stones, which remain and stand.

VIII. So may ye act, and so may ye honor us, whether present or absent, whether taking your part in our sermons, or preferring to do something else: and may ye be the children of God, pure and unblamable, in the midst of a crooked and perverse generation: and may ye never be entangled in the snares of the wicked that go round about, or bound with the chain of your sins. May the Word in you never be smothered with cares of this life and so ye become unfruitful: but may ye walk in the King's Highway, turning aside neither to the right hand nor to the left, but led by the Spirit through the strait gate. Then all our affairs shall prosper, both now and at the inquest There, in Christ Jesus our Lord, to Whom be the glory for ever. Amen.

Panegyric on his brother S Caesarius

The date of this Oration is probably the spring of A.D. 369. It is placed by S. Jerome first among S. Gregory's Orations. Caesarius, the Saint's younger brother, was born probably about A.D. 330. Educated in his early years at home, he studied later in the schools of Alexandria, where he attained great proficiency in mathematics, astronomy, and, especially, in medicine. On his return from Alexandria, he was offered by the Emperor Constantius, in response to a public petition, an honorable and lucrative post at Byzantium, but was prevailed upon by Gregory to return with him to Nazianzus. After a while he went back to Byzantium, and, on the accession of Julian, was pressed to retain his appointment at court, and did so, in spite of Gregory's reproaches, until Julian, who had long been trying to win him from Christianity, at last invited him to a public discussion. Caesarius, in spite of the specious arguments of the Emperor, gained the day, but, having now distinctly declared himself a Christian, could no longer remain at court. On the death of Julian, he was esteemed and promoted by successive Emperors, until he received from Valens the office of treasurer of Bithynia. The exact character of this office and its rank are still undecided by historical writers, some of whom attribute to him other offices not mentioned by S. Gregory, which most probably were filled by a namesake. On the 11th of October A.D. 368 the city of Nicaea was almost entirely destroyed by an earthquake and Caesarius miraculously escaped with his life. Impressed by his escape, he received Holy Baptism, and formed plans for retiring from office and (as it seems) devoting himself to a life of ascetic discipline, which were dissipated by his early and sudden death.

1 . It may be, my friends, my brethren, my fathers (ye who are dear to me in reality as well as in name) that you think that I, who am about to pay the sad tribute of lamentation to him who has departed, am eager to undertake the task, and shall, as most men delight to do, speak at great length and in eloquent style. And so some of you, who have had like sorrows to bear, are prepared to join in my mourning and lamentation, in order to bewail your own griefs in mine, and learn to feel pain at the afflictions of a friend, while others are looking to feast their ears in the enjoyment of my words. For they suppose that I must needs make my misfortune an occasion for display — as was once my wont, when possessed of a superabundance of earthly things, and ambitious, above all, of oratorical renown — before I looked up to Him Who is the true and highest Word, and gave all up to God, from Whom all things come, and took God for all in all. Now pray do not think this of me, if you wish to think of me aright. For I am neither going to lament for him who is gone more than is good — as I should not approve of such conduct even in others — nor am I going to praise him beyond due measure. Albeit that language is a dear and especially proper tribute to one gifted with it, and eulogy to one who was exceedingly fond of my words — aye, not only a tribute, but a debt, the most just of all debts. But even in my tears and admiration I must respect the law which regards such matters: nor is this alien to our philosophy; for he says The memory of the just is accompanied with eulogies, and also, Let tears fall

down over the dead, and begin to lament, as if thou hadst suffered great harm thyself: removing us equally from insensibility and immoderation. I shall proceed then, not only to exhibit the weakness of human nature, but also to put you in mind of the dignity of the soul, and, giving such consolation as is due to those who are in sorrow, transfer our grief, from that which concerns the flesh and temporal things, to those things which are spiritual and eternal.

2. The parents of Caesarius, to take first the point which best becomes me, are known to you all. Their excellence you are eager to notice, and hear of with admiration, and share in the task of setting it forth to any, if there be such, who know it not: for no single man is able to do so entirely, and the task is one beyond the powers of a single tongue, however laborious, however zealous. Among the many and great points for which they are to be celebrated (I trust I may not seem extravagant in praising my own family) the greatest of all, which more than any other stamps their character, is piety. By their hoar hairs they lay claim to reverence, but they are no less venerable for their virtue than for their age; for while their bodies are bent beneath the burden of their years, their souls renew their youth in God.

3. His father was well grafted out of the wild olive tree into the good one, and so far partook of its fatness as to be entrusted with the engrafting of others, and charged with the culture of souls, presiding in a manner becoming his high office over this people, like a second Aaron or Moses, bidden himself to draw near to God, and to convey the Divine Voice to the others who stand afar off; gentle, meek, calm in mien, fervent in spirit, a fine man in external appearance, but richer still in that which is out of sight. But why should I describe him whom you know? For I could not even by speaking at great length say as much as he deserves, or as much as each of you knows and expects to be said of him. It is then better to leave your own fancy to picture him, than mutilate by my words the object of your admiration.

4. His mother was consecrated to God by virtue of her descent from a saintly family, and was possessed of piety as a necessary inheritance, not only for herself, but also for her children — being indeed a holy lump from a holy firstfruits. And this she so far increased and amplified that some,(bold though the statement be, I will utter it,) have both believed and said that even her husband's perfection has been the work of none other than herself; and, oh how wonderful! she herself, as the reward of her piety, has received a greater and more perfect piety. Lovers of their children and of Christ as they both were, what is most extraordinary, they were far greater lovers of Christ than of their children: yea, even their one enjoyment of their children was that they should be acknowledged and named by Christ, and their one measure of their blessedness in their children was their virtue and close association with the Chief Good. Compassionate, sympathetic, snatching many a treasure from moths and robbers, and from the prince of this world, to transfer it from their sojourn here to the [true] habitation, laying up in store for

their children the heavenly splendor as their greatest inheritance. Thus have they reached a fair old age, equally reverend both for virtue and for years, and full of days, alike of those which abide and those which pass away; each one failing to secure the first prize here below only so far as equaled by the other; yea, they have fulfilled the measure of every happiness with the exception of this last trial, or discipline, whichever anyone may think we ought to call it; I mean their having to send before them the child who was, owing to his age, in greater danger of falling, and so to close their life in safety, and be translated with all their family to the realms above.

5. I have entered into these details, not from a desire to eulogize them, for this, I know well, it would be difficult worthily to do, if I made their praise the subject of my whole oration, but to set forth the excellence inherited from his parents by Caesarius, and so prevent you from being surprised or incredulous, that one sprung from such progenitors, should have deserved such praises himself; nay, strange indeed would it have been, had he looked to others and disregarded the examples of his kinsfolk at home. His early life was such as becomes those really well born and destined for a good life. I say little of his qualities evident to all, his beauty, his stature, his manifold gracefulness, and harmonious disposition, as shown in the tones of his voice — for it is not my office to laud qualities of this kind, however important they may seem to others — and proceed with what I have to say of the points which, even if I wished, I could with difficulty pass by.

6. Bred and reared under such influences, we were fully trained in the education afforded here, in which none could say how far he excelled most of us from the quickness and extent of his abilities — and how can I recall those days without my tears showing that, contrary to my promises, my feelings have overcome my philosophic restraint? The time came when it was decided that we should leave home, and then for the first time we were separated, for I studied rhetoric in the then flourishing schools of Palestine; he went to Alexandria, esteemed both then and now the home of every branch of learning. Which of his qualities shall I place first and foremost, or which can I omit with least injury to my description? Who was more faithful to his teacher than he? Who more kindly to his classmates? Who more carefully avoided the society and companionship of the depraved? Who attached himself more closely to that of the most excellent, and among others, of the most esteemed and illustrious of his countrymen? For he knew that we are strongly influenced to virtue or vice by our companions. And in consequence of all this, who was more honored by the authorities than he, and whom did the whole city (though all individuals are concealed in it, because of its size), esteem more highly for his discretion, or deem more illustrious for his intelligence?

7. What branch of learning did he not master, or rather, in what branch of study did he not surpass those who had made it their sole study? Whom did he allow even to approach him, not only of his own time and age, but even of his elders, who had

devoted many more years to study? All subjects he studied as one, and each as thoroughly as if he knew no other. The brilliant in intellect, he surpassed in industry, the devoted students in quickness of perception; nay, rather he outstripped in rapidity those who were rapid, in application those who were laborious, and in both respects those who were distinguished in both. From geometry and astronomy, that science so dangerous to anyone else, he gathered all that was helpful (I mean that he was led by the harmony and order of the heavenly bodies to reverence their Maker), and avoided what is injurious; not attributing all things that are or happen to the influence of the stars, like those who raise their own fellow-servant, the creation, in rebellion against the Creator, but referring, as is reasonable, the motion of these bodies, and all other things besides, to God. In arithmetic and mathematics, and in the wonderful art of medicine, in so far as it treats of physiology and temperament, and the causes of disease, in order to remove the roots and so destroy their offspring with them, who is there so ignorant or contentious as to think him inferior to himself, and not to be glad to be reckoned next to him, and carry off the second prize? This indeed is no unsupported assertion, but East and West alike, and every place which he afterward visited, are as pillars inscribed with the record of his learning.

8. But when, after gathering into his single soul every kind of excellence and knowledge, as a mighty merchantman gathers every sort of ware, he was voyaging to his own city, in order to communicate to others the fair cargo of his culture, there befell a wondrous thing, which I must, as its mention is most cheering to me and may delight you, briefly set forth. Our mother, in her motherly love for her children, had offered up a prayer that, as she had sent us forth together, she might see us together return home. For we seemed, to our mother at least, if not to others, to form a pair worthy of her prayers and glances, if seen together, though now, alas, our connection has been severed. And God, Who hears a righteous prayer, and honors the love of parents for well-disposed children, so ordered that, without any design or agreement on our part, the one from Alexandria, the other from Greece, the one by sea, the other by land, we arrived at the same city at the same time. This city was Byzantium, which now presides over Europe, in which Caesarius, after the lapse of a short time, gained such a repute, that public honors, an alliance with an illustrious family, and a seat in the council of state were offered him; and a mission was despatched to the Emperor by public decision, to beg that the first of cities be adorned and honored by the first of scholars (if he cared at all for its being indeed the first, and worthy of its name); and that to all its other titles to distinction this further one be added, that it was embellished by having Caesarius as its physician and its inhabitant, although its brilliancy was already assured by its throngs of great men both in philosophy and other branches of learning. But enough of this. At this time there happened what seemed to others a chance without reason or cause, such as frequently occurs of its own accord in our day, but was more than sufficiently manifest to devout minds as the result of the prayers to God-fearing parents, which were answered by the united arrival of their sons by land and sea.

9. Well, among the noble traits of Caesarius' character, we must not fail to note one, which perhaps is in others' eyes slight and unworthy of mention, but seemed to me, both at the time and since, of the highest import, if indeed brotherly love be a praiseworthy quality; nor shall I ever cease to place it in the first rank, in relating the story of his life. Although the metropolis strove to retain him by the honors I have mentioned, and declared that it would under no circumstances let him go, my influence, which he valued most highly on all occasions, prevailed upon him to listen to the prayer of his parents, to supply his country's need, and to grant me my own desire. And when he thus returned home in my company, he preferred me not only to cities and peoples, not only to honors and revenues, which had in part already flowed to him in abundance from many sources and in part were within his reach, but even to the Emperor himself and his imperial commands. From this time, then, having shaken off all ambition, as a hard master and a painful disorder, I resolved to practice philosophy and adapt myself to the higher life: or rather the desire was earlier born, the life came later. But my brother, who had dedicated to his country the firstfruits of his learning, and gained an admiration worthy of his efforts, was afterwards led by the desire of fame, and, as he persuaded me, of being the guardian of the city, to betake himself to court, not indeed according to my own wishes or judgment; for I will confess to you that I think it a better and grander thing to be in the lowest rank with God than to win the first place with an earthly king. Nevertheless I cannot blame him, for inasmuch as philosophy is the greatest, so is it the most difficult, of professions, which can be taken in hand by but few, and only by those who have been called forth by the Divine magnanimity, which gives its hand to those who are honored by its preference. Yet it is no small thing if one, who has chosen the lower form of life, follows after goodness, and sets greater store on God and his own salvation than on earthly luster; using it as a stage, or a manifold ephemeral mask while playing in the drama of this world, but himself living unto God with that image which he knows that he has received from Him, and must render to Him Who gave it. That this was certainly the purpose of Caesarius, we know full well.

10. Among physicians he gained the foremost place with no great trouble, by merely exhibiting his capacity, or rather some slight specimen of his capacity, and was forthwith numbered among the friends of the Emperor, and enjoyed the highest honors. But he placed the humane functions of his art at the disposal of the authorities free of cost, knowing that nothing leads to further advancement than virtue and renown for honorable deeds; so that he far surpassed in fame those to whom he was inferior in rank. By his modesty he so won the love of all that they entrusted their precious charges to his care, without requiring him to be sworn by Hippocrates, since the simplicity of Crates was nothing to his own: winning in general a respect beyond his rank; for besides the present repute he was ever thought to have justly won, a still greater one was anticipated for him, both by the Emperors themselves and by all who occupied the nearest positions to them. But, most important, neither by his fame, nor by the luxury which surrounded him, was

his nobility of soul corrupted; for amidst his many claims to honor, he himself cared most for being, and being known to be, a Christian, and, compared with this, all other things were to him but trifling toys. For they belong to the part we play before others on a stage which is very quickly set up and taken down again — perhaps indeed more quickly destroyed than put together, as we may see from the manifold changes of life, and fluctuations of prosperity; while the only real and securely abiding good thing is godliness.

11. Such was the philosophy of Caesarius, even at court: these were the ideas amidst which he lived and died, discovering and presenting to God, in the hidden man, a still deeper godliness than was publicly visible. And if I must pass by all else, his protection of his kinsmen in distress, his contempt for arrogance, his freedom from assumption towards friends, his boldness towards men in power, the numerous contests and arguments in which he engaged with many on behalf of the truth, not merely for the sake of argument, but with deep piety and fervor, I must speak of one point at least as especially worthy of note. The Emperor of unhappy memory was raging against us, whose madness in rejecting Christ, after making himself its first victim, had now rendered him intolerable to others; though he did not, like other fighters against Christ, grandly enlist himself on the side of impiety, but veiled his persecution under the form of equity; and, ruled by the crooked serpent which possessed his soul, dragged down into his own pit his wretched victims by manifold devices. His first artifice and contrivance was, to deprive us of the honor of our conflicts (for, noble man as he was, he grudged this to Christians), by causing us, who suffered for being Christians, to be punished as evil doers: the second was, to call this process persuasion, and not tyranny, so that the disgrace of those who chose to side with impiety might be greater than their danger. Some he won over by money, some by dignities, some by promises, some by various honors, which he bestowed, not royally but in right servile style, in the sight of all, while everyone was influenced by the witchery of his words, and his own example. At last he assailed Caesarius. How utter was the derangement and folly which could hope to take for his prey a man like Caesarius, my brother, the son of parents like ours!

12. However, that I may dwell awhile upon this point, and luxuriate in my story as men do who are eyewitnesses in some marvelous event, that noble man, fortified with the sign of Christ, and defending himself with His Mighty Word, entered the lists against an adversary experienced in arms and strong in his skill in argument. In no wise abashed at the sight, nor shrinking at all from his high purpose through flattery, he was an athlete ready, both in word and deed, to meet a rival of equal power. Such then was the arena, and so equipped the champion of godliness. The judge on one side was Christ, arming the athlete with His own sufferings: and on the other a dreadful tyrant, persuasive by his skill in argument, and overawing him by the weight of his authority; and as spectators, on either hand, both those who were still left on the side of godliness and those who had been snatched away by

him, watching whether victory inclined to their own side or to the other, and more anxious as to which would gain the day than the combatants themselves.

13. Didst thou not fear for Caesarius, lest aught unworthy of his zeal should befall him? Nay, be ye of good courage. For the victory is with Christ, Who overcame the world. Now for my part, be well assured, I should be highly interested in setting forth the details of the arguments and allegations used on that occasion, for indeed the discussion contains certain feats and elegances, which I dwell on with no slight pleasure; but this would be quite foreign to an occasion and discourse like the present. And when, after having torn to shreds all his opponent's sophistries, and thrust aside as mere child's play every assault, veiled or open, Caesarius in a loud clear voice declared that he was and remained a Christian — not even thus was he finally dismissed. For indeed, the Emperor was possessed by an eager desire to enjoy and be distinguished by his culture, and then uttered in the hearing of all his famous saying — O happy father, O unhappy sons! thus deigning to honor me, whose culture and godliness he had known at Athens, with a share in the dishonor of Caesarius, who was remanded for a further trial, (since Justice was fitly arming the Emperor against the Persians), and welcomed by us after his happy escape and bloodless victory, as more illustrious for his dishonor than for his celebrity.

14. This victory I esteem far more sublime and honorable than the Emperor's mighty power and splendid purple and costly diadem. I am more elated in describing it than if he had won from him the half of his Empire. During the evil days he lived in retirement, obedient herein to our Christian law, which bids us, when occasion offers, to make ventures on behalf of the truth, and not be traitors to our religion from cowardice; yet refrain, as long as may be, from rushing into danger, either in fear for our own souls, or to spare those who bring the danger upon us. But when the gloom had been dispersed, and the righteous sentence had been pronounced in a foreign land, and the glittering sword had struck down the ungodly, and power had returned to the hands of Christians, what boots it to say with what glory and honor, with how many and great testimonies, as if bestowing rather than receiving a favor, he was welcomed again at the Court; his new honor succeeding to that of former days; while tithe changed its Emperors, the repute and commanding influence of Caesarius with them was undisturbed, nay, they vied with each other in striving to attach him most closely to themselves, and be known as his special friends and acquaintances. Such was the godliness of Caesarius, such its results. Let all men, young and old, give ear, and press on through the same virtue to the same distinction, for glorious is the fruit of good labors, if they suppose this to be worth striving after, and a part of true happiness.

15. Again another wonder concerning him is a strong argument for his parents' piety and his own. He was living in Bithynia, holding an office of no small importance from the Emperor, viz., the stewardship of his revenue, and care of the exchequer: for this had been assigned to him by the Emperor as a prelude to the

highest offices. And when, a short time ago, the earthquake in Nicaea occurred, which is said to have been the most serious within the memory of man, overwhelming in a common destruction almost all the inhabitants and the beauty of the city, he alone, or with very few of the men of rank, survived the danger, being shielded by the very falling ruins in his incredible escape, and bearing slight traces of the peril; yet he allowed fear to lead him to a more important salvation, for he dedicated himself entirely to the Supreme Providence; he renounced the service of transitory things, and attached himself to another court. This he both purposed himself, and made the object of the united earnest prayers to which he invited me by letter, when I seized this opportunity to give him warning, as I never ceased to do when pained that his great nature should be occupied in affairs beneath it, and that a soul so fitted for philosophy should, like the sun behind a cloud, be obscured amid the whirl of public life. Unscathed though he had been by the earthquake, he was not proof against disease, since he was but human. His escape was peculiar to himself; his death common to all mankind; the one the token of his piety, the other the result of his nature. The former, for our consolation, preceded his fate, so that, though shaken by his death, we might exult in the extraordinary character of his preservation. And now our illustrious Caesarius has been restored to us, when his honored dust and celebrated coarse, after being escorted home amidst a succession of hymns and public orations, has been honored by the holy hands of his parents; while his mother, substituting the festal garments of religion for the trappings of woe, has overcome her tears by her philosophy, and lulled to sleep lamentations by psalmody, as her son enjoys honors worthy of his newly regenerate soul, which has been, through water, transformed by the Spirit.

16. This, Caesarius, is my funeral offering to thee, this the firstfruits of my words, which thou hast often blamed me for withholding, yet wouldst have stripped off, had they been bestowed on thee; with this ornament I adorn thee, an ornament, I know well, far dearer to thee than all others, though it be not of the soft flowing tissues of silk, in which while living, with virtue for thy sole adorning, thou didst not, like the many, rejoice; nor texture of transparent linen, nor outpouring of costly unguents, which thou hadst long resigned to the boudoirs of the fair, with their sweet savors lasting but a single day; nor any other small thing valued by small minds, which would have all been hidden today with thy fair form by this bitter stone. Far hence be games and stories of the Greeks, the honors of ill-fated youths, with their petty prizes for petty contests; and all the libations and firstfruits or garlands and newly plucked flowers, wherewith men honor the departed, in obedience to ancient custom and unreasoning grief, rather than reason. My gift is an oration, which perhaps succeeding time will receive at my hand and ever keep in motion, that it may not suffer him who has left us to be utterly lost to earth, but may ever keep him whom we honor in men's ears and minds, as it sets before them, more clearly than a portrait, the image of him for whom we mourn.

17. Such is my offering; if it be slight and inferior to his merit, God loveth that which is according to our power. Part of our gift is now complete, the remainder we will now pay by offering (those of us who still survive) every year our honors and memorials. And now for thee, sacred and holy soul, we pray for an entrance into heaven; mayest thou enjoy such repose as the bosom of Abraham affords, mayest thou behold the choir of Angels, and the glories and splendors of sainted men; aye, mayest thou be united to that choir and share in their joy, looking down from on high on all things here, on what men call wealth, and despicable dignities, and deceitful honors, and the errors of our senses, and the tangle of this life, and its confusion and ignorance, as if we were fighting in the dark; whilst thou art in attendance upon the Great King and filled with the light which streams forth from Him: and may it be ours hereafter, receiving therefrom no such slender rivulet, as is the object of our fancy in this day of mirrors and enigmas, to attain to the fount of good itself, gazing with pure mind upon the truth in its purity, and finding a reward for our eager toil here below on behalf of the good, in our more perfect possession and vision of the good on high: the end to which our sacred books and teachers foretell that our course of divine mysteries shall lead us.

18. What; now remains? To bring the healing of the Word to those in sorrow. And a powerful remedy for mourners is sympathy, for sufferers are best consoled by those who have to bear a like suffering. To such, then, I specially address myself, of whom I should be ashamed, if, with all other virtues, they do not show the elements of patience. For even if they surpass all others in love of their children, let them equally surpass them in love of wisdom and love of Christ, and in the special practice of meditation on our departure hence, impressing it likewise on their children, making even their whole life a preparation for death. But if your misfortune still clouds your reason and, like the moisture which dims our eyes, hides from you the clear view of your duty, come, ye elders, receive the consolation of a young man, ye fathers, that of a child, who ought to be admonished by men as old as you, who have admonished many and gathered experience from your many years. Yet wonder not, if in my youth I admonish the aged; and if in aught I can see better than the hoary, I offer it to you. How much longer have we to live, ye men of honored held, so near to God? How long are we to suffer here? Not even man's whole life is long, compared with the Eternity of the Divine Nature, still less the remains of life, and what I may call the parting of our human breath, the close of our frail existence. How much has Caesarius outstripped us? How long shall we be left to mourn his departure? Are we not hastening to the same abode? Shall we not soon be covered by the same stone? Shall we not shortly be reduced to the same dust? And what in these short days will be our gain, save that after it has been ours to see, or suffer, or perchance even to do, more ill, we must discharge the common and inexorable tribute to the law of nature, by following some, preceding others, to the tomb, mourning these, being lamented by those, and receiving from some that meed of tears which we ourselves had paid to others?

19. Such, my brethren, is our existence, who live this transient life, such our pastime upon earth: we come into existence out of non-existence, and after existing are dissolved. We are unsubstantial dreams, impalpable visions, like the flight of a passing bird, like a ship leaving no track upon the sea, a speck of dust, a vapor, an early dew, a flower that quickly blooms, and quickly fades. As for man his days are as grass, as a flower of the field, so he flourisheth. Well hath inspired David discoursed of our frailty, and again in these words, "Let me know the shortness of my days;" and he defines the days of man as "of a span long." And what wouldst thou say to Jeremiah, who complains of his mother in sorrow for his birth, and that on account of others' faults? I have seen all things, says the preacher, I have reviewed in thought all human things, wealth, pleasure, power, unstable glory, wisdom which evades us rather than is won; then pleasure again, wisdom again, often revolving the same objects, the pleasures of appetite, orchards, numbers of slaves, store of wealth, serving men and serving maids, singing men and singing women, arms, spearmen, subject nations, collected tributes, the pride of kings, all the necessaries and superfluities of life, in which I surpassed all the kings that were before me. And what does he say after all these things? Vanity of vanities, all is vanity and vexation of spirit, possibly meaning some unreasoning longing of the soul, and distraction of man condemned to this from the original fall: but hear, he says, the conclusion of the whole matter, Fear God. This is his stay in his perplexity, and this is thy only gain from life here below, to be guided through the disorder of the things which are seen and shaken, to the things which stand firm and are not moved.

20. Let us not then mourn Caesarius but ourselves, knowing what evils he has escaped to which we are left behind, and what treasure we shall lay up, unless, earnestly cleaving unto God and outstripping transitory things, we press towards the life above, deserting the earth while we are still upon the earth, and earnestly following the spirit which bears us upward. Painful as this is to the faint-hearted, it is as nothing to men of brave mind. And let us consider it thus. Caesarius will not reign, but rather will he be reigned over by others. He will strike terror into no one, but he will be free from fear of any harsh master, often himself unworthy even of a subject's position. He will not amass wealth, but neither will he be liable to envy, or be pained at lack of success, or be ever seeking to add to his gains as much again. For such is the disease of wealth, which knows no limit to its desire of more, and continues to make drinking the medicine for thirst. He will make no display of his power of speaking, yet for his speaking will he be admired. He will not discourse upon the dicta of Hippocrates and Galen, and their adversaries, but neither will he be troubled by diseases, and suffer pain at the misfortunes of others. He will not set forth the principles of Eucleides, Ptolemaeus, and Heron, but neither will he be pained by the tumid vaunts of uncultured men. He will make no display of the doctrines of Plato, and Aristotle, and Pyrrho, and the names of any Democritus, and Heracleitus, Anaxagoras, Cleanthes and Epicurus, and all the members of the venerable Porch and Academy: but neither will he trouble himself with the solution

of their cunning syllogisms. What need of further details? Yet here are some which all men honor or desire. Nor wife nor child will he have beside him, but he will escape mourning for, or being mourned by them, or leaving them to others, or being left behind himself as a memorial of misfortune. He will inherit no property: but he will have such heirs as are of the greatest service, such as he himself wished, so that he departed hence a rich man, bearing with him all that was his. What an ambition! What a new consolation! What magnanimity in his executors! A proclamation has been heard, worthy of the ears of all, and a mother's grief has been made void by a fair and holy promise, to give entirely to her son his wealth as a funeral offering on his behalf, leaving nothing to those who expected it.

21. Is this inadequate for our consolation? I will add a more potent remedy. I believe the words of the wise, that every fair and God-be-loved soul, when, set free from the bonds of the body, it departs hence, at once enjoys a sense and perception of the blessings which await it, inasmuch as that which darkened it has been purged away, or laid aside — I know not how else to term it — and feels a wondrous pleasure and exultation, and goes rejoicing to meet its Lord, having escaped as it were from the grievous poison of life here, and shaken off the fetters which bound it and held down the wings of the mind, and so enters on the enjoyment of the bliss laid up for it, of which it has even now some conception. Then, a little later, it receives its kindred flesh, which once shared in its pursuits of things above, from the earth which both gave and had been entrusted with it, and in some way known to God, who knit them together and dissolved them, enters with it upon the inheritance of the glory there. And, as it shared, through their close union, in its hardships, so also it bestows upon it a portion of its joys, gathering it up entirely into itself, and becoming with it one in spirit and in mind and in God, the mortal and mutable being swallowed up of life. Hear at least how the inspired Ezekiel discourses of the knitting together of bones and sinews, how after him Saint Paul speaks of the earthly tabernacle, and the house not made with hands, the one to be dissolved, the other laid up in heaven, alleging absence from the body to be presence with the Lord, and bewailing his life in it as an exile, and therefore longing for and hastening to his release. Why am I faint-hearted in my hopes? Why behave like a mere creature of a day? I await the voice of the Archangel, the last trumpet, the transformation of the heavens, the transfiguration of the earth, the liberation of the elements, the renovation of the universe. Then shall I see Caesarius himself, no longer in exile, no longer laid upon a bier, no longer the object of mourning and pity, but brilliant, glorious, heavenly, such as in my dreams I have often beheld thee, dearest and most loving of brothers, pictured thus by my desire, if not by the very truth.

22. But now, laying aside lamentation, I will look at myself, and examine my feelings, that I may not unconsciously have in myself anything to be lamented. O ye sons of men, for the words apply to you, how long will ye be hard-hearted and gross in mind? Why do ye love vanity and seek after leasing, supposing life here to

be a great thing and these few days many, and shrinking from this separation, welcome and pleasant as it is, as if it were really grievous and awful? Are we not to know ourselves? Are we not to cast away visible things? Are we not to look to the things unseen? Are we not, even if we are somewhat grieved, to be on the contrary distressed at our lengthened sojourn, like holy David, who calls things here the tents of darkness, and the place of affliction, and the deep mire, and the shadow of death; because we linger in the tombs we bear about with us, because, though we are gods, we die like men the death of sin? This is my fear, this day and night accompanies me, and will not let me breathe, on one side the glory, on the other the place of correction: the former I long for till I can say, "My soul fainteth for Thy salvation;" from the latter I shrink back shuddering; yet I am not afraid that this body of mine should utterly perish in dissolution and corruption; but that the glorious creature of God (for glorious it is if upright, just as it is dishonorable if sinful) in which is reason, morality, and hope, should be condemned to the same dishonor as the brutes, and be no better after death; a fate to be desired for the wicked, who are worthy of the fire yonder.

23. Would that I might mortify my members that are upon the earth, would that I might spend my all upon the spirit, walking in the way that is narrow and trodden by few, not that which is broad and easy. For glorious and great are its consequences, and our hope is greater than our desert. What is man, that Thou art mindful of him? What is this new mystery which concerns me? I am small and great, lowly and exalted, mortal and immortal, earthly and heavenly. I share one condition with the lower world, the other with God; one with the flesh, the other with the spirit. I must be buried with Christ, arise with Christ, be joint heir with Christ, become the son of God, yea, God Himself. See whither our argument has carried us in its progress. I almost own myself indebted to the disaster which has inspired me with such thoughts, and made me more enamored of my departure hence. This is the purpose of the great mystery for us. This is the purpose for us of God, Who for us was made man and became poor, to raise our flesh, and recover His image, and remodel man, that we might all be made one in Christ, who was perfectly made in all of us all that He Himself is, that we might no longer be male and female, barbarian, Scythian, bond or free (which are badges of the flesh), but might bear in ourselves only the stamp of God, by Whom and for Whom we were made, and have so far received our form and model from Him, that we are recognized by it alone.

24. Yea, would that what we hope for might be, according to the great kindness of our bountiful God, Who asks for little and bestows great things, both in the present and in the future, upon those who truly love Him; bearing all things, enduring all things for their love and hope of Him, giving thanks for all things favorable and unfavorable alike: I mean pleasant and painful, for reason knows that even these are often instruments of salvation; commending to Him our own souls and the souls of those fellow wayfarers who, being more ready, have gained their rest before us. And,

51

now that we have done this, let us cease from our discourse, and you too from your tears, hastening, as you now are, to your tomb, which as a sad abiding gift you have given to Caesarius, seasonably prepared as it was for 463 his parents in their old age, and now unexpectedly bestowed on their son in his youth, though not without reason in His eyes Who disposes our affairs. O Lord and Maker of all things, and specially of this our frame! O God and Father and Pilot of men who are Thine! O Lord of life and death! O Judge and Benefactor of our souls! O Maker and Transformer in due time of all things by Thy designing Word, according to the knowledge of the depth of Thy wisdom and providence! do Thou now receive Caesarius, the firstfruits of our pilgrimage; and if he who was last is first, we bow before Thy Word, by which the universe is ruled; yet do Thou receive us also afterwards, in a time when Thou mayest be found, having ordered us in the flesh as long as is for our profit; yea, receive us, prepared and not troubled by Thy fear, not departing from Thee in our last day, nor violently borne away from things here, like souls fond of the world and the flesh, but filled with eagerness for that blessed and enduring life which is in Christ Jesus, our Lord, to whom be glory, world without end. Amen.

On His Sister Gorgonia

The exact date of this Oration is uncertain. It is certainly later than the death of Caesarius, A.D. 369, and previous to the death of their father, A.D. 374. So much we gather from the Oration itself, and the references made by some authors to a poem of S. Gregory do not add anything certain to our knowledge (Poem. Hist. I. 1. v. v. 108, 227). The place in which it was delivered is, almost without doubt, the city in which her married life had been spent. The public details of that life are familiar to the audience. Gorgonia's parents, and the speaker himself, although known to them, are not spoken of in terms implying intimacy such as we find in Orations known to have been delivered at Nazianzus. The spiritual father and confidant of Gorgonia is present, certainly in a position of authority, probably seated in the Episcopal throne. The husband of Gorgonia (Epitaph. 24) was named Alypius. His home, as Clemencet and Benoit agree, on the authority of Elias, was at Iconium, of which city, at the time, Faustinus was bishop. The names of Gorgonia's two sons are unknown. Elias states that they both became bishops. S. Gregory mentions her three daughters, Alypiana, Eugenia, and Nonna, in his will. The oration is marked by an eloquence, piety, and tender feeling which make it a worthy companion of that on Caesarius. FUNERAL ORATION ON HIS SISTER GORGONIA

1. In praising my sister, I shall pay honor to one of my own family; yet my praise will not be false, because it is given to a relation, but, because it is true, will be worthy of commendation, and its truth is based not only upon its justice, but upon well-known facts. For, even if I wished, I should not be permitted to be partial; since everyone who hears me stands, like a skillful critic, between my oration and the truth, to discountenance exaggeration, yet, if he be a man of justice, demanding what is really due. So that my fear is not of outrunning the truth, but, on the contrary, of falling short of it, and lessening her just repute by the extreme inadequacy of my panegyric; for it is a hard task to match her excellences with suitable action and words. Let us not then be so unjust as to praise every characteristic of other folk, and disparage really valuable qualities because they are our own, so as to make some men gain by their absence of kindred with us, while others suffer for their relationship. For justice would be violated alike by the praise of the one and the neglect of the other, whereas if we make the truth our standard and rule, and look to her alone, disregarding all the objects of the vulgar and mean, we shall praise or pass over everything according to its merits.

2. Yet it would be most unreasonable of all, if, while we refuse to regard it as a righteous thing to defraud, insult, accuse, or treat unjustly in any way, great or small, those who are our kindred, and consider wrong done to those nearest to us the worst of all; we were yet to imagine that it would be an act of justice to deprive them of such an oration as is due most of all to the good, and spend more words upon those who are evil, and beg for indulgent treatment, than on those who are excellent and merely claim their due. For if we are not prevented, as would be far

more just, from praising men who have lived outside our own circle, because we do not know and cannot personally testify to their merits, shall we be prevented from praising those whom we do know, because of our friendship, or the envy of the multitude, and especially those who have departed hence, whom it is too late to ingratiate ourselves with, since they have escaped, amongst all other things, from the reach of praise or blame.

3. Having now made a sufficient defense on these points, and shown how necessary it is for me to be the speaker, come, let me proceed with my eulogy, rejecting all daintiness and elegance of style (for she whom we are praising was unadorned and the absence of ornament was to her, beauty), and yet performing, as a most indispensable debt, all those funeral rites which are her due, and further instructing everyone in a zealous imitation of the same virtue, since it is my object in every word and action to promote the perfection of those committed to my charge. The task of praising the country and family of our departed one I leave to another, more scrupulous in adhering to the rules of eulogy; nor will he lack many fair topics, if he wish to deck her with external ornaments, as men deck a splendid and beautiful form with gold and precious stones, and the artistic devices of the craftsman; which, while they accentuate ugliness by their contrast, can add no attractiveness to the beauty which surpasses them. For my part, I will only conform to such rules so far as to allude to our common parents, for it would not be reverent to pass unnoticed the great blessing of having such parents and teachers, and then speedily direct my attention to herself, without further taxing the patience of those who are eager to learn what manner of woman she was.

4. Who is there who knows not the Abraham and Sarah of these our latter days, Gregory and Nonna his wife? For it is not well to omit the incitement to virtue of mentioning their names. He has been justified by faith, she has dwelt with him who is faithful; he beyond all hope has been the father of many nations, she has spiritually travailed in their birth; he escaped from the bondage of his father's gods, she is the daughter as well as the mother of the free; he went out from kindred and home for the sake of the land of promise, she was the occasion of his exile; for on this head alone I venture to claim for her an honor higher than that of Sarah; he set forth on so noble a pilgrimage, she readily shared with him in its toils; he gave himself to the Lord, she both called her husband Lord and regarded him as such, and in part was thereby justified; whose was the promise, from whom, as far as in them lay, was born Isaac, and whose was the gift.

5. This good shepherd was the result of his wife's prayers and guidance, and it was from her that he learned his ideal of a good shepherd's life. He generously fled from his idols, and afterwards even put demons to flight; he never consented to eat salt with idolators: united together with a bond of one honor, of one mind, of one soul, concerned as much with virtue and fellowship with God as with the flesh; equal in length of life and hoary hairs, equal in prudence and brilliancy, rivals of each other,

soaring beyond all the rest, possessed in few respects by the flesh, and translated in spirit, even before dissolution: possessing not the world, and yet possessing it, by at once despising and rightly valuing it: forsaking riches and yet being rich through their noble pursuits; rejecting things here, and purchasing instead the things yonder: possessed of a scanty remnant of this life, left over from their piety, but of an abundant and long life for which they have labored. I will say but one word more about them: they have been rightly and fairly assigned, each to either sex; he is the ornament of men, she of women, and not only the ornament but the pattern of virtue.

6. From them Gorgonia derived both her existence and her reputation; they sowed in her the seeds of piety, they were the source of her fair life, and of her happy departure with better hopes. Fair privileges these, and such as are not easily attained by many of those who plume themselves highly upon their noble birth, and are proud of their ancestry. But, if I must treat of her case in a more philosophic and lofty strain, Gorgonia' s native land was Jerusalem above, the object, not of sight but of contemplation, wherein is our commonwealth, and whereto we are pressing on: whose citizen Christ is, and whose fellow-citizens are the assembly and church of the first born who are written in heaven, and feast around its great Founder in contemplation of His glory, and take part in the endless festival; her nobility consisted in the preservation of the Image, and the perfect likeness to the Archetype, which is produced by reason and virtue and pure desire, ever more and more conforming, in things pertaining to God, to those truly initiated into the heavenly mysteries; and in knowing whence, and of what character, and for what end we came into being.

7. This is what I know upon these points: and therefore it is that I both am aware and assert that her soul was more noble than those of the East, according to a better than the ordinary rule of noble or ignoble birth, whose distinctions depend not on blood but on character; nor does it classify those whom it praises or blames according to their families, but as individuals. But speaking as I do of her excellences among those who know her, let each one join in contributing some particular and aid me in my speech: for it is impossible for one man to take in every point, however gifted with observation and intelligence.

8. In modesty she so greatly excelled, and so far surpassed, those of her own day, to say nothing of those of old time who have been illustrious for modesty, that, in regard to the two divisions of the life of all, that is, the married and the unmarried state, the latter being higher and more divine, though more difficult and dangerous, while the former is more humble and more safe, she was able to avoid the disadvantages of each, and to select and combine all that is best in both, namely, the elevation of the one and the security of the other, thus becoming modest without pride, blending the excellence of the married with that of the unmarried state, and proving that neither of them absolutely binds us to, or separates us from,

God or the world (so that the one from its own nature must be utterly avoided, and the other altogether praised): but that it is mind which nobly presides over wedlock and maidenhood, and arranges and works upon them as the raw material of virtue under the master-hand of reason. For though she had entered upon a carnal union, she was not therefore separated from the spirit, nor, because her husband was her head, did she ignore her first Head: but, performing those few ministrations due to the world and nature, according to the will of the law of the flesh, or rather of Him who gave to the flesh these laws, she consecrated herself entirely to God. But what is most excellent and honorable, she also won over her husband to her side, and made of him a good fellow-servant, instead of an unreasonable master. And not only so, but she further made the fruit of her body, her children and her children's children, to be the fruit of her spirit, dedicating to God not her single soul, but the whole family and household, and making wedlock illustrious through her own acceptability in wedlock, and the fair harvest she had reaped thereby; presenting herself, as long as she lived, as an example to her offspring of all that was good, and when summoned hence, leaving her will behind her, as a silent exhortation to her house.

9. The divine Solomon, in his instructive wisdom, I mean his Proverbs, praises the woman who looks to her household and loves her husband, contrasting her with one who roams abroad, and is uncontrolled and dishonorable, and hunts for precious souls with wanton words and ways, while she manages well at home and bravely sets about her woman's duties, as her hands hold the distaff, and she prepares two coats for her husband, buying a field in due season, and makes good provision for the food of her servants, and welcomes her friends at a liberal table; with all the other details in which he sings the praises of the modest and industrious woman. Now, to praise my sister in these points would be to praise a statue for its shadow, or a lion for its claws, without allusion to its greatest perfections. Who was more deserving of renown, and yet who avoided it so much and made herself inaccessible to the eyes of man? Who knew better the due proportions of sobriety and cheerfulness, so that her sobriety should not seem inhuman, nor her tenderness immodest, but prudent in one, gentle in the other, her discretion was marked by a combination of sympathy and dignity? Listen, ye women addicted to ease and display, who despise the veil of shamefastness. Who ever so kept her eyes under control? Who so derided laughter, that the ripple of a smile seemed a great thing to her? Who more steadfastly closed her ears? And who opened them more to the Divine words, or rather, who installed the mind as ruler of the tongue in uttering the judgments of God? Who, as she, regulated her lips?

10. Here, if you will, is another point of her excellence: one of which neither she nor any truly modest and decorous woman thinks anything: but which we have been made to think much of, by those who are too fond of ornament and display, and refuse to listen to instruction on such matters. She was never adorned with gold wrought into artistic forms of surpassing beauty, nor flaxen tresses, fully or partially

displayed, nor spiral curls, nor dishonoring designs of men who construct erections on the honorable head, nor costly folds of flowing and transparent robes, nor graces of brilliant stones, which color the neighboring air, and cast a glow upon the form; nor the arts and witcheries of the painter, nor that cheap beauty of the infernal creator who works against the Divine, hiding with his treacherous pigments the creation of God, and putting it to shame with his honor, and setting before eager eyes the imitation of an harlot instead of the form of God, so that this bastard beauty may steal away that image which should be kept for God and for the world to come. But though she was aware of the many and various external ornaments of women, yet none of them was more precious to her than her own character, and the brilliancy stored up within. One red tint was dear to her, the blush of modesty; one white one, the sign of temperance: but pigments and pencilings, and living pictures, and flowing lines of beauty, she left to women of the stage and of the streets, and to all who think it a shame and a reproach to be ashamed.

11. Enough of such topics. Of her prudence and piety no adequate account can be given, nor many examples found besides those of her natural and spiritual parents, who were her only models, and of whose virtue she in no wise fell short, with this single exception most readily admitted, that they, as she both knew and acknowledged, were the source of her goodness, and the root of her own illumination. What could be keener than the intellect of her who was recognized as a common adviser not only by those of her family, those of the same people and of the one fold, but even by all men round about, who treated her counsels and advice as a law not to be broken? What more sagacious than her words? What more prudent than her silence? Having mentioned silence, I will proceed to that which was most characteristic of her, most becoming to women, and most serviceable to these times. Who had a fuller knowledge of the things of God, both from the Divine oracles, and from her own understanding? But who was less ready to speak, confining herself within the due limits of women? Moreover, as was the bounden duty of a woman who has learned true piety, and that which is the only honorable object of insatiate desire, who, as she, adorned temples with offerings, both others and this one, which will hardly, now she is gone, be so adorned again? Or rather, who so presented herself to God as a living temple? Who again paid such honor to Priests, especially to him who was her fellow soldier and teacher of piety, whose are the good seeds, and the pair of children consecrated to God.

12. Who opened her house to those who live according to God with a more graceful and bountiful welcome? And, which is greater than this, who bade them welcome with such modesty and godly greetings? Further, who showed a mind more unmoved in sufferings? Whose soul was more sympathetic to those in trouble? Whose hand more liberal to those in want? I should not hesitate to honor her with the words of Job: Her door was opened to all comers; the stranger did not lodge in the street. She was eyes to the blind, feet to the lame, a mother to the orphan. Why should I say more of her compassion to widows, than that its fruit

which she obtained was, never to be called a widow herself? Her house was a common abode to all the needy of her family; and her goods no less common to all in need than their own belonged to each. She hath dispersed abroad and given to the poor, and according to the infallible truth of the Gospel, she laid up much store in the wine -presses above, and oftentimes entertained Christ in the person of those whose benefactress she was. And, best of all, there was in her no unreal profession, but in secret she cultivated piety before Him who seeth secret things. Everything she rescued from the ruler of this world, everything she transferred to the safe garners. Nothing did she leave behind to earth, save her body. She bartered everything for the hopes above: the sole wealth she left to her children was the imitation of her example, and emulation of her merits.

13. But amid these tokens of incredible magnanimity, she did not surrender her body to luxury, and unrestrained pleasures of the appetite, that raging and tearing dog, as though presuming upon her acts of benevolence, as most men do, who redeem their luxury by compassion to the poor, and instead of healing evil with good, receive evil as a recompense for their good deeds. Nor did she, while subduing her dust by fasting, leave to another the medicine of hard lying; nor, while she found this of spiritual service, was she less restrained in sleep than anyone else; nor, while regulating her life on this point as if freed from the body, did she lie upon the ground, when others were passing the night erect, as the most mortified men struggle to do. Nay in this respect she was seen to surpass not only women, but the most devoted of men, by her intelligent chanting of the psalter, her converse with, and unfolding and apposite recollection of, the Divine oracles, her bending of her knees which had grown hard and almost taken root in the ground, her tears to cleanse her stains with contrite heart and spirit of lowliness, her prayer rising heavenward, her mind freed from wandering in rapture; in all these, or in any one of them, is there man or woman who can boast of having surpassed her? Besides, it is a great thing to say, but it is true, that while she was zealous in her endeavor after some points of excellence, of others she was the paragon: of some she was the discoverer, in others she excelled. And if in some single particular she was rivaled, her superiority consists in her complete grasp of all. Such was her success in all points, as none else attained even in a moderate degree in one: to such perfection did she attain in each particular, that any one might of itself have supplied the place of all.

14. O untended body, and squalid garments, whose only flower is virtue! O soul, clinging to the body, when reduced almost to an immaterial state through lack of food; or rather, when the body had been mortified by force, even before dissolution, that the soul might attain to freedom, and escape the entanglements of the senses! O nights of vigil, and psalmody, and standing which lasts from one day to another! O David, whose strains never seem tedious to faithful souls! O tender limbs, flung upon the earth and, contrary to nature, growing hard! O fountains of tears, sowing in affliction that they might reap in joy. O cry in the night, piercing

the clouds and reaching unto Him that dwelleth in the heavens! O fervor of spirit, waxing bold in prayerful longings against the dogs of night, and frosts and rain, and thunders, and hail, and darkness! O nature of woman overcoming that of man in the common struggle for salvation, and demonstrating that the distinction between male and female is one of body not of soul! O Baptismal purity, O soul, in the pure chamber of thy body, the bride of Christ! O bitter eating! O Eve mother of our race and of our sin! O subtle serpent, and death, overcome by her self-discipline! O self-emptying of Christ, and form of a servant, and sufferings, honored by her mortification!

15. Oh! how am I to count up all her traits, or pass over most of them without injury to those who know them not? Here however it is right to subjoin the rewards of her piety, for indeed I take it that you, who knew her life well, have long been eager and desirous to find in my speech not only things present, or her joys yonder, beyond the conception and hearing and sight of man, but also those which the righteous Rewarder bestowed upon her here: a matter which often tends to the edification of unbelievers, who from small things attain to faith in those which are great, and from things which are seen to those which are not seen. I will mention then some facts which are generally notorious, others which have been from most men kept secret; and that because her Christian principle made a point of not making a display of her [Divine] favors. You know how her maddened mules ran away with her carriage, and unfortunately overturned it, how horribly she Was dragged along, and seriously injured, to the scandal of unbelievers at the permission of such accidents to the righteous, and how quickly their unbelief was corrected: for, all crushed and bruised as she was, in bones and limbs, alike in those exposed and in those out of sight, she would have none of any physician, except Him Who had permitted it; both because she shrunk from the inspection and the hands of men, preserving, even in suffering, her modesty, and also awaiting her justification from Him Who allowed this to happen, so that she owed her preservation to none other than to Him: with the result that men were no less struck by her unhoped-for recovery than by her misfortune, and concluded that the tragedy had happened for her glorification through sufferings, the suffering being human, the recovery superhuman, and giving a lesson to those who come after, exhibiting in a high degree faith in the midst of suffering, and patience under calamity, but in a still higher degree the kindness of God to them that are such as she. For to the beautiful promise to the righteous "though he fall, he shall not be utterly broken," has been added one more recent, "though he be utterly broken, he shall speedily be raised up and glorified." For if her misfortune was unreasonable, her recovery was extraordinary, so that health soon stole away the injury, and the cure became more celebrated than the blow.

16. O remarkable and wonderful disaster! O injury more noble than security! O prophecy, "He hath smitten, and He will bind us up, and revive us, and after three days He will raise us up," portending indeed, as it did, a greater and more sublime

event, yet no less applicable to Gorgonia's sufferings! This then, notorious to all, even to those afar off, for the wonder spread to all, and the lesson was stored up in the tongues and ears of all, with the other wonderful works and powers of God. But the following incident, hitherto unknown and concealed from moot men by the Christian principle I spoke of, and her pious shrinking from vanity and display, dost thou bid me tell, O best and most perfect of shepherds, pastor of this holy sheep, and dost thou further give thy assent to it, since to us alone has this secret been entrusted, and we were mutual witnesses of the marvel, or are we still to keep our faith to her who is gone? Yet I do think, that as that was the time to be silent, this is the time to manifest it, not only for the glory of God, but also for the consolation of those in affliction.

17. She was sick in body, and dangerously ill of an extraordinary and malignant disease, her whole frame was incessantly fevered, her blood at one time agitated and boiling, then curdling with coma, incredible pallor, and paralysis of mind and limbs: and this not at long intervals, but sometimes very frequently. Its virulence seemed beyond human aid; the skill of physicians, who carefully examined the case, both singly and in consultation, was of no avail; nor the tears of her parents, which often have great power, nor public supplications and intercessions, in which all the people joined as earnestly as if for their own preservation: for her safety was the safety of all, as, on the contrary, her suffering and sickness was a common misfortune.

18. What then did this great soul, worthy offspring of the greatest, and what was the medicine for her disorder, for we have now come to the great secret? Despairing of all other aid, she betook herself to the Physician of all, and awaiting the silent hours of night, during a slight intermission of the disease, she approached the altar with faith, and, calling upon Him Who is honored thereon, with a mighty cry, and every kind of invocation, calling to mind all His former works of power, and well she knew those both of ancient and of later days, at last she ventured on an act of pious and splendid effrontery: she imitated the woman whose fountain of blood was dried up by the hem of Christ's garment. What did she do? Resting her head with another cry upon the altar, and with a wealth of tears, as she who once bedewed the feet of Christ, and declaring that she would not loose her hold until she was made whole, she then applied her medicine to her whole body, viz., such a portion of the antitypes of the Precious Body and Blood as she treasured in her hand, mingling therewith her tears, and, O the wonder, she went away feeling at once that she was saved, and with the lightness of health in body, soul, and mind, having received, as the reward of her hope, that which she hoped for, and having gained bodily by means of spiritual strength. Great though these things be, they are not untrue. Believe them all of you, whether sick or sound, that ye may either keep or regain your health. And that my story is no mere boastfulness is plain from the silence in which she kept, while alive, what I have revealed. Nor should I now have

published it, be well assured, had I not feared that so great a marvel would have been utterly hidden from the faithful and unbelieving of these and later days.

19. Such was her life. Most of its details I have left untold, lest my speech should grow to undue proportions, and lest I should seem to be too greedy for her fair fame: but perhaps we should be wronging her holy and illustrious death, did we not mention some of its excellences; especially as she so longed for and desired it. I will do so therefore, as concisely as I can. She longed for her dissolution, for indeed she had great boldness towards Him who called her, and preferred to be with Christ, beyond all things on earth. And there is none of the most amorous and unrestrained, who has such love for his body, as she had to fling away these fetters, and escape from the mire in which we spend our lives, and to associate in purity with Him Who is Fair, and entirely to hold her Beloved, Who is I will even say it, her Lover, by Whose rays, feeble though they now are, we are enlightened, and Whom, though separated from Him, we are able to know. Nor did she fail even of this desire, divine and sublime though it was, and, what is still greater, she had a foretaste of His Beauty through her forecast and constant watching. Her only sleep transferred her to exceeding joys, and her one vision embraced her departure at the foreappointed time, having been made aware of this day, so that according to the decision of God she might be prepared and yet not disturbed.

20. She had recently obtained the blessing of cleansing and perfection, which we have all received from God as a common gift and foundation of our new life. Or rather all her life was a cleansing and perfecting: and while she received regeneration from the Holy Spirit, its security was hers by virtue of her former life. And in her case almost alone, I will venture to say, the mystery was a seal rather than a gift of grace. And when her husband's perfection was her one remaining desire (and if you wish me briefly to describe the man, I do not know what more to say of him than that he was her husband) in order that she might be consecrated to God in her whole body, and not depart half-perfected, or leave behind her imperfect anything that was hers; she did not even fail of this petition, from Him Who fulfills the desire of them that fear Him, and accomplishes their requests.

21. And now when she had all things to her mind, and nothing was lacking of her desires, and the appointed time drew nigh, being thus prepared for death and departure, she fulfilled the law which prevails in such matters, and took to her bed. After many injunctions to her husband, her children, and her friends, as was to be expected from one who was full of conjugal, maternal, and brotherly love, and after making her last day a day of solemn festival with brilliant discourse upon the things above, she fell asleep, full not of the days of man, for which she had no desire, knowing them to be evil for her, and mainly occupied with our dust and wanderings, but more exceedingly full of the days of God, than I imagine any one even of those who have departed in a wealth of hoary hairs, and have numbered many terms of years. Thus she was set free, or, it is better to say, taken to God, or

flew away, or changed her abode, or anticipated by a little the departure of her body.

22. Yet what was I on the point of omitting? But perhaps thou, who art her spiritual father, wouldst not have allowed me, and hast carefully concealed the wonder, and made it known to me. It is a great point for her distinction, and in our memory of her virtue, and regret for her departure. But trembling and tears have seized upon me, at the recollection of the wonder. She was just passing away, and at her last breath, surrounded by a group of relatives and friends performing the last offices of kindness, while her aged mother bent over her, with her soul convulsed with envy of her departure, anguish and affection being blended in the minds of all. Some longed to hear some burning word to be branded in their recollection; others were eager to speak, yet no one dared; for tears were mute and the pangs of grief unconsoled, since it seemed sacrilegious, to think that mourning could be an honor to one who was thus passing away. So there was solemn silence, as if her death had been a religious ceremony. There she lay, to all appearance, breathless, motionless, speechless; the stillness of her body seemed paralysis, as though the organs of speech were dead, after that which could move them was gone. But as her pastor, who in this wonderful scene, was carefully watching her, perceived that her lips were gently moving, and placed his ear to them, which his disposition and sympathy emboldened him to do, — but do you expound the meaning of this mysterious calm, for no one can disbelieve it on your word! Under her breath she was repeating a psalm — the last words of a psalm — to say the truth, a testimony to the boldness with which she was departing, and blessed is he who can fall asleep with these words, "I will lay me down in peace, and take my rest." Thus wert thou singing, fairest of women, and thus it fell out unto thee; and the song became a reality, and attended on thy departure as a memorial of thee, who hast entered upon sweet peace after suffering, and received (over and above the rest which comes to all), that sleep which is due to the beloved, as befitted one who lived and died amid the words of piety.

23. Better, I know well, and far more precious than eye can see, is thy present lot, the song of them that keep holy-day, the throng of angels, the heavenly host, the vision of glory, and that splendor, pure and perfect beyond all other, of the Trinity Most High, no longer beyond the ken of the captive mind, dissipated by the senses, but entirely contemplated and possessed by the undivided mind, and flashing upon our souls with the whole light of Godhead: Mayest thou enjoy to the full all those things whose crumbs thou didst, while still upon earth, possess through the reality of thine inclination towards them. And if thou takest any account of our affairs, and holy souls receive from God this privilege, do thou accept these words of mine, in place of, and in preference to many panegyrics, which I have bestowed upon Caesarius before thee, and upon thee after him — since I have been preserved to pronounce panegyrics upon my brethren. If any one will, after you, pay me the like honor, I cannot say. Yet may my only honor be that which is in God, and may my

pilgrimage and my home be in Christ Jesus our Lord, to Whom, with the Father and the Holy Ghost, be glory for ever. Amen.

To his father when he entrusted him the care of the church in Nazianzen

This Oration was delivered A.D. 372. Two years earlier Valens had divided Cappadocia into two provinces. Anthimus, Bishop of Tyana, asserting that the ecclesiastical provinces were regulated by those of the empire, claimed metropolitical rights over the churches of Cappadocia Secunda, in opposition to S. Basil, who had hitherto been metropolitan of the undivided province. S. Basil, with the intention of vindicating the permanence of his former rights, created a new see at Sasima, on the borders of the two provinces, and with great difficulty prevailed upon S. Gregory to receive consecration as its first Bishop. S. Gregory, who had "bent his neck, but not his will," was for a long time reluctant to enter upon his Episcopal duties, and at last was prevailed upon by S. Gregory of Nyssa, S. Basil's brother, to make an attempt to do so. When, however, he found that Anthimus was prepared to bar his entrance by force of arms, he returned home, definitely resigned his see, and once more betook himself to the life of solitude which he so dearly loved. Recalled hence, he consented, at his father's earnest entreaty, to undertake provisionally the duties of Bishop-coadjutor of Nazianzus: and pronounced this short discourse on the occasion of his installation.

1 . I opened my mouth, and drew in the Spirit, and I give myself and my all to the Spirit, my action and speech, my inaction and silence, only let Him hold me and guide me, and move both hand and mind and tongue whither it is right, and He wills: and restrain them as it is right and expedient. I am an instrument of God, a rational instrument, an instrument tuned and struck by that skillful artist, the Spirit. Yesterday His work in me was silence. I mused on abstinence from speech. Does He strike upon my mind today? My speech shall be heard, and I will muse on utterance. I am neither so talkative, as to desire to speak, when He is bent on silence; nor so reserved and ignorant as to set a watch before my lips when it is the time to speak: but I open and close my door at the will of that Mind and Word and Spirit, Who is One kindred Deity.

2. I will speak then, since I am so bidden. And I will speak both to the good shepherd here, and to you, his holy flock, as I think is best both for me to speak, and for you to hear today. Why is it that you have begged for one to share your shepherd's toil? For my speech shall begin with you, O dear and honored head, worthy of that of Aaron, down which runs that spiritual and priestly ointment upon his beard and clothing. Why is it that, while yet able to stablish and guide many, and actually guiding them in the power of the Spirit, you support yourself with a staff and prop in your spiritual works? Is it because you have heard and know that even with the illustrious Aaron were anointed Eleazar and Ithamar, the sons of Aaron? For I pass over Nadab and Abihu, test the allusion be ill-omened: and Moses during his lifetime appoints Joshua in his stead, as lawgiver and general over those who were pressing on to the land of promise? The office of Aaron and Hur, supporting the hands of Moses on the mount where Amalek was warred down by the Cross, prefigured and typified long before, I feel willing to pass by, as not

very suitable or applicable to us: for Moses did not choose them to share his work as lawgiver, but as helpers in his prayer and supports for the weariness of his hands.

3. What is it then that ails you? What is your weakness? Is it physical? I am ready to sustain you, yea I have sustained, and been sustained, like Jacob of old, by your fatherly blessings. Is it spiritual? Who is stronger, and more fervent, especially now, when the powers of the flesh are ebbing and fading, like so many barriers which interfere with, and dim the brilliancy of a light? For these powers are wont, for the most part, to wage war upon and oppose one another, while the body's health is purchased by the sickness of the soul, and the soul flourishes and looks upward when pleasures are stilled and fade away along with the body. But, wonderful as your simplicity and nobility have seemed to me before, how is it that you have no fear, especially in times like these, that your spirit will be considered a pretext, and that most men will suppose, in spite of our spiritual professions, that we are undertaking this from carnal motives. For most men have made the office to be looked upon as great and princely, and accompanied with considerable enjoyment, even though a man have the charge and rule over a more slender flock than this, and one which affords more troubles than pleasures. Thus far of your simplicity, or parental preference, if it be so, which makes you neither admit yourself, nor readily suspect in others anything disgraceful; for a mind hardly roused to evil, is slow to suspect evil. My second duty is briefly to address this people of yours, or now even of mine.

4. I have been overpowered, my friends and brethren, for I will now, though I did not at the time, ask for your aid. I have been overpowered by the old age of my father, and, to use moderate terms, the kindliness of my friend. So, help me, each of you who can, and stretch out a hand to me who am pressed down and torn asunder by regret and enthusiasm. The one suggests flights, mountains and deserts, and calm of soul and body, and that the mind should retire into itself, and recall its powers from sensible things, in order to hold pure communion with God, and be clearly illumined by the flashing rays of the Spirit, with no admixture or disturbance of the divine light by anything earthly or clouded, Until we come to the source of the effulgence which we enjoy here, and regret and desire are alike stayed, when our mirrors pass away in the light of truth. The other wills that I should come forward, and bear fruit for the common good, and be helped by helping others; and publish the Divine light, and bring to God a people for His own possession, a holy nation, a royal priesthood, and His image cleansed in many souls. And this, because, as a park is better than and preferable to a tree, the whole heaven with its ornaments to a single star, and the body to a limb, so also, in the sight of God, is the reformation of a whole church preferable to the progress of a single soul: and therefore, I ought not to look only on my own interest, but also on that of others. For Christ also likewise, when it was possible for him to abide in His own honor and deity, not only so far emptied Himself as to take the form of a slave, but also endured the cross, despising the shame, that he might by His own

sufferings destroy sin, and by death slay death. The former are the imaginings of desire, the latter the teachings of the Spirit. And I, standing midway between the desire and the Spirit, and not knowing to which of the two I should rather yield, will impart to you what seems to me the best and safest course, that you may test it with me and take part in my design.

5. It seemed to me to be best and least dangerous to take a middle course between desire and fear, and to yield in part to desire, in part to the Spirit: and that this would be the case, if I neither altogether evaded the office, and so refused the grace, which would be dangerous, nor yet assumed a burden beyond my powers, for it is a heavy one. The former indeed is suited to the person of another, the latter to another' s power, or rather to undertake both would be madness. But piety and safety would alike advise me to proportion the office to my power, and as is the case with food, to accept that which is within my power and refuse what is beyond it for health is gained for the body, and tranquillity for the soul, by such a course of moderation. Therefore I now consent to share in the cares of my excellent father, like an eaglet, not quite vainly flying close to a mighty and high soaring eagle. But hereafter I will offer my wing to the Spirit to be borne whither, and as, He wills: no one shall force or drag me in any direction, contrary to His counsel. For sweet it is to inherit a father's toils, and this flock is more familiar than a strange and foreign one; I would even add, more precious in the sight of God, unless the spell of affection deceives me, and the force of habit robs me of perception: nor is there any more useful or safer course than that willing rulers should rule willing subjects: since it is our practice not to lead by force, or by compulsion, but by good will. For this would not hold together even another form of government, since that which is held in by force is wont, when opportunity offers, to strike for freedom: but freedom of will more than anything else it is, which holds together our — I will not call it rule, but — tutorship. For the mystery of godliness belongs to those who are willing, not to those who are overpowered.

6. This is my speech to you, my good men, uttered in simplicity and with all good will, and this is the secret of my mind. And may the victory rest with that which will be for the profit of both you and me, under the Spirit' s guidance of our affairs, (for our discourse comes back again to the same point,) to Whom we have given ourselves, and the head anointed with the oil of perfection, in the Almighty Father, and the Only -begotten Son, and the Holy Spirit, Who is God. For how long shall we hide the lamp under the bushel, and withhold from others the full knowledge of the Godhead, when it ought to be now put upon the lampstand and give light to all churches and souls and to the whole fullness of the world, no longer by means of metaphors, or intellectual sketches, but by distinct declaration? And this indeed is a most perfect setting forth of Theology to those Who have been deemed worthy of this grace in Christ Jesus Himself, our Lord, to Whom be glory, honor, and power for ever. Amen.

On his father's silence because of the plague of Hail

This Oration belongs to the year A.D. 373. A series of disasters had befallen the people of Nazianzus. A deadly cattle plague, which had devastated their herds, had been followed by a prolonged drought, and now their just ripened crops had been ruined by a storm of rain and hail. The people flocked to the church, and finding S. Gregory the elder so overwhelmed by his sense of these terrible misfortunes that he was unable to address them, implored his coadjutor to enter the pulpit. The occasion gave no time for preparation, so S. Gregory poured out his feelings in a discourse which was in the fullest sense of the words ex tempore, its present form, however, as Benoit suggests, may be due to a later polishing of notes taken down at the time of delivery.

1 . Why do you infringe upon the approved order of things? Why would you do violence to a tongue which is under obligation to the law? Why do you challenge a speech which is in subjection to the Spirit? Why, when you have excused the head, have you hastened to the feet? Why do you pass by Aaron and urge forward Eleazar? I cannot allow the fountain to be dammed up, while the rivulet runs its course; the sun to be hidden, while the star shines forth; hoar hairs to be in retirement, while youth lays down the law; wisdom to be silent, while inexperience speaks with assurance. A heavy rain is not always more useful than a gentle shower. Nay, indeed, if it be too violent, it sweeps away the earth, and increases the proportion of the farmer's loss: while a gentle fall, which sinks deep, enriches the soil, benefits the tiller and makes the corn grow to a fine crop. So the fluent Speech is not more profitable than the wise. For the one, though it perhaps gave a slight pleasure, passes away, and is dispersed as soon, and with as little effect, as the air on which it struck, though it charms with its eloquence the greedy ear. But the other sinks into the mind, and opening wide its mouth, fills it with the Spirit, and, showing itself nobler than its origin, produces a rich harvest by a few syllables.

2. I have not yet alluded to the true and first wisdom, for which our wonderful husbandman and shepherd is conspicuous. The first wisdom is a life worthy of praise, and kept pure for God, or being purified for Him Who is all-pure and all-luminous, Who demands of us, us His only sacrifice, purification — that is, a contrite heart and the sacrifice of praise, and a new creation in Christ, and the new man, and the like, as the Scripture loves to call it. The first wisdom is to despise that wisdom which consists of language and figures of speech, and spurious and unnecessary embellishments. Be it mine to speak five words with my understanding in the church, rather than ten thousand words in a tongue, and with the unmeaning voice of a trumpet, which does not rouse my soldier to the spiritual combat. This is the wisdom which I praise, which I welcome. By this the ignoble have won renown, and the despised have attained the highest honors. By this a crew of fishermen have taken the whole world in the meshes of the Gospel-net, and overcome by a word finished and cut short the wisdom that comes to naught. I count not wise the man who is clever in words, nor him who is of a ready tongue,

but unstable and undisciplined in soul, like the tombs which, fair and beautiful as they are outwardly, are fetid with corpses within, and full of manifold ill-savors; but him who speaks but little of virtue, yet gives many examples of it in his practice, and proves the trustworthiness of his language by his life.

3. Fairer in my eyes, is the beauty which we can gaze upon than that which is painted in words: of more value the wealth which our hands can hold, than that which is imagined in our dreams; and more real the wisdom of which we are convinced by deeds, than that which is set forth in splendid language. For "a good understanding," he saith, "have all they that do thereafter," not they who proclaim it. Time is the best touchstone of this wisdom, and "the hoary head is a crown of glory." For if, as it seems to me as well as to Solomon, we must "judge none blessed before his death," and it is uncertain" what a day may bring forth," since our life here below has many turnings, and the body of our humiliation is ever rising, falling and changing; surely he, who without fault has almost drained the cup of life, and nearly reached the haven of the common sea of existence is more secure, and therefore more enviable, than one who has yet a long voyage before him.

4. Do not thou, therefore, restrain a tongue whose noble utterances and fruits have been many, which has begotten many children of righteousness — yea, lift up thine eyes round about and see, how many are its sons, and what are its treasures; even this whole people, whom thou hast begotten in Christ through the Gospel. Grudge not to us those words which are excellent rather than many, and do not yet give us a foretaste of our impending loss. Speak in words which, if few, are dear and most sweet to me, which, if scarcely audible, are perceived from their spiritual cry, as God heard the silence of Moses, and said to him when interceding mentally, "Why criest thou unto Me?" Comfort this people, I pray thee, I, who was thy nursling, and have since been made Pastor, and now even Chief Pastor. Give a lesson, to me in the Pastor's art, to this people of obedience. Discourse awhile on our present heavy blow, about the just judgments of God, whether we grasp their meaning, or are ignorant of their great deep. How again "mercy is put in the balance," as holy Isaiah declares, for goodness is not without discernment, as the first laborers in the vineyard fancied, because they could not perceive any distinction between those who were paid alike: and how anger, which is called "the cup in the hand of the Lord," and "the cup of falling which is drained," is in proportion to transgressions, even though He abates to all somewhat of what is their due, and dilutes with compassion the unmixed draught of His wrath. For He inclines from severity to indulgence towards those who accept chastisement with fear, and who after a slight affliction conceive and are in pain with conversion, and bring forth the perfect spirit of salvation; but nevertheless he reserves the dregs, the last drop of His anger, that He may pour it out entire upon those who, instead of being healed by His kindness, grow obdurate, like the hard-hearted Pharaoh, that bitter taskmaster, who is set forth as an example of the power of God over the ungodly.

5. Tell us whence come such blows and scourges, and what account we can give of them. Is it some disordered and irregular motion or some unguided current, some unreason of the universe, as though there were no Ruler of the world, which is therefore borne along by chance, as is the doctrine of the foolishly wise, who are themselves borne along at random by the disorderly spirit of darkness? Or are the disturbances and changes of the universe, (which was originally constituted, blended, bound together, and set in motion in a harmony known only to Him Who gave it motion,) directed by reason and order under the guidance of the reins of Providence? Whence come famines and tornadoes and hailstorms, our present warning blow? Whence pestilences, diseases, earthquakes, tidal waves, and fearful things in the heavens? And how is the creation, once ordered for the enjoyment of men, their common and equal delight, changed for the punishment of the ungodly, in order that we may be chastised through that for which, when honored with it, we did not give thanks, and recognize in our sufferings that power which we did not recognize in our benefits? How is it that some receive at the Lord's hand double for their sins, and the measure of their wickedness is doubly filled up, as in the correction of Israel, while the sins of others are done away by a sevenfold recompense into their bosom? What is the measure of the Amorites that is not yet full? And how is the sinner either let go, or chastised again, let go perhaps, because reserved for the other world, chastised, because healed thereby in this? Under what circumstances again is the righteous, when unfortunate, possibly being put to the test, or, when prosperous, being observed, to see if he be poor in mind or not very far superior to visible things, as indeed conscience, our interior and unerring tribunal, tells us. What is our calamity, and what its cause? Is it a test of virtue, or a touchstone of wickedness? And is it better to bow beneath it as a chastisement, even though it be not so, and humble ourselves under the mighty hand of God, or, considering it as a trial, to rise superior to it? On these points give us instruction and warning, lest we be too much discouraged by our present calamity, or fall into the gulf of evil and despise it; for some such feeling is very general; but rather that we may bear our admonition quietly, and not provoke one more severe by our insensibility to this.

6. Terrible is an unfruitful season, and the loss of the crops. It could not be otherwise, when men are already rejoicing in their hopes, and counting on their all but harvested stores. Terrible again is an unseasonable harvest, when the farmers labor with heavy hearts, sitting as it were beside the grave of their crops, which the gentle rain nourished, but the wild storm has rooted up, whereof the mower filleth not his hand, neither he that bindeth up the sheaves his bosom, nor have they obtained the blessing which passers-by bestow upon the farmers. Wretched indeed is the sight of the ground devastated, cleared, and shorn of its ornaments, over which the blessed Joel wails in his most tragic picture of the desolation of the land, and the scourge of famine; while another prophet wails, as he contrasts with its former beauty its final disorder, and thus discourses on the anger of the Lord when He smites the land: before him is the garden of Eden, behind Him a desolate

wilderness. Terrible indeed these things are, and more than terrible, when we are grieved only at what is present, and are not yet distressed by the feeling of a severer blow: since, as in sickness, the suffering which pains us from time to time is more distressing than that which is not present. But more terrible still are those which the treasures of God's wrath contain, of which God forbid that you should make trial; nor will you, if you fly for refuge to the mercies of God, and win over by your tears Him Who will have mercy, and avert by your conversion what remains of His wrath. As yet, this is gentleness and loving-kindness and gentle reproof, and the first elements of a scourge to train our tender years: as yet, the smoke of His anger, the prelude of His torments; not yet has fallen the flaming fire, the climax of His being moved; not yet the kindled coals, the final scourge, part of which He threatened, when He lifted up the other over us, part He held back by force, when He brought the other upon us; using the threat and the blow alike for our instruction, and making a way for His indignation, in the excess of His goodness; beginning with what is slight, so that the more severe may not be needed; but ready to instruct us by what is greater, if He be forced so to do.

7. I know the glittering sword, and the blade made drunk in heaven, bidden to slay, to bring to naught, to make childless, and to spare neither flesh, nor marrow, nor bones. I know Him, Who, though free from passion, meets us like a bear robbed of her whelps, like a leopard in the way of the Assyrians, not only those of that day, but if anyone now is an Assyrian in wickedness: nor is it possible to escape the might and speed of His wrath when He watches over our impieties, and His jealousy, which knoweth to devour His adversaries, pursues His enemies to the death. I know the emptying, the making void, the making waste, the melting of the heart, and knocking of the knees together, such are the punishments of the ungodly. I do not dwell on the judgments to come, to which indulgence in this world delivers us, as it is better to be punished and cleansed now than to be transmitted to the torment to come, when it is the time of chastisement, not of cleansing. For as he who remembers God here is conqueror of death (as David has most excellently sung) so the departed have not in the grave confession and restoration; for God has confined life and action to this world, and to the future the scrutiny of what has been done.

8. What shall we do in the day of visitation, with which one of the Prophets terrifies me, whether that of the righteous sentence of God against us, or that upon the mountains and hills, of which we have heard, or whatever and whenever it may be, when He will reason with us, and oppose us, and set before us those bitter accusers, our sins, comparing our wrongdoings with our benefits, and striking thought with thought, and scrutinizing action with action, and calling us to account for the image which has been blurred and spoilt by wickedness, till at last He leads us away self-convicted and self-condemned, no longer able to say that we are being unjustly treated — a thought which is able even here sometimes to console in their condemnation those who are suffering.

70

9. But then what advocate shall we have? What pretext? What false excuse? What plausible artifice? What device contrary to the truth will impose upon the court, and rob it of its right judgment, which places in the balance for us all, our entire life, action, word, and thought, and weighs against the evil that which is better, until that which preponderates wins the day, and the decision is given in favor of the main tendency; after which there is no appeal, no higher court, no defense on the ground of subsequent conduct, no oil obtained from the wise virgins, or from them that sell, for the lamps going out, no repentance of the rich man wasting away in the flame, and begging for repentance for his friends, no statute of limitations; but only that final and fearful judgment- seat, more just even than fearful; or rather more fearful because it is also just; when the thrones are set and the Ancient of days takes His seat, and the books are opened, and the fiery stream comes forth, and the light before Him, and the darkness prepared; and they that have done good shall go into the resurrection of life, now hid in Christ and to be manifested hereafter with Him, and they that have done evil, into the resurrection of judgment, to which they who have not believed have been condemned already by the word which judges them. Some will be welcomed by the unspeakable light and the vision of the holy and royal Trinity, Which now shines upon them with greater brilliancy and purity and unites Itself wholly to the whole soul, in which solely and beyond all else I take it that the kingdom of heaven consists. The others among other torments, but above and before them all must endure the being outcast from God, and the shame of conscience which has no limit. But of these anon.

10. What are we to do now, my brethren, when crushed, cast down, and drunken but not with strong drink nor with wine, which excites and obfuscates but for a while, but with the blow which the Lord has inflicted upon us, Who says, And thou, O heart, be stirred and shaken, and gives to the despisers the spirit of sorrow and deep sleep to drink: to whom He also says, See, ye despisers, behold, and wonder and perish? How shall we bear His convictions; or what reply shall we make, when He reproaches us not only with the multitude of the benefits for which we have continued ungrateful, but also with His chastisements, and reckons up the remedies with which we have refused to be healed? Calling us His children indeed, but unworthy children, and His sons, but strange sons who have stumbled from lameness out of their paths, in the trackless and rough ground. How and by what means could I have instructed you, and I have not done so? By gentler measures? I have applied them. I passed by the blood drunk in Egypt from the wells and rivers and all reservoirs of water in the first plague: I passed over the next scourges, the frogs, lice, and flies. I began with the flocks and the cattle and the sheep, the fifth plague, and, sparing as yet the rational creatures, I struck the animals. You made light of the stroke, and treated me with less reason and attention than the beasts who were struck. I withheld from you the rain; one piece was rained upon, and the piece whereupon it rained not withered, and ye said "We will brave it." I brought the hail upon you, chastising you with the opposite kind of blow, I uprooted your vineyards and shrubberies, and crops, but I failed to shatter your wickedness.

71

11. Perchance He will say to me, who am not reformed even by blows, I know that thou art obstinate, and thy neck is an iron sinew, the heedless is heedless and the lawless man acts lawlessly, naught is the heavenly correction, naught the scourges. The bellows are burnt, the lead is consumed, as I once reproached you by the mouth of Jeremiah, the founder melted the silver in vain, your wickednesses are not melted away. Can ye abide my wrath, saith the Lord. Has not My hand the power to inflict upon you other plagues also? There are still at My command the blains breaking forth from the ashes of the furnace, by sprinkling which toward heaven, Moses, or any other minister of God's action, may chastise Egypt with disease. There remain also the locusts, the darkness that may be felt, and the plague which, last in order, was first in suffering and power, the destruction and death of the firstborn, and, to escape this, and to turn aside the destroyer, it were better to sprinkle the doorposts of our mind, contemplation and action, with the great and saving token, with the blood of the new covenant, by being crucified and dying with Christ, that we may both rise and be glorified and reign with Him both now and at His final appearing, and not be broken and crushed, and made to lament, when the grievous destroyer smites us all too late in this life of darkness, and destroys our firstborn, the offspring and results of our life which we had dedicated to God.

12. Far be it from me that I should ever, among other chastisements, be thus reproached by Him Who is good, but walks contrary to me in fury because of my own contrariness: I have smitten you with blasting and mildew, and blight; without result. The sword from without made you childless, yet have ye not returned unto Me, saith the Lord. May I not become the vine of the beloved, which after being planted and entrenched, and made sure with a fence and tower and every means which was possible, when it ran wild and bore thorns, was consequently despised, and had its tower broken down and its fence taken away, and was not pruned nor digged, but was devoured and laid waste and trodden down by all! This is what I feel I must say as to my fears, thus have I been pained by this blow, and this, I will further tell you, is my prayer. We have sinned, we have done amiss, and have dealt wickedly, for we have forgotten Thy commandments and walked after our own evil thought, for we have behaved ourselves unworthily of the calling and gospel of Thy Christ, and of His holy sufferings and humiliation for us; we have become a reproach to Thy beloved, priest and people, we have erred together, we have all gone out of the way, we have together become unprofitable, there is none that doeth judgment and justice, no not one. We have cut short Thy mercies and kindness and the bowels and compassion of our God, by our wickedness and the perversity of our doings, in which we have turned away. Thou art good, but we have done amiss; Thou art long-suffering, but we are worthy of stripes; we acknowledge Thy goodness, though we are without understanding, we have been scourged for but few of our faults; Thou art terrible, and who will resist Thee? the mountains will tremble before Thee; and who will strive against the might of Thine arm? If Thou shut the heaven, who will open it? And if Thou let loose Thy

torrents, who will restrain them? It is a light thing in Thine eyes to make poor and to make rich, to make alive and to kill, to strike and to heal, and Thy will is perfect action. Thou art angry, and we have sinned, says one of old, making confession; and it is now time for me to say the opposite, "We have sinned, and Thou art angry:" therefore have we become a reproach to our neighbors. Thou didst turn Thy face from us, and we were filled with dishonor. But stay, Lord, cease, Lord, forgive, Lord, deliver us not up for ever because of our iniquities, and let not our chastisements be a warning for others, when we might learn wisdom from the trials of others. Of whom? Of the nations which know Thee not, and kingdoms which have not been subject to Thy power. But we are Thy people, O Lord, the rod of Thine inheritance; therefore correct us, but in goodness and not in Thine anger, lest Thou bring us to nothingness and contempt among all that dwell on the earth.

13. With these words I invoke mercy: and if it were possible to propitiate His wrath with whole burnt offerings or sacrifices, I would not even have spared these. Do you also yourselves imitate your trembling priest, you, my beloved children, sharers with me alike of the Divine correction and loving-kindness. Possess your souls in tears, and stay His wrath by amending your way of life. Sanctify a fast, call a solemn assembly, as blessed Joel with us charges you: gather the elders, and the babes that suck the breasts, whose tender age wins our pity, and is specially worthy of the loving-kindness of God. I know also what he enjoins both upon me, the minister of God, and upon you, who have been thought worthy of the same honor, that we should enter His house in sackcloth and lament night and day between the porch and the altar, in piteous array, and with more piteous voices, crying aloud without ceasing on behalf of ourselves and the people, sparing nothing, either toil or word, which may propitiate God: saying "Spare, O Lord, Thy people, and give not Thine heritage to reproach," and the rest of the prayer; surpassing the people in our sense of the affliction as much as in our rank, instructing them in our own persons in compunction and correction of wickedness, and in the consequent long-suffering of God, and cessation of the scourge.

14. Come then, all of you, my brethren, let us worship and fall down, and weep before the Lord our Maker; let us appoint a public mourning, in our various ages and families, let us raise the voice of supplication; and let this, instead of the cry which He hates, enter into the ears of the Lord of Sabaoth. Let us anticipate His anger by confession; let us desire to see Him appeased, after He was wroth. Who knoweth, he says, if He will turn and repent, and leave a blessing behind Him? This I know certainly, I the sponsor of the loving-kindness of God. And when He has laid aside that which is unnatural to Him, His anger, He will betake Himself to that which is natural, His mercy. To the one He is forced by us, to the other He is inclined. And if He is forced to strike, surely He will refrain, according to His Nature. Only let us have mercy on ourselves, and open a road for our Father's righteous affections. Let us sow in tears, that we may reap in joy, let us show ourselves men of Nineveh, not of Sodom. Let us amend our wickedness, lest we be

consumed with it; let us listen to the preaching of Jonah, lest we be overwhelmed by fire and brimstone, and if we have departed from Sodom let us escape to the mountain, let us flee to Zoar, let us enter it as the sun rises; let us not stay in all the plain, let us not look around us, lest we be frozen into a pillar of salt, a really immortal pillar, to accuse the soul which returns to wickedness.

15. Let us be assured that to do no wrong is really superhuman, and belongs to God alone. I say nothing about the Angels, that we may give no room for wrong feelings, nor opportunity for harmful altercations. Our unhealed condition arises from our evil and unsubdued nature, and from the exercise of its powers. Our repentance when we sin, is a human action, but an action which bespeaks a good man, belonging to that portion which is in the way of salvation. For if even our dust contracts somewhat of wickedness, and the earthly tabernacle presseth down the upward flight of the soul, which at least was created to fly upward, yet let the image be Cleansed from filth, and raise aloft the flesh, its yoke-fellow, lifting it on the wings of reason; and, what is better, let us neither need this cleansing, nor have to be cleansed, by preserving our original dignity, to which we are hastening through our training here, and let us not by the bitter taste of sin be banished from the tree of life: though it is better to turn again when we err, than to be free from correction when we stumble. For whom the Lord loveth He chasteneth, and a rebuke is a fatherly action; while every soul which is unchastized, is unhealed. Is not then freedom from chastisement a hard thing? But to fail to be corrected by the chastisement is still harder. One of the prophets, speaking of Israel, whose heart was hard and uncircumcised, says, Lord, Thou hast stricken them, but they have not grieved, Thou hast consumed them but they have refused to receive correction; and again, The people turned not to Him that smiteth them; and Why is my people slid-den back by a perpetual backsliding, because of which it will be utterly crushed and destroyed?

16. It is a fearful thing, my brethren, to fall into the hands of a living God, and fearful is the face of the Lord against them that do evil, and abolishing wickedness with utter destruction. Fearful is the ear of God, listening even to the voice of Abel speaking through his silent blood. Fearful His feet, which overtake evildoing. Fearful also His filling of the universe, so that it is impossible anywhere to escape the action of God, not even by flying up to heaven, or entering Hades, or by escaping to the far East, or concealing ourselves in the depths and ends of the sea. Nahum the Elkoshite was afraid before me, when he proclaimed the burden of Nineveh, God is jealous, and the Lord takes vengeance in wrath upon His adversaries, and uses such abundance of severity that no room is left for further vengeance upon the wicked. For whenever I hear Isaiah threaten the people of Sodom and rulers of Gomorrah, and say Why will ye be smitten any more, adding sin to sin? I am almost filled with horror, and melted to tears. It is impossible, he says, to find any blow to add to those which are past, because of your newly added sins; so completely have you run through the whole, and exhausted every form of

chastisement, ever calling upon yourselves some new one by your wickedness. There is not a wound, nor bruise, nor putrefying sore; the plague affects the whole body and is incurable: for it is impossible to apply a plaster, or ointment or bandages. I pass over the rest of the threatenings, that I may not press upon you more heavily than your present plague.

17. Only let us recognize the purpose of the evil. Why have the crops withered, our storehouses been emptied, the pastures of our flocks failed, the fruits of the earth been withheld, and the plains been filled with shame instead of with fatness: why have valleys lamented and not abounded in corn, the mountains not dropped sweetness, as they shall do hereafter to the righteous, but been stript and dishonored, and received on the contrary the curse of Gilboa? The whole earth has become as it was in the beginning, before it was adorned with its beauties. Thou visitedst the earth, and madest it to drink — but the visitation has been for evil, and the draught destructive. Alas! what a spectacle! Our prolific crops reduced to stubble, the seed we sowed is recognized by scanty remains, and our harvest, the approach of which we reckon from the number of the months, instead of from the ripening corn, scarcely bears the firstfruits for the Lord. Such is the wealth of the ungodly, such the harvest of the careless sower; as the ancient curse runs, to look for much, and bring in little, to sow and not reap, to plant and not press, ten acres of vineyard to yield one hath: and to hear of fertile harvests in other lands, and be ourselves pressed by famine. Why is this, and what is the cause of the breach? Let us not wait to be convicted by others, let us be our own examiners. An important medicine for evil is confession, and care to avoid stumbling. I will be first to do so, as I have made my report to my people from on high, and performed the duty of a watcher. For I did not conceal the coming of the sword that I might save my own soul and those of my hearers. So will I now announce the disobedience of my people, making what is theirs my own, if I may perchance thus obtain some tenderness and relief.

18. One of us has oppressed the poor, and wrested from him his portion of land, and wrongly encroached upon his landmark by fraud or violence, and joined house to house, and field to field, to rob his neighbor of something, and been eager to have no neighbor, so as to dwell alone on the earth. Another has defiled the land with usury and interest, both gathering where he had not sowed and reaping where he had not strawed, farming, not the land, but the necessity of the needy. Another has robbed God, the giver of all, of the firstfruits of the barnfloor and winepress, showing himself at once thankless and senseless, in neither giving thanks for what he has had, nor prudently providing, at least, for the future. Another has had no pity on the widow and orphan, and not imparted his bread and meager nourishment to the needy, or rather to Christ, Who is nourished in the persons of those who are nourished even in a slight degree; a man perhaps of much property unexpectedly gained, for this is the most unjust of all, who finds his many barns too narrow for him, filling some and emptying others, to build greater ones for future

75

crops, not knowing that he is being snatched away with hopes unrealized, to give an account of his riches and fancies, and proved to have been a bad steward of another' s goods. Another has turned aside the way of the meek, and turned aside the just among the unjust; another has hated him that reproveth in the gates, and abhorred him that speaketh uprightly; another has sacrificed to his net which catches much, and keeping the spoil of the poor in his house, has either remembered not God, or remembered Him ill — by saying "Blessed be the Lord, for we are rich," and wickedly supposed that he received these things from Him by Whom he will be punished. For because of these things cometh the wrath of God upon the children of disobedience. Because of these things the heaven is shut, or opened for our punishment; and much more, if we do not repent, even when smitten, and draw near to Him, Who approaches us through the powers of nature.

19. What shall be said to this by those of us who are buyers and sellers of corn, and watch the hardships of the seasons, in order to grow prosperous, and luxuriate in the misfortunes of others, and acquire, not, like Joseph, the property of the Egyptians, as a part of a wide policy, (for he could both collect and supply corn duly, as he also could foresee the famine, and provide against it afar off,) but the property of their fellow countrymen in an illegal manner, for they say, "When will the new moon be gone, that we may sell, and the sabbaths, that we may open our stores?" And they corrupt justice with divers measures and balances, and draw upon themselves the ephah of lead. What shall we say to these things who know no limit to our getting, who worship gold and silver, as those of old worshipped Baal, and Astarte and the abomination Chemosh? Who give heed to the brilliance of costly stones, and soft flowing garments, the prey of moths, and the plunder of robbers and tyrants and thieves; who are proud of their multitude of slaves and animals, and spread themselves over plains and mountains, with their possessions and gains and schemes, like Solomon's horseleach which cannot be satisfied, any more than the grave, and the earth, and fire, and water; who seek for another world for their possession, and find fault with the bounds of God, as too small for their insatiable cupidity? What of those who sit on lofty thrones and raise the stage of government, with a brow loftier than that of the theater, taking no account of the God over all, and the height of the true kingdom that none can approach unto, so as to rule their subjects as fellow-servants, as needing themselves no less loving-kindness? Look also, I pray you, at those who stretch themselves upon beds of ivory, whom the divine Amos fitly upbraids, who anoint themselves with the chief ointments, and chant to the sound of instruments of music, and attach themselves to transitory things as though they were stable, but have not grieved nor had compassion for the affliction of Joseph; though they ought to have been kind to those who had met with disaster before them, and by mercy have obtained mercy; as the fir-tree should howl, because the cedar had fallen, and be instructed by their neighbors' chastisement, and be led by others' ills to regulate their own lives, having the advantage of being saved by their predecessors' fate, instead of being themselves a warning to others.

76

20. Join with us, thou divine and sacred person, in considering these questions, with the store of experience, that source of wisdom, which thou hast gathered in thy long life. Herewith instruct thy people. Teach them to break their bread to the hungry, to gather together the poor that have no shelter, to cover their nakedness and not neglect those of the same blood, and now especially that we may gain a benefit from our need instead of from abundance, a result which pleases God more than plentiful offerings and large gifts. After this, nay before it, show thyself, I pray, a Moses, or Phinehas to day. Stand on our behalf and make atonement, and let the plague be stayed, either by the spiritual sacrifice, or by prayer and reasonable intercession. Restrain the anger of the Lord by thy mediation: avert any succeeding blows of the scourge. He knoweth to respect the hoar hairs of a father interceding for his children. Intreat for our past wickedness: be our surety for the future. Present a people purified by suffering and fear. Beg for bodily sustenance, but beg rather for the angels' food that cometh down from heaven. So doing, thou wilt make God to be our God, wilt conciliate heaven, wilt restore the former and latter rain: the Lord shall show loving-kindness and our land shall yield her fruit; our earthly land its fruit which lasts for the day, and our frame, which is but dust, the fruit which is eternal, which we shall store up in the heavenly winepresses by thy hands, who presentest both us and ours in Christ

On the death of his father in the Presence of Basil

This Oration was delivered A. D. 374. S. Gregory the eider died early in that year, according to the Greek Menaea on the 1st of January, though Clemencet and some others place his death a few months later. His wife, S. Nonna, survived him, and was present to hear the Oration, as was also S. Basil, who desired to honor one who had consecrated him to the Episcopate. The aged Saint, who died in his hundredth year, had originally belonged to a sect called Hypsistarii. Our knowledge of the existence and tenets of this sect is due to this Oration and to a few sentences in that of S. Greg. Nyssen. (c. Eunom. I. ed. 1615, p. 12), by whom they are called Hypsistians. He was converted by the prayers, influence and example of his wife, S. Nonna, and, soon after his baptism, consecrated Bishop of Nazianzus. He was eminent as an able administrator, a devout Christian, an orthodox teacher, a steadfast Confessor of the faith, a sympathetic Pastor, an affectionate father. In his life and work he was seconded by his wife, and followed by his three children, Gregory, Gorgonia, and Caesarius, whose names are all to be found upon the roll of the Saints.

1. O man of God, and faithful servant, and steward of the mysteries of God, and man of desires of the Spirit: for thus Scripture speaks of men advanced and lofty, superior to visible things. I will call you also a God to Pharaoh and all the Egyptian and hostile power, and pillar and ground of the Church and will of God and light in the world, holding forth the word of life, and prop of the faith and resting place of the Spirit. But why should I enumerate all the titles which your virtue, in its varied forms, has won for and applied to you as your own?

2. Tell me, however, whence do you come, what is your business, and what favor do you bring us? Since I know that you are entirely moved with and by God, and for the benefit of those who receive you. Are you come to inspect us, or to seek for the pastor, or to take the oversight of the flock? You find us no longer in existence, but for the most part having passed away with him, unable to bear with the place of our affliction, especially now that we have lost our skillful steersman, our light of life, to whom we looked to direct our course as the blazing beacon of salvation above us: he has departed with all his excellence, and all the power of pastoral organization, which he had gathered in a long time, full of days and wisdom, and crowned, to use the words of Solomon, with the hoary head of glory. His flock is desolate and downcast, filled, as you see, with despondency and dejection, no longer reposing in the green pasture, and reared up by the water of comfort, but seeking precipices, deserts and pits, in which it will be scattered and perish; in despair of ever obtaining another wise pastor, absolutely persuaded that it cannot find such an one as he, content if it be one who will not be far inferior.

3. There are, as I said, three causes to necessitate your presence, all of equal weight, ourselves, the pastor, and the flock: come then, and according to the spirit of ministry which is in you, assign to each its due, and guide your words in judgment,

so that we may more than ever marvel at your wisdom. And how will you guide them? First by bestowing seemly praise upon his virtue, not only as a pure sepulchral tribute of speech to him who was pure, but also to set forth to others his conduct and example as a mark of true piety. Then bestow upon us some brief counsels concerning life and death, and the union and severance of body and soul, and the two worlds, the one present but transitory, the other spiritually perceived and abiding; and persuade us to despise that which is deceitful and disordered and uneven, carrying us and being carried, like the waves, now up, now down; but to cling to that which is firm and stable and divine and constant, free from all disturbance and confusion. For this would lessen our pain because of friends departed before us, nay we should rejoice if your words should carry us hence and set us on high, and hide distress of the present in the future, and persuade us that we also are pressing on to a good Master, and that our home is better than our pilgrimage; and that translation and removal thither is to us who are tempest-tost here like a calm haven to men at sea; or as ease and relief from toil come to men who, at the close of a long journey, escape the troubles of the wayfarer, so to those who attain to the hostel yonder comes a better and more tolerable existence than that of those who still tread the crooked and precipitous path of this life.

4. Thus might you console us; but what of the flock? Would you first promise the oversight and leadership of yourself, a man under whose wings we all would gladly repose, and for whose words we thirst more eagerly than men suffering from thirst for the purest fountain? Secondly, persuade us that the good shepherd who laid down his life for the sheep has not even now left us; but is present, and tends and guides, and knows his own, and is known of his own, and, though bodily invisible, is spiritually recognized, and defends his flock against the wolves, and allows no one to climb over into the fold as a robber and traitor; to pervert and steal away, by the voice of strangers, souls under the fair guidance of the truth. Aye, I am well assured that his intercession is of more avail now than was his instruction in former days, since he is closer to God, now that he has shaken off his bodily fetters, and freed his mind from the clay which obscured it, and holds intercourse naked with the nakedness of the prime and purest Mind; being promoted, if it be not rash to say so, to the rank and confidence of an angel. This, with your power of speech and spirit, you will set forth and discuss better than I can sketch it. But in order that, through ignorance of his excellences, your language may not fall very far short of his deserts, I will, from my own knowledge of the departed, briefly draw an outline, and preliminary plan of an eulogy to be handed to you, the illustrious artist of such subjects, for the details of the beauty of his virtue to be filled in and transmitted to the ears and minds of all.

5. Leaving to the laws of panegyric the description of his country, his family, his nobility of figure, his external magnificence, and the other subjects of human pride, I begin with what is of most consequence and comes closest to ourselves. He sprang from a stock unrenowned, and not well suited for piety, for I am not ashamed of

his origin, in my confidence in the close of his life, one that was not planted in the house of God, but far removed and estranged, the combined product of two of the greatest opposites — Greek error and legal imposture, some parts of each of which it escaped, of others it was compounded. For, on the one side, they reject idols and sacrifices, but reverence fire and lights; on the other, they observe the Sabbath and petty regulations as to certain meats, but despise circumcision. These lowly men call themselves Hypsistarii, and the Almighty is, so they say, the only object of their worship. What was the result of this double tendency to impiety? I know not whether to praise more highly the grace which called him, or his own purpose. However, he so purged the eye of his mind from the humors which obscured it, and ran towards the truth with such speed that he endured the loss of his mother and his property for a while, for the sake of his heavenly Father and the true inheritance: and submitted more readily to this dishonor, than others to the greatest honors, and, most wonderful as this is, I wonder at it but little. Why? Because this glory is common to him with many others, and all must come into the great net of God, and be caught by the words of the fishers, although some are earlier, some later, enclosed by the Gospel. But what does especially in his life move my wonder, it is needful for me to mention.

6. Even before he was of our fold, he was ours. His character made him one of us. For, as many of our own are not with us, whose life alienates them from the common body, so, many of those without are on our side, whose character anticipates their faith, and need only the name of that which indeed they possess. My father was one of these, an alien shoot, but inclined by his life towards us. He was so far advanced in self control, that he became at once most beloved and most modest, two qualities difficult to combine. What greater and more splendid testimony can there be to his justice than his exercise of a position second to none in the state, without enriching himself by a single farthing, although he saw everyone else casting the hands of Briareus upon the public funds, and swollen with ill-gotten gain? For thus do I term unrighteous wealth. Of his prudence this also is no slight proof, but in the course of my speech further details will be given. It was as a reward for such conduct, I think, that he attained to the faith. How this came about, a matter too important to be passed over, I would now set forth.

7. I have heard the Scripture say: Who can find a valiant woman? and declare that she is a divine gift, and that a good marriage is brought about by the Lord. Even those without are of the same mind; if they say that a man can win no fairer prize than a good wife, nor a worse one than her opposite. But we can mention none who has been in this respect more fortunate than he. For I think that, had anyone from the ends of the earth and from every race of men attempted to bring about the best of marriages, he could not have found a better or more harmonious one than this. For the most excellent of men and of women were so united that their marriage was a union of virtue rather than of bodies: since, while they excelled all

others, they could not excel each other, because in virtue they were quite equally matched.

8. She indeed who was given to Adam as a help meet for him, because it was not good for man to be alone, instead of an assistant became an enemy, and instead of a yoke-fellow, an opponent, and beguiling the man by means of pleasure, estranged him through the tree of knowledge from the tree of life. But she who was given by God to my father became not only, as is less wonderful, his assistant, but even his leader, drawing him on by her influence in deed and word to the highest excellence; judging it best in all other respects to be overruled by her husband according to the law of marriage, but not being ashamed, in regard of piety, even to offer herself as his teacher. Admirable indeed as was this conduct of hers, it was still more admirable that he should readily acquiesce in it. She is a woman who while others have been honored and extolled for natural and artificial beauty, has acknowledged but one kind of beauty, that of the soul, and the preservation, or the restoration as far as possible, of the Divine image. Pigments and devices for adornment she has rejected as worthy of women on the stage. The only genuine form of noble birth she recognized is piety, and the knowledge of whence we are sprung and whither we are tending. The only safe and inviolable form of wealth is, she considered, to strip oneself of wealth for God and the poor, and especially for those of our own kin who are unfortunate; and such help only as is necessary, she held to be rather a reminder, than a relief of their distress, while a more liberal beneficence brings stable honor and most perfect consolation. Some women have excelled in thrifty management, others in piety, while she, difficult as it is to unite the two virtues, has surpassed all in both of them, both by her eminence in each, and by the fact that she alone has combined them together. To as great a degree has she, by her care and skill, secured the prosperity of her household, according to the injunctions and laws of Solomon as to the valiant woman, as if she had had no knowledge of piety; and she applied herself to God and Divine things as closely as if absolutely released from household cares, allowing neither branch of her duty to interfere with the other, but rather making each of them support the other.

9. What time or place for prayer ever escaped her? To this she was drawn before all other things in the day; or rather, who had such hope of receiving an immediate answer to her requests? Who paid such reverence to the hand and countenance of the priests? Or honored all kinds of philosophy? Who reduced the flesh by more constant fast and vigil? Or stood like a pillar at the night long and daily psalmody? Who had a greater love for virginity, though patient of the marriage bond herself? Who was a better patron of the orphan and the widow? Who aided as much in the alleviation of the misfortunes of the mourner? These things, small as they are, and perhaps contemptible in the eyes of some, because not easily attainable by most people (for that which is unattainable comes, through envy, to be thought not even credible), are in my eyes most honorable, since they were the discoveries of her faith and the undertakings of her spiritual fervor. So also in the holy assemblies, or

places, her voice was never to be heard except in the necessary responses of the service.

10. And if it was a great thing for the altar never to have had an iron tool lifted upon it, and that no chisel should be seen or heard, with greater reason, since everything dedicated to God ought to be natural and free from artificiality, it was also surely a great thing that she reverenced the sanctuary by her silence; that she never turned her back to the venerable table, nor spat upon the divine pavement; that she never grasped the hand or kissed the lips of any heathen woman, however honorable in other respects, or closely related she might be; nor would she ever share the salt, I say not willingly but even under compulsion, of those who came from the profane and unholy table; nor could she bear, against the law of conscience, to pass by or look upon a polluted house; nor to have her ears or tongue, which had received and uttered divine things, defiled by Grecian tales or theatrical songs, on the ground that what is unholy is unbecoming to holy things; and what is still more wonderful, she never so far yielded to the external signs of grief, although greatly moved even by the misfortunes of strangers, as to allow a sound of woe to burst forth before the Eucharist, or a tear to fall from the eye mystically sealed, or any trace of mourning to be left on the occasion of a festival, however frequent her own sorrows might be; inasmuch as the God-loving soul should subject every human experience to the things of God.

11. I pass by in silence what is still more ineffable, of which God is witness, and those of the faithful handmaidens to whom she has confided such things. That which concerns myself is perhaps undeserving of mention, since I have proved unworthy of the hope cherished in regard to me: yet it was on her part a great undertaking to promise me to God before my birth, with no fear of the future, and to dedicate me immediately after I was born. Through God's goodness has it been that she has not utterly failed in her prayer, and that the auspicious sacrifice was not rejected. Some of these things were already in existence, others were in the future, growing up by means of gradual additions. And as the sun which most pleasantly casts its morning rays, becomes at midday hotter and more brilliant, so also did she, who from the first gave no slight evidence of piety, shine forth at last with fuller light. Then indeed he, who had established her in his house, had at home no slight spur to piety, possessed, by her origin and descent, of the love of God and Christ, and having received virtue as her patrimony; not, as he had been, cut out of the wild olive and grafted into the good olive, yet unable to bear, in the excess of her faith, to be unequally yoked; for, though surpassing all others in endurance and fortitude, she could not brook this, the being but half united to God, because of the estrangement of him who was a part of herself, and the failure to add to the bodily union, a close connection in the spirit: on this account, she fell before God night and day, entreating for the salvation of her head with many fastings and tears, and assiduously devoting herself to her husband, and influencing him in many ways, by means of reproaches, admonitions, attentions, estrangements, and above all by her

own character with its fervor for piety, by which the soul is specially prevailed upon and softened, and willingly submits to virtuous pressure. The drop of water constantly striking the rock was destined to hollow it, and at length attain its longing, as the sequel shows.

12. These were the objects of her prayers and hopes, in the fervor of faith rather than of youth. Indeed, none was as confident of things present as she of things hoped for, from her experience of the generosity of God. For the salvation of my father there was a concurrence of the gradual conviction of his reason, and the vision of dreams which God often bestows upon a soul worthy of salvation. What was the vision? This is to me the most pleasing part of the story. He thought that he was singing, as he had never done before, though his wife was frequent in her supplications and prayers, this verse from the psalms of holy David: I was glad when they said unto me, we will go into the house of the Lord. The psalm was a strange one to him, and along with its words the desire came to him. As soon as she heard it, having thus obtained her prayer, she seized the opportunity, replying that the vision would bring the greatest pleasure, if accompanied by its fulfillment, and, manifesting by her joy the greatness of the benefit, she urged forward his salvation, before anything could intervene to hinder the call, and dissipate the object of her longing. At that very time it happened that a number of Bishops were hastening to Nicaea, to oppose the madness of Arius, since the wickedness of dividing the Godhead had just arisen; so my father yielded himself to God and to the heralds of the truth, and confessed his desire, and requested from them the common salvation, one of them being the celebrated Leontius, at that time our own metropolitan. It would be a great wrong to grace, were I to pass by in silence the wonder which then was bestowed upon him by grace. The witnesses of the wonder are not few. The teachers of accuracy were spiritually at fault, and the grace was a forecast of the future, and the formula of the priesthood was mingled with the admission of the catechumen. O involuntary initiation! bending his knee, he received the form of admission to the state of a catechumen in such wise, that many, not only of the highest, but even of the lowest, intellect, prophesied the future, being assured by no indistinct signs of what was to be.

13. After a short interval, wonder succeeded wonder. I will commend the account of it to the ears of the faithful, for to profane minds nothing that is good is trustworthy. He was approaching that regeneration by water and the Spirit, by which we confess to God the formation and completion of the Christlike man, and the transformation and reformation from the earthy to the Spirit. He was approaching the layer with warm desire and bright hope, after all the purgation possible, and a far greater purification of soul and body than that of the men who were to receive the tables from Moses. Their purification extended only to their dress, and a slight restriction of the belly, and a temporary continence. The whole of his past life had been a preparation for the enlightenment, and a preliminary purification making sure the gift, in order that perfection might be entrusted to

purity, and that the blessing might incur no risk in a soul which was confident in its possession of the grace. And as he was ascending out of the water, there flashed around him a light and a glory worthy of the disposition with which he approached the gift of faith; this was manifest even to some others, who for the time concealed the wonder, from fear of speaking of a sight which each one thought had been only his own, but shortly afterwards communicated it to one another. To the baptizer and initiator, however, it was so clear and visible, that he could not even hold back the mystery, but publicly cried out that he was anointing with the Spirit his own successor.

14. Nor indeed would anyone disbelieve this who has heard and knows that Moses, when little in the eyes of men, and not yet of any account, was called from the bush which burned but was not consumed, or rather by Him who appeared in the bush, and was encouraged by that first wonder: Moses, I say, for whom the sea was divided, and manna rained down, and the rock poured out a fountain, and the pillar of fire and cloud led the way in turn, and the stretching out of his hands gained a victory, and the representation of the cross overcame tens of thousands. Isaiah, again, who beheld the glory of the Seraphim, and after him Jeremiah, who was entrusted with great power against nations and kings; the one heard the divine voice and was cleansed by a live coal for his prophetic office, and the other was known before his formation and sanctified before his birth. Paul, also, while yet a persecutor, who became the great herald of the truth and teacher of the Gentiles in faith, was surrounded by a light and acknowledged Him whom he was persecuting, and was entrusted with his great ministry, and filled every ear and mind with the gospel.

15. Why need I count up all those who have been called to Himself by God and associated with such wonders as confirmed him in his piety? Nor was it the case that after such and so incredible and startling beginnings, any of the former things was put to shame by his subsequent conduct, as happens with those who very soon acquire a distaste for what is good, and so neglect all further progress, if they do not utterly relapse into vice. This cannot be said of him, for he was most consistent with himself and his early days, and kept in harmony his life before the priesthood with its excellence, and his life after it with what had gone before, since it would have been unbecoming to begin in one way and end in another, or to advance to a different end from that which he had in view at first. He was next entrusted with the priesthood, not with the facility and disorder of the present day, but after a brief interval, in order to add to his own cleansing the skill and power to cleanse others; for this is the law of spiritual sequence. And when he had been entrusted with it, the grace was the more glorified, being really the grace of God, and not of men, and not, as the preacher says, an independent impulse and purpose of spirit.

16. He received a woodland and rustic church, the pastoral care and oversight of which had not been bestowed from a distance, but it had been cared for by one of

84

his predecessors of admirable and angelic disposition, and a more simple man than our present rulers of the people; but, after he had been speedily taken to God, it had, in consequence of the loss of its leader, for the most part grown careless and run wild; accordingly, he at first strove without harshness to soften the habits of the people, both by words of pastoral knowledge, and by setting himself before them as an example, like a spiritual statue, polished into the beauty of all excellent conduct. He next, by constant meditation on the divine words, though a late student of such matters, gathered together so much wisdom within a short time that he was in no wise excelled by those who had spent the greatest toil upon them, and received this special grace from God, that he became the father and teacher of orthodoxy — not, like our modern wise men, yielding to the spirit of the age, nor defending our faith by indefinite and sophistical language, as if they bad no fixity of faith, or were adulterating the truth; but, he was more pious than those who possessed rhetorical power, more skilled in rhetoric than those who were upright in mind; or rather, while he took the second place as an orator, he surpassed all in piety. He acknowledged One God worshipped in Trinity, and Three, Who are united in One Godhead; neither Sabellianising as to the One, nor Arianising as to the Three; either by contracting and so atheistically annihilating the Godhead, or by tearing It asunder by distinctions of unequal greatness or nature. For, seeing that Its every quality is incomprehensible and beyond the power of our intellect, how can we either perceive or express by definition on such a subject, that which is beyond our ken? How can the immeasurable be measured, and the Godhead be reduced to the condition of finite things, and measured by degrees of greater or less?

17. What else must we say of this great man of God, the true Divine, under the influence, in regard to these subjects, of the Holy Ghost, but that through his perception of these points, he, like the great Noah, the father of this second world, made this church to be called the new Jerusalem, and a second ark borne up upon the waters; since it both surmounted the deluge of souls, and the insults of the heretics, and excelled all others in reputation riotless than it fell behind them in numbers; and has had the same fortune as the sacred Bethlehem, which can without contradiction be at once said to be a little city and the metropolis of the world, since it is the nurse and mother of Christ, Who both made and overcame the world.

18. To give a proof of what I say. When a tumult of the over- zealous part of the Church was raised against us, and we had been decoyed by a document and artful terms into association with evil, he alone was believed to have an unwounded mind, and a soul unstained by ink, even when he had been imposed upon in his simplicity, and failed from his guilelessness of soul to be on his guard against guile. He it was alone, or rather first of all, who by his zeal for piety reconciled to himself and the rest of the church the faction opposed to us, which was the last to leave us, the first to return, owing to both their reverence for the man and the purity of his doctrine, so that the serious storm in the churches was allayed, and the hurricane

reduced to a breeze under the influence of his prayers and admonitions; while, if I may make a boastful remark, I was his partner in piety and activity, aiding him in every effort on behalf of what is good, accompanying and running beside him, and being permitted on this occasion to contribute a very great share of the toil. Here my account of these matters, which is a little premature, must come to an end.

19. Who could enumerate the full tale of his excellences, or, if he wished to pass by most of them, discover without difficulty what can be omitted? For each trait, as it occurs to the mind, seems superior to what has gone before; it takes possession of me, and I feel more at a loss to know what I ought to pass by, than other panegyrists are as to what they ought to say. So that the abundance of material is to some extent a hindrance to me, and my mind is itself put to the test in its efforts to test his qualities, and its inability, where all are equal, to find one which surpasses the rest. So that, just as when we see a pebble falling into still water, it becomes the center and starting-point of circle after circle, each by its continuous agitation breaking up that which lies outside of it; this is exactly the case with myself. For as soon as one thing enters my mind, another follows and displaces it; and I am wearied out in making a choice, as what I have already grasped is ever retiring in favor of that which follows in its train.

20. Who was more anxious than he for the common weal? Who more wise in domestic affairs, since God, who orders all things in due variation, assigned to him a house and suitable fortune? Who was more sympathetic in mind, more bounteous in hand, towards the poor, that most dishonored portion of the nature to which equal honor is due? For he actually treated his own property as if it were another's, of which he was but the steward, relieving poverty as far as he could, and expending not only his superfluities but his necessities — a manifest proof of love for the poor, giving a portion, not only to seven, according to the injunction of Solomon, but if an eighth came forward, not even in his case being niggardly, but more pleased to dispose of his wealth than we know others are to acquire it; taking away the yoke and election (which means, as I think, all meanness in testing as to whether the recipient is worthy or not) and word of murmuring in benevolence. This is what most men do: they give indeed, but without that readiness, which is a greater and more perfect thing than the mere offering. For he thought it much better to be generous even to the undeserving for the sake of the deserving, than from fear of the undeserving to deprive those who were deserving. And this seems to be the duty of casting our bread upon the waters, since it will not be swept away or perish in the eyes of the just Investigator, but will arrive yonder where all that is ours is laid up, and will meet with us in due time, even though we think it not.

21. But what is best and greatest of all, his magnanimity was accompanied by freedom from ambition. Its extent and character I will proceed to show. In considering their wealth to be common to all, and in liberality in bestowing it, he and his consort rivaled each other in their struggles after excellence; but he

intrusted the greater part of this bounty to her hand, as being a most excellent and trusty steward of such matters. What a woman she is? Not even the Atlantic Ocean, or if there be a greater one, could meet her drafts upon it. So great and so boundless is her love of liberality. In the contrary sense she has rivaled the horse-leech of Solomon, by her insatiable longing for progress, overcoming the tendency to backsliding, and unable to satisfy her zeal for benevolence. She not only considered all the property which they originally possessed, and what accrued to them later, as unable to suffice her own longing, but she would, as I have often heard her say, have gladly sold herself and her children into slavery, had there been any means of doing so, to expend the proceeds upon the poor. Thus entirely did she give the rein to her generosity. This is, I imagine, far more convincing than any instance of it could be. Magnanimity in regard to money may be found without difficulty in the case of others, whether it be dissipated in the public rivalries of the state, or lent to God through the poor, the only mode of treasuring it up for those who spend it: but it is not easy to discover a man who has renounced the consequent reputation. For it is desire for reputation which supplies to most men their readiness to spend. And where the bounty must be secret, there the disposition to it is less keen.

22. So bounteous was his hand — further details I leave to those who knew him, so that if anything of the kind is borne witness to in regard to myself, it proceeds from that fountain, and is a portion of that stream. Who was more trader the Divine guidance in admitting men to the sanctuary, or in resenting dishonor done to it, or in cleansing the holy table with awe from the unholy? Who with such unbiassed judgment, and with the scales of justice, either decided a suit, or hated vice, or honored virtue, or promoted the most excellent? Who was so compassionate for the sinner, or sympathetic towards those who were running well? Who better knew the right time for using the rod and the staff, yet relied most upon the staff? Whose eyes were more upon the faithful in the land, especially upon those who, in the monastic and unwedded life, have despised the earth and the things of earth?

23. Who did more to rebuke pride and foster lowliness? And that in no assumed or external way, as most of those who now make profession of virtue, and are in appearance as elegant as the most mindless women, who, for lack of beauty of their own, take refuge in pigments, and are, if I may say so, splendidly made up, uncomely in their comeliness, and more ugly than they originally were. For his lowliness was no matter of dress, but of spiritual disposition: nor was it expressed by a bent neck, or lowered voice, or downcast look, or length of beard, or close-shaven head, or measured gait, which can be adopted for a while, but are very quickly exposed, for nothing which is affected can be permanent. No! he was ever most lofty in life, most lowly in mind; inaccessible in virtue, most accessible in intercourse. His dress had in it nothing remarkable, avoiding equally magnificence and sordidness, while his internal brilliancy was supereminent. The disease and insatiability of the belly, he, if anyone, held in check, but without ostentation; so that he might be kept down without being puffed up, from having encouraged a

new vice by his pursuit of reputation. For he held that doing and saying everything by which fame among externs might be won, is the characteristic of the politician, whose chief happiness is found in the present life: but that the spiritual and Christian man should look to one object alone, his salvation, and think much of what may contribute to this, but detest as of no value what does not; and accordingly despise what is visible, but be occupied with interior perfection alone, and estimate most highly whatever promotes his own improvement, and attracts others through himself to that which is supremely good.

24. But what was most excellent and most characteristic, though least generally recognized, was his simplicity, and freedom from guile and resentment. For among men of ancient and modern days, each is supposed to have had some special success, as to have received from God some particular virtue: Job unconquered patience in misfortune, Moses and David meekness, Samuel prophecy, seeing into the future, Phineas zeal, for which he has a name, Peter and Paul eagerness in preaching, the sons of Zebedee magniloquence, whence also they were entitled Sons of thunder. But why should I enumerate them all, speaking as I do among those who know this? Now the specially distinguishing mark of Stephen and of my father was the absence of malice. For not even when in peril did Stephen hate his assailants, but was stoned while praying for those who were stoning him as a disciple of Christ, on Whose behalf he was allowed to suffer, and so, in his long-suffering, bearing for God a nobler fruit than his death: my father, in allowing no interval between assault and forgiveness, so that he was almost robbed of pain itself by the speed of pardon.

25. We both believe in and hear of the dregs of the anger of God, the residuum of His dealings with those who deserve it: For the Lord is a God of vengeance. For although He is disposed by His kindness to gentleness rather than severity, yet He does not absolutely pardon sinners, lest they should be made worse by His goodness. Yet my father kept no grudge against those who provoked him, indeed he was absolutely uninfluenced by anger, although in spiritual things exceedingly overcome by zeal: except when he had been prepared and armed and set in hostile array against that which was advancing to injure him. So that this sweet disposition of his would not, as the saying goes, have been stirred by tens of thousands. For the wrath which he had was not like that of the serpent, smoldering within, ready to defend itself, eager to burst forth, and longing to strike back at once on being disturbed; but like the sting of the bee, which does not bring death with its stroke; while his kindness was superhuman. The wheel and scourge were often threatened, and those who could apply them stood near; and the danger ended in being pinched on the ear, patted on the face, or buffeted on the temple: thus he mitigated the threat. His dress and sandals were dragged off, and the scoundrel was felled to the ground: then his anger was directed not against his assailant, but against his eager succorer, as a minister of evil. How could anyone be more conclusively proved to be good, and worthy to offer the gifts to God? For often, instead of being

himself roused, he made excuses for the man who assailed him, blushing for his faults as if they had been his own.

26. The dew would more easily resist the morning rays of the sun, than any remains of anger continue in him; but as soon as he had spoken, his indignation departed with his words, leaving behind only his love for what is good, and never outlasting the sun; nor did he cherish anger which destroys even the prudent, or show any bodily trace of vice within, nay, even when roused, he preserved calmness. The result of this was most unusual, not that he was the only one to give rebuke, but the only one to be both loved and admired by those whom he reproved, from the victory which his goodness gained over warmth of feeling; and it was felt to be more serviceable to be punished by a just man than besmeared by a bad one, for in one case the severity becomes pleasant for its utility, in the other the kindliness is suspected because of the evil of the man's character. But though his soul and character were so simple and divine, his piety nevertheless inspired the insolent with awe: or rather, the cause of their respect was the simplicity which they despised. For it was impossible to him to utter either prayer or curse without the immediate bestowal of permanent blessing or transient pain. The one proceeded from his inmost soul, the other merely rested upon his lips as a paternal reproof. Many indeed of those who had injured him incurred neither lingering requital nor, as the poet says, "vengeance which dogs men's steps;" but at the very moment of their passion they were struck and converted, came forward, knelt before him, and were pardoned, going away gloriously vanquished, and amended both by the chastisement and the forgiveness. Indeed, a forgiving spirit often has great saving power, checking the wrongdoer by the sense of shame, and bringing him back from fear to love, a far more secure state of mind. In chastisement some were tossed by oxen oppressed by the yoke, which suddenly attacked them, though they had never done anything of the kind before; others were thrown and trampled upon by most obedient and quiet horses; others seized by intolerable fevers, and apparitions of their daring deeds; others being punished in different ways, and learning obedience from the things which they suffered.

27. Such and so remarkable being his gentleness, did he yield the palm to others in industry and practical virtue? By no means. Gentle as he was, he possessed, if any one did, an energy corresponding to his gentleness. For although, for the most part, the two virtues of benevolence and severity are at variance and opposed to each other, the one being gentle but without practical qualities, the other practical but unsympathetic, in his case there was a wonderful combination of the two, his action being as energetic as that of a severe man, but combined with gentleness; while his readiness to yield seemed unpractical but was accompanied with energy, in his patronage, his freedom of speech, and every kind of official duty. He united the wisdom of the serpent, in regard to evil, with the harmlessness of the dove, in regard to good, neither allowing the wisdom to degenerate into knavery, nor the simplicity into silliness, but as far as in him lay, he combined the two in one perfect

form of virtue. Such being his birth, such his exercise of the priestly office, such the reputation which he won at the hands of all, what wonder if he was thought worthy of the miracles by which God establishes true religion?

28. One of the wonders which concern him was that he suffered from sickness and bodily pain. But what wonder is it for even holy men to be distressed, either for the cleansing of their clay, slight though it may be, or a touchstone of virtue and test of philosophy, or for the education of the weaker, who learn from their example to be patient instead of giving way under their misfortunes? Well, he was sick, the time was the holy and illustrious Easter, the queen of days, the brilliant night which dissipates the darkness of sin, upon which with abundant light we keep the feast of our salvation, putting ourselves to death along with the Light once put to death for us, and rising again with Him who rose. This was the time of his sufferings. Of what kind they were, I will briefly explain. His whole frame was on fire with an excessive, burning fever, his strength had failed, he was unable to take food, his sleep had departed from him, he was in the greatest distress, and agitated by palpitations. Within his mouth, the palate and the whole of the upper surface was so completely and painfully ulcerated, that it was difficult and dangerous to swallow even water. The skill of physicians, the prayers, most earnest though they were, of his friends, and every possible attention were alike of no avail. He himself in this desperate condition, while his breath came short and fast, had no perception of present things, but was entirely absent, immersed in the objects he had long desired, now made ready for him. We were in the temple, mingling supplications with the sacred rites, for, in despair, of all others, we had betaken ourselves to the Great Physician, to the power of that night, and to the last succor, with the intention, shall I say, of keeping a feast, or of mourning; of holding festival, or paying funeral honors to one no longer here? O those tears! which were shed at that time by all the people. O voices, and cries, and hymns blended with the psalmody! From the temple they sought the priest, from the sacred rite the celebrant, from God their worthy ruler, with my Miriam to lead them and strike the timbrel not of triumph, but of supplication; learning then for the first time to be put to shame by misfortune, and calling at once upon the people and upon God; upon the former to sympathize with her distress, and to be lavish of their tears, upon the latter, to listen to her petitions, as, with the inventive genius of suffering, she rehearsed before Him all His wonders of old time.

29. What then was the response of Him who was the God of that night and of the sick man? A shudder comes over me as I proceed with my story. And though you, my hearers, may shudder, do not disbelieve: for that would be impious, when I am the speaker, and in reference to him. The time of the mystery was come, and the reverend station and order, when silence is kept for the solemn rites; and then he was raised up by Him who quickeneth the dead, and by the holy night. At first he moved slightly, then more decidedly; then in a feeble and indistinct voice he called by name one of the servants who was in attendance upon him, and bade him come,

and bring his clothes, and support him with his hand. He came in alarm, and gladly waited upon him, while he, leaning upon his hand as upon a staff, imitates Moses upon the mount, arranges his feeble hands in prayer, and in union with, or on behalf of, his people eagerly celebrates the mysteries, in such few words as his strength allowed, but, as it seems to me, with a most perfect intention. What a miracle! In the sanctuary without a sanctuary, sacrificing without an altar, a priest far from the sacred rites: yet all these were present to him in the power of the spirit, recognized by him, though unseen by those who were there. Then, after adding the customary words of thanksgiving, and after blessing the people, he retired again to his bed, and after taking a little food, and enjoying a sleep, he recalled his spirit, and, his health being gradually recovered, on the new day of the feast, as we call the first Sunday after the festival of the Resurrection, he entered the temple and inaugurated his life which had been preserved, with the full complement of clergy, and offered the sacrifice of thanksgiving. To me this seems no less remarkable than the miracle in the case of Hezekiah, who was glorified by God in his sickness and prayers with an extension of life, and this was signified by the return of the shadow of the degrees, according to the request of the king who was restored, whom God honored at once by the favor and the sign, assuring him of the extension of his days by the extension of the day.

30. The same miracle occurred in the case of my mother not long afterwards. I do not think it would be proper to pass by this either: for we shall both pay the meed of honor which is due to her, if to anyone at all, and gratify him, by her being associated with him in our recital. She, who had always been strong and vigorous and free from disease all her life, was herself attacked by sickness. In consequence of much distress, not to prolong my story, caused above all by inability to eat, her life was for many days in danger, and no remedy for the disease could be found. How did God sustain her? Not by raining down manna, as for Israel of old or opening the rock, in order to give drink to His thirsting people, or feasting her by means of ravens, as Elijah, or feeding her by a prophet carried through the air, as He did to Daniel when a-hungered in the den. But how? She thought she saw me, who was her favorite, for not even in her dreams did she prefer any other of us, coming up to her suddenly at night, with a basket of pure white loaves, which I blessed and crossed as I was wont to do, and then fed and strengthened her, and she became stronger. The nocturnal vision was a real action. For, in consequence, she became more herself and of better hope, as is manifest by a clear and evident token. Next morning, when I paid her an early visit, I saw at once that she was brighter, and when I asked, as usual, what kind of a night she had passed, and if she wished for anything, she replied, "My child, you most readily and kindly fed me, and then you ask how I am. I am very well and at ease." Her maids too made signs to me to offer no resistance, and to accept her answer at once, lest she should be thrown back into despondency, if the truth were laid bare. I will add one more instance common to them both.

31.I was on a voyage from Alexandria to Greece over the Parthenian Sea. The voyage was quite unseasonable, undertaken in an Aeginetan vessel, under the impulse of eager desire; for what specially induced me was that I had fallen in with a crew who were well known to me. After making some way on the voyage, a terrible storm came upon us, and such an one as my shipmates said they had but seldom seen before. While we were all in fear of a common death, spiritual death was what I was most afraid of; for I was in danger of departing in misery, being unbaptized, and I longed for the spiritual water among the waters of death. On this account I cried and begged and besought a slight respite. My shipmates, even in their common danger, joined in my cries, as not even my own relatives would have done, kindly souls as they were, having learned sympathy from their dangers. In this my condition, my parents felt for me, my danger having been communicated to them by a nightly vision, and they aided me from the land, soothing the waves by prayer, as I afterwards learned by calculating the time, after I had landed. This was also shown me in a wholesome sleep, of which I had experience during a slight lull of the tempest. I seemed to be holding a Fury, of fearful aspect, boding danger; for the night presented her clearly to my eyes. Another of my shipmates, a boy most kindly disposed and dear to me, and exceedingly anxious on my behalf, in my then present condition, thought he saw my mother walk upon the sea, and seize and drag the ship to land with no great exertion. We had confidence in the vision, for the sea began to grow calm, and we soon reached Rhodes after the intervention of no great discomfort. We ourselves became an offering in consequence of that peril; for we promised ourselves if we were saved, to God, and, when we had been saved, gave ourselves to Him.

32. Such were their common experiences. But I imagine that some of those who have had an accurate knowledge of his life must have been for a long while wondering why we have dwelt upon these points, as if we thought them his only title to renown, and postponed the mention of the difficulties of his times, against which he conspicuously arrayed himself, as though we were either ignorant of them, or thought them to be of no great consequence. Come, then, we will proceed to speak upon this topic. The first, and I think the last, evil of our day, was the Emperor who apostatized from God and from reason, and thought it a small matter to conquer the Persians, but a great one to subject to himself the Christians; and so, together with the demons who led and prevailed upon him, he failed in no form of impiety, but by means of persuasions, threats, and sophistries, strove to draw men to him, and even added to his various artifices the use of force. His design, however, was exposed, whether he strove to conceal persecution under sophistical devices, or manifestly made use of his authority — namely by one means or the other — either by cozening or by violence, to get us into his power. Who can be found who more utterly despised or defeated him? One sign, among many others, of his contempt, is the mission to our sacred buildings of the police and their commissary, with the intention of taking either voluntary or forcible possession of them: he had attacked many others, and came hither with like intent, demanding the surrender of the

temple according to the Imperial decree, but was so far from succeeding in any of his wishes that, had he not speedily given way before my father, either from his own good sense or according to some advice given to him, he would have had to retire with his feet mangled, with such wrath and zeal did the priest boil against him in defense of his shrine. And who had a manifestly greater share in bringing about his end, both in public, by the prayers and united supplications which he directed against the accursed one, without regard to the [dangers of] the time; and in private, arraying against him his nightly armory, of sleeping on the ground, by which he wore away his aged and tender frame, and of tears, with whose fountains he watered the ground for almost a whole year, directing these practices to the Searcher of hearts alone, while he tried to escape our notice, in his retiring piety of which I have spoken. And he would have been utterly unobserved, had I not once suddenly rushed into his room, and noticing the tokens of his lying upon the ground, inquired of his attendants what they meant, and so learned the mystery of the night.

33. A further story of the same period and the same courage. The city of Caesarea was in an uproar about the election of a bishop; for one had just departed, and another must be found, amidst heated partisanship not easily to be soothed. For the city was naturally exposed to party spirit, owing to the fervor of its faith, and the rivalry was increased by the illustrious position of the see. Such was the state of affairs; several Bishops had arrived to consecrate the Bishop; the populace was divided into several parties, each with its own candidate, as is usual in such cases, owing to the influences of private friendship or devotion to God; but at last the whole people came to an agreement, and, with the aid of a band of soldiers at that time quartered there, seized one of their leading citizens, a man of excellent life, but not yet sealed with the divine baptism, brought him against his will to the sanctuary, and setting him before the Bishops, begged, with entreaties mingled with violence, that he might be consecrated and proclaimed, not in the best of order, but with all sincerity and ardor. Nor is it possible to say whom time pointed out as more illustrious and religious than he was. What then took place, as the result of the uproar? Their resistance was overcome, they purified him, they proclaimed him, they enthroned him, by external action, rather than by spiritual judgment and disposition, as the sequel shows. They were glad to retire and regain freedom of judgment, and agreed upon a plan — I do not know that it was inspired by the Spirit — to hold nothing which had been done to be valid, and the institution to have been void, pleading violence on the part of him who had had no less violence done to himself, and laying hold of certain words which had been uttered on the occasion with greater vigor than wisdom. But the great high-priest and just examiner of actions was not carried away by this plan of theirs, and did not approve of their judgment, but remained as uninfluenced and unmoved as if no pressure at all had been put upon him. For he saw that, the violence having been common, if they brought any charge against him, they were themselves liable to a counter-charge, or, if they acquitted him, they themselves might be acquitted, or rather with

still more justice, they were unable to secure their own acquittal, even by acquitting him: for if they were deserving of excuse, so assuredly was he, and if he was not, much less were they: for it would have been far better to have at the time run the risk of resistance to the last extremity, than afterwards to enter into designs against him, especially at such a juncture, when it was better to put an end to existing enmities than to devise new ones. For the state of affairs was as follows.

34. The Emperor had come, raging against the Christians; he was angry at the election and threatened the elect, and the city stood in imminent peril as to whether, after that day it should cease to exist, or escape and be treated with some degree of mercy. The innovation in regard to the election was a new ground of exasperation, in addition to the destruction of the temple of Fortune in a time of prosperity, and was looked upon as an invasion of his rights. The governor of the province also was eager to turn the opportunity to his own account, and was ill disposed to the new bishop, with whom he had never had friendly relations, in consequence of their different political views. Accordingly he sent letters to summon the consecrators to invalidate the election, and in no gentle terms, for they were threatened as if by command of the Emperor. Hereupon, when the letter reached him, without fear or delay, he replied — consider the courage and spirit of his answer — "Most excellent governor, we have one Censor of all our actions, and one Emperor, against whom his enemies are in arms. He will review the present consecration, which we have legitimately performed according to His will. In regard to any other matter, you may, if you will, use violence with the greatest ease against us. But no one can prevent us from vindicating the legitimacy and justice of our action in this case; unless you should make a law on this point, you, who have no right to interfere in our affairs." This letter excited the admiration of its recipient, although he was for a while annoyed at it, as we have been told by many who know the facts well. It also stayed the action of the Emperor, and delivered the city from peril, and ourselves, it is not amiss to add, from disgrace. This was the work of the occupant of an unimportant and suffragan see. Is not a presidency of this kind far preferable to a title derived from a superior see, and a power which is based upon action rather than upon a name.

35. Who is so distant from this world of ours, as to be ignorant of what is last in order, but the first and greatest proof of his power? The same city was again in an uproar for the same reason, in consequence of the sudden removal of the Bishop chosen with such honorable violence, who had now departed to God, on Whose behalf he had nobly and bravely contended in the persecutions. The heat of the disturbance was in proportion to its unreasonableness. The man of eminence was not unknown, but was more conspicuous than the sun amidst the stars, in the eyes not only of all others, but especially of that select and most pure portion of the people, whose business is in the sanctuary, and the Nazarites amongst us, to whom such appointments should, if not entirely, as much as possible belong, and so the church would be free from harm, instead of to the most opulent and powerful, or

94

the violent and unreasonable portion of the people, and especially the most corrupt of them. Indeed, I am almost inclined to believe that the civil government is more orderly than ours, to which divine grace is attributed, and that such matters are better regulated by fear than by reason. For what man in his senses could ever have approached another, to the neglect of your divine and sacred person, who have been beautified by the hands of the Lord, the unwedded the destitute of property and almost of flesh and blood, who in your words come next to the Word Himself, who are wise among philosophers, superior to the world among worldlings, my companion and workfellow, and to speak more daringly, the sharer with me of a common soul, the partaker of my life and education. Would that I could speak at liberty and describe you before others without being obliged by your presence, in dwelling upon such topics, to pass over the greater part of them, lest I should incur the suspicion of flattery. But, as I began by saying, the Spirit must needs have known him as His own; yet he was the mark of envy, at the hands of those whom I am ashamed to mention, and would that it were not possible to hear their names from others who studiously ridicule our affairs. Let us pass this by like a rock in the midstream of a river, and treat with respectful silence a subject which ought to be forgotten, as we pass on to the remainder of our subject.

36. The things of the Spirit were exactly known to the man of the Spirit, and he felt that he must take up no submissive position, nor side with factions and prejudices which depend upon favor rather than upon God, but must make the advantage of the Church and the common salvation his sole object. Accordingly he wrote, gave advice, strove to unite the people and the clergy, whether ministering in the sanctuary or not, gave his testimony, his decision and his vote, even in his absence, and assumed, in virtue of his gray hairs, the exercise of authority among strangers no less than among his own flock. At last, since it was necessary that the consecration should be canonical, and there was lacking one of the proper number of Bishops for the proclamation, he tore himself from his couch, exhausted as he was by age and disease, and manfully went to the city, or rather was borne, with his boy dead though just breathing, persuaded that, if anything were to happen to him, this devotion would be a noble winding-sheet. Hereupon once more there was a prodigy, not unworthy of credit. He received strength from his toil, new life from his zeal, presided at the function, took his place in the conflict, enthroned the Bishop, and was conducted home, no longer borne upon a bier, but in a divine ark. His long-suffering, over whose praises I have already lingered, was in this case further exhibited. For his colleagues were annoyed at the shame Of being overcome, and at the public influence of the old man, and allowed their annoyance to show itself in abuse of him; but such was the strength of his endurance that he was superior even to this, finding in modesty a most powerful ally, and refusing to bandy abuse with them. For he felt that it would be a terrible thing, after really gaining the victory, to be vanquished by the tongue. In consequence, he so won upon them by his long-suffering, that, when time had lent its aid to his judgment, they exchanged their annoyance for admiration, and knelt before him to ask his

pardon, in shame for their previous conduct, and flinging away their hatred, submitted to him as their patriarch, lawgiver, and judge.

37. From the same zeal proceeded his opposition to the heretics, when, with the aid of the Emperor's impiety, they made their expedition, in the hope of overpowering us also, and adding us to the number of the others whom they had, in almost all cases, succeeded in enslaving. For in this he afforded us no slight assistance, both in himself, and by hounding us on like well-bred dogs against these most savage beasts, through his training in piety. On one point I blame you both, and pray do not take amiss my plainspeaking. if I should annoy you by expressing the cause of my pain. When I was disgusted at the evils of life, and longing, if anyone of our day has longed, for solitude, and eager, as speedily as possible, to escape to some haven of safety, from the surge and dust of public life, it was you who, somehow or other seized and gave me up by the noble title of the priesthood to this base and treacherous mart of souls. In consequence, evils have already befallen me, and others are yet to be anticipated. For past experience renders a man somewhat distrustful of the future, in spite of the better suggestions of reason to the contrary.

38. Another of his excellences I must not leave unnoticed. In general, he was a man of great endurance, and superior to his robe of flesh: but during the pain of his last sickness, a serious addition to the risks and burdens of old age, his weakness was common to him and all other men; but this fitting sequel to the other marvels, so far from being common, was peculiarly his own. He was at no time free from the anguish of pain, but often in the day, sometimes in the hour, his only relief was the liturgy, to which the pain yielded, as if to an edict of banishment. At last, after a life of almost a hundred years, exceeding David's limit of our age, forty-five of these, the average life of man, having been spent in the priesthood, he brought it to a close in a good old age. And in what manner? With the words and forms of prayer, leaving behind no trace of vice, and many recollections of virtue. The reverence felt for him was thus greater than falls to the lot of man, both on the lips and in the hearts of all. Nor is it easy to find anyone who recollects him, and does not, as the Scripture says, lay his hand upon his mouth and salute his memory. Such was his life, and such its completion and perfection.

39. And since some living memorial of his munificence ought to be left behind, what other is required than this temple, which he reared for God and for us, with very little contribution from the people in addition to the expenditure of his private fortune? An exploit which should not be buried in silence, since in size it is superior to most others, in beauty absolutely to all. It surrounds itself with eight regular equilaterals, and is raised aloft by the beauty of two stories of pillars and porticos, while the statues placed upon them are true to the life; its vault flashes down upon us from above, and it dazzles our eyes with abundant sources of light on every side, being indeed the dwelling-place of light. It is surrounded by excrescent equiangular ambulatories of most splendid material, with a wide area in the midst, while its

96

doors and vestibules shed around it the luster of their gracefulness, and offer from a distance their welcome to those who are drawing nigh. I have not yet mentioned the external ornament, the beauty and size of the squared and dove-tailed stonework, whether it be of marble in the bases and capitals, which divide the angles, or from our own quarries, which are in no wise inferior to those abroad; nor of the belts of many shapes and colors, projecting or inlaid from the foundation to the roof-tree, which robs the spectator by limiting his view. How could anyone with due brevity describe a work which cost so much time and toil and skill: or will it suffice to say that amid all the works, private and public, which adorn other cities, this has of itself been able to secure us celebrity among the majority of mankind? When for such a temple a priest was needed, he also at his own expense provided one, whether worthy of the temple or no, it is not for me to say. And when sacrifices were required, he supplied them also, in the misfortunes of his son, and his patience under trials, that God might receive at his hands a reasonable whole burnt offering and spiritual priesthood, to be honorably consumed, instead of the sacrifice of the Law.

40. What sayest thou, my father? Is this sufficient, and dost thou find an ample recompense for all thy toils, which thou didst undergo for my learning, in this eulogy of farewell or of entombment? And dost thou, as of old, impose silence on my tongue, and bid me stop in due time, and so avoid excess? Or dost thou require some addition? I know thou bidst me cease, for I have said enough. Yet stiffer me to add this. Make known to us where thou art in glory, and the light which encircles thee, and receive into the same abode thy partner soon to follow thee, and the children whom thou hadst laid to rest before thee, and me also, after no further, or but a slight addition to the ills of this life: and before reaching that abode receive me in this sweet stone, which thou didst erect for both of us, to the honor even here of thy consecrated namesake, and excuse me from the care both of the people which I have already resigned, and of that which for thy sake I have since accepted: and mayest thou guide and free from peril, as I earnestly entreat, the whole flock and all the clergy, whose father thou art said to be, but especially him who was overpowered by thy paternal and spiritual coercion, so that he may not entirely consider that act of tyranny obnoxious to blame.

41. And what do you think of us, O judge of my words and motions? If we have spoken adequately, and to the satisfaction of your desire, confirm it by your decision, and we accept it: for your decision is entirely the decision of God. But if it falls far short of his glory and of your hope, my ally is not far to seek. Let fall thy voice, which is awaited by his merits like a seasonable shower. And indeed he has upon you the highest claims, those of a pastor upon a pastor and of a father upon his son in grace. What wonder if he, who has through your voice thundered throughout the world, should himself have some enjoyment of it? What more is needed? Only to unite with our spiritual Sarah, the consort and fellow-traveler through life of our great father Abraham, in the last Christian offices.

42. The nature of God, my mother, is not the same as that of men; indeed, to speak generally, the nature of divine things is not the same as that of earthly things. They possess unchangeableness and immortality, and absolute being with its consequences, for sure are the properties of things sure. But how is it with what is ours? It is in a state of flux and corruption, constantly undergoing some fresh change. Life and death, as they are called, apparently so different, are in a sense resolved into, and successive to, each other. For the one takes its rise from the corruption which is our mother, runs its course through the corruption which is the displacement of all that is present, and comes to an end in the corruption which is the dissolution of this life; while the other, which is able to set us free from the ills of this life, and oftentimes translates us to the life above, is not in my opinion accurately called death, and is more dreadful in name than in reality; so that we are in danger of irrationally being afraid of what is not fearful, and courting as preferable what we really ought to fear. There is one life, to look to life. There is one death, sin, for it is the destruction of the soul. But all else, of which some are proud, is a dream- vision, making sport of realities, and a series of phantasms which lead the soul astray. If this be our condition, mother, we Shall neither be proud of life, nor greatly hurt, by death. What grievance can we find in being transferred hence to the true life? In being freed from the vicissitudes, the agitation, the disgust, and all the vile tribute we must pay to this life, to find ourselves, amid stable things, which know no flux, while as lesser lights, we circle round the great light?

43. Does the sense of separation cause you pain? Let hope cheer you. Is widowhood grievous to you? Yet it is not so to him. And what is the good of love, if it gives itself easy things, and assigns the more difficult to its neighbor? And why should it be grievous at all, to one who is soon to pass away? The appointed day is at hand, the pain will not last long. Let us not, by ignoble reasonings, make a burden of things which are really light. We have endured a great loss — because the privilege we enjoyed was great. Loss is common to all, such a privilege to few. Let us rise superior to the one thought by the consolation of the other. For it is more reasonable, that that which is better should win the day. You have borne, in a most brave, Christian spirit, the loss of children, who were still in their prime and qualified for life; bear also the laying aside of his aged body by one who was weary of life, although his vigor of mind preserved for him his senses unimpaired. Do you want some one to care for you? Where is your Isaac, whom he left behind for you, to take his place in all respects? Ask of him small things, the support of his hand and service, and requite him with greater things, a mother's blessing and prayers, and the consequent freedom. Are you vexed at being admonished? I praise you for it. For you have admonished many whom your long life has brought under your notice. What I have said can have no application to you, who are so truly wise; but let it be a general medicine of consolation for mourners, so that they may know that they are mortals following mortals to the grave.

On the Great Athanasius, Bishop of Alexandria

The reference in 22 to "the Council which sat first at Seleucia… and afterwards at this mighty city," leaves no room for doubting that the Oration was delivered at Constantinople. Further local color is found in the allusions of 5. We are assured by the panegyric on S. Cyprian (Orat. xxiv. I) that it was already the custom of the Church of Constantinople to observe annual festivals in honor of the Saints: and at present two days are kept by the Eastern Church, viz., Jan. 18th, as the day of the actual death of S. Athanasius, and May ad, in memory of the translation of his remains to the church of S. Sophia at Constantinople. Probably, therefore, this Oration was delivered on the former day, on which Assemani holds that S. Athanasius died. Papebroke and (with some hesitation) Dr. Bright pronounce in favor of May 2d. Tillemont supposes that A.D. 379 is the year of its delivery; in which case it must have been very shortly after S. Gregory's arrival in the city. Since, however, no allusion is made to this, it seems, on the whole, more likely that it should be assigned to A.D. 380. The sermon takes high rank, even among S. Gregory's discourses, as the model of an ecclesiastical panegyric. It lacks, however, the charm of personal affection and intimate acquaintance with the inner life, which is characteristic of the orations concerned with his own relatives and friends.

1 . In praising Athanasius, I shall be praising virtue. To speak of him and to praise virtue are identical, because he had, or, to speak more truly, has embraced virtue in its entirety. For all who have lived according to God still live unto God, though they have departed hence. For this reason, God is called the God of Abraham, Isaac and Jacob, since He is the God, not of the dead, but of the living. Again, in praising virtue, I shall be praising God, who gives virtue to men and lifts them up, or lifts them up again, to Himself by the enlightenment which is akin to Himself. For many and great as are our blessings — none can say how many and how great — which we have and shall have from God, this is the greatest and kindliest of all, our inclination and relationship to Him. For God is to intelligible things what the sun is to the things of sense. The one lightens the visible, the other the invisible, world. The one makes our bodily eyes to see the sun, the other makes our intellectual natures to see God. And, as that, which bestows on the things which see and are seen the power of seeing and being seen, is itself the most beautiful of visible things; so God, who creates, for those who think, and that which is thought of, the power of thinking and being thought of, is Himself the highest of the objects of thought, in Whom every desire finds its borne, beyond Whom it can no further go. For not even the most philosophic, the most piercing, the most curious intellect has, or can ever have, a more exalted object. For this is the utmost of things desirable, and they who arrive at it find an entire rest from speculation.

2. Whoever has been permitted to escape by reason and contemplation from matter and this fleshly cloud or veil (whichever it should be called) and to hold communion with God, and be associated, as far as man's nature can attain, with the purest Light, blessed is he, both from his ascent from hence, and for his deification

there, which is conferred by true philosophy, and by rising superior to the dualism of matter, through the unity which is perceived in the Trinity. And whosoever has been depraved by being knit to the flesh, and so far oppressed by the clay that he cannot look at the rays of truth, nor rise above things below, though he is born from above, and called to things above, I hold him to be miserable in his blindness, even though he may abound in things of this world; and all the more, because he is the sport of his abundance, and is persuaded by it that something else is beautiful instead of that which is really beautiful, reaping, as the poor fruit of his poor opinion, the sentence of darkness, or the seeing Him to be fire, Whom he did not recognize as light.

3. Such has been the philosophy of few, both nowadays and of old — for few are the men of God, though all are His handiwork, — among lawgivers, generals, priests, Prophets, Evangelists, Apostles, shepherds, teachers, and all the spiritual host and band — and, among them all, of him whom now we praise. And whom do I mean by these? Men like Enoch, Noah, Abraham, Isaac, Jacob, the twelve Patriarchs, Moses, Aaron, Joshua, the Judges, Samuel, David, to some extent Solomon, Elijah, Elisha, the Prophets before the captivity, those after the captivity, and, though last in order, first in truth, those who were concerned with Christ's Incarnation or taking of our nature, the lamp before the Light, the voice before the Word, the mediator before the Mediator, the mediator between the old covenant and the new, the famous John, the disciples of Christ, those after Christ, who were set over the people, or illustrious in word, or conspicuous for miracles, or made perfect through their blood.

4. With some of these Athanasius vied, by some he was slightly excelled, and others, if it is not bold to say so, he surpassed: some he made his models in mental power, others in activity, others in meekness, others in zeal, others in dangers, others in most respects, others in all, gathering from one and another various forms of beauty (like men who paint figures of ideal excellence), and combining them in his single soul, he made one perfect form of virtue out of all, excelling in action men of intellectual capacity, in intellect men of action; or, if you will, surpassing in intellect men renowned for intellect, in action those of the greatest active power; outstripping those who had moderate reputation in both respects, by his eminence in either, and those who stood highest in one or other, by his powers in both; and, if it is a great thing for those who have received an example, so to use it as to attach themselves to virtue, he has no inferior title to fame, who for our advantage has set an example to those who come after him.

5. To speak of and admire him fully, would perhaps be too long a task for the present purpose of my discourse, and would take the form of a history rather than of a panegyric: a history which it has been the object of my desires to commit to writing for the pleasure and instruction of posterity, as he himself wrote the life of the divine Antony, and set forth, in the form of a narrative, the laws of the

monastic life. Accordingly, after entering into a few of the many details of his history, such as memory suggests at the moment as most noteworthy, in order both to satisfy my own longing and fulfill the duty which befits the festival, we will leave the many others to those who know them. For indeed, it is neither pious nor safe, while the lives of the ungodly are honored by recollection, to pass by in silence those who have lived piously, especially in a city which could hardly be saved by many examples of virtue, making sport, as it does, of Divine things, no less than of the horse-race and the theater.

6. He was brought up, from the first, in religious habits and practices, after a brief study of literature and philosophy, so that he might not be utterly unskilled in such subjects, or ignorant of matters which he had determined to despise. For his generous and eager soul could not brook being occupied in vanities, like unskilled athletes, who beat the air instead of their antagonists and lose the prize. From meditating on every book of the Old and New Testament, with a depth such as none else has applied even to one of them, he grew rich in contemplation, rich in splendor of life, combining them in wondrous sort by that golden bond which few can weave; using life as the guide of contemplation, contemplation as the seal of life. For the fear of the Lord is the beginning of wisdom, and, so to say, its first swathing band; but, when wisdom has burst the bonds of fear and risen up to love, it makes us friends of God, and sons instead of bondsmen.

7. Thus brought up and trained, as even now those should be who are to preside over the people, and take the direction of the mighty body of Christ, according to the will and foreknowledge of God, which lays long before the foundations of great deeds, he was invested with this important ministry, and made one of those who draw near to the God Who draws near to us, and deemed worthy of the holy office and rank, and, after passing through the entire series of orders, he was (to make my story short) entrusted with the chief rule over the people, in other words, the charge of the whole world: nor can I say whether he received the priesthood as the reward of virtue, or to be the fountain and life of the Church. For she, like Ishmael, fainting from her thirst for the truth, needed to be given to drink, or, like Elijah, to be refreshed from the brook, when the land was parched by drought; and, when but faintly breathing, to be restored to life and left as a seed to Israel, that we might not become like Sodom and Gomorrah, whose destruction by the rain of fire and brimstone is only more notorious than their wickedness. Therefore, when we were cast down, a horn of salvation was raised up for us, and a chief corner stone, knitting us to itself and to one another, was laid in due season, or a fire to purify our base and evil matter, or a farmer's fan to winnow the light from the weighty in doctrine, or a sword to cut out the roots of wickedness; and so the Word finds him as his own ally, and the Spirit takes possession of one who will breathe on His behalf.

8. Thus, and for these reasons, by the vote of the whole people, not in the evil fashion which has since prevailed, nor by means of bloodshed and oppression, but in an apostolic and spiritual manner, he is led up to the throne of Saint Mark, to succeed him in piety, no less than in office; in the latter indeed at a great distance from him, in the former, which is the genuine right of succession, following him closely. For unity in doctrine deserves unity in office; and a rival teacher sets up a rival throne; the one is a successor in reality, the other but in name. For it is not the intruder, but he whose rights are intruded upon, who is the successor, not the lawbreaker, but the lawfully appointed, not the man of contrary opinions, but the man of the same faith; if this is not what we mean by successor, he succeeds in the same sense as disease to health, darkness to light, storm to calm, and frenzy to sound sense.

9. The duties of his office he discharged in the same spirit as that in which he had been preferred to it. For he did not at once, after taking possession of his throne, like men who have unexpectedly seized upon some sovereignty or inheritance, grow insolent from intoxication. This is the conduct of illegitimate and intrusive priests, who are unworthy of their vocation; whose preparation for the priesthood has cost them nothing, who have endured no inconvenience for the sake of virtue, who only begin to study religion when appointed to teach it, and undertake the cleansing of others before being cleansed themselves; yesterday sacrilegious, today sacerdotal; yesterday excluded from the sanctuary, today its officiants; proficient in vice, novices in piety; the product of the favor of man, not of the grace of the Spirit; who, having run through the whole gamut of violence, at last tyrannize over even piety; who, instead of gaining credit for their office by their character, need for their character the credit of their office, thus subverting the due relation between them; who ought to offer more sacrifices for themselves than for the ignorances of the people; who inevitably fall into one of two errors, either, from their own need of indulgence, being excessively indulgent, and so even teaching, instead of checking, vice, or cloaking their own sins under the harshness of their rule. Both these extremes he avoided; he was sublime in action, lowly in mind; inaccessible in virtue, most accessible in intercourse; gentle, free from anger, sympathetic, sweet in words, sweeter in disposition; angelic in appearance, more angelic in mind; calm in rebuke, persuasive in praise, without spoiling the good effect of either by excess, but rebuking with the tenderness of a father, praising with the dignity of a ruler, his tenderness was not dissipated, nor his severity sour; for the one was reasonable, the other prudent, and both truly wise; his disposition sufficed for the training of his spiritual children, with very little need of words; his words with very little need of the rod, and his moderate use of the rod with still less for the knife.

10. But why should I paint for you the portrait of the man? St. Paul has sketched him by anticipation. This he does, when he sings the praises of the great High-priest, who hath passed through the heavens (for I will venture to say even this, since Scripture can call those who live according to Christ by the name of Christs):

and again when by the rules in his letter to Timothy, he gives a model for future Bishops: for if you will apply the law as a test to him who deserves these praises, you will clearly perceive his perfect exactness. Come then to aid me in my panegyric; for I am laboring heavily in my speech, and though I desire to pass by point after point, they seize upon me one after another, and I can find no surpassing excellence in a form which is in all respects well proportioned and beautiful; for each as it occurs to me seems fairer than the rest and so takes by storm my speech. Come then I pray, you who have been his admirers and witnesses, divide among yourselves his excellences, contend bravely with one another, men and women alike, young men and maidens, old men and children, priests and people, solitaries and cenobites, men of simple or of exact life, contemplatives or practically minded. Let one praise him in his fastings and prayers as if he had been disembodied and immaterial, another his unweariedness and zeal for vigils and psalmody, another his patronage of the needy, another his dauntlessness towards the powerful, or his condescension to the lowly. Let the virgins celebrate the friend of the Bridegroom; those under the yoke their restrainer, hermits him who lent wings to their course, cenobites their lawgiver, simple folk their guide, contemplatives the divine, the joyous their bridle, the unfortunate their consolation, the hoary-headed their staff, youths their instructor, the poor their resource, the wealthy their steward. Even the widows will, methinks, praise their protector, even the orphans their father, even the poor their benefactor, strangers their entertainer, brethren the man of brotherly love, the sick their physician, in whatever sickness or treatment you will, the healthy the guard of health, yea all men him who made himself all things to all men that he might gain almost, if not quite, all.

11. On these grounds, as I have said, I leave others, who have leisure to admire the minor details of his character, to admire and extol him. I call them minor details only in comparing him and his character with his own standard, for that which hath been made glorious hath not been made glorious, even though it be exceeding splendid by reason of the glory that surpasseth, as we are told; for indeed the minor points of his excellence would suffice to win celebrity for others. But since it would be intolerable for me to leave the word and serve less important details, I must turn to that which is his chief characteristic; and God alone, on Whose behalf I am speaking, can enable me to say anything worthy of a soul so noble and so mighty in the word.

12. In the palmy days of the Church, when all was well, the present elaborate, far-fetched and artificial treatment of Theology had not made its way into the schools of divinity, but playing with pebbles which deceive the eye by the quickness of their changes, or dancing before an audience with varied and effeminate contortions, were looked upon as all one with speaking or hearing of God in a way unusual or frivolous. But since the Sextuses and Pyrrhos, and the antithetic style, like a dire and malignant disease, have infected our churches, and babbling is reputed culture, and, as the book of the Acts says of the Athenians, we spend our time in nothing

else but either to tell or to hear some new thing. O what Jeremiah will bewail our confusion and blind madness; he alone could utter lamentations befitting our misfortunes.

13. The beginning of this madness was Arius (whose name is derived from frenzy), who paid the penalty of his unbridled tongue by his death in a profane spot, brought about by prayer not by disease, when he like Judas burst asunder for his similar treachery to the Word. Then others, catching the infection, organized an art of impiety, and, confining Deity to the Unbegotten, expelled from Deity not only the Begotten, but also the Proceeding one, and honored the Trinity with communion in name alone, or even refused to retain this for it. Not so that blessed one, Who was indeed a man of God and a mighty trumpet of truth: but being aware that to contract the Three Persons to a numerical Unity is heretical, and the innovation of Sabellius, who first devised a contraction of Deity; and that to sever the Three Persons by a distinction of nature, is an unnatural mutilation of Deity; he both happily preserved the Unity, which belongs to the Godhead, and religiously taught the Trinity, which refers to Personality, neither confounding the Three Persons in the Unity, nor dividing the Substance among the Three Persons, but abiding within the bounds of piety, by avoiding excessive inclination or opposition to either side.

14. And therefore, first in the holy Synod of Nicaea, the gathering of the three hundred and eighteen chosen men, united by the Holy Ghost, as far as in him lay, he stayed the disease. Though not yet ranked among the Bishops, he held the first rank among the members of the Council, for preference was given to virtue just as much as to office. Afterwards, when the flame had been fanned by the blasts of the evil one, and had spread very widely (hence came the tragedies of which almost the whole earth and sea are full), the fight raged fiercely around him who was the noble champion of the Word. For the assault is hottest upon the point of resistance, while various dangers surround it on every side: for impiety is skillful in designing evils, and excessively daring in taking them in hand: and how would they spare men, who had not spared the Godhead? Yet one of the assaults was the most dangerous of all: and I myself contribute somewhat to this scene; yea, let me plead for the innocence of my dear fatherland, for the wickedness was not due to the land that bore them, but to the men who undertook it. For holy indeed is that land, and everywhere noted for its piety, but these men are unworthy of the Church which bore them, and ye have heard of a briar growing in a vine; and the traitor was Judas, one of the disciples.

15. There are some who do not excuse even my namesake from blame; who, living at Alexandria at the time for the sake of culture, although he had been most kindly treated by him, as if the dearest of his children, and received his special confidence, yet joined in the revolutionary plot against 534 his father and patron: for, though others took the active part in it, the hand of Absalom was with them, as the saying

goes. If any of you had heard of the hand which was produced by fraud against the Saint, and the corpse of the living man, and the unjust banishment, he knows what I mean. But this I will gladly forget. For on doubtful points, I am disposed to think we ought to incline to the charitable side, and acquit rather than condemn the accused. For a bad man would speedily condemn even a good man, while a good man would not be ready to condemn even a bad one. For one who is not ready to do ill, is not inclined even to suspect it. I come now to what is matter of fact, not of report, what is vouched for as truth instead of unverified suspicion.

16. There was a monster from Cappadocia, born on our farthest confines, of low birth, and lower mind, whose blood was not perfectly free, but mongrel, as we know that of mules to be; at first, dependent on the table of others, whose price was a barley cake, who had learnt to say and do everything with an eye to his stomach, and, at last, after sneaking into public life, and filling its lowest offices, such as that of contractor for swine's flesh, the soldiers' rations, and then having proved himself a scoundrel for the sake of greed in this public trust, and been stripped to the skin, contrived to escape, and after passing, as exiles do, from country to country and city to city, last of all, in an evil hour for the Christian community, like one of the plagues of Egypt, he reached Alexandria. There, his wanderings being stayed, he began his villainy. Good for nothing in all other respects, without culture, without fluency in conversation, without even the form and pretense of reverence, his skill in working villainy and confusion was unequaled.

17. His acts of insolence towards the saint you all know in full detail. Often were the righteous given into the hands of the wicked, not that the latter might be honored, but that the former might be tested: and though the wicked come, as it is written, to an awful death, nevertheless for the present the godly are a laughing stock, while the goodness of God and the great treasuries of what is in store for each of them hereafter are concealed. Then indeed word and deed and thought will be weighed in the just balances of God, as He arises to judge the earth, gathering together counsel and works, and revealing what He had kept sealed up. Of this let the words and sufferings of Job convince thee, who was a truthful, blameless, just, godfearing man, with all those other qualities which are testified of him, and yet was smitten with such a succession of remarkable visitations, at the hands of him who begged for power over him, that, although many have often suffered in the whole course of time, and some even have, as is probable, been grievously afflicted, yet none can be compared with him in misfortunes. For he not only suffered, without being allowed space to mourn for his losses in their rapid succession, the loss of his money, his possessions, his large and fair family, blessings for which all men care; but was at last smitten with an incurable disease horrible to look upon, and, to crown his misfortunes, had a wife whose only comfort was evil counsel. For his surpassing troubles were those of his soul added to those of the body. He had also among his friends truly miserable comforters, as he calls them, who could not help him. For when they saw his suffering, in ignorance of its hidden meaning, they

supposed his disaster to be the punishment of vice and not the touchstone of virtue. And they not only thought this, but were not even ashamed to reproach him with his lot, at a time when, even if he had been suffering for vice, they ought to have treated his grief with words of consolation.

18. Such was the lot of Job: such at first sight his history. In reality it was a contest between virtue and envy: the one straining every nerve to overcome the good, the other enduring everything, that it might abide unsubdued; the one striving to smooth the way for vice, by means of the chastisement of the upright, the other to retain its hold upon the good, even if they do exceed others in misfortunes. What then of Him who answered Job out of the whirlwind and cloud, Who is slow to chastise and swift to help, Who suffers not utterly the rod of the wicked to come into the lot of the righteous, lest the righteous should learn iniquity? At the end of the contests He declares the victory of the athlete in a splendid proclamation and lays bare the secret of his calamities, saying: "Thinkest thou that I have dealt with thee for any other purpose than the manifestation of thy righteousness?" This is the balm for his wounds, this is the crown of the contest, this the reward for his patience. For perhaps his subsequent prosperity was small, great as it may seem to some, and ordained for the sake of small minds, even though he received again twice as much as he had lost.

19. In this case then it is not wonderful, if George had the advantage of Athanasius; nay it would be more wonderful, if the righteous were not tried in the fire of contumely; nor is this very wonderful, as it would have been had the flames availed for more than this. Then he was in retirement, and arranged his exile most excellently, for he betook himself to the holy and divine homes of contemplation in Egypt, where, secluding themselves from the world, and welcoming the desert, men live to God more than all who exist in the body. Some struggle on in an utterly monastic and solitary life, speaking to themselves alone and to God, and all the world they know is what meets their eyes in the desert. Others, cherishing the law of love in community, are at once Solitaries and Coenobites, dead to all other men and to the eddies of public affairs which whirl us and are whirled about themselves and make sport of us in their sudden changes, being the world to one another and whetting the edge of their love in emulation. During his intercourse with them, the great Athanasius, who was always the mediator and reconciler of all other men, like Him Who made peace through His blood between things which were at variance, reconciled the solitary with the community life: by showing that the Priesthood is capable of contemplation, and that contemplation is in need of a spiritual guide.

20. Thus he combined the two, and so united the partisans of both calm action and of active calm, as to convince them that the monastic life is characterized by steadfastness of disposition rather than by bodily retirement. Accordingly the great David was a man of at once the most active and most solitary life, if any one thinks the verse, I am in solitude, till I pass away, of value and authority in the exposition

of this subject. Therefore, though they surpass all others in virtue, they fell further short of his mind than others fell short of their own, and while contributing little to the perfection of his priesthood, they gained in return greater assistance in contemplation. Whatever he thought, was a law for them, whatever on the contrary he disapproved, they abjured: his decisions were to them the tables of Moses, and they paid him more reverence than is due from men to the Saints. Aye, and when men came to hunt the Saint like a wild beast, and, after searching for him everywhere, failed to find him, they vouchsafed these emissaries not a single word, and offered their necks to the sword, as risking their lives for Christ's sake, and considering the most cruel sufferings on behalf of Athanasius to be an important step to contemplation, and far more divine and sublime than the long fasts and hard lying and mortifications in which they constantly revel.

21. Such were his surrounding when he approved the wise counsel of Solomon that their is a time to every purpose: so he hid himself for a while, escaping during the time of war, to show himself when the time of peace came, as it did soon afterwards. Meanwhile George, there being absolutely no one to resist him, overran Egypt, and desolated Syria, in the might of ungodliness. He seized upon the East also as far as he could, ever attracting the weak, as torrents roll down objects in their course, and assailing the unstable or faint-hearted. He won over also the simplicity of the Emperor, for thus I must term his instability, though I respect his pious motives. For, to say the truth, he had zeal, but not according to knowledge. He purchased those in authority who were lovers of money rather than lovers of Christ — for he was well supplied with the funds for the poor, which he embezzled — especially the effeminate and unmanly men, of doubtful sex, but of manifest impiety; to whom, I know not how or why, Emperors of the Romans entrusted authority over men, though their proper function was the charge of women. In this lay the power of that servant of the wicked one, that sower of tares, that forerunner of Antichrist; foremost in speech of the orators of his time among the Bishops; if any one likes to call him an orator who was not so much an impious, as he was a hostile and contentious reasoner, — his name I will gladly pass by: he was the hand of his party, perverting the truth by the gold subscribed for pious uses, which the wicked made an instrument of their impiety.

22. The crowning feat of this faction was the council which sat first at Seleucia, the city of the holy and illustrious virgin Thekla, and afterwards at this mighty city, thus connecting their names, no longer with noble associations, but with these of deepest disgrace; whether we must call that council, which subverted and disturbed everything, a tower of Chalane, which deservedly confounded the tongues — would that theirs had been confounded for their harmony in evil! — or a Sanhedrim of Caiaphas where Christ was condemned, or some other like name. The ancient and pious doctrine which defended the Trinity was abolished, by setting up a palisade and battering down the Consubstantial: opening the door to impiety by means of what is written, using as their pretext, their reverence for

Scripture and for the use of approved terms, but really introducing unscriptural Arianism. For the phrase "like, according to the Scriptures," was a bait to the simple, concealing the hook of impiety, a figure seeming to look in the direction of all who passed by, a boot fitting either foot, a winnowing with every wind, gaining authority from the newly written villainy and device against the truth. For they were wise to do evil, but to do good they had no knowledge.

23. Hence came their pretended condemnation of the heretics, whom they renounced in words, in order to gain plausibility for their efforts, but in reality furthered; charging them not with unbounded impiety, but with exaggerated language. Hence came the profane judges of the Saints, and the new combination, and public view and discussion of mysterious questions, and the illegal enquiry into the actions of life, and the hired informers, and the purchased sentences. Some were unjustly deposed from their sees, others intruded, and among other necessary qualifications, made to sign the bonds of iniquity: the ink was ready, the informer at hand. This the majority even of us, who were not overcome, had to endure, not falling in mind, though prevailed upon to sign, and so uniting with men who were in both respects wicked, and involving ourselves in the smoke, if not in the flame. Over this I have often wept, when contemplating the con-fission of impiety at that time, and the persecution of the orthodox teaching which now arose at the hands of the patrons of the Word.

24. For in reality, as the Scripture says, the shepherds became brutish, and many shepherds destroyed My vineyard, and defiled my pleasant portion, I mean the Church of God, which has been gathered together by the sweat and blood of many toilers and victims both before and after Christ, aye, even the great sufferings of God for us. For with very few exceptions, and these either men who from their insignificance were disregarded, or from their virtue manfully resisted, being left unto Israel, as was ordained, for a seed and root, to blossom and come to life again amid the streams of the Spirit, everyone yielded to the influences of the time, distinguished only by the fact that some did so earlier, some later, that some became the champions and leaders of impiety, while such others were assigned a lower rank, as had been shaken by fear, enslaved by need, fascinated by flattery, or beguiled in ignorance; the last being the least guilty, if indeed we can allow even this to be a valid excuse for men entrusted with the leadership of the people. For just as the force of lions and other animals, or of men and of women, or of old and of young men is not the same, but there is a considerable difference due to age or species — so it is also with rulers and their subjects. For while we might pardon laymen in such a case, and often they escape, because not put to the test, yet how can we excuse a teacher, whose duty it is, unless he is falsely so-called, to correct the ignorance of others. For is it not absurd, while no one, however great his boorishness and want of education, is allowed to be ignorant of the Roman law, and while there is no law in favor of sins of ignorance, that the teachers of the mysteries of salvation should be ignorant of the first principles of salvation, however

simple and shallow their minds may be in regard to other subjects. But, even granting indulgence to them who erred in ignorance, what can be said for the rest, who lay claim to subtlety of intellect, and yet yielded to the court-party for the reasons I have mentioned, and after playing the part of piety for a long while, failed in the hour of trial.

25. "Yet once more," I hear the Scripture say that the heaven and the earth shall be shaken, inasmuch as this has befallen them before, signifying, as I suppose, a manifest renovation of all things. And we must believe S. Paul when he says that this last shaking is none other than the second coming of Christ, and the transformation and changing of the universe to a condition of stability which cannot be shaken. And I imagine that this present shaking, in which the contemplatives and lovers of God, who before the time exercise their heavenly citizenship, are shaken from us, is of no less consequence than any of former days. For, however peaceful and moderate in other respects these men are, yet they cannot bear to carry their reasonableness so far as to be traitors to the cause of God for quietness' sake: nay on this point they are excessively warlike and sturdy in fight; such is the heat of their zeal, that they would sooner proceed to excess in disturbance, than fail to notice anything that is amiss. And no small portion of the people is breaking away with them, flying away, as a flock of birds does, with those who lead the flight, and even now does not cease to fly with them.

26. Such was Athanasius to us, when present, the pillar of the Church; and such, even when he retired before the insults of the wicked. For those who have plotted the capture of some strong fort, when they see no other easy means of approaching or taking it, betake themselves to arts, and then, after seducing the commander by money or guile, without any effort possess themselves of the stronghold, or, if you will, as those who plotted against Samson first cut off his hair, in which his strength lay, and then seized upon the judge, and made sport of him at will, to requite him for his former power: so did our foreign foes, after getting rid of our source of strength, and shearing off the glory of the Church, revel in like manner in utterances and deeds of impiety. Then the supporter and patron of the hostile shepherd died, crowning his reign, which had not been evil, with an evil close, and unprofitably repenting, as they say, with his last breath, when each man, in view of the higher judge-merit seat, is a prudent judge of his own conduct. For of these three evils, which were unworthy of his reign, he said that he was conscious, the murder of his kinsmen, the proclamation of the Apostate, and the innovation upon the faith; and with these words he is said to have departed. Thus there was once more authority to teach the word of truth, and those who had suffered violence had now undisturbed freedom of speech, while jealousy was whetting the weapons of its wrath. Thus it was with the people of Alexandria, who, with their usual impatience of the insolent, could not brook the excesses of the man, and therefore marked his wickedness by an unusual death, and his death by an unusual ignominy. For you know that camel, and its strange burden, and the new form of elevation, and the

first and, I think, the only procession, with which to this day the insolent are threatened.

27. But when from this hurricane of unrighteousness, this corrupter of godliness, this precursor of the wicked one, such satisfaction had been exacted, in a way I cannot praise, for we must consider not what he ought to have suffered, but what we ought to do: exacted however it was, as the result of the public anger and excitement: and thereupon, our champion was restored from his illustrious banishment, for so I term his exile on behalf of, and under the blessing of, the Trinity, amid such delight of the people of the city and of almost all Egypt, that they ran together from every side, from the furthest limits of the country, simply to hear the voice of Athanasius, or feast their eyes upon the sight of him, nay even, as we are told of the Apostles, that they might be hallowed by the shadows and unsubstantial image of his body: so that, many as are the honors, and welcomes bestowed on frequent occasions in the course of time upon various individuals, not only upon public rulers and bishops, but also upon the most illustrious of private citizens, not one has been recorded more numerously attended or more brilliant than this. And only one honor can be compared with it by Athanasius himself, which had been conferred upon him on his former entrance into the city, when returning from the same exile for the same reasons.

28. With reference to this honor there was also current some such report as the following; for I will take leave to mention it, even though it be superfluous, as a kind of flavoring to my speech, or a flower scattered in honor of his entry. After that entry, a certain officer, who had been twice Consul, was riding into the city; he was one of us, among the most noted of Cappadocians. I am sure that you know that I mean Philagrius, who won upon our affections far beyond any one else, and was honored as much as he was loved, if I may thus briefly set forth all his distinctions: who had been for a second time entrusted with the government of the city, at the request of the citizens, by the decision of the Emperor. Then one of the common people present, thinking the crowd enormous, like an ocean whose bound no eye can see, is reported to have said to one of his comrades and friends — as often happens in such a case iTell me, my good fellow, have you ever before seen the people pour out in such numbers and so enthusiastically to do honor to any one man?" "No!" said the young man, "and I fancy that not even Constantius himself would be so treated;" indicating, by the mention of the Emperor, the climax of possible honor. "Do you speak of that," said the other with a sweet and merry laugh, "as something wonderfully great? I can scarcely believe that even the great Athanasius would be welcomed like this," adding at the same time one of our native oaths in confirmation of his words. Now the point of what he said, as I suppose you also plainly see, is this, that he set the subject of our eulogy before the Emperor himself.

110

29. So great was the reverence of all for the man, and so amazing even now seems the reception which I have described. For if divided according to birth, age and profession,(and the city is most usually arranged in this way, when a public honor is bestowed on anyone) how can I set forth in words that mighty spectacle? They formed one river, and it were indeed a poet's task to describe that Nile, of really golden stream and rich in crops, flowing back again from the city to the Chaereum, a day's journey, I take it, and more. Permit me to revel a while longer in my description: for I am going there, and it is not easy to bring back even my words from that ceremony. He rode upon a colt, almost, blame me not for folly, as my Jesus did upon that other colt, whether it were the people of the Gentiles, whom He mounts in kindness, by setting it free from the bonds of ignorance, or something else, which the Scripture sets forth. He was welcomed with branches of trees, and garments with many Bowers and of varied hue were torn off and strewn before him and under his feet: there alone was all that was glorious and costly and peerless treated with dishonor. Like, once more, to the entry of Christ were those that went before with shouts and followed with dances; only the crowd which sung his praises was not of children only, but every tongue was harmonious, as men contended only to outdo one another. I pass by the universal cheers, and the pouring forth of unguents, and the nightlong festivities, and the whole city gleaming with light, and the feasting in public and at home, and all the means of testifying to a city's joy, which were then in lavish and incredible profusion bestowed upon him. Thus did this marvelous man, with such a concourse, regain his own city.

30. He lived then as becomes the rulers of such a people, but did he fail to teach as he lived? Were his contests out of harmony with his teaching? Were his dangers less than those of men who have contended for any truth? Were his honors inferior to the objects for which he contended? Did he after his reception in any way disgrace that reception? By no means. Everything was harmonious, as an air upon a single lyre, and in the same key; his life, his teaching, his struggles, his dangers, his return, and his conduct after his return. For immediately on his restoration to his Church, he was not like those who are blinded by unrestrained passion, who, under the dominion of their anger, thrust away or strike at once whatever comes in their way, even though it might well be spared. But, thinking this to be a special time for him to consult his reputation, since one who is ill-treated is usually restrained, and one who has the power to requite a wrong is ungoverned, he treated so mildly and gently those who had injured him, that even they themselves, if I may say so, did not find his restoration distasteful.

31. He cleansed the temple of those who made merchandise of God, and trafficked in the things of Christ, imitating Christ in this also; only it was with persuasive words, not with a twisted scourge that this was wrought. He reconciled also those who were at variance, both with one another and with him, without the aid of any coadjutor. Those who had been wronged he set free from oppression, making no

distinction as to whether they were of his own or of the opposite party. He restored too the teaching which had been overthrown: the Trinity was once more boldly spoken of, and set upon the lampstand, flashing with the brilliant light of the One Godhead into the souls of all. He legislated again for the whole world, and brought all minds trader his influence, by letters to some, by invitations to others, instructing some, who visited him uninvited, and proposing as the single law to all — Good will. For this alone was able to conduct them to the true issue. In brief, he exemplified the virtues of two celebrated stones — for to those who assailed him he was adamant, and to those at variance a magnet, which by some secret natural power draws iron to itself, and influences the hardest of substances.

32. But yet it was not likely that envy could brook all this, or see the Church restored again to the same glory and health as in former days, by the speedy healing over, as in the body, of the wounds of separation. Therefore it was, that he raised up against Athanasius the Emperor, a rebel like himself, and his peer in villainy, inferior to him only from lack of time, the first of Christian Emperors to rage against Christ, bringing forth all at once the basilisk of impiety with which he had long been in labor, when he obtained an opportunity, and shewing himself, at the time when he was proclaimed Emperor, to be a traitor to the Emperor who had entrusted him with the empire, and a traitor double dyed to the God who had saved him. He devised the most inhuman of all the persecutions by blending speciousness with cruelty, in his envy of the honor won by the martyrs in their struggles; and so he called in question their repute for courage, by making verbal twists and quibbles a part of his character, or to speak the real truth, devoting himself to them with an eagerness born of his natural disposition, and imitating in varied craft the Evil one who dwelt within him. The subjugation of the whole race of Christians he thought a simple task; but found it a great one to overcome Athanasius and the power of his teaching over us. For he saw that no success could he gained in the plot against us, because of this man's resistance and opposition; the places of the Christians cut down being at once filled up, surprising though it seems, by the accession of Gentiles and the prudence of Athanasius. In full view therefore of this, the crafty perverter and persecutor, clinging no longer to his cloak of illiberal sophistry, laid bare his wickedness and openly banished the Bishop from the city. For the illustrious warrior must needs conquer in three struggles and thus make good his perfect title to fame.

33. Brief was the interval before Justice pronounced sentence, and handed over the offender to the Persians: sending him forth an ambitious monarch — and bringing him back a corpse for which no one even felt pity; which, as I have heard, was not allowed to rest in the grave, but was shaken out and thrown up by the earth which he had shaken: a prelude — I take it — to his future chastisement. Then another king arose, not shameless in countenance like the former, nor an oppressor of Israel with cruel tasks and taskmasters, but most pious and gentle. In order to lay the best of foundations for his empire, and begin, as is right, by an act of justice, he recalled

from exile all the Bishops, but in the first place him who stood first in virtue and had conspicuously championed the cause of piety. Further, he inquired into the truth of our faith which had been turn asunder, confused, and parceled out into various opinions and portions by many; with the intention, if it were possible, of reducing the whole world to harmony and union by the co-operation of the Spirit: and, should he fail in this, of attaching himself to the best party, so as to aid and be aided by it, thus giving token of the exceeding loftiness and magnificence of his ideas on questions of the greatest moment. Here too was shown in a very high degree the simple-mindedness of Athanasius, and the steadfastness of his faith in Christ. For, when all the rest who sympathized with us were divided into three parties, and many were faltering in their conception of the Son, and still more in that of the Holy Ghost, (a point on which to be only slightly in error was to be orthodox) and few indeed were sound upon both points, he was the first and only one, or with the concurrence of but a few, to venture to confess in writing, with entire clearness and distinctness, the Unity of Godhead and Essence of the Three Persons, and thus to attain in later days, under the influence of inspiration, to the same faith in regard to the Holy Ghost, as had been bestowed at an earlier time on most of the Fathers in regard to the Son. This confession, a truly royal and magnificent gift, he presented to the Emperor, opposing to the unwritten innovation, a written account the orthodox faith, so that an emperor might be overcome by an emperor, reason by reason, treatise by treatise.

34. This confession was, it seems, greeted with respect by all, both in West and East, who were capable of life; some cherishing piety within their own bosoms, if we may credit what they say, but advancing no further, like a still-born child which dies within its mother's womb; others kindling to some extent, as it were, sparks, so far as to escape the difficulties of the time, arising either from the more fervent of the orthodox, or the devotion of the people; while others spoke the truth with boldness, on whose side I would be, for I dare make no further boast; no longer consulting my own fearfulness — in other words, the views of men more unsound than myself (for this we have done enough and to spare, without either gaining anything from others, or guarding from injury that which was our own, just as bad stewards do) but bringing forth to light my offspring, nourishing it with eagerness, and exposing it, in its constant growth, to the eyes of all.

35. This, however, is less admirable than his conduct. What wonder that he, who had already made actual ventures on behalf of the truth, should confess it in writing? Yet this point I will add to what has been said, as it seems to me especially wonderful and cannot with impunity be passed over in a time so fertile in disagreements as this. For his action, if we take note of him, will afford instruction even to the men of this clay. For as, in the case of one and the same quantity of water, there is separated from it, not only the residue which is left behind by the hand when drawing it, but also those drops, once contained in the hand, which trickle out through the fingers; so also there is a separation between us anti, not

only those who hold aloof in their impiety, but also those who are most pious, and that, both in regard to such doctrines as are of small consequence (a matter of less moment) and also in regard to expressions intended to bear the same meaning. We use in an orthodox sense the terms one Essence and three Hypostases, the one to denote the nature of the Godhead, the other the properties of the Three; the Italians mean the same, but, owing to the scantiness of their vocabulary, and its poverty of terms, they are unable to distinguish between Essence and Hypostases, and therefore introduce the term Persons, to avoid being understood to assert three Essences. The result, were it not piteous, would be laughable. This slight difference of sound was taken to indicate a difference of faith. Then, Sabellianism was suspected in the doctrine of Three Persons, Arianism in that of Three Hypostases, both being the offspring of a contentious spirit. And then, from the gradual but constant growth of irritation (the unfailing result of contentiousness) there was a danger of the whole world being torn asunder in the strife about syllables. Seeing and hearing this, our blessed one, true man of God and great steward of souls as he was, felt it inconsistent with his duty to overlook so absurd and unreasonable a rending of the word, and applied his medicine to the disease. In what manner? He conferred in his gentle and sympathetic way with both parties, anti after be had carefully weighed the meaning of their expressions, and found that they had the same sense, and were in nowise different in doctrine, by permit-ring each party to use its own terms, he bound them together in unity of action.

36. This in itself was more profitable than the long course of labors and teaching on which all writers enlarge, for in it somewhat of ambition mingled, and consequently, perhaps, somewhat of novelty in expressions. This again was of more value than his many vigils and acts of discipline, the advantage of which is limited to those who perform them. This Was worthy of our hero's famous banishments and flights; for the object, in view of which he chose to endure such sufferings, he still pursued when the sufferings were past. Nor did he cease to cherish the same ardor in others, praising some, gently rebuking others; rousing the sluggishness of these, restraining the passion of those; in some cases eager to prevent a fall, in others devising means of recovery after a fall; simple in disposition, manifold in the arts of government; clever in argument, more clever still in mind; condescending to the more lowly, outsoaring the more lofty; hospitable, protector of suppliants, averted of evils, really combining in himself alone the whole of the attributes parceled out by the sons of Greece among their deities. Further he was the patron of the wedded and virgin state alike, both peaceable and a peacemaker, and attendant upon those who are passing from hence. Oh, how many a title does his virtue afford me, if I would detail its many-sided excellence.

37. After such a course, as taught and teacher, that his life and habits form the ideal of an Episcopate, and his teaching the law of orthodoxy, what reward does he win for his piety? It is not indeed right to pass this by. In a good old age he closed his life, and was gathered to his fathers, the Patriarchs, and Prophets, and Apostles, and

Martyrs, who contended for the truth. To be brief in my epitaph, the honors at his departure surpassed even those of his return from exile; the object of many tears, his glory, stored up in the minds of all, outshines all its visible tokens. Yet, O thou dear and holy one, who didst thyself, with all thy fair renown, so especially illustrate the due proportions of speech and of silence, do thou stay here my words, falling short as they do of thy true meed of praise, though they have claimed the full exercise of all my powers. And mayest thou cast upon us from above a propitious glance, and conduct this people in its perfect worship of the perfect Trinity, which, as Father, Son, Holy Ghost, we contemplate and adore. And mayest thou, if my lot be peaceful, possess and aid me in my pastoral charge, or if it pass through struggles, uphold me, or take me to thee, and set me with thyself and those like thee (though I have asked a great thing) in Christ Himself, our Lord, to whom be all glory, honor, and power for evermore. Amen.

A preliminary discourse against the Eunominans

I. I am to speak against persons who pride themselves on their eloquence; so, to begin with a text of Scripture, "Behold, I am against thee, O thou proud one," not only in thy system of teaching, but also in thy hearing, and in thy tone of mind. For there are certain persons who have not only their ears and their tongues, but even, as I now perceive, their hands too, itching for our words; who delight in profane babblings, and oppositions of science falsely so called, and strifes about words, which tend to no profit; for so Paul, the Preacher and Establisher of the "Word cut short," the disciple and teacher of the Fishermen, calls all that is excessive or superfluous in discourse. But as to those to whom we refer, would that they, whose tongue is so voluble and clever in applying itself to noble and approved language, would likewise pay some attention to actions. For then perhaps in a little while they would become less sophistical, and less absurd and strange acrobats of words, if I may use a ridiculous expression about a ridiculous subject.

II. But since they neglect every path of righteousness, and look only to this one point, namely, which of the propositions submitted to them they shall bind or loose, (like those persons who in the theatres perform wrestling matches in public, but not that kind of wrestling in which the victory is won according to the rules of the sport, but a kind to deceive the eyes of those who are ignorant in such matters, and to catch applause), and every marketplace must buzz with their talking; and every dinner party be worried to death with silly talk and boredom; and every festival be made unfestive and full of dejection, and every occasion of mourning be consoled by a greater calamity — their questions — and all the women's apartments accustomed to simplicity be thrown into confusion and be robbed of its flower of modesty by the torrent of their words... since, I say this is so, the evil is intolerable and not to be borne, and our Great Mystery is in danger of being made a thing of little moment. Well then, let these spies bear with us, moved as we are with fatherly compassion, and as holy Jeremiah says, torn in our hearts; let them bear with us so far as not to give a savage reception to our discourse upon this subject; and let them, if indeed they can, restrain their tongues for a short while and lend us their ears. However that may be, you shall at any rate suffer no loss. For either we shall have spoken in the ears of them that will hear, and our words will bear some fruit, namely an advantage to you (since the Sower soweth the Word upon every kind of mind; and the good and fertile bears fruit), or else you will depart despising this discourse of ours as you have despised others, and having drawn from it further material for gainsaying and railing at us, upon which to feast yourselves yet more. And you must not be astonished if I speak a language which is strange to you and contrary to your custom, who profess to know everything and to teach everything in a too impetuous and generous manner... not to pain you by saying ignorant and rash.

III. Not to every one, my friends, does it belong to philosophize about God; not to every one; the Subject is not so cheap and low; and I will add, not before every audience, nor at all times, nor on all points; but on certain occasions, and before certain persons, and within certain limits. Not to all men, because it is permitted only to those who have been examined, and are passed masters in meditation, and who have been previously purified in soul and body, or at the very least are being purified. For the impure to touch the pure is, we may safely say, not safe, just as it is unsafe to fix weak eyes upon the sun's rays. And what is the permitted occasion? It is when we are free from all external defilement or disturbance, and when that which rules within us is not confused with vexatious or erring images; like persons mixing up good writing with bad, or filth with the sweet odors of unguents. For it is necessary to be truly at leisure to know God; and when we can get a convenient season, to discern the straight road of the things divine. And who are the permitted persons? They to whom the subject is of real concern, and not they who make it a matter of pleasant gossip, like any other thing, after the races, or the theater, or a concert, or a dinner, or still lower employments. To such men as these, idle jests and pretty contradictions about these subjects are a part of their amusement.

IV. Next, on what subjects and to what extent may we philosophize? On matters within our reach, and to such an extent as the mental power and grasp of our audience may extend. No further, lest, as excessively loud sounds injure the hearing, or excess of food the body, or, if you will, as excessive burdens beyond the strength injure those who bear them, or excessive rains the earth; so these too, being pressed down and overweighted by the stiffness, if I may use the expression, of the arguments should suffer loss even in respect of the strength they originally possessed.

V. Now, I am not saying that it is not needful to remember God at all times;… I must not be misunderstood, or I shall be having these nimble and quick people down upon me again. For we ought to think of God even more often than we draw our breath; and if the expression is permissible, we ought to do nothing else. Yea, I am one of those who entirely approve that Word which bids us meditate day and night, and tell at eventide and morning and noon day, and praise the Lord at every tithe; or, to use Moses' words, whether a man lie down, or rise up, or walk by the way, or whatever else he be doing — and by this recollection we are to be molded to purity. So that it is not the continual remembrance of God that I would hinder, but only the talking about God; nor even that as in itself wrong, but only when unseasonable; nor all teaching, but only want of moderation. As of even honey repletion and satiety, though it be of honey, produce vomiting; and, as Solomon says and I think, there is a time for every thing, and that which is good ceases to be good if it be not done in a good way; just as a flower is quite out of season in winter, and just as a man's dress does not become a woman, nor a woman's a man; and as geometry is out of place in mourning, or tears at a carousal; shall we in this instance alone disregard the proper time, in a matter in which most of all due season should be respected? Surely not, my friends and brethren (for I will still call you Brethren, though you do not behave like brothers). Let us not think so nor yet, like hot tempered and hard mouthed horses, throwing off our rider Reason, and casting away Reverence, that keeps us within due limits, run far away from the turning point? but let us philosophize within our proper bounds, and not be carried away into Egypt, nor be swept down into Assyria, nor sing the Lord's song in a strange land, by which I mean before any kind of audience, strangers or kindred, hostile or friendly, kindly or the reverse, who watch what we do with over great care, and would like the spark of what is wrong in us to become a flame, and secretly kindle and fan it and raise it to heaven with their breath and make it higher than the Babylonian flame which burnt up every thing around it. For since their strength lies not in their own dogmas, they hunt for it in our weak points. And therefore they apply themselves to our — shall I say "misfortunes" or "failings"? — like flies to wounds. But let us at least be no longer ignorant of ourselves, or pay too little attention to the due order in these matters. And if it be impossible to put an end to the existing hostility, let us at least agree upon this, that we will utter Mysteries under our breath, and holy things in a holy manner, and we will not cast to ears profane that which may not be uttered, nor give evidence that we possess less gravity than those who worship demons, and serve shameful fables and deeds; for they would sooner give their blood to the uninitiated than certain words. But let us recognize that as in dress and diet and laughter and demeanor there is a certain decorum, so there is also in speech and silence; since among so many titles and powers of God, we pay the highest honor to The Word. Let even our disputings then be kept within bounds.

VI. Why should a man who is a hostile listener to such words be allowed to hear about the Generation of God, or his creation, or how God was made out of things which had no existence, or of section and analysis and division? Why do we make our accusers judges? Why do we put swords into the hands of oar enemies? How, thinkest thou, or with what temper, will the arguments about such subjects be received by one who approves of adulteries, and corruption of children, and who worships the passions and cannot conceive of aught higher than the body... who till very lately set up gods for himself, and gods too who were noted for the vilest deeds? Will it not first be from a material standpoint, shamefully and ignorantly, and in the sense to which he has been accustomed? Will he not make thy Theology a defense for his own gods and passions? For if we ourselves wantonly misuse these words, it will be a long time before we shall persuade them to accept our philosophy. And if they are in their own persons inventors of evil things, how should they refrain from grasping at such things when offered to them? Such results come to us from mutual contest. Such results follow to those who fight for the Word beyond what the Word approves; they are behaving like mad people, who set their own house on fire, or tear their own children, or disavow their own parents, taking them for strangers.

VII. But when we have put away from the conversation those who are strangers to it, and sent the great legion on its way to the abyss into the herd of swine, the next thing is to look to ourselves, and polish our theological self to beauty like a statue. The first point to be considered is — What is this great rivalry of speech and endless talking? What is this new disease of insatiability? Why have we tied our hands and armed our tongues? We do not praise either hospitality, or brotherly love, or conjugal affection, or virginity; nor do we admire liberality to the poor, or the chanting of Psalms, or nightlong vigils, or tears. We do not keep under the body by fasting, or go forth to God by prayer; nor do we subject the worse to the better — I mean the dust to the spirit — as they would do who form a just judgment of our composite nature; we do not make our life a preparation for death; nor do we make ourselves masters of our passions, mindful of our heavenly nobility; nor tame our anger when it swells and rages, nor our pride that bringeth to a fall, nor unreasonable grief, nor unchastened pleasure, nor meretricious laughter, nor undisciplined eyes, nor insatiable ears, nor excessive talk, nor absurd thoughts, nor aught of the occasions which the Evil One gets against us from sources within ourselves; bringing upon us the death that comes through the windows, as Holy Scripture saith; that is, through the senses. Nay we do the very opposite, and have given liberty to the passions of others, as kings give releases from service in honor of a victory, only on condition that they incline to our side, and make their assault upon God more boldly, or more impiously. And we give them an evil reward for a thing which is not good, license of tongue for their impiety.

VIII. And yet, O talkative Dialectician, I will ask thee one small question, and answer thou me, as He saith to Job, Who through whirlwind and cloud giveth Divine admonitions. Are there many mansions in God's House, as thou hast heard, or only one? Of course you will admit that there are many, and not only one. Now, are they all to be filled, or only some, and others not; so that some will be left empty, and will have been prepared to no purpose? Of course all will be filled, for nothing can be in vain which has been done by God. And can you tell me what you will consider this Mansion to be? Is it the rest and glory which is in store There for the Blessed, or something else? — No, not anything else. Since then we are agreed upon this point, let us further examine another also. Is there any thing that procures these Mansions, as I think there is; or is there nothing? — Certainly there is — What is it? Is it not that there are various modes of conduct, and various purposes, one leading one way, another way, according to the proportion of faith, and these we call Ways? Must we, then, travel all, or some of these Ways... the same individual along them all, if that be possible; or, if not, along as many as may be; or else along some of them? And even if this may not be, it would still be a great thing, at least as it appears to me, to travel excellently along even one. — "You are right in your conception." — What then when you hear there is but One way, and that a narrow one, does the word seem to you to shew? That there is but one on account of its excellence. For it is but one, even though it be split into many parts. And narrow because of its difficulties, and because it is trodden by few in

119

comparison with the multitrade of the adversaries, and of those who travel along the road of wickedness. "So I think too." Well, then, my good friend, since this is so, why do you, as though condemning our doctrine for a certain poverty, rush headlong down that one which leads through what you call arguments and speculations, but I frivolities and quackeries? Let Paul reprove you with those bitter reproaches, in which, after his list of the Gifts of Grace, he says, Are all Apostles? Are all Prophets? etc.

IX. But, be it so. Lofty thou art, even beyond the lofty, even above the clouds, if thou wilt, a spectator of things invisible, a hearer of things unspeakable; one who hast ascended after Elias, and who after Moses hast been deemed worthy of the Vision of God, and after Paul hast been taken up into heaven why dost thou mold the rest of thy fellows in one day into Saints, and ordain them Theologians, and as it were breathe into them instruction, and make them many councils of ignorant oracles? Why dost thou entangle those who are weaker in thy spider's web, as if it were something great and wise? Why dost thou stir up wasps' nests against the Faith? Why dost thou suddenly spring a flood of dialectics upon us, as the fables of old did the Giants? Why hast thou collected all that is frivolous and unmanly among men, like a rabble, into one torrent, and having made them more effeminate by flattery, fashioned a new workshop, cleverly making a harvest for thyself out of their want of understanding? Dost thou deny that this is so, and are the other matters of no account to thee? Must thy tongue rule at any cost, and canst thou not restrain the birthpang of thy speech? Thou mayest find many other honorable subjects for discussion. To these turn this disease of thine with some advantage. Attack the silence of Pythagoras, and the Orphic beans, and the novel brag about "The Master said." Attack the ideas of Plato, and the transmigrations and courses of our souls, and the reminiscences, and the unlovely loves of the soul for lovely bodies. Attack the atheism of Epicurus, and his atoms, and his unphilosophic pleasure; or Aristotle's petty Providence, and his artificial system, and his discourses about the mortality of the soul, and the humanitarianism of his doctrine. Attack the superciliousness of the Stoa, or the greed and vulgarity of the Cynic. Attack the "Void and Full" (what nonsense), and all the details about the gods and the sacrifices and the idols and demons, whether beneficent or malignant, and all the tricks that people play with divination, evoking of gods, or of souls, and the power of the stars. And if these things seem to thee unworthy of discussion as petty and already often confuted, and thou wilt keep to thy line, and seek the satisfaction of thy ambition in it; then here too I will provide thee with broad paths. Philosophize about the world or worlds; about matter; about soul; about natures endowed with reason, good or bad; about resurrection, about judgment, about reward, or the Sufferings of Christ. For in these subjects to hit the mark is not useless, and to miss it is not dangerous. But with God we shall have converse, in this life only in a small degree; but a little later, it may be, more perfectly, in the Same, our Lord Jesus Christ, to Whom be glory for ever. Amen.

I. In the former Discourse we laid down clearly with respect to the Theologian, both what sort of character he ought to bear, and on what kind of subject he may philosophize, and when, and to what extent. We saw that he ought to be, as far as may be, pure, in order that light may be apprehended by light; and that he ought to consort with serious men, in order that his word be not fruitless through failing on an unfruitful soil; and that the suitable season is when we have a calm within from the whirl of outward things; so as not like madmen to lose our breath; and that the extent to which we may go is that to which we have ourselves advanced, or to which we are advancing. Since then these things are so, and we have broken up for ourselves the fallows of Divinity? so as not to sow upon thorns, and have made plain the face of the ground, being molded and molding others by Holy Scripture... let us now enter upon Theological questions, setting at the head thereof the Father, the Son, and the Holy Ghost, of Whom we are to treat; that the Father may be well pleased, and the Son may help us, and the Holy Ghost may inspire us; or rather that one illumination may come upon us from the One God, One in diversity, diverse in Unity, wherein is a marvel.

II. Now when I go up eagerly into the Mount — or, to use a truer expression, when I both eagerly long, and at the same time am afraid (the one through my hope and the other through my weakness) to enter within the Cloud, and hold converse with God, for so God commands; if any be an Aaron, let him go up with me, and let him stand near, being ready, if it must be so, to remain outside the Cloud. But if any be a Nadad or an Abihu, or of the Order of the Elders, let him go up indeed, but let him stand afar off, according to the value of his purification. But if any be of the multitude, who are unworthy of this height of contemplation, if he be altogether impure let him not approach at all, for it would be dangerous to him; but if he be at least temporarily purified, let him remain below and listen to the Voice alone, and the trumpet, the bare words of piety, and let him see the Mountain smoking and lightening, a terror at once and a marvel to those who cannot get up. But if any is an evil and savage beast, and altogether incapable of taking in the subject matter of Contemplation and Theology, let him not hurtfully and malignantly lurk in his den among the woods, to catch hold of some dogma or saying by a sudden spring, and to tear sound doctrine to pieces by his misrepresentations, but let him stand yet afar off and withdraw from the Mount, or he shall be stoned and crushed, and shall perish miserably in his wickedness. For to those who are like wild beasts true and sound discourses are stones. If he be a leopard let him die with his spots. If a ravening and roaring lion, seeking what he may devour of our souls or of our words; or a wild boar, trampling under foot the precious and translucent pearls of the Truth; or an Arabian and alien wolf, or one keener even than these in tricks of argument; or a fox, that is a treacherous and faithless soul, changing its shape according to circumstances or necessities, feeding on dead or putrid bodies, or on little vineyards when the large ones have escaped them; or any other carnivorous beast, rejected by the Law as unclean for food or enjoyment; our discourse must withdraw from such and be engraved on solid tables of stone, and that on both sides because the Law is partly visible, and partly hidden; the one part belonging to the mass who remain below, the other to the few who press upward into the Mount.

III. What is this that has happened to me, O friends, and initiates, and fellow-lovers of the truth? I was running to lay hold on God, and thus I went up into the Mount, and drew aside the curtain of the Cloud, and entered away from matter and material things, and as far as I could I withdrew within myself. And then when I looked up, I scarce saw the back parts of God; although I was sheltered by the Rock, the Word that was made flesh for us. And when I looked a little closer, I saw, not the First and unmingled Nature, known to Itself — to the Trinity, I mean; not That which abideth within the first veil, and is hidden by the Cherubim; but only that Nature, which at last even reaches to us. And that is, as far as I can learn, the Majesty, or as holy David calls it, the Glory which is manifested among the creatures, which It has produced and governs. For these are the Back Parts of God, which He leaves behind Him, as tokens of Himself like the shadows and reflection of the sun in the water, which shew the sun to our weak eyes, because we cannot look at the sun himself, for by his unmixed light he is too strong for our power of perception. In this way then shalt thou discourse of God; even wert thou a Moses and a God to Pharaoh; even wert thou caught up like Paul to the Third Heaven, and hadst heard unspeakable words; even wert thou raised above them both, and exalted to Angelic or Archangelic place and dignity. For though a thing be all heavenly, or above heaven, and far higher in nature and nearer to God than we, yet it is farther distant from God, and from the complete comprehension of His Nature, than it is lifted above our complex and lowly and earthward sinking composition.

IV. Therefore we must begin again thus. It is difficult to conceive God but to define Him in words is an impossibility, as one of the Greek teachers of Divinity taught, not unskillfully, as it appears to me; with the intention that he might be thought to have apprehended Him; in that he says it is a hard thing to do; and yet may escape being convicted of ignorance because of the impossibility of giving expression to the apprehension, But in my opinion it is impossible to express Him, and yet more impossible to conceive Him. For that which may be conceived may perhaps be made clear by language, if not fairly well, at any rate imperfectly, to any one who is not quite deprived of his hearing, or slothful of understanding. But to comprehend the whole of so great a Subject as this is quite impossible and impracticable, not merely to the utterly careless and ignorant, but even to those who are highly exalted, and who love God, and in like manner to every created nature; seeing that the darkness of this world and the thick covering of the flesh is an obstacle to the full understanding of the truth. I do not know whether it is the same with the higher natures and purer Intelligences which because of their nearness to God, and because they are illumined with all His Light, may possibly see, if not the whole, at any rate more perfectly and distinctly than we do; some perhaps more, some less than others, in proportion to their rank.

V. But enough has been said on this point. As to what concerns us, it is not only the Peace of God which passeth all understanding and knowledge, nor only the things which God hath stored up in promise for the righteous, which "eye hath not seen, nor ear heard, nor mind conceived" except in a very small degree, nor the accurate knowledge of the Creation. For even of this I would have you know that you have only a shadow when you hear the words, "I will consider the heavens, the work of Thy fingers, the moon and the stars," and the settled order therein; not as if he were considering them now, but as destined to do so hereafter. But far before them is That nature Which is above them, and Out of which they spring, the Incomprehensible and Illimitable — not, I mean, as to the fact of His being, but as to Its nature. For our preaching is not empty, nor our Faith vain, nor is this the doctrine we proclaim; for we would not have you take our candid statement as a starting point for a quibbling denial of God, or of arrogance on account of our confession of ignorance. For it is one thing to be persuaded of the existence of a thing, and quite another to know what it is.

VI. Now our very eyes and the Law of Nature teach us that God exists and that He is the Efficient and Maintaining Cause of all things: our eyes, because they fall on visible objects, and see them in beautiful stability and progress, immovably moving and revolving if I may so say; natural Law, because through these visible things and their order, it reasons back to their Author. For how could this Universe have come into being or been put together, unless God had called it into existence, and held it together? For every one who sees a beautifully made lute, and considers the skill with which it has been fitted together and arranged, or who hears its melody, would think of none but the lutemaker, or the luteplayer, and would recur to him in mind, though he might not know him by sight. And thus to us also is manifested That which made and moves and preserves all created things, even though He be not comprehended by the mind. And very wanting in sense is he who will not willingly go thus far in following natural proofs; but not even this which we have fancied or formed, or which reason has sketched for us, proves the existence of a God. But if any one has got even to some extent a comprehension of this, how is God' s Being to bedemonstrated? Who ever reached this extremity of wisdom? Who was ever deemed worthy of so great a gift? Who has opened the mouth of his mind and drawn in the Spirit, so as by Him that searcheth all things, yea the deep thing of God, to take in God, and no longer to need progress, since he already possesses the Extreme Object of desire, and That to which all the social life and all the intelligence of the best men press forward?

VII. For what will you conceive the Deity to be, if you rely upon all the approximations of reason? Or to what will reason carry you, O most philosophic of men and best of Theologians, who boast of your familiarity with the Unlimited? Is

He a body? How then is He the Infinite and Limitless, and formless, and intangible, and invisible? or are these attributes of a body? What arrogance for such is not the nature of a body! Or will you say that He has a body, but not these attributes? O stupidity, that a Deity should possess nothing more than we do. For how is He an object of worship if He be circumscribed? Or how shall He escape being made of elements, and therefore subject to be resolved into them again, or even altogether dissolved? For every compound is a starting point of strife, and strife of separation, and separation of dissolution. But dissolution is altogether foreign to God and to the First Nature. Therefore there can be no separation, that there may be no dissolution, and no strife that there may be no separation, and no composition that there may be no strife. Thus also them must be no body, that there may be no composition, and so the argument is established by going back from last to first.

VIII. And how shall we preserve the truth that God pervades all things and fills all, as it is written "Do not I fill heaven and earth? saith the Lord," and "The Spirit of the Lord filleth the world," if God partly contains and partly is contained? For either He will occupy an empty Universe, and so all things will have vanished for us, with this result, that we shall have insulted God by making Him a body, and by robbing Him of all things which He has made; or else He will be a body contained in other bodies, which is impossible; or He will be enfolded in them, or contrasted with them, as liquids are mixed, and one divides and is divided by another; — a view which is more absurd and anile than even the atoms of Epicurus and so this argument Concerning the body will fall through, and have no body and no solid basis at all. But if we are to assert that He is immaterial (as for example that Fifth Element which some have imagined), and that He is carried round in the circular movement... let us assume that He is immaterial, and that He is the Fifth Element; and, if they please, let Him be also bodiless in accordance with the independent drift and arrangement of their argument; for I will not at present differ with them on this point; in what respect then will He be one of those things which are in movement and agitation, to say nothing of the insult involved in making the Creator subject to the same move-merit as the creatures, and Him That carries all (if they will allow even this) one with those whom He carries. Again, what is the force that moves your Fifth Element, and what is it that moves all things, and what moves that, and what is the force that moves that? And so on ad infinitum. And how can He help being altogether contained in space if He be subject to motion? But if they assert that He is something other than this Fifth Element; suppose it is an angelic nature that they attribute to Him, how will they shew that Angels are corporeal, or what sort of bodies they have? And how far in that case could God, to Whom the Angels minister, be superior to the Angels? And if He is above them, there is again brought in an irrational swarm of bodies, and a depth of nonsense, that has no possible basis to stand upon.

IX. And thus we see that God is not a body. For no inspired teacher has yet asserted or admitted such a notion, nor has the sentence of our own Court allowed it. Nothing then remains but to conceive of Him as incorporeal. But this term Incorporeal, though granted, does not yet set before us — or contain within itself His Essence, any more than Unbegotten, or Unoriginate, or Unchanging, or Incorruptible, or any other predicate which is used concerning God or in reference to Him. For what effect is produced upon His Being or Substance by His having no beginning, and being incapable of change or limitation? Nay, the whole question of His Being is still left for the further consideration and exposition of him who truly has the mind of God and is advanced in contemplation. For just as to say "It is a body," or "It was begotten," is not sufficient to present clearly to the mind the various objects of which these predicates are used, but you must also express the subject of which you use them, if you would present the object of your thought clearly and adequately (for every one of these predicates, corporeal, begotten, mortal, may be used of a man, or a cow, or a horse). Just so he who is eagerly pursuing the nature of the Self-existent will not stop at saying what He is not, but must go on beyond what He is not, and say what He is; inasmuch as it is easier to take in some single point than to go on disowning point after point in endless detail, in order, both by the elimination of negatives and the assertion of positives to arrive at a comprehension of this subject. But a man who states what God is not without going on to say what He is, acts much in the same way as one would who when asked how many twice five make, should answer, "Not two, nor three, nor four, nor five, nor twenty, nor thirty, nor in short any number below ten, nor any multiple of ten;" but would not answer "ten," nor settle the mind of his questioner upon the firm ground of the answer. For it is much easier, and more concise to shew what a thing is not from what it is, than to demonstrate what it is by stripping it of what it is not. And this surely is evident to every one.

X. Now since we have ascertained that God is incorporeal, let us proceed a little further with our examination. Is He Nowhere or Somewhere. For if He is Nowhere, then some person of a very inquiring turn of mind might ask, How is it then that He can even exist? For if the non-existent is nowhere, then that which is nowhere is also perhaps non-existent. But if He is Somewhere, He must be either in the Universe, or above the Universe. And if He is in the Universe, then He must be either in some part or in the whole. If in some part, then He will be circumscribed by that part which is less than Himself; but if everywhere, then by one which is further and greater — I mean the Universal, which contains the Particular; if the Universe is to be contained by the Universe, and no place is to be free from circumscription. This follows if He is contained in the Universe. And besides, where was He before the Universe was created, for this is a point of no little difficulty. But if He is above the Universe, is there nothing to distinguish this from the Universe, and where is this above situated? And how could this Transcendence and that which is transcended be distinguished in thought, if there is not a limit to divide and define them? Is it not necessary that there shall be some mean to mark off the Universe from that which is above the Universe? And what could this be but Place, which we have already rejected? For I have not yet brought forward the point that God would be altogether circumscript, if He were even comprehensible in thought: for comprehension is one form of circumscription.

XI Now, why have I gone into all this, perhaps too minutely for most people to listen to, and in accordance with the present manner of discourse, which despises noble simplicity, and has introduced a crooked and intricate style? That the tree may be known by its fruits; I mean, that the darkness which is at work in such teaching may be known by the obscurity of the arguments. For my purpose in doing so was, not to get credit for myself for astonishing utterances, or excessive wisdom, through tying knots and solving difficulties (this was the great miraculous gift of Daniel), but to make clear the point at which my argument has aimed from the first. And what was this? That the Divine Nature cannot be apprehended by human reason, and that we cannot even represent to ourselves all its greatness. And this not out of envy, for envy is far from the Divine Nature, which is passionless, and only good and Lord of all; especially envy of that which is the most honorable of all His creatures. For what does the Word prefer to the rational and speaking creatures? Why, even their very existence is a proof of His supreme goodness. Nor yet is this incomprehensibility for the sake of His own glory and honor, Who is full, as if His possession of His glory and majesty depended upon the impossibility of approaching Him. For it is utterly sophistical and foreign to the character, I will not say of God, but of any moderately good man, who has any right ideas about himself, to seek his own supremacy by throwing a hindrance in the way of another.

XII. But whether there be other causes for it also, let them see who are nearer God, and are eye witnesses and spectators of His unsearchable judgments; if there are any who are so eminent in virtue, and who walk in the paths of the Infinite, as the saying is. As far, however, as we have attained, who measure with our little measure things hard to be understood, perhaps one reason is to prevent us from too readily throwing away the possession because it was so easily come by. For people cling tightly to that which they acquire with labor; but that which they acquire easily they quickly throw away, because it can be easily recovered. And so it is turned into a blessing, at least to all men who are sensible, that this blessing is not too easy. Or perhaps it is in order that we may not share the fate of Lucifer, who fell, and in consequence of receiving the full light make our necks stiff against the Lord Almighty, and suffer a fall, of all things most pitiable, from the height we had attained. Or perhaps it may be to give a greater reward hereafter for their labor and glorious life to those who have here been purified, and have exercised long patience in respect of that which they desired. Therefore this darkness of the body has been placed between us and God, like the cloud of old between the Egyptians and the Hebrews; and this is perhaps what is meant by "He made darkness His secret place," namely our dullness, through which few can see even a little. But as to this point, let those discuss it whose business it is; and let them ascend as far as possible in the examination. To us who are (as Jeremiah saith), "prisoners of the earth," and covered with the denseness of carnal nature, this at all events is known, that as it is impossible for a man to step over his own shadow, however fast he may move (for the shadow will always move on as fast as it is being overtaken) or, as it is impossible for the eye to draw near to visible objects apart from the intervening air and light, or for a fish to glide about outside of the waters; so it is quite impracticable for those who are in the body to be conversant with objects of pure thought apart altogether from bodily objects. For something in our own environment is ever creeping in, even when the mind has most fully detached itself from the visible, and collected itself, and is attempting to apply itself to those invisible things which are akin to itself.

XIII. This will be made clear to you as follows: — Are not Spirit, and Fire, and Light, Love, and Wisdom, and Righteousness, and Mind and Reason, and the like, the names of the First Nature? What then? Can you conceive of Spirit apart from motion and diffusion; or of Fire without its fuel and its upward motion, and its proper color and form? Or of Light unmingled with air, and loosed from that which is as it were its father and source? And how do you conceive of a mind? Is it not that which is inherent in some person not itself, and are not its movements thoughts, silent or uttered? And Reason... what else can you think it than that which is either silent within ourselves, or else outpoured (for I shrink from saying loosed)? And if you conceive of Wisdom, what is it but the habit of mind which you know as such, and which is concerned with contemplations either divine or human? And Justice and Love, are they not praiseworthy dispositions, the one opposed to injustice, the other to hate, and at one time intensifying themselves, at another relaxed, now taking possession of us, now leaving us alone, and in a word, making Its what we are, and changing us as colors do bodies? Or are we rather to leave all these things, and to look at the Deity absolutely, as best we can, collecting a fragmentary perception of It from Its images? What then is this subtle thing, which is of these, and yet is not these, or how can that Unity which is in its Nature uncomposite and incomparable, still be all of these, and each one of them perfectly? Thus our mind faints to transcend corporeal things, and to consort with the Incorporeal, stripped of all clothing of corporeal ideas, as long as it has to look with its inherent weakness at things above its strength. For every rational nature longs for God and for the First Cause, but is unable to grasp Him, for the reasons I have mentioned. Faint therefore with the desire, and as it were restive and impatient of the disability, it tries a second course, either to look at visible things, and out of some of them to make a God... (a poor contrivance, for in what respect and to what extent can that which is seen be higher and more godlike than that which sees, that this should worship that?) or else through the beauty and order of visible things to attain to that which is above sight; but not to suffer the loss of God through the magnificence of visible things.

XIV. From this cause some have made a God of the Sun, others of the Moon, others of the host of Stars, others of heaven itself with all its hosts, to which they have attributed the guiding of the Universe, according to the quality or quantity of their movement. Others again of the Elements, earth, air, water, fire, because of their useful nature, since without them human life cannot possibly exist. Others again have worshipped any chance visible objects, setting up the most beautiful of what they saw as their gods. And there are those who worship pictures and images, at first indeed of their own ancestors — at least, this is the case with the more affectionate and sensual — and honor the departed with memorials; and afterwards even those of strangers are worshipped by men of a later generation separated froth them by a long interval; through ignorance of the First Nature, and following the traditional honor as lawful and necessary; for usage when confirmed by time was held to be Law. And I think that some who were courtiers of arbitrary power and extolled bodily strength and admired beauty, made a God in time out of him whom they honored, perhaps getting hold of some fable to help on their imposture.

XV. And those of them who were most subject to passion deified their passions, or honored them among their gods; Anger and Blood-thirstiness, Lust and Drunkenness, and every similar wickedness; and made out of this an ignoble and unjust excuse for their own sins. And some they left on earth, and some they hid beneath the earth (this being the only sign of wisdom about them), and some they raised to heaven. O ridiculous distribution of inheritance! Then they gave to each of these concepts the name of some God or demon, by the authority and private judgment of their error, and set up statues whose costliness is a snare, and thought to honor them with blood and the steam of sacrifices, and sometimes even by most shameful actions, frenzies and manslaughter. For such honors were the fitting due of such gods. And before now men have insulted themselves by worshipping monsters, and fourfooted beasts, and creeping things? and of the very vilest and most absurd, and have made an offering to them of the glory of God; so that it is not easy to decide whether we ought most to despise the worshippers or the objects of their worship. Probably the worshippers are far the most contemptible, for though they are of a rational nature, and have received grace from God, they have set up the worse as the better. And this was the trick of the Evil One, who abused good to an evil purpose, as in most of his evil deeds. For he laid hold of their desire in its wandering in search of God, in order to distort to himself the power, and steal the desire, leading it by the hand, like a blind man asking a road; and he hurled down and scattered some in one direction and some in another, into one pit of death and destruction.

XVI. This was their course. But reason receiving us in our desire for God, and in our sense of the impossibility of being without a leader and guide, and then making us apply ourselves to things visible and meeting with the things which have been since the beginning, doth not stay its course even here. For it was not the part of Wisdom to grant the sovereignty to things which are, as observation tells us, of equal rank. By these then it leads to that which is above these, and by which being is given to these. For what is it which ordered things in heaven and things in earth, and those which pass through air, and those which live in water; or rather the things which were before these, heaven and earth, air and water? Who mingled these, and who distributed them? What is it that each has in common with the other, and their mutual dependence and agreement? For I commend the man, though he was a heathen, who said, What gave movement to these, and drives their ceaseless and unhindered motion? Is it not the Artificer of them Who implanted reason in them all, in accordance with which the Universe is moved and controlled? Is it not He who made them and brought them into being? For we cannot attribute such a power to the Accidental. For, suppose that its existence is accidental, to what will you let us ascribe its order? And if you like we will grant you this: to what then will you ascribe its preservation and protection in accordance with the terms of its first creation. Do these belong to the Accidental, or to something else? Surely not to the Accidental. And what can this Something Else be but God? Thus reason that proceeds from God, that is implanted in all from the beginning and is the first law in us, and is bound up in all, leads us up to God through visible things. Let us begin again, and reason this out.

XVII. What God is in nature and essence, no man ever yet has discovered or can discover. Whether it will ever be discovered is a question which he who will may examine and decide. In my opinion it will be discovered when that within us which is godlike and divine, I mean our mind and reason, shall have mingled with its Like, and the image shall have ascended to the Archetype, of which it has now the desire. And this I think is the solution of that vexed problem as to "We shall know even as we are known." But in our present life all that comes to us is but a little effluence, and as it were a small effulgence from a great Light. So that if anyone has known God, or has had the testimony of Scripture to his knowledge of God, we are to understand such an one to have possessed a degree of knowledge which gave him the appearance of being more fully enlightened than another who did not enjoy the same degree of illumination; and this relative superiority is spoken of as if it were absolute knowledge, not because it is really such, but by comparison with the power of that other.

XVIII. Thus Enos "hoped to call upon the Name of the Lord." Hope was that for which he is commended; and that, not that he should know God, but that he should call upon him. And Enoch was translated, but it is not yet clear whether it was because he already comprehended the Divine Nature, or in order that he might comprehend it. And Noah's "glory was that he was pleasing to God; he who was entrusted with the saving of the whole world from the waters, or rather of the Seeds of the world, escaped the Deluge in a small Ark. And Abraham, great Patriarch though he was, was justified by faith, and offered a strange victim, the type of the Great Sacrifice. Yet he saw not God as God, but gave Him food as a man. He was approved because he worshipped as far as he comprehended. And Jacob dreamed of a lofty ladder and stair of Angels, and in a mystery anointed a pillar — perhaps to signify the Rock that was anointed for our sake — and gave to a place the name of The House of God in honor of Him whom he saw; and wrestled with God in human form; whatever this wrestling of God with man may mean… possibly it refers to the comparison of man's virtue with God's; and he bore on his body the marks of the wrestling, setting forth the defeat of the created nature; and for a reward of his reverence he received a change of his name; being named, instead of Jacob, Israel — that great and honorable name. Yet neither he nor any one on his behalf, unto this day, of all the Twelve Tribes who where his children, could boast that he comprehended the whole nature or the pure sight of God.

XIX. To Elias neither the strong wind, nor the fire, nor the earthquake, as you learn from the story, but a light breeze adumbrated the Presence of God, and not even this His Nature. And who was this Elias? The man whom a chariot of fire took up to heaven, signifying the superhuman excellency of the righteous man. And are you not amazed at Manoah the Judge of yore, and at Peter the disciple in later days; the one being unable to endure the sight even of one in whom was a representation of God; and saying, "We are undone, O wife, we have seen God;" speaking as though even a vision of God could not be grasped by human beings, let alone the Nature of God; and the other unable to endure the Presence of Christ in his boat and therefore bidding Him depart; and this though Peter was more zealous than the others for the knowledge of Christ, and received a blessing for this,' and was entrusted with the greatest gifts. What would you say of Isaiah or Ezekiel, who was an eyewitness of very great mysteries, and of the other Prophets; for one of these saw the Lord of Sabaoth sitting on the Throne of glory, and encircled and praised and hidden by the sixwinged Seraphim, and was himself purged by the live coal, and equipped for his prophetic office. And the other describes the Cherubic Chariot of God, and the Throne upon them, and the Firmament over it, and Him that shewed Himself in the Firmament, and Voices, and Forces, and Deeds. And whether this was an appearance by day, only visible to Saints, or an unerring vision of the night, or an impression on the mind holding converse with the future as if it were the present; or some other ineffable form of prophecy, I cannot say; the God of the Prophets knoweth, and they know who are thus inspired. But neither these of whom I am speaking, nor any of their fellows ever stood before the Council and Essence of God, as it is written, or saw, or proclaimed the Nature of God.

XX. If it had been permitted to Paul to utter what the Third Heaven contained, and his own advance, or ascension, or assumption thither, perhaps we should know something more about God's Nature, if this was the mystery of the rapture. But since it was ineffable, we too will honor it by silence. Thus much we will hear Paul say about it, that we know in part and we prophesy in part. This and the like to this are the confessions of one who is not rude in knowledge, who threatens to give proof of Christ speaking in him, the great doctor and champion of the truth. Wherefore he estimates all knowledge on earth only as through a glass darkly, as taking its stand upon little images of the truth. Now, unless I appear to anyone too careful, and over anxious about the examination of this matter, perhaps it was of this and nothing else that the Word Himself intimated that there were things which could not now be borne, but which should be borne and cleared up hereafter,' and which John the Forerunner of the Word and great Voice of the Truth declared even the whole world could not contain.

XXI. The truth then, and the whole Word is full of difficulty and obscurity; and as it were with a small instrument we are undertaking a great work, when with merely human wisdom we pursue the knowledge of the Self-existent, and in company with, or not apart from, the senses, by which we are borne hither and thither, and led into error, we apply ourselves to the search after things which are only to be grasped by the mind, and we are unable by meeting bare realities with bare intellect to approximate somewhat more closely to the truth, and to mold the mind by its concepts. Now the subject of God is more hard to come at, in proportion as it is more perfect than any other, and is open to more objections, and the solutions of them are more laborious. For every objection, however small, stops and hinders the course of our argument, and cuts off its further advance, just like men who suddenly check with the rein the horses in full career, and turn them right round by the unexpected shock. Thus Solomon, who was the wisest of all men, whether before him or in his own time, to whom God gave breadth of heart, and a flood of contemplation, more abundant than the sand, even he, the more he entered into the depth, the more dizzy he became, and declared the furthest point of wisdom to be the discovery of how very far off she was from him. Paul also tries to arrive at, I will not say the nature of God, for this he knew was utterly impossible, but only the judgments of God; and since he finds no way out, and no halting place in the ascent, and moreover, since the earnest searching of his mind after knowledge does not end in any definite conclusion, because some fresh unattained point is being continually disclosed to him (O marvel, that I have a like experience), he closes his discourse with astonishment, and calls this the riches of God, and the depth, and confesses the unsearchableness of the judgments of God, in almost the very words of David, who at one time calls God's judgments the great deep whose foundations cannot be reached by measure or sense; and at another says that His knowledge of him and of his own constitution was marvelous, and had attained greater strength than was in his own power or grasp.

XXII. For if, he says, I leave everything else alone, and consider myself and the whole nature and constitution of man, and how we are mingled, and what is our movement, and how the mortal was compounded with the immortal, and how it is that I flow downwards, and yet am borne upwards, and how the soul is circumscribed; and how it gives life and shares in feelings; and how the mind is at once circumscribed and unlimited, abiding in us and yet traveling over the Universe in swift motion and flow; how it is both received and imparted by word, and passes through air, and enters with all things; how it shares in sense, and enshrouds itself away from sense. And even before these questions — what was our first molding and composition in the workshop of nature, and what is our last formation and completion? What is the desire for and imparting of nourishment, and who brought us spontaneously to those first springs and sources of life? How is the body nourished by food, and the soul by reason? What is the drawing of nature, and the mutual relation between parents and children, that it should be held together by a spell of love? How is it that species are permanent, and are different in their characteristics, although there are so many that their individual marks cannot be described? How is it that the same animal is both mortal and immortal the one by decease, the other by coming into being? For one departs, and another takes its place, just like the flow of a river, which is never still, yet ever constant. And you might discuss many more points concerning men's members and parts, and their mutual adaptation both for use and beauty, and how some are connected and others disjoined, some are more excellent and others less comely, some are united and others divided, some contain and others are contained, according to the law and reason of Nature. Much too might be said about voices and ears. How is it that the voice is carried by the vocal organs, and received by the ears, and both are joined by the smiting and resounding of the medium of the air? Much too of the eyes, which have an indescribable communion with visible objects, and which are moved by the will alone, and that together, and are affected exactly as is the mind. For with equal speed the mind is joined to the objects of thought, the eye to those of sight. Much too concerning the other senses, not objects of the research of reason. And much concerning our rest in sleep, and the figments of dreams, and of memory and remembrance; of calculation, and anger, and desire; and in a word, all by which this little world called Man is swayed.

XXIII. Shall I reckon up for you the differences of the other animals, both from us and from each other, — differences of nature, and of production, and of nourishment, and of region, and of temper, and as it were of social life? How is it that some are gregarious and others solitary, some herbivorous and others carnivorous, some fierce and others tame, some fond of man and domesticated, others untamable and free? And some we might call bordering on reason and power of learning, while others are altogether destitute of reason, and incapable of being taught. Some with fuller senses, others with less; some immovable, and some with the power of walking, and some very swift, and some very slow; some surpassing in size or beauty, or in one or other of these respects; others very small or very ugly, or both; some strong, others weak, some apt at self-defense, others timid and crafty and others again are unguarded. Some are laborious and thrifty, others altogether idle and improvident. And before we come to such points as these, how is it that some are crawling things, and others upright; some attached to one spot, some amphibious; some delight in beauty and others are unadorned; some are married and some single; some temperate and others intemperate; some have numerous offspring and others not; some are long-lived and others have but short lives? It would be a weary discourse to go through all the details.

XXIV. Look also at the fishy tribe gliding through the waters, and as it were flying through the liquid element, and breathing its own air, but in danger when in contact with ours, as we are in the waters; and mark their habits and dispositions, their intercourse and their births, their size and their beauty, and their affection for places, and their wanderings, and their assemblings and departings, and their properties which so nearly resemble those of the animals that dwell on land; in some cases community, in others contrast of properties, both in name and shape. And consider the tribes of birds, and their varieties of form and color, both of those which are voiceless and of songbirds. What is the reason of their melody, and from whom came it? Who gave to the grasshopper the lute in his breast, and the songs and chirruping on the branches, when they are moved by the sun to make their midday music, and sing among the groves, and escort the wayfarer with their voices? Who wove the song for the swan when he spreads his wings to the breezes, and makes melody of their rustling? For I will not speak of the forced voices, and all the rest that art contrives against the truth. Whence does the peacock, that boastful bird of Media, get his love of beauty and of praise (for he is fully conscious of his own beauty), so that when he sees any one approaching, or when, as they say, he would make a show before his hens, raising his neck and spreading his tail in circle around him, glittering like gold and studded with stars, he makes a spectacle of his beauty to his lovers with pompous strides? Now Holy Scripture admires the cleverness in weaving even of women, saying, Who gave to woman skill in weaving and cleverness in the art of embroidery? This belongeth to a living creature that hath reason, and exceedeth in wisdom and maketh way even as far as the things of heaven.

XXV. But I would have you marvel at the natural knowledge even of irrational creatures, and if you can, explain its cause. How is it that birds have for nests rocks and trees and roofs, and adapt them both for safety and beauty, and suitably for the comfort of their nurslings? Whence do bees and spiders get their love of work and art, by which the former plan their honeycombs, and join them together by hexagonal and co-ordinate tubes, and construct the foundation by means of a partition and an alternation of the angles with straight lines; and this, as is the case, in such dusky hives and dark combs; and the latter weave their intricate webs by such light and almost airy threads stretched in divers ways, and this from almost invisible beginnings, to be at once a precious dwelling, and a trap for weaker creatures with a view to enjoyment of food? What Euclid ever imitated these, while pursuing philosophical enquiries with lines that have no real existence, and wearying himself with demonstrations? From what Palamedes came the tactics, and, as the saying is, the movements and configurations of cranes, and the systems of their movement in ranks and their complicated flight? Who were their Phidiae and Zeuxides, and who were the Parrhasii and Aglaophons who knew how to draw and mold excessively beautiful things? What harmonious Gnossian chorus of Daedalus, wrought for a girl to the highest pitch of beauty? What Cretan Labyrinth, hard to get through, hard to unravel, as the poem say, and continually crossing itself through the tricks of its construction? I will not speak of the ants' storehouses and storekeepers, and of their treasurings of wood in quantities corresponding to the time for which it is wanted, and all the other details which we know are told of their marches and leaders and their good order in their works.

XXVI. If this knowledge has come within your reach and you are familiar with these branches of science, look at the differences of plants also, up to the artistic fashion of the leaves, which is adapted both to give the utmost pleasure to the eye, and to be of the greatest advantage to the fruit. Look too at the variety and lavish abundance of fruits, and most of all at the wondrous beauty of such as are most necessary. And consider the power of roots, and juices, and flowers, and odors, not only so very sweet, but also serviceable as medicines; and the graces and qualities of colors; and again the costly value, and the brilliant transparency of precious stones. Since nature has set before you all things as in an abundant banquet free to all, both the necessaries and the luxuries of life, in order that, if nothing else, you may at any rate know God by His benefits, and by your own sense of want be made wiser than you were. Next, I pray you, traverse the length and breadth of earth, the common mother of all, and the gulfs of the sea bound together with one another and with the land, and the beautiful forests, and the rivers and springs abundant and perennial, not only of waters cold and fit for drinking, and on the surface of the earth; but also such as running beneath the earth, and flowing under caverns, are then forced out by a violent blast, and repelled, and then filled with heat by this violence of strife and repulsion, burst out by little and little wherever they get a chance, and hence supply our need of hot baths in many parts of the earth, and in conjunction with the cold give us a healing which is without cost and spontaneous. Tell me how and whence are these things? What is this great web unwrought by art? These things are no less worthy of admiration, in respect of their mutual relations than when considered separately. How is it that the earth stands solid and unswerving? On what is it supported? What is it that props it up, and on what does that rest? For indeed even reason has nothing to lean upon, but only the Will of God. And how is it that part of it is drawn up into mountain summits, and part laid down in plains, and this in various and differing ways? And because the variations are individually small, it both supplies our needs more liberally, and is more beautiful by its variety; part being distributed into habitations, and part left uninhabited, namely all the great height of Mountains, and the various clefts of its coast line cut off from it. Is not this the clearest proof of the majestic working of God?

XXVII. And with respect to the Sea even if I did not marvel at its greatness, yet I should have marveled at its gentleness, in that although loose it stands within its boundaries; and if not at its gentleness, yet surely at its greatness; but since I marvel at both, I will praise the Power that is in both. What collected it? What bounded it? How is it raised and lulled to rest, as though respecting its neighbor earth? How, moreover, does it receive all the rivers, and yet remain the same, through the very superabundance of its immensity, if that term be permissible? How is the boundary of it, though it be an element of such magnitude, only sand? Have your natural philosophers with their knowledge of useless details anything to tell us, those men I mean who are really endeavoring to measure the sea with a wineglass, and such mighty works by their own conceptions? Or shall I give the really scientific explanation of it from Scripture concisely, and yet more satisfactorily and truly than by the longest arguments? "He hath fenced the face of the water with His command." This is the chain of fluid nature. And how doth He bring upon it the Nautilus that inhabits the dry land (i.e., man) in a little vessel, and with a little breeze (dost thou not marvel at the sight of this, — is not thy mind astonished?), that earth and sea may be bound together by needs and commerce, and that things so widely separated by nature should be thus brought together into one for man? What are the first fountains of springs? Seek, O man, if you can trace out or find any of these things. And who was it who cleft the plains and the mountains for the rivers, and gave them an unhindered course? And how comes the marvel on the other side, that the Sea never overflows, nor the Rivers cease to flow? And what is the nourishing power of water, and what the difference therein; for some things are irrigated from above, and others drink from their roots, if I may luxuriate a little in my language when speaking of the luxuriant gifts of God.

XXVIII. And now, leaving the earth and the things of earth, soar into the air on the wings of thought, that our argument may advance in due path; and thence I will take you up to heavenly things, and to heaven itself, and things which are above heaven; for to that which is beyond my discourse hesitates to ascend, but still it shall ascend as far as may be. Who poured forth the air, that great and abundant wealth, not measured to men by their rank or fortunes; not restrained by boundaries; not divided out according to people's ages; but like the distribution of the Manna, received in sufficiency, and valued for its equality of distribution; the chariot of the winged creation; the seat of the winds; the moderator of the seasons; the quickener of living things, or rather the preserver of natural life in the body; in which bodies have their being, and by which we speak; in which is the light and all that it shines upon, and the sight' which flows through it? And mark, if you please, what follows. I cannot give to the air the whole empire of all that is thought to belong to the air. What are the storehouses of the winds? What are the treasuries of the snow? Who, as Scripture hath said, hath begotten the drops of dew? Out of Whose womb came the ice? arid Who bindeth the waters in the clouds, and, fixing part in the clouds (O marvel!) held by His Word though its nature is to flow, poureth out the rest upon the face of the whole earth, and scattereth it abroad in due season, and in just proportions, and neither suffereth the whole substance of moisture to go out free and uncontrolled (for sufficient was the cleansing in the days of Noah; and He who cannot lie is not forgetful of His own covenant);... nor yet restraineth it entirely that we should not again stand in need of an Elias to bring the drought to an end. If He shall shut up heaven, it saith, who shall open it? If He open the floodgates, who shall shut them up? Who can bring an excess or withhold a sufficiency of rain, unless he govern the Universe by his own measures and balances? What scientific laws, pray, can you lay down concerning thunder and lightning, O you who thunder from the earth, and cannot shine with even little sparks of truth? To what vapors from earth will you attribute the creation of cloud, or is it due to some thickening of the air, or pressure or crash of clouds of excessive rarity, so as to make you think the pressure the cause of the lightning, and the crash that which makes the thunder? Or what compression of wind having no outlet will account to you for the lightning by its compression, and for the thunder by its bursting out? Now if you have in your thought passed through the air and all the things of air, reach with me to heaven and the things of heaven. And let faith lead us rather than reason, if at least you have learnt the feebleness of the latter in matters nearer to you, and have known reason by knowing the things that are beyond reason, so as not to be altogether on the earth or of the earth, because you are ignorant even of your ignorance.

XXIX. Who spread the sky around us, and set the stars in order? Or rather, first, can you tell me, of your own knowledge of the things in heaven, what are the sky and the stars; you who know not what lies at your very feet, and cannot even take the measure of yourself, and yet must busy yourself about what is above your nature, and gape at the illimitable? For, granted that you understand orbits and periods, and waxings and wanings, and settings and risings, and some degrees and minutes, and all the other things which make you so proud of your wonderful knowledge; you have not arrived at comprehension of the realities themselves, but only at an observation of some movement, which, when confirmed by longer practice, and drawing the observations of many individuals into one generalization, and thence deducing a law, has acquired the name of Science (just as the lunar phenomena have become generally known to our sight), being the basis of this knowledge. But if you are very scientific on this subject, and have a just claim to admiration, tell me what is the cause of this order and this movement. How came the sun to be a beacon-fire to the whole world, and to all eyes like the leader of some chorus, concealing all the rest of the stars by his brightness, more completely than some of them conceal others. The proof of this is that they shine against him, but he outshines them and does not even allow it to be perceived that they rose simultaneously with him, fair as a bridegroom, swift and great as a giant for I will not let his praises be sung from any other source than my own Scriptures — so mighty in strength that from one end to the other of the world he embraces all things in his heat, and there is nothing hid from the feeling thereof, but it fills both every eye with light, and every embodied creature with heat; warming, yet not burning, by the gentleness of its temper, and the order of its movement, present to all, and equally embracing all.

XXX. Have you considered the importance of the fact that a heathen writer" speaks of the sun as holding the same position among material objects as God does among objects of thought? For the one gives light to the eyes, as the Other does to the mind; and is the most beautiful of the objects of sight, as God is of those of thought. But who gave him motion at first? And what is it which ever moves him in his circuit, though in his nature stable and immovable, truly unwearied, and the giver and sustainer of life, and all the rest of the titles which the poets justly sing of him, and never resting in his course or his benefits? How comes he to be the creator of day when above the earth, and of night when below it? or whatever may be the right expression when one contemplates the sun? What are the mutual aggressions and concessions of day and night, and their regular irregularities — to use a somewhat strange expression? How comes he to be the maker and divider of the seasons, that come and depart in regular order, and as in a dance interweave with each other, or stand apart by a law of love on the one hand, and of order on the other, and mingle little by little, and steal on their neighbor, just as nights and days do, so as not to give us pain by their suddenness. This will be enough about the sun. Do you know the nature and phenomena of the Moon, and the measures and courses of light, and how it is that the sun bears rule over the day, and the moon presides over the night; and while She gives confidence to wild beasts, He stirs Man up to work, raising or lowering himself as may be most serviceable? Know you the bond of Pleiades, or the fence of Orion as He who counteth the number of the stars and calleth them all by their names? Know you the differences of the glory of each, and the order of their movement, that I should trust you, when by them you weave the web of human concerns, and arm the creature against the Creator?

XXXI. What say you? Shall we pause here, after discussing nothing further than matter and visible things, or, since the Word knows the Tabernacle of Moses to be a figure of the whole creation — I mean the entire system of things visible and invisible — shall we pass the first veil, and stepping beyond the realm of sense, shall we look into the Holy Place, the Intellectual and Celestial creation? But not even this can we see in an incorporeal way, though it is incorporeal, since it is called — or is — Fire and Spirit. For He is said to make His Angels spirits, and His Ministers a flame of fire… though perhaps this "making" means preserving by that Word by which they Came into existence. The Angel then is called spirit and fire; Spirit, as being a creature of the intellectual sphere; Fire, as being of a purifying nature; for I know that the same names belong to the First Nature. But, relatively to us at least, we must reckon the Angelic Nature incorporeal, or at any rate as nearly so as possible. Do you see how we get dizzy over this subject, and cannot advance to any point, unless it be as far as this, that we know there are Angels and Archangels, Thrones, Dominions, Princedoms, Powers, Splendors, Ascents, Intelligent Powers or Intelligencies, pure natures and unalloyed, immovable to evil, or scarcely movable; ever circling in chorus round the First Cause (or how should we sing their praises?) illuminated thence with the purest Illumination, or one in one degree and one in another, proportionally to their nature and rank… so conformed to beauty and molded that they become secondary Lights, and can enlighten others by the overflowings and largesses of the First Light? Ministrants of God's Will, strong with both inborn and imparted strength, traversing all space, readily present to all at any place through their zeal for ministry and the agility of their nature... different individuals of them embracing different parts of the world, or appointed over different districts of the Universe, as He knoweth who ordered and distributed it all. Combining all things in one, solely with a view to the consent of the Creator of all things; Hymners of the Majesty of the Godhead, eternally contemplating the Eternal Glory, not that God may thereby gain an increase of glory, for nothing can be added to that which is full — to Him, who supplies good to all outside Himself but that there may never be a cessation of blessings to these first natures after God. If we have told these things as they deserve, it is by the grace of the Trinity, and of the one Godhead in Three Persons; but if less perfectly than we have desired, yet even so our discourse has gained its purpose. For this is what we were laboring to shew, that even the secondary natures surpass the power of our intellect; much more then the First and (for I fear to say merely That which is above all), the only Nature.

On the Son.

I. This then is what might be said to cut short our opponents' readiness to argue and their hastiness with its consequent insecurity in all matters, but above all in those discussions which relate to God. But since to rebuke others is a matter of no difficulty whatever, but a very easy thing, which any one who likes can do; whereas to substitute one's own belief for theirs is the part of a pious and intelligent man; let us, relying on the Holy Ghost, Who among them is dishonored, but among us is adored, bring forth to the light our own conceptions about the Godhead, whatever these may be, like some noble and timely birth. Not that I have at other times been silent; for on this subject alone I am full of youthful strength and daring; but the fact is that under present circumstances I am even more bold to declare the truth, that I may not (to use the words of Scripture) by drawing back fall into the condemnation of being displeasing to God. And since every discourse is of a twofold nature, the one part establishing one's own, and the other overthrowing one's opponents' position; let us first of all state our own position, and then try to controvert that of our opponents; — and both as briefly as possible, so that our arguments may be taken in at a glance (like those of the elementary treatises which they have devised to deceive simple or foolish persons), and that our thoughts may not be scattered by reason of the length of the discourse, like water which is not contained in a channel, but flows to waste over the open land.

II. The three most ancient opinions concerning God are Anarchia, Polyarchia, and Monarchia. The first two are the sport of the children of Hellas, and may they continue to be so. For Anarchy is a thing without order; and the Rule of Many is factious, and thus anarchical, and thus disorderly. For both these tend to the same thing, namely disorder; and this to dissolution, for disorder is the first step to dissolution. But Monarchy is that which we hold in honor. It is, however, a Monarchy that is not limited to one Person, for it is possible for Unity if at variance with itself to come into a condition of plurality; but one which is made of an equality of Nature and a Union of mind, and an identity of motion, and a convergence of its elements to unity — a thing which is impossible to the created nature — so that though numerically distinct there is no severance of Essence. Therefore Unity having from all eternity arrived by motion at Duality, found its rest in Trinity. This is what we mean by Father and Son and Holy Ghost. The Father is the Begetter and the Emitter; without passion of course, and without reference to time, and not in a corporeal manner. The Son is the Begotten, and the Holy Ghost the Emission; for I know not how this could be expressed in terms altogether excluding visible things. For we shall not venture to speak of "an overflow of goodness," as one of the Greek Philosophers dared to say, as if it were a bowl overflowing, and this in plain words in his Discourse on the First and Second Causes. Let us not ever look on this Generation as involuntary, like some natural overflow, hard to be retained, and by no means befitting our conception of Deity. Therefore let us confine ourselves within our limits, and speak of the Unbegotten and the Begotten and That which proceeds from the Father, as somewhere God the Word Himself saith.

III. When did these come into being? They are above all "When." But, if I am to speak with something more of boldness, — when the Father did. And when did the Father come into being. There never was a time when He was not. And the same thing is true of the Son and the Holy Ghost. Ask me again, and again I will answer you, When was the Son begotten? When the Father was not begotten. And when did the Holy Ghost proceed? When the Son was, not proceeding but, begotten — beyond the sphere of time, and above the grasp of reason; although we cannot set forth that which is above time, if we avoid as we desire any expression which conveys the idea of time. For such expressions as "when" and "before" and "after" and "from the beginning" are not timeless, however much we may force them; unless indeed we were to take the Aeon, that interval which is coextensive with the eternal things, and is not divided or measured by any motion, or by the revolution of the sun, as time is measured. How then are They not alike unoriginate, if They are coeternal? Because They are from Him, though not after Him. For that which is unoriginate is eternal, but that which is eternal is not necessarily unoriginate, so long as it may be referred to the Father as its origin. Therefore in respect of Cause They are not unoriginate; but it is evident that the Cause is not necessarily prior to its effects, for the sun is not prior to its light. And yet They are in some sense unoriginate, in respect of time, even though you would scare simple minds with your quibbles, for the Sources of Time are not subject to time.

IV. But how can this generation be passionless? In that it is incorporeal. For if corporeal generation involves passion, incorporeal generation excludes it. And I will ask of you in turn, How is He God if He is created? For that which is created is not God. I refrain from reminding you that here too is passion if we take the creation in a bodily sense, as time, desire, imagination, thought, hope, pain, risk, failure, success, all of which and more than all find a place in the creature, as is evident to every one. Nay, I marvel that you do not venture so far as to conceive of marriages and times of pregnancy, and dangers of miscarriage, as if the Father could not have begotten at all if He had not begotten thus; or again, that you did not count up the modes of generation of birds and beasts and fishes, and bring under some one of them the Divine and Ineffable Generation, or even eliminate the Son out of your new hypothesis. And you cannot even see this, that as His Generation according to the flesh differs from all others (for where among men do you know of a Virgin Mother?), so does He differ also in His spiritual Generation; or rather He, Whose Existence is not the same as ours, differs from us also in His Generation.

V. Who then is that Father Who had no beginning? One Whose very Existence had no beginning; for one whose existence had a beginning must also have begun to be a Father. He did not then become a Father after He began to be, for His being had no beginning. And He is Father in the absolute sense, for He is not also Son; just as the Son is Son in the absolute sense, because He is not also Father. These names do not belong to us in the absolute sense, because we are both, and not one more than the other; and we are of both, and not of one only; and so we are divided, and by degrees become men, and perhaps not even men, and such as we did not desire, leaving and being left, so that only the relations remain, without the underlying facts. But, the objector says, the very form of the expression "He begat" and "He was begotten," brings in the idea of a beginning of generation. But what if you do not use this expression, but say, "He had been begotten from the beginning" so as readily to evade your far-fetched and time-loving objections? Will you bring Scripture against us, as if we were forging something contrary to Scripture and to the truth? Why, every one knows that in practice we very often find tenses interchanged when time is spoken of; and especially is this the custom of Holy Scripture, not only in respect of the past tense, and of the present; but even of the future, as for instance "Why did the heathen rage?" when they had not yet raged and "they shall cross over the river on foot," where the meaning is they did cross over. It would be a long task to reckon up all the expressions of this kind which students have noticed.

VI. So much for this point. What is their next objection, how full of contentiousness and impudence? He, they say, either voluntarily begat the Son, or else involuntarily. Next, as they think, they bind us on both sides with cords; these however are not strong, but very weak. For, they say, if it was involuntarily He was under the sway of some one, and who exercised this sway? And how is He, over whom it is exercised, God? But if voluntarily, the Son is a Son of Will; how then is He of the Father? — and they thus invent a new sort of Mother for him, — the Will, — in place of the Father. There is one good point which they may allege about this argument of theirs; namely, that they desert Passion, and take refuge in Will. For Will is not Passion. Secondly, let us look at the strength of their argument. And it were best to wrestle with them at first at close quarters. You yourself, who so recklessly assert whatever takes your fancy; were you begotten voluntarily or involuntarily by your father? If involuntarily, then he was under some tyrant's sway (O terrible violence!) and who was the tyrant? You will hardly say it was nature, — for nature is tolerant of chastity. If it was voluntarily, then by a few syllables your father is done away with, for you are shewn to be the son of Will, and not of your father. But I pass to the relation between God and the creature, and I put your own question to your own wisdom. Did God create all things voluntarily or under compulsion? If under compulsion, here also is the tyranny, and one who played the tyrant; if voluntarily, the creatures also are deprived of their God, and you before the rest, who invent such arguments and tricks of logic. For a partition is set up between the Creator and the creatures in the shape of Will. And yet I think that the Person who wills is distinct from the Act of willing; He who begets from the Act of begetting; the Speaker from the speech, or else we are all very stupid. On the one side we have the mover, and on the other that which is, so to speak, the motion. Thus the thing willed is not the child of will, for it does not always result therefrom; nor is that which is begotten the child of generation, nor that which is heard the child of speech, but of the Person who willed, or begat, or spoke. But the things of God are beyond all this, for with Him perhaps the Will to beget is generation, and there is no intermediate action (if we may accept this altogether, and not rather consider generation superior to will).

VII. Will you then let me play a little upon this word Father, for your example encourages me to be so bold? The Father is God either willingly or unwillingly; and how will you escape from your own excessive acuteness? If willingly, when did He begin to will? It could not have been before He began to be, for there was nothing prior to Him. Or is one part of Him Will and another the object of Will? If so, He is divisible. So the question arises, as the result of your argument, whether He Himself is not the Child of Will. And if unwillingly, what compelled Him to exist, and how is He God if He was compelled — and that to nothing less than to be God? How then was He begotten, says my opponent. How was He created, if as you say, He was created? For this is a part of the same difficulty. Perhaps you would say, By Will and Word. You have not yet solved the whole difficulty; for it yet remains for you to shew how Will and Word gained the power of action. For man was not created in this way.

VIII. How then was He begotten? This Generation would have been no great thing, if you could have comprehended it who have no real knowledge even of your own generation, or at least who comprehend very little of it, and of that little you are ashamed to speak; and then do you think you know the whole? You will have to undergo much labor before you discover the laws of composition, formation, manifestation, and the bond whereby soul is united to body, — mind to soul, and reason to mind; and movement, increase, assimilation of food, sense, memory, recollection, and all the rest of the parts of which you are compounded; and which of them belongs to the soul and body together, and which to each independently of the other, and which is received from each other. For those parts whose maturity comes later, yet received their laws at the time of conception. Tell me what these laws are? And do not even then venture to speculate on the Generation of God; for that would be unsafe. For even if you knew all about your own, yet you do not by any means know about God's. And if you do not understand your own, how can you know about God's? For in proportion as God is harder to trace out than man, so is the heavenly Generation harder to comprehend than your own. But if you assert that because you cannot comprehend it, therefore He cannot have been begotten, it will be time for you to strike out many existing things which you cannot comprehend; and first of all God Himself. For you cannot say what He is, even if you are very reckless, and excessively proud of your intelligence. First, cast away your notions of flow and divisions and sections, and your conceptions of immaterial as if it were material birth, and then you may perhaps worthily conceive of the Divine Generation. How was He begotten? — I repeat the question in indignation. The Begetting of God must be honored by silence. It is a great thing for you to learn that He was begotten. But the manner of His generation we will not admit that even Angels can conceive, much less you. Shall I tell you how it was? It was in a manner known to the Father Who begat, and to the Son Who was begotten. Anything more than this is hidden by a cloud, and escapes your dim sight.

IX. Well, but the Father begat a Son who either was or was not in existence. What utter nonsense! This is a question which applies to you or me, who on the one hand were in existence, as for instance Levi in the loins of Abraham; and on the other hand came into existence; and so in some sense we are partly of what existed, and partly of what was nonexistent; whereas the contrary is the case with the original matter, which was certainly created out of what was non-existent, notwithstanding that some pretend that it is unbegotten. But in this case "to be begotten," even from the beginning, is concurrent with "to be." On what then will you base this captious question? For what is older than that which is from the beginning, if we may place there the previous existence or non-existence of the Son? In either case we destroy its claim to be the Beginning. Or perhaps you will say, if we were to ask you whether the Father was of existent or non-existent substance, that he is twofold, partly pre-existing, partly existing; or that His case is the same with that of the Son; that is, that He was created out of non-existing matter, because of your ridiculous questions and your houses of sand, which cannot stand against the merest ripple. I do not admit either solution, and I declare that your question contains an absurdity, and not a difficulty to answer. If however you think, in accordance with your dialectic assumptions, that one or other of these alternatives must necessarily be true in every case, let me ask you one little question: Is time in time, or is it not in time? If it is contained in time, then in what time, and what is it but that time, and how does it contain it? But if it is not contained in time, what is that surpassing wisdom which can conceive of a time which is timeless? Now, in regard to this expression, "I am now telling a lie," admit one of these alternatives, either that it is true, or that it is a falsehood, without qualification (for we cannot admit that it is both). But this cannot be. For necessarily he either is lying, and so is telling the truth, or else he is telling the truth, and so is lying. What wonder is it then that, as in this case contraries are true, so in that case they should both be untrue, and so your clever puzzle prove mere foolishness? Solve me one more riddle. Were you present at your own generation, and are you now present to yourself, or is neither the case? If you were and are present, who were you, and with whom are you present? And how did your single self become thus both subject and object? But if neither of the above is the case, how did you get separated from yourself, and what is the cause of this disjoining? But, you will say, it is stupid to make a fuss about the question whether or no a single individual is present to himself; for the expression is not used of oneself but of others. Well, you may be certain that it is even more stupid to discuss the question whether That which was begotten from the beginning existed before its generation or not. For such a question arises only as to matter divisible by time.

X. But they say, The Unbegotten and the Begotten are not the same; and if this is so, neither is the Son the same as the Father. It is clear, without saying so, that this line of argument manifestly excludes either the Son or the Father from the Godhead. For if to be Unbegotten is the Essence of God, to be begotten is not that Essence; if the opposite is the case, the Unbegotten is excluded. What argument can contradict this? Choose then whichever blasphemy you prefer, my good inventor of a new theology, if indeed you are anxious at all costs to embrace a blasphemy. In the next place, in what sense do you assert that the Unbegotten and the Begotten are not the same? If you mean that the Uncreated and the created are not the same, I agree with you; for certainly the Unoriginate and the created are not of the same nature. But if you say that He That begat and That which is begotten are not the same, the statement is inaccurate. For it is in fact a necessary truth that they are the same. For the nature of the relation of Father to Child is this, that the offspring is of the same nature with the parent. Or we may argue thus again. What do you mean by Unbegotten and Begotten, for if you mean the simple fact of being unbegotten or begotten, these are not the same; but if you mean Those to Whom these terms apply, how are They not the same? For example, Wisdom and Unwisdom are not the same in themselves, but yet both are attributes of man, who is the same; and they mark not a difference of essence, but one external to the essence, (a) Are immortality and innocence and immutability also the essence of God? If so God has many essences and not one; or Deity is a compound of these. For He cannot be all these without composition, if they be essences.

XI They do not however assert this, for these qualities are common also to other beings. But God's Essence is that which belongs to God alone, and is proper to Him. But they, who consider matter and form to be unbegotten, would not allow that to be unbegotten is the property of God alone (for we must cast away even further the darkness of the Manichaeans. But suppose that it is the property of God alone. What of Adam? Was he not alone the direct creature of God? Yes, you will say. Was he then the only human being? By no means. And why, but because humanity does not consist in direct creation? For that which is begotten is also human. Just so neither is He Who is Unbegotten alone God, though He alone is Father. But grant that He Who is Begotten is God; for He is of God, as you must allow, even though you cling to your Unbegotten. Then how do you describe the Essence of God? Not by declaring what it is, but by rejecting what it is not. For your word signifies that He is not begotten; it does not present to you what is the real nature or condition of that which has no generation. What then is the Essence of God? It is for your infatuation to define this, since you are so anxious about His Generation too; but to us it will be a very great thing, if ever, even in the future, we learn this, when this darkness and dullness is done away for us, as He has promised Who cannot lie. This then may be the thought and hope of those who are purifying themselves with a view to this. Thus much we for our part will be bold to say, that if it is a great thing for the Father to be Unoriginate, it is no less a thing for the Son to have been Begotten of such a Father. For not only would He share the glory of the Unoriginate, since he is of the Unoriginate, but he has the added glory of His Generation, a thing so great and august in the eyes of all those who are not altogether groveling and material in mind.

XII. But, they say, if the Son is the Same as the Father in respect of Essence, then if the Father is unbegotten, the Son must be so likewise. Quite so — if the Essence of God consists in being unbegotten; and so He would be a strange mixture, begottenly unbegotten. If, however, the difference is outside the Essence, how can you be so certain in speaking of this? Are you also your father's father, so as in no respect to fall short of your father, since you are the same with him in essence? Is it not evident that our enquiry into the Nature of the Essence of God, if we make it, will leave Personality absolutely unaffected? But that Unbegotten is not a synonym of God is proved thus. If it were so, it would be necessary that since God is a relative term, Unbegotten should be so likewise; or that since Unbegotten is an absolute term, so must God be.... God of no one. For words which are absolutely identical are similarly applied. But the word Unbegotten is not used relatively. For to what is it relative? And of what things is God the God? Why, of all things. How then can God and Unbegotten be identical terms? And again, since Begotten and Unbegotten are contradictories, like possession and deprivation, it would follow that contradictory essences would co-exist, which is impossible. Or again, since possessions are prior to deprivations, and the latter are destructive of the former, not only must the Essence of the Son be prior to that of the Father, but it must be destroyed by the Father, on your hypothesis.

XIII. What now remains of their invincible arguments? Perhaps the last they will take refuge in is this. If God has never ceased to beget, the Generation is imperfect; and when will He cease? But if He has ceased, then He must have begun. Thus again these carnal minds bring forward carnal arguments. Whether He is eternally begotten or not, I do not yet say, until I have looked into the statement, "Before all the hills He begetteth Me," more accurately. But I cannot see the necessity of their conclusion. For if, as they say, everything that is to come to an end had also a beginning, then surely that which has no end had no beginning. What then will they decide concerning the soul, or the Angelic nature? If it had a beginning, it will also have an end; and if it has no end, it is evident that according to them it had no beginning. But the truth is that it had a beginning, and will never have an end. Their assertion, then, that which will have an end had also a beginning, is untrue. Our position, however, is, that as in the case of a horse, or an ox, or a man, the same definition applies to all the individuals of the same species, and whatever shares the definition has also a right to the Name; so In the very same way there is One Essence of God, and One Nature, and One Name; although in accordance with a distinction in our thoughts we use distinct Names and that whatever is properly called by this Name really is God; and what He is in Nature, That He is truly called — if at least we are to hold that Truth is a matter not of names but of realities. But our opponents, as if they were afraid of leaving any stone unturned to subvert the Truth, acknowledge indeed that the Son is God when they are compelled to do so by arguments and evidences; but they only mean that He is God in an ambiguous sense, and that He only shares the Name.

XIV. And when we advance this objection against them, "What do you mean to say then? That the Son is not properly God, just as a picture of an animal is not properly an animal? And if not properly God, in what sense is He God at all?" They reply, Why should not these terms be ambiguous, and in both cases be used in a proper sense? And they will give us such instances as the land-dog and the dogfish; where the word Dog is ambiguous, and yet in both cases is properly used, for there is such a species among the ambiguously named, or any other case in which the same appellative is used for two things of different nature, But, my good friend, in this case, when you include two natures under the same name, you do not assert that either is better than the other, or that the one is prior and the other posterior, or that one is in a greater degree and the other in a lesser that which is predicated of them both, for there is no connecting link which forces this necessity upon them. One is not a dog more than the other, and one less so; either the dogfish more than the land-dog, or the land-dog than the dogfish. Why should they be, or on what principle? But the community of name is here between things of equal value, though of different nature. But in the case of which we are speaking, you couple the Name of God with adorable Majesty, and make It surpass every essence and nature (an attribute of God alone), and then you ascribe this Name to the Father, while you deprive the Son of it, and make Him subject to the Father, and give Him only a secondary honor and worship; and even if in words you bestow on Him one which is Equal, yet in practice you cut off His Deity, and pass malignantly from a use of the same Name implying an exact equality, to one which connects things which are not equal. And so the pictured and the living man are in your mouth an apter illustration of the relations of Deity than the dogs which I instanced. Or else you must concede to both an equal dignity of nature as well as a common name — even though you introduced these natures into your argument as different; and thus you destroy the analogy of your dogs, which you invented as an instance of inequality. For what is the force of your instance of ambiguity, if those whom you distinguish are not equal in honor? For it was not to prove an equality but an inequality that you took refuge in your dogs. How could anybody be more clearly convicted of fighting both against his own arguments, and against the Deity?

XV. And if, when we admit that in respect of being the Cause the Father is greater than the Son, they should assume the premise that He is the Cause by Nature, and then deduce the conclusion that He is greater by Nature also, it is difficult to say whether they mislead most themselves or those with whom they are arguing. For it does not absolutely follow that all that is predicated of a class can also be predicated of all the individuals composing it; for the different particulars may belong to different individuals. For what hinders me, if I assume the same premise, namely, that the Father is greater by Nature, and then add this other, Yet not by nature in every respect greater nor yet Father — from concluding, Therefore the Greater is not in every respect greater, nor the Father in every respect Father? Or, if you prefer it, let us put it in this way: God is an Essence: But an Essence is not in every case God; and draw the conclusion for yourself — Therefore God is not in every case God. I think the fallacy here is the arguing from a conditioned to an unconditioned use of a term, to use the technical expression of the logicians. For while we assign this word Greater to His Nature viewed as a Cause, they infer it of His Nature viewed in itself. It is just as if when we said that such a one was a dead man they were to infer simply that he was a Man.

XVI. How shall we pass over the following point, which is no less amazing than the rest? Father, they say, is a name either of an essence or of an Action, thinking to bind us down on both sides. If we say that it is a name of an essence, they will say that we agree with them that the Son is of another Essence, since there is but one Essence of God, and this, according to them, is preoccupied by the Father. On the other hand, if we say that it is the name of an Action, we shall be supposed to acknowledge plainly that the Son is created and not begotten. For where there is an Agent there must also be an Effect. And they will say they wonder how that which is made can be identical with That which made it. I should myself have been frightened with your distinction, if it had been necessary to accept one or other of the alternatives, and not rather put both aside, and state a third and truer one, namely, that Father is not a name either of an essence or of an action, most clever sirs. But it is the name of the Relation in which the Father stands to the Son, and the Son to the Father. For as with us these names make known a genuine and intimate relation, so, in the case before us too, they denote an identity of nature between Him That is begotten and Him That begets. But let us concede to you that Father is a name of essence, it will still bring in the idea of Son, and will not make it of a different nature, according to common ideas and the force of these names. Let it be, if it so please you, the name of an action; you will not defeat us in this way either. The Homoousion would be indeed the result of this action, or otherwise the conception of an action in this matter would be absurd. You see then how, even though you try to fight unfairly, we avoid your sophistries. But now, since we have ascertained how invincible you are in your arguments and sophistries, let us look at your strength in the Oracles of God, if perchance you may choose to persuade us out of them.

XVII. For we have learnt to believe in and to teach the Deity of the Son from their great and lofty utterances. And what utterances are these? These: God — The Word — He That Was In The Beginning and With The Beginning, and The Beginning. "In the Beginning was The Word, and the Word was with God, and the Word was God," and "With Thee is the Beginning," and "He who calleth her The Beginning from generations." Then the Son is Only -begotten: The only "begotten Son which is in the bosom of the Father, it says, He hath declared Him." The Way, the Truth, the Life, the Light. "I am the Way, the Truth, and the Life;"

and "I am the Light of the World." Wisdom and Power, "Christ, the Wisdom of God, and the Power of God." The Effulgence, the Impress, the Image, the Seal; "Who being the Effulgence of His glory and the Impress of His Essence," and "the Image of His Goodness," and "Him hath God the Father sealed." Lord, King, He That Is, The Almighty. "The Lord rained down fire from the Lord; " and "A scepter of righteousness is the scepter of Thy Kingdom;" and "Which is and was and is to come, the Almighty" — all which are clearly spoken of the Son, with all the other passages of the same force, none of which is an afterthought, or added later to the Son or the Spirit, any more than to the Father Himself. For Their Perfection is not affected by additions. There never was a time when He was without the Word, or when He was not the Father, or when He was not true, or not wise, or not powerful, or devoid of life, or of splendor, or of goodness. But in opposition to all these, do you reckon up for me the expressions which make for your ignorant arrogance, such as "My God and your God," or greater, or created, or made, or sanctified; Add, if you like, Servant and Obedient and Gave and Learnt, and was commanded, was sent, can do nothing of Himself, either say, or judge, or give, or will. And further these, — His ignorance, subjection, prayer, asking, increase, being made perfect. And if you like even more humble than these; such as speak of His sleeping, hungering, being in an agony, and fearing; or perhaps you would make even His Cross and Death a matter of reproach to Him. His Resurrection and Ascension I fancy you will leave to me, for in these is found something to support our position. A good many other things too you might pick up, if you desire to put together that equivocal and intruded God of yours, Who to us is True God, and equal to the Father. For every one of these points, taken separately, may very easily, if we go through them one by one, be explained to you in the most reverent sense, and the stumbling-block of the letter be cleaned away — that is, if your stumbling at it be honest, and not willfully malicious. To give you the explanation in one sentence. What is lofty you are to apply to the Godhead, and to that Nature in Him which is superior to sufferings and incorporeal; but all that is lowly to the composite condition of Him who for your sakes made Himself of no reputation and was Incarnate-yes, for it is no worse thing to say, was made Man, and afterwards was also exalted. The result will be that you will abandon these carnal and groveling doctrines, and learn to be more sublime, and to ascend with His Godhead, and you will not remain permanently among the things of sight, but will rise up with Him into the world of thought, and come to know which passages refer to His Nature, and which to His assumption of Human Nature.

XIX. For He Whom you now treat with contempt was once above you. He Who is now Man was once the Uncompounded. What He was He continued to be; what He was not He took to Himself. In the beginning He was, uncaused; for what is the Cause of God? But afterwards for a cause He was born. And that came was that you might be saved, who insult Him and despise His Godhead, because of this, that He took upon Him your denser nature, having converse with Flesh by means of

Mind. While His inferior Nature, the Humanity, became God, because it was united to God, and became One Person because the Higher Nature prevailed in order that I too might be made Goal so far as He is made Man. He was born — but He had been begotten: He was born of a woman — but she was a Virgin. The first is human the second Divine. In His Human nature He had no Father, but also in His Divine Nature no Mother. Both these belong to Godhead. He dwelt in the womb — but He was recognized by the Prophet, himself still in the womb, leaping before the Word, for Whose sake He came into being. He was wrapped in swaddling clothes — but He took off the swathing bands of the grave by His rising again. He was laid in a manger — but He was glorified by Angels, and proclaimed by a star, and worshipped by the Magi. Why are you offended by that which is presented to your sight, because you will not look at that which is presented to your mind? He was driven into exile into Egypt — but He drove away the Egyptian idols. He had no form nor comeliness in the eyes of the Jews — but to David He is fairer than the children of men. And on the Mountain He was bright as the lightning, and became more luminous than the sun, initiating us into the mystery of the future.

XX. He was baptized as Man — but He remitted sins as God — not because He needed purificatory rites Himself, but that He might sanctify the element of water. He was tempted as Man, but He conquered as God; yea, He bids us be of good cheer, for He has overcome the world. He hungered — but He fed thousands; yea, He is the Bread that giveth life, and That is of heaven. He thirsted — but He cried, If any man thirst, let him come unto Me and drink. Yea, He promised that fountains should flow from them that believe. He was wearied, but He is the Rest of them that are weary and heavy laden. He was heavy with sleep, but He walked lightly over the sea. He rebuked the winds, He made Peter light as he began to sink. He pays tribute, but it is out of a fish; yea, He is the King of those who demanded it. He is called a Samaritan and a demoniac; — but He saves him that came down from Jerusalem and fell among thieves; the demons acknowledge Him, and He drives out demons and sinks in the sea legions of foul spirits, and sees the Prince of the demons falling like lightning. He is stoned, but is not taken. He prays, but He hears prayer. He weeps, but He causes tears to cease. He asks where Lazarus was laid, for He was Man; but He raises Lazarus, for He was God. He is sold, and very cheap, for it is only for thirty pieces of silver; but He redeems the world, and that at a great price, for the Price was His own blood. As a sheep He is led to the slaughter, but He is the Shepherd of Israel, and now of the whole world also. As a Lamb He is silent, yet He is the Word, and is proclaimed by the Voice of one crying in the wilderness. He is bruised and wounded, but He healeth every disease and every infirmity. He is lifted up and nailed to the Tree, but by the Tree of Life He restoreth us; yea, He saveth even the Robber crucified with Him; yea, He wrapped the visible world in darkness. He is given vinegar to drink mingled with gall. Who? He who turned the water into wine? who is the destroyer of the bitter taste, who is Sweetness and altogether desire. He lays down His life, but He has power to take it again; and the veil is rent, for the mysterious doors of Heaven are opened; the rocks are cleft, the dead arise. He dies, but He gives life, and by His death destroys death. He is buried, but He rises again; He goes down into Hell, but He brings up the souls; He ascends to Heaven, and shall come again to judge the quick and the dead, and to put to the test such words as yours. If the one give you a starting point for your error, let the others put an end to it.

XXI. This, then, is our reply to those who would puzzle us; not given willingly indeed (for light talk and contradictions of words are not agreeable to the faith fill, and one Adversary is enough for us), but of necessity, for the sake of our assailants (for medicines exist because of diseases), that they may be led to see that they are not all-wise nor invincible in those superfluous arguments which make void the Gospel. For when we leave off believing, and protect ourselves by mere strength of argument, and destroy the claim which the Spirit has upon our faith by questionings, and then our argument is not strong enough for the importance of the subject (and this must necessarily be the case, since it is put in motion by an organ of so little power as is our mind), what is the result? The weakness of the argument appears to belong to the mystery, and thus elegance of language makes void the Cross, as Paul also thought. For faith is that which completes our argument. But may He who proclaimeth unions and looseth those that are bound, and who putteth into our minds to solve the knots of their unnatural dogmas, if it may be, change these men and make them faithful instead of rhetoricians, Christians instead of that which they now are called. This indeed we entreat and beg for Christ' s sake. Be ye reconciled to God, and quench not the Spirit; or rather, may Christ be reconciled to you, and may the Spirit enlighten you, though so late. But if you are too fond of your quarrel, we at any rate will hold fast to the Trinity, and by the Trinity may we be saved, remaining pure and without offense, until the more perfect shewing forth of that which we desire, in Him, Christ our Lord, to Whom be the glory for ever. Amen.

150

Which is the second concerning the Son

I. Since I have by the power of the Spirit sufficiently overthrown the subtleties and intricacies of the arguments, and already solved in the mass the objections and oppositions drawn from Holy Scripture, with which these sacrilegious robbers of the Bible and thieves of the sense of its contents draw over the multitude to their side, and confuse the way of truth; and that not without clearness, as I believe all candid persons will say; attributing to the Deity the higher and diviner expressions, and the lower and more human to Him Who for us men was the Second Adam, and was God made capable of suffering to strive against sin; yet we have not yet gone through the passages in detail, because of the haste of our argument. But since you demand of us a brief explanation of each of them, that you may not be carried away by the plausibilities of their arguments, we will therefore state the explanations summarily, dividing them into numbers for the sake of carrying them more easily in mind.

II. In their eyes the following is only too ready to hand "The Lord created me at the beginning of His ways with a view to His works." How shall we meet this? Shall we bring an accusation against Solomon, or reject his former words because of his fall in after-life? Shall we say that the words are those of Wisdom herself, as it were of Knowledge and the Creator-word, in accordance with which all things were made? For Scripture often personifies many even lifeless objects; as for instance, "The Sea said" so and so; and, "The Depth saith, It is not in me;" and "The Heavens declare the glory of God;" and again a command is given to the Sword; and the Mountains and Hills are asked the reason of their skipping. We do not allege any of these, though some of our predecessors used them as powerful arguments. But let us grant that the expression is used of our Savior Himself, the true Wisdom. Let us consider one small point together. What among all things that exist is unoriginate? The Godhead. For no one can tell the origin of God, that otherwise would be older than God. But what is the cause of the Manhood, which for our sake God assumed? It was surely our Salvation. What else could it be? Since then we find here clearly both the Created and the Begetteth Me, the argument is simple. Whatever we find joined with a cause we are to refer to the Manhood, but all that is absolute and unoriginate we are to reckon to the account of His Godhead. Well, then, is not this "Created" said in connection with a cause? He created Me, it so says, as the beginning of His ways, with a view to his works. Now, the Works of His Hands are verity and judgment; for whose sake He was anointed with Godhead;; for this anointing is of the Manhood; but the "He begetteth Me" is not connected with a cause; or it is for you to shew the adjunct. What argument then will disprove that Wisdom is called a creature, in connection with the lower generation, but Begotten in respect of the first and more incomprehensible?

III. Next is the fact of His being called Servant and serving many well, and that it is a great thing for Him to be called the Child of God. For in truth He was in

151

servitude to flesh and to birth and to the conditions of our life with a view to our liberation, and to that of all those whom He has saved, who were in bondage under sin. What greater destiny can befall man's humility than that he should be intermingled with God, and by this intermingling should be deified, and that we should be so visited by the Dayspring from on high, that even that Holy Thing that should be born should be called the Son of the Highest, and that there should be bestowed upon Him a Name which is above every name? And what else can this be than God? — and that every knee should bow to Him That was made of no reputation for us, and That mingled the Form of God with the form of a servant, and that all the House of Israel should know that God hath made Him both Lord and Christ? For all this was done by the action of the Begotten, and by the good pleasure of Him That begat Him.

IV. Well, what is the second of their great irresistible passages? "He must reign," till such and such a time... and "be received by heaven until the time of restitution," and "have the seat at the Right Hand until the overthrow of His enemies." But after this? Must He cease to be King, or be removed from Heaven? Why, who shall make Him cease, or for what cause? What a bold and very anarchical interpreter you are; and yet you have heard that Of His Kingdom there shall be no end. Your mistake arises from not understanding that Until is not always exclusive of that which comes after, but asserts up to that time, without denying what comes after it. To take a single instance — how else would you understand, "Lo, I am with you always, even unto the end of the world?" Does it mean that He will no longer be so afterwards. And for what reason? But this is not the only cause of your error; you also fail to distinguish between the things that are signified. He is said to reign in one sense as the Almighty King, both of the willing and the unwilling; but in another as producing in us submission, and placing us under His Kingship as willingly acknowledging His Sovereignty. Of His Kingdom, considered in the former sense, there shall be no end. But in the second sense, what end will there be? His taking us as His servants, on our entrance into a state of salvation. For what need is there to Work Submission in us when we have already submitted? After which He arises to judge the earth, and to separate the saved from the lost. After that He is to stand as God in the midst of gods, that is, of the saved, distinguishing and deciding of what honor and of what mansion each is worthy.

V. Take, in the next place, the subjection by which you subject the Son to the Father. What, you say, is He not now subject, or must He, if He is God, be subject to God? You are fashioning your argument as if it concerned some robber, or some hostile deity. But look at it in this manner: that as for my sake He was called a curse, Who destroyed my curse; and sin, who taketh away the sin of the world; and became a new Adam to take the place of the old, just so He makes my disobedience His own as Head of the whole body. As long then as I am disobedient and rebellious, both by denial of God and by my passions, so long Christ also is called disobedient on my account. But when all things shall be subdued unto Him on the one hand by acknowledgment of Him, and on the other by a reformation, then He Himself also will have fulfilled His submission, bringing me whom He has saved to God. For this, according to my view, is the subjection of Christ; namely, the fulfilling of the Father's Will. But as the Son subjects all to the Father, so does the Father to the Son; the One by His Work, the Other by His good pleasure, as we have already said. And thus He Who subjects presents to God that which he has subjected, making our condition His own. Of the same kind, it appears to me, is the expression, "My God, My God, why hast Thou forsaken Me?" It was not He who was forsaken either by the Father, or by His own Godhead, as some have thought, as if It were afraid of the Passion, and therefore withdrew Itself from Him in His Sufferings (for who compelled Him either to be born on earth at all, or to be lifted up on the Cross?) But as I said, He was in His own Person representing us. For we were the forsaken and despised before, but now by the Sufferings of Him Who could not suffer, we were taken up and saved. Similarly, He makes His own our folly and our transgressions; and says what follows in the Psalm, for it is very evident that the Twenty-first Psalm refers to Christ.

VI. The same consideration applies to another passage, "He learnt obedience by the things which He suffered," and to His "strong crying and tears," and His "Entreaties," and His "being heard," and His" Reverence," all of which He wonderfully wrought out, like a drama whose plot was devised on our behalf. For in His character of the Word He was neither obedient nor disobedient. For such expressions belong to servants, and inferiors, and the one applies to the better sort of them, while the other belongs to those who deserve punishment. But, in the character of the Form of a Servant, He condescends to His fellow servants, nay, to His servants, and takes upon Him a strange form, bearing all me and mine in Himself, that in Himself He may exhaust the bad, as fire does wax, or as the sun does the mists of earth; and that I may partake of His nature by the blending. Thus He honors obedience by His action, and proves it experimentally by His Passion. For to possess the disposition is not enough, just as it would not be enough for us, unless we also proved it by our acts; for action is the proof of disposition. And perhaps it would not be wrong to assume this also, that by the art of His love for man He gauges our obedience, and measures all by comparison with His own Sufferings, so that He may know our condition by His own, and how much is demanded of us, and how much we yield, taking into the account, along with our environment, our weakness also. For if the Light shining through the veil upon the darkness, that is upon this life, was persecuted by the other darkness (I mean, the Evil One and the Tempter), how much more will the darkness be persecuted, as being weaker than it? And what marvel is it, that though He entirely escaped, we have been, at any rate in part, overtaken? For it is a more wonderful thing that He should have been chased than that we should have been captured; — at least to the minds of all who reason aright on the subject. I will add yet another passage to those I have mentioned, because I think that it clearly tends to the same sense. I mean "In that He hath suffered being tempted, He is able to succor them that are tempted." But God will be all in all in the time of restitution; not in the sense that the Father alone will Be; and the Son be wholly resolved into Him, like a torch into a great pyre, from which it was reft away for a little space, and then put back (for I would not have even the Sabellians injured by such an expression); but the entire Godhead when we shall be no longer divided (as we now are by movements and passions), and containing nothing at all of God, or very little, but shall be entirely like.

VII. As your third point you count the Word Greater; and as your fourth, To My God and your God. And indeed, if He had been called greater, and the word equal had not occurred, this might perhaps have been a point in their favor. But if we find both words clearly used what will these gentlemen have to say? How will it strengthen their argument? How will they reconcile the irreconcilable? For that the same thing should be at once greater than and equal to the same thing is an impossibility; and the evident solution is that the Greater refers to origination, while the Equal belongs to the Nature; and this we acknowledge with much good will. But perhaps some one else will back up our attack on your argument, and assert, that That which is from such a Cause is not inferior to that which has no Cause; for it would share the glory of the Unoriginate, because it is from the Unoriginate. And there is, besides, the Generation, which is to all men a matter so marvelous and of such Majesty. For to say that he is greater than the Son considered as man, is true indeed, but is no great thing. For what marvel is it if God is greater than man? Surely that is enough to say in answer to their talk about Greater.

VIII. As to the other passages, My God would be used in respect, not of the Word, but of the Visible Word. For how could there be a God of Him Who is properly God? In the same way He is Father, not of the Visible, but of the Word; for our Lord was of two Natures; so that one expression is used properly, the other improperly in each of the two cases; but exactly the opposite way to their use in respect of us. For with respect to us God is properly our God, but not properly our Father. And this is the cause of the error of the Heretics, namely the joining of these two Names, which are interchanged because of the Union of the Natures. And an indication of this is found in the fact that wherever the Natures are distinguished in our thoughts from one another, the Names are also distinguished; as you hear in Paul's words, "The God of our Lord Jesus Christ, the Father of Glory." The God of Christ, but the Father of glory. For although these two terms express but one Person, yet this is not by a Unity of Nature, but by a Union of the two. What could be clearer?

IX. Fifthly, let it be alleged that it is said of Him that He receives life, judgment, inheritance of the Gentiles, or power over all flesh, or glory, or disciples, or whatever else is mentioned. This also belongs to the Manhood; and yet if you were to ascribe it to the Godhead, it would be no absurdity. For you would not so ascribe it as if it were newly acquired, but as belonging to Him from the beginning by reason of nature, and not as an act of favor.

X. Sixthly, let it be asserted that it is written, The Son can do nothing of Himself, but what He seeth the Father do. The solution of this is as follows: — Can and Cannot are not words with only one meaning, but have many meanings. On the one hand they are used sometimes in respect of deficiency of strength, sometimes in respect of time, and sometimes relatively to a certain object; as for instance, A Child cannot be an Athlete, or, A Puppy cannot see, or fight with so and so. Perhaps some day the child will be an athlete, the puppy will see, will fight with that other, though it may still be unable to fight with Any other. Or again, they may be used of that which is Generally true. For instance, — A city that is set on a hill cannot be hid; while yet it might possibly be hidden by another higher hill being in a line with it. Or in another sense they are used of a thing which is not reasonable; as, Can the Children of the Bridechamber fast while the Bridegroom is with them; whether He be considered as visible in bodily form (for the time of His sojourning among us was not one of mourning, but of gladness), or, as the Word. For why should they keep a bodily fast who are cleansed by the Word? Or, again, they are used of that which is contrary to the will; as in, He could do no mighty works there because of their unbelief, — i.e. of those who should receive them. For since in order to healing there is need of both faith in the patient and power in the Healer, when one of the two failed the other was impossible. But probably this sense also is to be referred to the head of the unreasonable. For healing is not reasonable in the case of those who would afterwards be injured by unbelief. The sentence The world cannot hate you, comes under the same head, as does also How can ye, being evil, speak good things? For in what sense is either impossible, except that it is contrary to the will? There is a somewhat similar meaning in the expressions which imply that a thing impossible by nature is possible to God if He so wills; as that a man cannot be born a second time, or that a needle will not let a camel through it. For what could prevent either of these things happening, if God so willed?

XI And besides all this, there is the absolutely impossible and inadmissible, as that which we are now examining. For as we assert that it is impossible for God to be evil, or not to exist — for this would be indicative of weakness in God rather than of strength — or for the non-existent to exist, or for two and two to make both four and ten, so it is impossible and inconceivable that the Son should do anything that the Father doeth not. For all things that the Father hath are the Son's; and on the other hand, all that belongs to the Son is the Father's. Nothing then is peculiar, because all things are in common. For Their Being itself is common and equal, even though the Son receive it from the Father. It is in respect of this that it is said I live by the Father; not as though His Life and Being were kept together by the Father, but because He has His Being from Him beyond all time, and beyond all cause. But how does He see the Father doing, and do likewise? Is it like those who copy pictures and letters, because they cannot attain the truth unless by looking at the original, and being led by the hand by it? But how shall Wisdom stand in need of a teacher, or be incapable of acting unless taught? And in what sense does the Father "Do" in the present or in the past? Did He make another world before this one, or is He going to make a world to come? And did the Son look at that and make this? Or will He look at the other, and make one like it? According to this argument there must be Four worlds, two made by the Father, and two by the Son. What an absurdity! He cleanses lepers, and delivers men from evil spirits, and diseases, and quickens the dead, and walks upon the sea, and does all His other works; but in what case, or when did the Father do these acts before Him? Is it not clear that the Father impressed the ideas of these same actions, and the Word brings them to pass, yet not in slavish or unskillful fashion, but with full knowledge and in a masterly way, or, to speak more properly, like the Father? For in this sense I understand the words that whatsoever is done by the Father, these things doeth the Son likewise; not, that is, because of the likeness of the things done, but in respect of the Authority. This might well also be the meaning of the passage which says that the Father worketh hitherto and the Son also; and not only so but it refers also to the government and preservation of the things which He has made; as is shewn by the passage which says that He maketh His Angels Spirits, and that the earth is founded upon its steadfastness (though once for all these things were fixed and made) and that the thunder is made firm and the wind created. Of all these things the Word was given once, but the Action is continuous even now.

XII. Let them quote in the seventh place that The Son came down from Heaven, not to do His own Will, but the Will of Him That sent Him. Well, if this had not been said by Himself Who came down, we should say that the phrase was modeled as issuing from the Human Nature, not from Him who is conceived of in His character as the Savior, for His Human Will cannot be opposed to God, seeing it is altogether taken into God; but conceived of simply as in our nature, inasmuch as the human will does not completely follow the Divine, but for the most part struggles against and resists it. For we understand in the same way the words, Father, if it be possible, let this cup pass from Me; Nevertheless let not what I will but Thy Will prevail. For it is not likely that He did not know whether it was possible or not, or that He would oppose will to will. But since, as this is the language of Him Who assumed our Nature (for He it was Who came down), and not of the Nature which He assumed, we must meet the objection in this way, that the passage does not mean that the Son has a special will of His own, besides that of the Father, but that He has not; so that the meaning would be, "not to do Mine own Will, for there is none of Mine apart from, but that which is common to, Me and Thee; for as We have one Godhead, so We have one Will." For many such expressions are used in relation to this Community, and are expressed not positively but negatively; as, e.g., God giveth not the Spirit by measure, for as a matter of fact He does not give the Spirit to the Son, nor does He measure It, for God is not measured by God; or again, Not my transgression nor my sin. The words are not used because He has these things, but because He has them not. And again, Not for our righteousness which we have done, for we have not done any. And this meaning is evident also in the clauses which follow. For what, says He, is the Will of My Father? That everyone that believeth on the Son should be saved, and obtain the final Resurrection. Now is this the Will of the Father, but not of the Son? Or does He preach the Gospel, and receive men's faith against His will? Who could believe that? Moreover, that passage, too, which says that the Word which is heard is not the Son's but the Father's has the same force. For I cannot see how that which is common to two can be said to belong to one alone, however much I consider it, and I do not think any one else can. If then you hold this opinion concerning the Will, you will be right and reverent in your opinion, as I think, and as every right-minded person thinks.

XIII. The eighth passage is, That they may know Thee, the only true God, and Jesus Christ Whom Thou hast sent; and There is none good save one, that is, God. The solution of this appears to me very easy. For if you attribute this only to the Father, where will you place the Very Truth? For if you conceive in this manner of the meaning of To the only wise God, or Who only hath Immortality, Dwelling in the light which no man can approach unto, or of to the king of the Ages, immortal, invisible, and only wise God, then the Son has vanished under sentence of death, or of darkness, or at any rate condemned to be neither wise nor king, nor invisible, nor God at all, which sums up all these points. And how will you prevent His Goodness, which especially belongs to God alone, from perishing with the rest? I, however, think that the passage That they may know Thee the only true God, was said to overthrow those gods which are falsely so called, for He would not have added and Jesus Christ Whom Thou hast sent, if The Only True God were contrasted with Him, and the sentence did not proceed upon the basis of a common Godhead. The "None is Good" meets the tempting Lawyer, who was testifying to His Goodness viewed as Man. For perfect goodness, He says, is God's alone, even if a man is called perfectly good. As for instance, A good man out of the good treasure of his heart bringeth forth good things. And, I will give the kingdom to one who is good above Thee.... Words of God, speaking to Saul about David. Or again, Do good, O Lord, unto the good... and all other like expressions concerning those of us who are praised, upon whom it is a kind of effluence from the Supreme Good, and has come to them in a secondary degree. It will be best of all if we can persuade you of this. But if not, what will you say to the suggestion on the other side, that on your hypothesis the Son has been called the only God. In what passage? Why, in this: — This is your God; no other shall be accounted of in comparison with Him, and a little further on, after this did He shew Himself upon earth, and conversed with men. This addition proves clearly that the words are not used of the Father, but of the Son; for it was He Who in bodily form companied with us, and was in this lower world. Now, if we should determine to take these words as said in contrast with the Father, and not with the imaginary gods, we lose the Father by the very terms which we were pressing against the Son. And what could be more disastrous than such a victory?

XIV. Ninthly, they allege, seeing He ever liveth to make intercession for us. O, how beautiful and mystical and kind. For to intercede does not imply to seek for vengeance, as is most men's way (for in that there would be something of humiliation), but it is to plead for us by reason of His Mediator ship, just as the Spirit also is said to make intercession for us. For there is One God, and One Mediator between God and Man, the Man Christ Jesus. For He still pleads even now as Man for my salvation; for He continues to wear the Body which He assumed, until He make me God by the power of His Incarnation; although He is no longer known after the flesh — I mean, the passions of the flesh, the same, except sin, as ours. Thus too, we have an Advocate, Jesus Christ, not indeed prostrating Himself for us before the Father, and falling down before Him in slavish fashion… Away with a suspicion so truly slavish and unworthy of the Spirit! For neither is it seemly for the Father to require this, nor for the Son to submit to it; nor is it just to think it of God. But by what He suffered as Man, He as the Word and the Counselor persuades Him to be patient. I think this is the meaning of His Advocacy.

XV. Their tenth objection is the ignorance, and the statement that Of the last day and hour knoweth no man, not even the Son Himself, but the Father. And yet how can Wisdom be ignorant of anything — that is, Wisdom Who made the worlds, Who perfects them, Who remodels them, Who is the Limit of all things that were made, Who knoweth the things of God as the spirit of a man knows the things that are in him? For what can be more perfect than this knowledge? How then can you say that all things before that hour He knows accurately, and all things that are to happen about the time of the end, but of the hour itself He is ignorant? For such a thing would be like a riddle; as if one were to say that he knew accurately all that was in front of the wall, but did not know the wall itself; or that, knowing the end of the day, he did not know the beginning of the night — where knowledge of the one necessarily brings in the other. Thus everyone must see that He knows as God, and knows not as Man; — if one may separate the visible from that which is discerned by thought alone. For the absolute and unconditioned use of the Name "The Son" in this passage, without the addition of whose Son, gives us this thought, that we are to understand the ignorance in the most reverent sense, by attributing it to the Manhood, and not to the Godhead.

XVI. If then this argument is sufficient, let us stop here, and not enquire further. But if not, our second argument is as follows: — Just as we do in all other instances, so let us refer His knowledge of the greatest events, in honor of the Father, to The Cause. And I think that anyone, even if he did not read it in the way that one of our own Students did, would soon perceive that not even the Son knows the day or hour otherwise than as the Father does. For what do we conclude from this? That since the Father knows, therefore also does the Son, as it is evident that this cannot be known or comprehended by any but the First Nature. There remains for us to interpret the passage about His receiving commandment, and

158

having kept His Commandments, and done always those things that please Him; and further concerning His being made perfect, and His exaltation, and His learning obedience by the things which He suffered; and also His High Priesthood, and His Oblation, and His Betrayal, and His prayer to Him That was able to save Him from death, and His Agony and Bloody Sweat and Prayer, and such like things; if it were not evident to every one that such words are concerned, not with That Nature Which is unchangeable and above all capacity of suffering, but with the passible Humanity. This, then, is the argument concerning these objections, so far as to be a sort of foundation and memorandum for the use of those who are better able to conduct the enquiry to a more complete working out. It may, however, be worth while, and will be consistent with what has been already said, instead of passing over without remark the actual Titles of the Son (there are many of them, and they are concerned with many of His Attributes), to set before you the meaning of each of them, and to point out the mystical meaning of the names.

XVII. We will begin thus. The Deity cannot be expressed in words. And this is proved to us, not only by argument, but by the wisest and most ancient of the Hebrews, so far as they have given us reason for conjecture. For they appropriated certain characters to the honor of the Deity, and would not even allow the name of anything inferior to God to be written with the same letters as that of God, because to their minds it was improper that the Deity should even to that extent admit any of His creatures to a share with Himself. How then could they have admitted that the invisible and separate Nature can be explained by divisible words? For neither has any one yet breathed the whole air, nor has any mind entirely comprehended, or speech exhaustively contained the Being of God. But we sketch Him by His Attributes, and so obtain a certain faint and feeble and partial idea concerning Him, and our best Theologian is he who has, not indeed discovered the whole, for our present chain does not allow of our seeing the whole, but conceived of Him to a greater extent than another, and gathered in himself more of the Likeness or adumbration of the Truth, or whatever we may call it.

XVIII. As far then as we can reach, He Who Is, and God, are the special names of His Essence; and of these especially He Who Is, not only because when He spake to Moses in the mount, and Moses asked what His Name was, this was what He called Himself, bidding him say to the people "I Am hath sent me," but also because we find that this Name is the more strictly appropriate. For the Name 6eo<; (God), even if, as those who are skillful in these matters say, it were derived from 0eeiv (to run) or from AiGeiv (to blaze), from continual motion, and because He consumes evil conditions of things (from which fact He is also called A Consuming Fire), would still be one of the Relative Names, and not an Absolute one; as again is the case with Lord, which also is called a name of God. I am the Lord Thy God, He says, that is My name; and, The Lord is His name. But we are enquiring into a Nature Whose Being is absolute and not into Being bound up with something else. But Being is in its proper sense peculiar to God, and belongs

159

to Him entirely, and is not limited or cut short by any Before or After, for indeed in him there is no past or future.

XIX. Of the other titles, some are evidently names of His Authority, others of His Government of the world, and of this viewed under a twofold aspect, the one before the other in the Incarnation. For instance the Almighty, the King of Glory, or of The Ages, or of The Powers, or of The Beloved, or of Kings. Or again the Lord of Sabaoth, that is of Hosts, or of Powers, or of Lords; these are clearly titles belonging to His Authority. But the God either of Salvation or of Vengeance, or of Peace, or of Righteousness; or of Abraham, Isaac, and Jacob, and of all the spiritual Israel that seeth God, — these belong to His Government. For since we are governed by these three things, the fear of punishment, the hope of salvation and of glory besides, and the practice of the virtues by which these are attained, the Name of the God of Vengeance governs fear, and that of the God of Salvation our hope, and that of the God of Virtues our practice; that whoever attains to any of these may, as carrying God in himself, press on yet more unto perfection, and to that affinity which arises out of virtues. Now these are Names common to the Godhead, but the Proper Name of the Unoriginate is Father, and that of the unoriginately Begotten is Son, and that of the unbegottenly Proceeding or going forth is The Holy Ghost. Let us proceed then to the Names of the Son, which were our starting point in this part of our argument.

XX. In my opinion He is called Son because He is identical with the Father in Essence; and not only for this reason, but also because He is Of Him. And He is called Only-Begotten, not because He is the only Son and of the Father alone, and only a Son; but also because the manner of His Sonship is peculiar to Himself and not shared by bodies. And He is called the Word, because He is related to the Father as Word to Mind; not only on account of His passionless Generation, but also because of the Union, and of His declaratory function. Perhaps too this relation might be compared to that between the Definition and the Thing defined since this also is called Aoyoc;. For, it says, he that hath mental perception of the Son (for this is the meaning of Hath Seen) hath also perceived the Father; and the Son is a concise demonstration and easy setting forth of the Father's Nature. For every thing that is begotten is a silent word of him that begat it. And if any one should say that this Name was given Him because He exists in all things that are, he would not be wrong. For what is there that consists but by the word? He is also called Wisdom, as the Knowledge of things divine and human. For how is it possible that He Who made all things should be ignorant of the reasons of what He has made? And Power, as the Sustainer of all created things, and the Furnisher to them of power to keep themselves together. And Truth, as being in nature One and not many (for truth is one and falsehood is manifold), and as the pure Seal of the Father and His most unerring Impress. And the Image as of one substance with Him, and because He is of the Father, and not the Father of Him. For this is of the Nature of an Image, to be the reproduction of its Archetype, and of that whose

160

name it bears; only that there is more here. For in ordinary language an image is a motionless representation of that which has motion; but in this case it is the living reproduction of the Living One, and is more exactly like than was Seth to Adam, or any son to his father. For such is the nature of simple Existences, that it is not correct to say of them that they are Like in one particular and Unlike in another; but they are a complete resemblance, and should rather be called Identical than Like. Moreover he is called Light as being the Brightness of souls cleansed by word and life. For if ignorance and sin be darkness, knowledge and a godly life will be Light…. And He is called Life, because He is Light, and is the constituting and creating Power of every reasonable soul. For in Him we live and move and have our being, according to the double power of that Breathing into us; for we were all inspired by Him with breath, and as many of us as were capable of it, and in so far as we open the mouth of our mind, with God the Holy Ghost. He is Righteousness, because He distributes according to that which we deserve, and is a righteous Arbiter both for those who are under the Law and for those who are under Grace, for soul and body, so that the former should rule, and the latter obey, and the higher have supremacy over the lower; that the worse may not rise in rebellion against the better. He is Sanctification, as being Purity, that the Pure may be contained by Purity. And Redemption, because He sets us free, who were held captive under sin, giving Himself a Ransom for us, the Sacrifice to make expiation for the world. And Resurrection, because He raises up from hence, and brings to life again us, who were slain by sin.

XXI. These names however are still common to Him Who is above us, and to Him Who came for our sake. But others are peculiarly our own, and belong to that nature which He assumed. So He is called Man, not only that through His Body He may be apprehended by embodied creatures, whereas otherwise this would be impossible because of His incomprehensible nature; but also that by Himself He may sanctify humanity, and be as it were a leaven to the whole lump; and by uniting to Himself that which was condemned may release it from all condemnation, becoming for all men all things that we are, except sin; — body, soul, mind and all through which death reaches — and thus He became Man, who is the combination of all these; God in visible form, because He retained that which is perceived by mind alone. He is Son of Man, both on account of Adam, and of the Virgin from Whom He came; from the one as a forefather, from the other as His Mother, both in accordance with the law of generation, and apart from it. He is Christ, because of His Godhead. For this is the Anointing of His Manhood, and does not, as is the case with all other Anointed Ones, sanctify by its action, but by the Presence in His Fullness of the Anointing One; the effect of which is that That which anoints is called Man, and makes that which is anointed God. He is The Way, because He leads us through Himself; The Door, as letting us in; the Shepherd, as making us dwell in a place of green pastures, and bringing us up by waters of rest, and leading us there, and protecting us from wild beasts, converting the erring, bringing back that which was lost, binding up that which was broken, guarding the strong, and bringing them together in the Fold beyond, with words of pastoral knowledge. The Sheep, as the Victim: The Lamb, as being perfect: the Highpriest, as the Offerer; Melchisedec, as without Mother in that Nature which is above us, and without Father in ours; and without genealogy above (for who, it says, shall declare His generation?) and moreover, as King of Salem, which means Peace, and King of Righteousness, and as receiving tithes from Patriarchs, when they prevail over powers of evil. They are the titles of the Son. Walk through them, those that are lofty in a godlike manner; those that belong to the body in a manner suitable to them; or rather, altogether in a godlike manner, that thou mayest become a God, ascending from below, for His sake Who came down from on high for ours. In all and above all keep to this, and thou shalt never err, either in the loftier or the lowlier names; Jesus Christ is the Same yesterday and today in the Incarnation, and in the Spirit for ever and ever. Amen.

On the Holy Spirit

I. Such then is the account of the Son, and in this manner He has escaped those who would stone Him, passing through the midst of them. For the Word is not stoned, but cats stones when He pleases; and uses a sling against wild beasts — that is, words — approaching the Mount in an unholy way. But, they go on, what have you to say about the Holy Ghost? From whence are you bringing in upon us this strange God, of Whom Scripture is silent? And even they who keep within bounds as to the Son speak thus. And just as we find in the case of roads and rivers, that they split off from one another and join again, so it happens also in this case, through the superabundance of impiety, that people who differ in all other respects have here some points of agreement, so that you never can tell for certain either where they are of one mind, or where they are in conflict.

II. Now the subject of the Holy Spirit presents a special difficulty, not only because when these men have become weary in their disputations concerning the Son, they struggle with greater heat against the Spirit (for it seems to be absolutely necessary for them to have some object on which to give expression to their impiety, or life would appear to them no longer worth living), but further because we ourselves also, being worn out by the multitude of their questions, are in something of the same condition with men who have lost their appetite; who having taken a dislike to some particular kind of food, shrink from all food; so we in like manner have an aversion from all discussions. Yet may the Spirit grant it to us, and then the discourse will proceed, and God will be glorified. Well then, we will leave to others who have worked upon this subject for us as well as for themselves, as we have worked upon it for them, the task of examining carefully and distinguishing in how many senses the word Spirit or the word Holy is used and understood in Holy Scripture, with the evidence suitable to such an enquiry; and of shewing how besides these the combination of the two words — I mean, Holy Spirit — is used in a peculiar sense; but we will apply ourselves to the remainder of the subject.

III. They then who are angry with us on the ground that we are bringing in a strange or interpolated God, viz.: — the Holy Ghost, and who fight so very hard for the letter, should know that they are afraid where no fear is; and I would have them clearly understand that their love for the letter is but a cloak for their impiety, as shall be shewn later on, when we refute their objections to the utmost of our power. But we have so much confidence in the Deity of the Spirit Whom we adore, that we will begin our teaching concerning His Godhead by fitting to Him the Names which belong to the Trinity, even though some persons may think us too bold. The Father was the True Light which lighteneth every man coming into the world. The Son was the True Light which lighteneth every man coming into the world. The Other Comforter was the True Light which lighteneth every man coming into the world, Was and Was and Was, but Was One Thing. Light thrice repeated; but One Light and One God. This was what David represented to himself long before when he said. In Thy Light shall we see Light. And now we have both seen and proclaim concisely and simply the doctrine of God the Trinity, comprehending out of Light (the Father), Light (the Son), in Light (the Holy Ghost). He that rejects it, let him reject it; and he that doeth iniquity, let him do iniquity; we proclaim that which we have understood. We will get us up into a high mountain, and will shout, if we be not heard, below; we will exalt the Spirit; we will not be afraid; or if we are afraid, it shall be of keeping silence, not of proclaiming.

IV. If ever there was a time when the Father was not, then there was a time when the Son was not. If ever there was a time when the Son was not, then there was a time when the Spirit was not. If the One was from the beginning, then the Three were so too. If you throw down the One, I am bold to assert that you do not set up the other Two. For what profit is there in an imperfect Godhead? Or rather, what Godhead can there be if It is not perfect? And how can that be perfect which lacks something of perfection? And surely there is something lacking if it hath not the Holy, and how would it have this if it were without the Spirit? For either holiness is something different from Him, and if so let some one tell me what it is conceived to be; or if it is the same, how is it not from the beginning, as if it were better for God to be at one time imperfect and apart from the Spirit? If He is not from the beginning, He is in the same rank with myself, even though a little before me; for we are both parted from Godhead by time. If He is in the same rank with myself, how can He make me God, or join me with Godhead?

V. Or rather, let me reason with you about Him from a somewhat earlier point, for we have already discussed the Trinity. The Sadducees altogether denied the existence of the Holy Spirit, just as they did that of Angels and the Resurrection; rejecting, I know not upon what ground, the important testimonies concerning Him in the Old Testament. And of the Greeks those who are more inclined to speak of God, and who approach nearest to us, have formed some conception of Him, as it seems to me, though they have differed as to His Name, and have addressed Him as the Mind of the World, or the External Mind, and the like. But of the wise men amongst ourselves, some have conceived of him as an Activity, some as a Creature, some as God; and some have been uncertain which to call Him, out of reverence for Scripture, they say, as though it did not make the matter clear either way. And therefore they neither worship Him nor treat Him with dishonor, but take up a neutral position, or rather a very miserable one, with respect to Him. And of those who consider Him to be God, some are orthodox in mind only, while others venture to be so with the lips also. And I have heard of some who are even more clever, and measure Deity; and these agree with us that there are Three Conceptions; but they have separated these from one another so completely as to make one of them infinite both in essence and power, and the second in power but not in essence, and the third circumscribed in both; thus imitating in another way those who call them the Creator, the Co-operator, and the Minister, and consider that the same order and dignity which belongs to these names is also a sequence in the facts.

VI. But we cannot enter into any discussion with those who do not even believe in His existence, nor with the Greek babblers (for we would not be enriched in our argument with the oil of sinners). With the others, however, we will argue thus. The Holy Ghost must certainly be conceived of either as in the category of the Self-existent, or as in that of the things which are contemplated in another; of which classes those who are skilled in such matters call the one Substance and the other Accident. Now if He were an Accident, He would be an Activity of God, for what else, or of whom else, could He be, for surely this is what most avoids composition? And if He is an Activity, He will be effected, but will not effect and will cease to exist as soon as He has been effected, for this is the nature of an Activity. How is it then that He acts and says such and such things, and defines, and is grieved, and is angered, and has all the qualities which belong clearly to one that moves, and not to movement? But if He is a Substance and not an attribute of Substance, He will be conceived of either as a Creature of God, or as God. For anything between these two, whether having nothing in common with either, or a compound of both, not even they who invented the goat-stag could imagine. Now, if He is a creature, how do we believe in Him, how are we made perfect in Him? For it is not the same thing to believe In a thing and to believe About it. The one belongs to Deity, the other to — any thing. But if He is God, then He is neither a creature, nor a thing made, nor a fellow servant, nor any of these lowly appellations.

VII. There — the word is with you. Let the slings be let go; let the syllogism be woven. Either He is altogether Unbegotten, or else He is Begotten. If He is Unbegotten, there are two Unoriginates. If he is Begotten, you must make a further subdivision. He is so either by the Father or by the Son. And if by the Father, there are two Sons, and they are Brothers. And you may make them twins if you like, or the one older and the other younger, since you are so very fond of the bodily conceptions. But if by the Son, then such a one will say, we get a glimpse of a Grandson God, than which nothing could be more absurd. For my part however, if I saw the necessity of the distinction, I should have acknowledged the facts without fear of the names. For it does not follow that because the Son is the Son in some higher relation (inasmuch as we could not in any other way than this point out that He is of God and Consubstantial), it would also be necessary to think that all the names of this lower world and of our kindred should be transferred to the Godhead. Or may be you would consider our God to be a male, according to the same arguments, because he is called God and Father, and that Deity is feminine, from the gender of the word, and Spirit neuter, because It has nothing to do with generation; But if you would be silly enough to say, with the old myths and fables, that God begat the Son by a marriage with His own Will, we should be introduced to the Hermaphrodite God of Marcion and Valentinus who imagined these newfangled Aeons.

165

VIII. But since we do not admit your first division, which declares that there is no mean between Begotten and Unbegotten, at once, along with your magnificent division, away go your Brothers and your Grandsons, as when the first link of an intricate chain is broken they are broken with it, and disappear from your system of divinity. For, tell me, what position will you assign to that which Proceeds, which has started up between the two terms of your division, and is introduced by a better Theologian than you, our Savior Himself? Or perhaps you have taken that word out of your Gospels for the sake of your Third Testament, The Holy Ghost, which proceedeth from the Father; Who, inasmuch as He proceedeth from That Source, is no Creature; and inasmuch as He is not Begotten is no Son; and inasmuch as He is between the Unbegotten and the Begotten is God. And thus escaping the toils of your syllogisms, He has manifested himself as God, stronger than your divisions. What then is Procession? Do you tell me what is the Unbegottenness of the Father, and I will explain to you the physiology of the Generation of the Son and the Procession of the Spirit, and we shall both of us be frenzy- stricken for prying into the mystery of God. And who are we to do these things, we who cannot even see what lies at our feet, or number the sand of the sea, or the drops of rain, or the days of Eternity, much less enter into the Depths of God, and supply an account of that Nature which is so unspeakable and transcending all words?

IX. What then, say they, is there lacking to the Spirit which prevents His being a Son, for if there were not something lacking He would be a Son? We assert that there is nothing lacking — for God has no deficiency. But the difference of manifestation, if I may so express myself, or rather of their mutual relations one to another, has caused the difference of their Names. For indeed it is not some deficiency in the Son which prevents His being Father (for Sonship is not a deficiency), and yet He is not Father. According to this line of argument there must be some deficiency in the Father, in respect of His not being Son. For the Father is not Son, and yet this is not due to either deficiency or subjection of Essence; but the very fact of being Unbegotten or Begotten, or Proceeding has given the name of Father to the First, of the Son to the Second, and of the Third, Him of Whom we are speaking, of the Holy Ghost that the distinction of the Three Persons may be preserved in the one nature and dignity of the Godhead. For neither is the Son Father, for the Father is One, but He is what the Father is; nor is the Spirit Son because He is of God, for the Only-begotten is One, but He is what the Son is. The Three are One in Godhead, and the One Three in properties; so that neither is the Unity a Sabellian one, nor does the Trinity countenance the present evil distinction.

X. What then? Is the Spirit God? Most certainly. Well then, is He Consubstantial? Yes, if He is God. Grant me, says my opponent, that there spring from the same Source One who is a Son, and One who is not a Son, and these of One Substance with the Source, and I admit a God and a God. Nay, if you will grant me that there is another God and another nature of God I will give you the same Trinity with the same name and facts. But since God is One and the Supreme Nature is One, how can I present to you the Likeness? Or will you seek it again in lower regions and in your own surroundings? It is very shameful, and not only shameful, but very foolish, to take from things below a guess at things above, and from a fluctuating nature at the things that are unchanging, and as Isaiah says, to seek the Living among the dead. But yet I will try, for your sake, to give you some assistance for your argument, even from that source. I think I will pass over other points, though I might bring forward many from animal history, some generally known, others only known to a few, of what nature has contrived with wonderful art in connection with the generation of animals. For not only are likes said to beget likes, and things diverse to beget things diverse, but also likes to be begotten by things diverse, and things diverse by likes. And if we may believe the story, there is yet another mode of generation, when an animal is self-consumed and self -begotten. There are also creatures which depart in some sort from their true natures, and undergo change and transformation from one creature into another, by a magnificence of nature. And indeed sometimes in the same species part may be generated and part not; and yet all of one substance; which is more like our present subject. I will just mention one fact of our own nature which every one knows, and then I will pass on to another part of the subject.

XI What was Adam? A creature of God. What then was Eve? A fragment of the creature. And what was Seth? The begotten of both. Does it then seem to you that Creature and Fragment and Begotten are the same thing? Of course it does not. But were not these persons consubstantial? Of course they were. Well then, here it is an acknowledged fact that different persons may have the same substance. I say this, not that I would attribute creation or fraction or any property of body to the Godhead (let none of your contenders for a word be down upon me again), but that I may contemplate in these, as on a stage, things which are objects of thought alone. For it is not possible to trace out any image exactly to the whole extent of the truth. But, they say, what is the meaning of all this? For is not the one an offspring, and the other a something else of the One? Did not both Eve and Seth come from the one Adam? And were they both begotten by him? No; but the one was a fragment of him, and the other was begotten by him. And yet the two were one and the same thing; both were human beings; no one will deny that. Will you then give up your contention against the Spirit, that He must be either altogether begotten, or else cannot be consubstantial, or be God; and admit from human examples the possibility of our position? I think it will be well for you, unless you are determined to be very quarrelsome, and to fight against what is proved to demonstration.

XII. But, he says, who in ancient or modern times ever worshipped the Spirit? Who ever prayed to Him? Where is it written that we ought to worship Him, or to pray to Him, and whence have you derived this tenet of yours? We will give the more perfect reason hereafter, when we discuss the question of the unwritten; for the present it will suffice to say that it is the Spirit in Whom we worship, and in Whom we pray. For Scripture says, God is a Spirit, and they that worship Him must worship Him in Spirit and in truth. And again, — We know not what we should pray for as we ought; but the Spirit Itself maketh intercession for us with groanings which cannot be uttered; and I will pray with the Spirit and I will pray with the understanding also; — that is, in the mind and in the Spirit. Therefore to adore or to pray to the Spirit seems to me to be simply Himself offering prayer or adoration to Himself. And what godly or learned man would disapprove of this, because in fact the adoration of One is the adoration of the Three, because of the equality of honor and Deity. between the Three? So I will not be frightened by the argument that all things are said to have been made by the Son; as if the Holy Spirit also were one of these things. For it says all things that were made, and not simply all things. For the Father was not, nor were any of the things that were not made. Prove that He was made, and then give Him to the Son, and number Him among the creatures; but until you can prove this you will gain nothing for your impiety from this comprehensive phrase. For if He was made, it was certainly through Christ; I myself would not deny that. But if He was not made, how can He be either one of the All, or through Christ? Cease then to dishonor the Father in your opposition to the Only-begotten (for it is no real honor, by presenting to Him a creature to rob Him of what is more valuable, a Son), and to dishonor the Son in your opposition to the Spirit. For He is not the Maker of a Fellow servant, but He is glorified with One of co-equal honor. Rank no part of the Trinity with thyself, lest thou fall away from the Trinity; cut not off from Either the One and equally august Nature; because if thou overthrow any of the Three thou wilt have overthrown the whole. Better to take a meager view of the Unity than to venture on a complete impiety.

XIII. Our argument has now come to its principal point; and I am grieved that a problem that was long dead, and that had given way to faith, is now stirred up afresh; yet it is necessary to stand against these praters, and not to let judgment go by default, when we have the Word on our side, and are pleading the cause of the Spirit. If, say they, there is God and God and God, how is it that there are not Three Gods, or how is it that what is glorified is not a plurality of Principles? Who is it who say this? Those who have reached a more complete ungodliness, or even those who have taken the secondary part; I mean who are moderate in a sense in respect of the Son. For my argument is partly against both in common, partly against these latter in particular. What I have to say in answer to these is as follows: — What right have you who worship the Son, even though you have revolted from the Spirit, to call us Tritheists? Are not you Ditheists? For if you deny also the worship of the Only Begotten, you have clearly ranged yourself among our adversaries. And why should we deal kindly with you as not quite dead? But if you do worship Him, and are so far in the way of salvation, we will ask you what reasons you have to give for your ditheism, if you are charged with it? If there is in you a word of wisdom answer, and open to us also a way to an answer. For the very same reason with which you will repel a charge of Ditheism will prove sufficient for us against one of Tritheism. And thus we shall win the day by making use of you our accusers as our Advocates, than which nothing can be more generous.

XIV. What is our quarrel and dispute with both? To us there is One God, for the Godhead is One, and all that proceedeth from Him is referred to One, though we believe in Three Persons. For one is not more and another less God; nor is One before and another after; nor are They divided in will or parted in power; nor can you find here any of the qualities of divisible things; but the Godhead is, to speak concisely, undivided in separate Persons; and there is one mingling of Light, as it were of three suns joined to each other. When then we look at the Godhead, or the First Cause, or the Monarchia, that which we conceive is One; but when we look at the Persons in Whom the Godhead dwells, and at Those Who tunelessly and with equal glory have their Being from the First Cause — there are Three Whom we worship.

XV. What of that, they will say perhaps; do not the Greeks also believe in one Godhead, as their more advanced philosophers declare? And with us Humanity is one, namely the entire race; but yet they have many gods, not One, just as there are many men. But in this case the common nature has a unity which is only conceivable in thought; and the individuals are parted from one another very far indeed, both by time and by dispositions and by power. For we are not only compound beings, but also contrasted beings, both with one another and with ourselves; nor do we remain entirely the same for a single day, to say nothing of a whole lifetime, but both in body and in soul are in a perpetual state of flow and change. And perhaps the same may be said of the Angels and the whole of that superior nature which is second to the Trinity alone; although they are simple in some measure and more fixed in good, owing to their nearness to the highest Good.

XVI. Nor do those whom the Greeks worship as gods, and (to use their own expression) demons, need us in any respect for their accusers, but are convicted upon the testimony of their own theologians, some as subject to passion, some as given to faction, and full of innumerable evils and changes, and in a state of opposition, not only to one another, but even to their first causes, whom they call Oceani and Tethyes and Phanetes, and by several other names; and last of all a certain God who hated his children through his lust of rule, and swallowed up all the rest through his greediness that he might become the father of all men and gods whom he miserably devoured, and then vomited forth again. And if these are but myths and fables, as they say in order to escape the shamefulness of the story, what will they say in reference to the dictum that all things are divided into three parts, and that each God presides over a different part of the Universe, having a distinct province as well as a distinct rank? But our faith is not like this, nor is this the portion of Jacob, says my Theologian. But each of these Persons possesses Unity, not less with that which is United to it than with itself, by reason of the identity of Essence and Power. And this is the account of the Unity, so far as we have apprehended it. If then this account is the true one, let us thank God for the glimpse He has granted us; if it is not let us seek for a better.

XVII. As for the arguments with which you would overthrow the Union which we support, I know not whether we should say you are jesting or in earnest. For what is this argument? "Things of one essence, you say, are counted together," and by this "counted together," you mean that they are collected into one number. But things which are not of one essence are not thus counted. ..so that you cannot avoid speaking of three gods, according to this account, while we do not run any risk at all of it, inasmuch as we assert that they are not consubstantial. And so by a single word you have freed yourselves from trouble, and have gained a pernicious victory, for in fact you have done something like what men do when they hang themselves for fear of death. For to save yourselves trouble in your championship of the Monarchia you have denied the Godhead, and abandoned the question to your opponents. But for my part, even if labor should be necessary, I will not abandon the Object of my adoration. And yet on this point I cannot see where the difficulty is.

XVIII. You say, Things of one essence are counted together, but those which are not con- substantial are reckoned one by one. Where did you get this from? From what teachers of dogma or mythology? Do you not know that every number expresses the quantity of what is included under it, and not the nature of the things? But I am so old fashioned, or perhaps I should say so unlearned, as to use the word Three of that number of things, even if they are of a different nature, and to use One and One and One in a different way of so many units, even if they are united in essence, looking not so much at the things themselves as at the quantity of the things in respect of which the enumeration is made. But since you hold so very close to the letter (although you are contending against the letter), pray take your demonstrations from this source. There are in the Book of Proverbs three things which go well, a lion, a goat, and a cock; and to these is added a fourth; — a King making a speech before the people, to pass over the other sets of four which are there counted up, although things of various natures. And I find in Moses two Cherubim counted singly. But now, in your technology, could either the former things be called three, when they differ so greatly in their nature, or the latter be treated as units when they are so closely connected and of one nature? For if I were to speak of God and Mammon, as two masters, reckoned under one head, when they are so very different from each other, I should probably be still more laughed at for such a connumeration.

XIX. But to my mind, he says, those things are said to be connumerated and of the same essence of which the names also correspond, as Three Men, or Three gods, but not Three this and that. What does this concession amount to? It is suitable to one laying down the law as to names, not to one who is asserting the truth. For I also will assert that Peter and James and John are not three or consubstantial, so long as I cannot say Three Peters, or Three Jameses, or Three Johns; for what you have reserved for common names we demand also for proper names, in accordance with your arrangement; or else you will be unfair in not conceding to others what you assume for yourself. What about John then, when in his Catholic Epistle he says that there are Three that bear witness, the Spirit and the Water and the Blood? Do you think he is talking nonsense? First, because he has ventured to reckon under one numeral things which are not consubstantial, though you say this ought to be done only in the case of things which are consubstantial. For who would assert that these are consubstantial? Secondly, because he has not been consistent in the way he has happened upon his terms; for after using Three in the masculine gender he adds three words which are neuter, contrary to the definitions and laws which you and your grammarians have laid down. For what is the difference between putting a masculine Three first, and then adding One and One and One in the neuter, or after a masculine One and One and One to use the Three not in the masculine but in the neuter, which you yourself disclaim in the case of Deity? What have you to say about the Crab, which may mean either an animal, or an instrument, or a constellation? And what about the Dog, now terrestrial, now aquatic, now celestial? Do you not see that three crabs or dogs are spoken of? Why of course it is so. Well then, are they therefore of one substance? None but a fool would say that. So you see how completely your argument from con-numeration has broken down, and is refuted by all these instances. For if things that are of one substance are not always counted under one numeral, and things not of one substance are thus counted, and the pronunciation of the name once for all is used in both cases, what advantage do you gain towards your doctrine?

XX. I will look also at this further point, which is not without its bearing on the subject. One and One added together make Two; and Two resolved again becomes One and One, as is perfectly evident. If, however, elements which are added together must, as your theory requires, be consubstantial, and those which are separate be heterogeneous, then it will follow that the same things must be both consubstantial and heterogeneous. No: I laugh at your Counting Before and your Counting After, of which you are so proud, as if the facts themselves depended upon the order of their names. If this were so, according to the same law, since the same things are in consequence of the equality of their nature counted in Holy Scripture, sometimes in an earlier, sometimes in a later place, what prevents them from being at once more honorable and less honorable than themselves? I say the same of the names God and Lord, and of the prepositions Of Whom, and By Whom, and In Whom, by which you describe the Deity according to the rules of art for us, attributing the first to the Father, the second to the Son, and the third to the Holy Ghost. For what would you have done, if each of these expressions were constantly allotted to Each Person, when, the fact being that they are used of all the Persons, as is evident to those who have studied the question, you even so make them the ground of such inequality both of nature and dignity. This is sufficient for all who are not altogether wanting in sense. But since it is a matter of difficulty for you after you have once made an assault upon the Spirit, to check your rush, and not rather like a furious boar to push your quarrel to the bitter end, and to thrust yourself upon the knife until you have received the whole wound in your own breast; let us go on to see what further argument remains to you.

XXI. Over and over again you turn upon us the silence of Scripture. But that it is not a strange doctrine, nor an afterthought, but acknowledged and plainly set forth both by the ancients and many of our own day, is already demonstrated by many persons who have treated of this subject, and who have handled the Holy Scriptures, not with indifference or as a mere pastime, but have gone beneath the letter and looked into the inner meaning, and have been deemed worthy to see the hidden beauty, and have been irradiated by the light of knowledge. We, however in our turn will briefly prove it as far as may be, in order not to seem to be over-curious or improperly ambitious, building on another's foundation. But since the fact, that Scripture does not very clearly or very often write Him God in express words (as it does first the Father and afterwards the Son), becomes to you an occasion of blasphemy and of this excessive wordiness and impiety, we will release you from this inconvenience by a short discussion of things and names, and especially of their use in Holy Scripture.

XXII. Some things have no existence, but are spoken of; others which do exist are not spoken of; some neither exist nor are spoken of, and some both exist and are spoken of. Do you ask me for proof of this? I am ready to give it. According to Scripture God sleeps and is awake, is angry, walks, has the Cherubim for His Throne. And yet when did He become liable to passion, and have you ever heard that God has a body? This then is, though not really fact, a figure of speech. For we have given names according to our own comprehension from our own attributes to those of God. His remaining silent apart from us, and as it were not caring for us, for reasons known to Himself, is what we call His sleeping; for our own sleep is such a state of inactivity. And again, His sudden turning to do us good is the waking up; for waking is the dissolution of sleep, as visitation is of turning away. And when He punishes, we say He is angry; for so it is with us, punishment is the result of anger. And His working, now here now there, we call walking; for walking is change from one place to another. His resting among the Holy Hosts, and as it were loving to dwell among them, is His sitting and being enthroned; this, too, from ourselves, for God resteth nowhere as He doth upon the Saints. His swiftness of moving is called flying, and His watchful care is called His Face, and his giving and bestowing is His hand; and, in a word, every other of the powers or activities of God has depicted for us some other corporeal one.

XXIII. Again, where do you get your Unbegotten and Unoriginate, those two citadels of your position, or we our Immortal? Show me these in so many words, or we shall either set them aside, or erase them as not contained in Scripture; and you are slain by your own principle, the names you rely on being overthrown, and therewith the wall of refuge in which you trusted. Is it not evident that they are due to passages which imply them, though the words do not actually occur? What are these passages? — I am the first, and I am the last, and before Me there was no God, neither shall there be after Me. For all that depends on that Am makes for my side, for it has neither beginning nor ending. When you accept this, that nothing is before Him, and that He has not an older Cause, you have implicitly given Him the titles Unbegotten and Unoriginate. And to say that He has no end of Being is to call Him Immortal and Indestructible. The first pairs, then, that I referred to are accounted for thus. But what are the things which neither exist in fact nor are said? That God is evil; that a sphere is square; that the past is present; that man is not a compound being. Have you ever known a man of such stupidity as to venture either to think or to assert any such thing? It remains to shew what are the things which exist, both in fact and in language. God, Man, Angel, Judgment, Vanity (viz., such arguments as yours), and the subversion of faith and emptying of the mystery.

XXIV. Since, then, there is so much difference in terms and things, why are you such a slave to the letter, and a partisan of the Jewish wisdom, and a follower of syllables at the expense of facts? But if, when you said twice five or twice seven, I concluded from your words that you meant Ten or Fourteen; or if, when you spoke of a rational and mortal animal, that you meant Man, should you think me to be talking nonsense? Surely not, because I should be merely repeating your own meaning; for words do not belong more to the speaker of them than to him who called them forth. As, then, in this case, I should have been looking, not so much at the terms used, as at the thoughts they were meant to convey; so neither, if I found something else either not at all or not clearly expressed in the Words of Scripture to be included in the meaning, should I avoid giving it utterance, out of fear of your sophistical trick about terms. In this way, then, we shall hold our own against the semi-orthodox — among whom I may not count you. For since you deny the Titles of the Son, which are so many and so clear, it is quite evident that even if you learnt a great many more and clearer ones you would not be moved to reverence. But now I will take up the argument again a little way further back, and shew you, though you are so clever, the reason for this entire system of secrecy.

XXV. There have been in the whole period of the duration of the world two conspicuous changes of men's lives, which are also called two Testaments, or, on account of the wide fame of the matter, two Earthquakes; the one from idols to the Law, the other from the Law to the Gospel. And we are taught in the Gospel of a third earthquake, namely, from this Earth to that which cannot be shaken or moved. Now the two Testaments are alike in this respect, that the change was not made on a sudden, nor at the first movement of the endeavor. Why not (for this is a point on which we must have information)? That no violence might be done to us, but that we might be moved by persuasion. For nothing that is involuntary is durable; like streams or trees which are kept back by force. But that which is voluntary is more durable and safe. The former is due to one who uses force, the latter is ours; the one is due to the gentleness of God, the other to a tyrannical authority. Wherefore God did not think it behooved Him to benefit the unwilling, but to do good to the willing. And therefore like a Tutor or Physician He partly removes and partly condones ancestral habits, conceding some little of what tended to pleasure, just as medical men do with their patients, that their medicine may be taken, being artfully blended with what is nice. For it is no very easy matter to change from those habits which custom and use have made honorable. For instance, the first cut off the idol, but left the sacrifices; the second, while it destroyed the sacrifices did not forbid circumcision. Then, when once men had submitted to the curtailment, they also yielded that which had been conceded to them; in the first instance the sacrifices, in the second circumcision; and became instead of Gentiles, Jews, and instead of Jews, Christians, being beguiled into the Gospel by gradual changes. Paul is a proof of this; for having at one time administered circumcision, and submitted to legal purification, he advanced till he could say, and I, brethren, if I yet preach circumcision, why do I yet suffer persecution? His former conduct belonged to the temporary dispensation, his latter to maturity.

XXVI. To this I may compare the case of Theology except that it proceeds the reverse way. For in the case by which I have illustrated it the change is made by successive subtractions; whereas here perfection is reached by additions. For the matter stands thus. The Old Testament proclaimed the Father openly, and the Son more obscurely. The New manifested the Son, and suggested the Deity of the Spirit. Now the Spirit Himself dwells among us, and supplies us with a clearer demonstration of Himself. For it was not safe, when the Godhead of the Father was not yet acknowledged, plainly to proclaim the Son; nor when that of the Son was not yet received to burden us further (if I may use so bold an expression) with the Holy Ghost; lest perhaps people might, like men loaded with food beyond their strength, and presenting eyes as yet too weak to bear it to the sun's light, risk the loss even of that which was within the reach of their powers; but that by gradual additions, and, as David says, Goings up, and advances and progress from glory to glory, the Light of the Trinity might shine upon the more illuminated. For this reason it was, I think, that He gradually came to dwell in the Disciples, measuring Himself out to them according to their capacity to receive Him, at the beginning of the Gospel, after the Passion, after the Ascension, making perfect their powers, being breathed upon them, and appearing in fiery tongues. And indeed it is by little and little that He is declared by Jesus, as you will learn for yourself if you will read more carefully. I will ask the Father, He says, and He will send you another Comforter, even the spirit of Truth. This He said that He might not seem to be a rival God, or to make His discourses to them by another authority. Again, He shall send Him, but it is in My Name. He leaves out the I will ask, but He keeps the Shall send, then again, I will send, — His own dignity. Then shall come, the authority of the Spirit.

XXVII. You see lights breaking upon us, gradually; and the order of Theology, which it is better for us to keep, neither proclaiming things too suddenly, nor yet keeping them hidden to the end. For the former course would be unscientific, the latter atheistical; and the former would be calculated to startle outsiders, the latter to alienate our own people. I will add another point to what I have said; one which may readily have come into the mind of some others, but which I think a fruit of my own thought. Our Savior had some things which, He said, could not be borne at that time by His disciples (though they were filled with many teachings), perhaps for the reasons I have mentioned; and therefore they were hidden. And again He said that all things should be taught us by the Spirit when He should come to dwell amongst us. Of these things one, I take it, was the Deity of the Spirit Himself, made clear later on when such knowledge should be seasonable and capable of being received after our Savior's restoration, when it would no longer be received with incredulity because of its marvelous character. For what greater thing than this did either He promise, or the Spirit teach. If indeed anything is to be considered great and worthy of the Majesty of God, which was either promised or taught.

XXVIII. This, then, is my position with regard to these things, and I hope it may be always my position, and that of whosoever is dear to me; to worship God the Father, God the Son, and God the Holy Ghost, Three Persons, One Godhead, undivided in honor and glory and substance and kingdom, as one of our own inspired philosophers not long departed shewed. Let him not see the rising of the Morning Star, as Scripture saith, nor the glory of its brightness, who is otherwise minded, or who follows the temper of the times, at one time being of one mind and of another at another time, and thinking unsoundly in the highest matters. For if He is not to be worshipped, how can He deify me by Baptism? but if He is to be worshipped, surely He is an Object of adoration, and if an Object of adoration He must be God; the one is linked to the other, a truly golden and saving chain. And indeed from the Spirit comes our New Birth, and from the New Birth our new creation, and from the new creation our deeper knowledge of the dignity of Him from Whom it is derived.

XXIX. This, then, is what may be said by one who admits the silence of Scripture. But now the swarm of testimonies shall burst upon you from which the Deity of the Holy Ghost shall be shewn to all who are not excessively stupid, or else altogether enemies to the Spirit, to be most clearly recognized in Scripture. Look at these facts: — Christ is born; the Spirit is His Forerunner. He is baptized; the Spirit bears witness. He is tempted; the Spirit leads Him up. He works miracles; the Spirit accompanies them. He ascends; the Spirit takes His place. What great things are there in the idea of God which are not in His power? What titles which belong to God are not applied to Him, except only Unbegotten and Begotten? For it was needful that the distinctive properties of the Father and the Son should remain peculiar to Them, lest there should be confusion in the Godhead Which brings all things, even disorder itself, into due arrangement and good order. Indeed I tremble when I think of the abundance of the titles, and how many Names they outrage who fall foul of the Spirit. He is called the Spirit of God, the Spirit of Christ, the Mind of Christ, the Spirit of The Lord, and Himself The Lord, the Spirit of Adoption, of Truth, of Liberty; the Spirit of Wisdom, of Understanding, of Counsel, of Might, of Knowledge, of Godliness, of the Fear of God. For He is the Maker of all these, filling all with His Essence, containing all things, filling the world in His Essence, yet incapable of being comprehended in His power by the world; good, upright, princely, by nature not by adoption; sanctifying, not sanctified; measuring, not measured; shared, not sharing; filling, not filled; containing, not contained; inherited, glorified, reckoned with the Father and the Son; held out as a threat; the Finger of God; fire like God; to manifest, as I take it, His consubstantiality); the Creator- Spirit, Who by Baptism and by Resurrection creates anew; the Spirit That knoweth all things, That teacheth, That bloweth where and to what extent He listeth; That guideth, talketh, sendeth forth, separateth, is angry or tempted; That revealeth, illumineth, quickeneth, or rather is the very Light and Life; That maketh Temples; That deifieth; That perfecteth so as even to anticipate Baptism, yet after Baptism to be sought as a separate gift; That doeth all things that God doeth; divided into fiery tongues; dividing gifts; making Apostles, Prophets, Evangelists, Pastors, and Teachers; understanding manifold, clear, piercing, undefiled, unhindered, which is the same thing as Most wise and varied in His actions; and making all things clear and plain; and of independent power, unchangeable, Almighty, all-seeing, penetrating all spirits that are intelligent, pure, most subtle (the Angel Hosts I think); and also all prophetic spirits and apostolic in the same manner and not in the same places; for they lived in different places; thus showing that He is uncircumscript.

XXX. They who say and teach these things, and moreover call Him another Paraclete in the sense of another God, who know that blasphemy against Him alone cannot be forgiven, and who branded with such fearful infamy Ananias and Sapphira for having lied to the Holy Ghost, what do you think of these men? Do they proclaim the Spirit God, or something else? Now really, you must be extraordinarily dull and far from the Spirit if you have any doubt about this and need some one to teach you. So important then, and so vivid are His Names. Why is it necessary to lay before you the testimony contained in the very words? And whatever in this case also is said in more lowly fashion, as that He is Given, Sent, Divided; that He is the Gift, the Bounty, the Inspiration, the Promise, the Intercession for us, and, not to go into any further detail, any other expressions of the sort, is to be referred to the First Cause, that it may be shewn from Whom He is, and that men may not in heathen fashion admit Three Principles. For it is equally impious to confuse the Persons with the Sabellians, or to divide the Natures with the Arians.

XXXI. I have very carefully considered this matter in my own mind, and have looked at it in every point of view, in order to find some illustration of this most important subject, but I have been unable to discover any thing on earth with which to compare the nature of the Godhead. For even if I did happen upon some tiny likeness it escaped me for the most part, and left me down below with my example. I picture to myself an eye, a fountain, a river, as others have done before, to see if the first might be analogous to the Father, the second to the Son, and the third to the Holy Ghost. For in these there is no distinction in time, nor are they torn away from their connection with each other, though they seem to be parted by three personalities. But I was afraid in the first place that I should present a flow in the Godhead, incapable of standing still; and secondly that by this figure a numerical unity would be introduced. For the eye and the spring and the river are numerically one, though in different forms.

XXXII. Again I thought of the sun and a ray and light. But here again there was a fear lest people should get an idea of composition in the Uncompounded Nature, such as there is in the Sun and the things that are in the Sun. And in the second place lest we should give Essence to the Father but deny Personality to the Others, and make Them only Powers of God, existing in Him and not Personal. For neither the ray nor the light is another sun, but they are only effulgences from the Sun, and qualities of His essence. And lest we should thus, as far as the illustration goes, attribute both Being and Not-being to God, which is even more monstrous. I have also heard that some one has suggested an illustration of the following kind. A ray of the Sun flashing upon a wall and trembling with the movement of the moisture which the beam has taken up in mid air, and then, being checked by the hard body, has set up a strange quivering. For it quivers with many rapid movements, and is not one rather than it is many, nor yet many rather than one; because by the swiftness of its union and separating it escapes before the eye can see it.

XXXIII. But it is not possible for me to make use of even this; because it is very evident what gives the ray its motion; but there is nothing prior to God which could set Him in motion; for He is Himself the Cause of all things, and He has no prior Cause. And secondly because in this case also there is a suggestion of such things as composition, diffusion, and an unsettled and unstable nature... none of which we can suppose in the Godhead. In a word, there is nothing which presents a standing point to my mind in these illustrations from which to consider the Object which I am trying to represent to myself, unless one may indulgently accept one point of the image while rejecting the rest. Finally, then, it seems best to me to let the images and the shadows go, as being deceitful and very far short of the truth; and clinging myself to the more reverent conception, and resting upon few words, using the guidance of the Holy Ghost, keeping to the end as my genuine comrade and companion the enlightenment which I have received from Him, and passing through this world to persuade all others also to the best of my power to worship Father, Son, and Holy Ghost, the One Godhead and Power. To Him belongs all glory and honor and might for ever and ever. Amen.

Against the Arians and concerning Himself.

Delivered at Constantinople about the middle of the year 380.

I. Where are they who reproach us with our poverty, and boast themselves of their own riches; who define the Church by numbers, and scorn the little flock; and who measure Godhead, and weigh the people in the balance, who honor the sand, and despise the luminaries of heaven; who treasure pebbles and overlook pearls; for they know not that sand is not in a greater degree more abundant than stars, and pebbles than lustrous stones — that the former are purer and more precious than the latter? Are you again indignant? Do you again arm yourselves? Do you again insult us? Is this a new faith? Restrain your threats a little while that I may speak. We will not insult you, but we will convict you; we will not threaten, but we will reproach you; we will not strike, but we will heal. This too appears an insult! What pride! Do you here also regard your equal as your slave? If not, permit me to speak openly; for even a brother chides his brother if he has been defrauded by him.

II. Would you like me to utter to you the words of God to Israel, stiff-necked and hardened? "O my people what have I done unto thee, or wherein have I injured thee, or wherein have I wearied thee?" This language indeed is fitter from me to you who insult me. It is a sad thing that we watch for opportunities against each other, and having destroyed our fellowship of spirit by diversities of opinion have become almost more inhuman and savage to one another than even the barbarians who are now engaged in war against us, banded together against us by the Trinity whom we have separated; with this difference that we are not foreigners making forays and raids upon foreigners, nor nations of different language, which is some little consolation in the calamity, but are making war upon one another, and almost upon those of the same household; or if you will, we the members of the same body are consuming and being consumed by one another. Nor is this, bad though it be, the extent of our calamity, for we even regard our diminution as a gain. But since we are in such a condition, and regulate our faith by the times, let us compare the times with one another; you your Emperor, and I my Sovereigns; you Ahab and I Josias. Tell me of your moderation, and I will proclaim my violence. But indeed yours is proclaimed by many books and tongues, which I think future ages will accept as an immortal pillory for your actions and I will declare my own.

III. What tumultuous mob have I led against you? What soldiers have I armed? What general boiling with rage, and more savage than his employers, and not even a Christian, but one who offers his impiety against us as his private worship to his own gods? Whom have I besieged while engaged in prayer and lifting up their hands to God? When have I put a stop to psalmody with trumpets? or mingled the Sacramental Blood with blood of massacre? What spiritual sighs have I put an end to by cries of death, or tears of penitence by tears of tragedy? What House of prayer have I made a burialplace? What liturgical vessels which the multitude may not touch have I given over to the hands of the wicked, of a Nebuzaradan, chief of the cooks, or of a Belshazzar, who wickedly used the sacred vessels for his revels, and then paid a worthy penalty for his madness? "Altars beloved" as Holy Scripture saith, but "now defiled." And what licentious youth has insulted you for our sake with shameful writhings and contortions? O precious Throne, seat and rest of precious men, which hast been occupied by a succession of pious Priests, who from ancient times have taught the divine Mysteries, what heathen popular speaker and evil tongue hath mounted thee to inveigh against the Christian's faith? O modesty and majesty of Virgins, that cannot endure the looks of even virtuous men, which of us hath shamed thee, and outraged thee by the exposure of what may not be seen, and showed to the eyes of the impious a pitiable sight, worthy of the fires of Sodom? I say nothing of deaths, which were more endurable than this shame.

IV. What wild beasts have we let loose upon the bodies of Saints, — like some who have prostituted human nature, — on one single accusation, that of not consenting to their impiety; or defiled ourselves by communion with them, which we avoid like the poison of a snake, not because it injures the body, but because it blackens the depths of the soul? Against whom have we made it a matter of criminal accusation that they buried the dead, whom the very beasts reverenced? And what a charge, worthy of another theater and of other beasts! What Bishop's aged flesh have we carded with hooks in the presence of their disciples, impotent to help them save by tears, hung up with Christ, conquering by suffering, and sprinkling the people with their precious blood, and at last carried away to death, to be both crucified and buried and glorified with Christ; with Christ Who conquered the world by such victims and sacrifices? What priests have those contrary elements fire and water divided, raising a strange beacon over the sea, and set on fire together with the ship in which they put to sea? Who (to cover the more numerous part of our woes with a veil of silence) have been accused of inhumanity by the very magistrates who conferred such favor on them? For even if they did obey the lusts of those men, yet at any rate they hated the cruelty of their purpose. The one was opportunism, the other calculation; the one came of the lawlessness of the Emperor, the other of a consciousness of the laws by which they had to judge.

V. And to speak of older things, for they too belong to the same fraternity; whose hands living or dead have I cut off — to bring a lying accusation against Saints, and to triumph over the faith by bluster? Whose exiles have I numbered as benefits, and failed to reverence even the sacred colleges of sacred philosophers, whence I sought their suppliants? Nay the very contrary is the case; I have reckoned as Martyrs those who incurred anger for the truth. Upon whom have I, whom you accuse of licentiousness of language, brought harlots when they were almost fleshless and bloodless? Which of the faithful have I exiled from their country and given over to the hands of lawless men, that they might be kept like wild beasts in rooms without light, and (for this is the saddest part of the tragedy) left separated from each other to endure the hardships of hunger and thirst, with food measured out to them, which they had to receive through narrow openings, so that they might not be permitted even to see their companions in misery. And what were they who suffered thus? Men of whom the world was not worthy. Is it thus that you honor faith? Is this your kind treatment of it? Ye know not the greater part of these things, and that reasonably, because of the number of these facts and the pleasure of the action. But he who suffers has a better memory. There have been even some more cruel than the times themselves, like wild boars hurled against a fence. I demand your victim of yesterday the old man, the Abraham-like Father, whom on his return from exile you greeted with stones in the middle of the day and in the middle of the city. But we, if it is not invidious to say so, begged off even our murderers from their danger. God says somewhere in Scripture, How shall I pardon thee for this? Which of these things shall I praise; or rather for which shall I bind a wreath upon you?

VI. Now since your antecedents are such, I should be glad if you too will tell me of my crimes, that I may either amend my life or be put to shame. My greatest wish is that I may be found free from wrong altogether; but if this may not be, at least to be converted from my crime; for this is the second best portion of the prudent. For if like the just man I do not become my own accuser in the first instance, yet at any rate I gladly receive healing from another. "Your City, you say to me, is a little one, or rather is no city at all, but only a village, arid, without beauty, and with few inhabitants." But, my good friend, this is my misfortune, rather than my fault; — if indeed it be a misfortune; and if it is against my will, I am to be pitied for my bad luck, if I may put it so; but if it be willingly, I am a philosopher. Which of these is a crime? Would anyone abuse a dolphin for not being a land animal, or an ox because it is not aquatic, or a lamprey because it is amphibious? But we, you go on, have walls and theatres and racecourses and palaces, and beautiful great Porticoes, and that marvelous work the underground and overhead river, and the splendid and admired column, and the crowded marketplace and a restless people, and a famous senate of highborn men.

VII. Why do you not also mention the convenience of the site, and what I may call the contest between land and sea as to which owns the City, and which adorns our Royal City with all their good things? This then is our crime, that while you are great and splendid, we are small and come from a small place? Many others do you this wrong, indeed all those whom you excel; and must we die because we have not reared a city, nor built walls around it, nor can boast of our racecourse, or our stadia, and pack of hounds, and all the follies that are connected with these things; nor have to boast of the beauty and splendor of our baths, and the costliness of their marbles and pictures and golden embroideries of all sorts of species, almost rivaling nature? Nor have we yet rounded off the sea for ourselves, or mingled the seasons, as of course you, the new Creators, have done, that we may live in what is at once the pleasantest and the safest way. Add if you like other charges, you who say, The silver is mine and the gold is mine, those words of God. We neither think much of riches, on which, if they increase, our Law forbids us to set our hearts, nor do we count up yearly and daily revenues; nor do we rival one another in loading our tables with enchantments for our senseless belly. For neither do we highly esteem those things which after we have swallowed them are all of the same worth, or rather I should say worthlessness, and are rejected. But we live so simply and from hand to mouth, as to differ but little from beasts whose sustenance is without apparatus and inartificial.

VIII. Do you also find fault with the raggedness of my dress, and the want of elegance in the disposition of my face? for these are the points upon which I see that some persons who are very insignificant pride themselves. Will you leave my head alone, and not jeer at it, as the children did at Elissaeus? What followed I will not mention. And will you leave out of your allegations my want of education, and what seems to you the roughness and rusticity of my elocution? And where will you put the fact that I am not full of small talk, nor a jester popular with company, nor great hunter of the marketplace, nor given to chatter and gossip with any chance people upon all sorts of subjects, so as to make even conversation grievous; nor a frequenter of Zeuxippus, that new Jerusalem; nor one who strolls from house to house flattering and stuffing himself; but for the most part staying at home, of low spirits and with a melancholy cast of countenance, quietly associating with myself, the genuine critic of my actions; and perhaps worthy of imprisonment for my uselessness? How is it that you pardon me for all this, and do not blame me for it? How sweet and kind you are.

IX. But I am so old fashioned and such a philosopher as to believe that one heaven is common to all; and that so is the revolution of the sun and the moon, and the order and arrangement of the stars; and that all have in Common an equal share and profit in day and night, and also change of seasons, rains, fruits, and quickening power of the air; and that the flowing rivers are a common and abundant wealth to all; and that one and the same is the Earth, the mother and the tomb, from which we were taken, and to which we shall return, none having a greater share than another. And further, above this, we have in common reason, the Law, the Prophets, the very Sufferings of Christ, by which we were all without exception created anew, who partake of the same Adam, and were led astray by the serpent and slain by sin, and are saved by the heavenly Adam and brought back by the tree of shame to the tree of life from whence we had fallen.

X. I was deceived too by the Ramah of Samuel, that little fatherland of the great man; which was no dishonor to the Prophet, for it drew its honor not so much from itself as from him; nor was he hindered on its account from being given to God before his birth, or from uttering oracles, and foreseeing the future; nor only so, but also anointing Kings and Priests, and judging the men of illustrious cities. I heard also of Saul, how while seeking his father's asses he found a kingdom. And even David himself was taken from the sheepfolds to be the shepherd of Israel.

What of Amos? Was he not, while a goatherd and scraper of sycamore fruit entrusted with the gifts of prophecy? How is it that I have passed over Joseph, who was both a slave and the giver of corn to Egypt, and the father of many myriads who were promised before to Abraham? Aye and I was deceived by the Carmel of Elias, who received the car of fire; and by the sheepskin of Elissaeus that had more power than a silken web or than gold forced into garments. I was deceived by the desert of John, which held the greatest among them that are born of women, with that clothing, that food, that girdle, which we know. And I ventured even beyond these, and found God Himself the Patron of my rusticity. I will range myself with Bethlehem, and will share the ignominy of the Manger; for since you refuse on this account honor to God, it is no wonder that on the same account you despise His herald also. And I will bring up to you the Fishermen, and the poor to whom the Gospel is preached, as preferred before many rich. Will you ever leave off priding yourselves upon your cities? Will you ever revere that wilderness which you abominate and despise? I do not yet say that gold has its birthplace in sand; nor that translucent stones are the product and gifts of rocks; for if to these I should oppose all that is dishonorable in cities perhaps it would be to no good end that I should use my freedom of speech.

XI But perhaps some one who is very circumscribed and carnally minded will say, "But our herald is a stranger and a foreigner." What of the Apostles? Were not they strangers to the many nations and cities among whom they were divided, that the Gospel might have free course everywhere, that nothing might miss the illumination of the Threefold Light, or be unenlightened by the Truth; but that the night of ignorance might be dissolved for those who sat in darkness and the shadow of death? You have heard the words of Paul, "that we might go the Gentiles, and they to the Circumcision." Be it that Judaea is Peter's home; what has Paul in common with the Gentiles, Luke with Achaia, Andrew with Epirus, John with Ephesus, Thomas with India, Marc with Italy, or the rest, not to go into particulars, with those to whom they went? So that you must either blame them or excuse me, or else prove that you, the ambassadors of the true Gospel, are being insulted by trifling. But since I have argued with you in a petty way about these matters, I will now proceed to take a larger and more philosophic view of them.

XII. My friend, every one that is of high mind has one Country, the Heavenly Jerusalem, in which we store up our Citizenship. All have one family — if you look at what is here below the dust — or if you look higher, that In-breathing of which we are partakers, and which we were bidden to keep, and with which I must stand before my Judge to give an account of my heavenly nobility, and of the Divine Image. Everyone then is noble who has guarded this through virtue and consent to his Archetype. On the other hand, everyone is ignoble who has mingled with evil, and put upon himself another form, that of the serpent. And these earthly countries and families are the playthings of this our temporary life and scene. For our country is whatever each may have first occupied, either as tyrant, or in misfortune; and in this we are all alike strangers and pilgrims, however much we may play with names. And the family is accounted noble which is either rich from old days, or is recently raised; and of ignoble birth that which is of poor parents, either owing to misfortune or to want of ambition. For how can a nobility be given from above which is at one time beginning and at another coming to an end; and which is not given to some, but is bestowed on others by letters patent? Such is my mind on this matter. Therefore I leave it to you to pride yourself on tombs or in myths, and I endeavor as far as I can, to purify myself from deceits, that I may keep if possible my nobility, or else may recover it.

XIII. It is thus then and for these reasons that I, who am small and of a country without repute, have come upon you, and that not of my own accord, nor self-sent, like many of those who now seize upon the chief places; but because I was invited, and compelled, and have followed the scruples of my conscience and the Call of the Spirit. If it be otherwise, may I continue to fight here to no purpose, and deliver no one from his error, but may they obtain their desire who seek the barrenness of my soul, if I lie. But since I am come, and perchance with no contemptible power (if I may boast myself a little of my folly), which of those who are insatiable have I copied, what have I emulated of opportunism, although I have such examples, even apart from which it is hard and rare not to be bad? Concerning what churches or property have I disputed with you; though you have more than enough of both, and the others too little? What imperial edict have we rejected and emulated? What rulers have we fawned upon against you? Whose boldness have we denounced? And what has been done on the other side against me? "Lord, lay not this sin to their charge," even then I said, for I remembered in season the words of Stephen, and so I pray now. Being reviled, we bless: being blasphemed we retreat.

XIV. And if I am doing wrong in this, that when tyrannized over I endure it, forgive me this wrong; I have borne to be tyrannized over by others too; and I am thankful that my moderation has brought upon me the charge of folly. For I reckon thus, using considerations altogether higher than any of yours; what a mere fraction are these trials of the spittings and blows which Christ, for Whom and by Whose aid we encounter these dangers, endured. I do not count them, taken altogether, worth the one crown of thorns which robbed our conqueror of his crown, for whose sake also I learn that I am crowned for the hardness of life. I do not reckon them worth the one reed by which the rotten empire was destroyed; of the gall alone, the vinegar alone, by which we were cured of the bitter taste; of the gentleness alone which He shewed in His Passion. Was He betrayed with a kiss? He reproves with a kiss, but smites not. Is he suddenly arrested? He reproaches indeed, but follows; and if through zeal thou cuttest off the ear of Malchus with the sword, He will be angry, and will restore it. And if one flee in a linen sheet, he will defend him. And if you ask for the fire of Sodom upon his captors, he will not pour it forth; and if he take a thief hanging upon the cross for his crime he will bring him into Paradise through His Goodness. Let all the acts of one that loves men be loving, as were all the sufferings of Christ, to which we could add nothing greater than, when God even died for us, to refuse on our part to forgive even the smallest wrongs of our fellowmen.

XV. Moreover this also I reckoned and still reckon with myself; and do you see if it is not quite correct. I have often discussed it with you before. These men have the houses, but we the Dweller in the house; they the Temples, we the God; and besides it is ours to be living temples of the Living God, lively sacrifices, reasonable burnt-offerings, perfect sacrifices, yea, gods through the adoration of the Trinity. They have the people, we the Angels; they rash boldness, we faith; they threatenings, we prayer; they smiting, we endurance; they gold and silver, we the pure word. "Thou hast built for thyself a wide house and large chambers (recognize the words of Scripture), a house celled and pierced with windows." But not yet is this loftier than my faith, and than the heavens to which I am being borne onwards. Is mine a little flock? But it is not being carried over a precipice. Is mine a narrow fold? But it is unapproachable by wolves; it cannot be entered by a robber, nor climbed by thieves and strangers. I shall yet see it, I know well, wider. And many of those who are now wolves, I must reckon among my sheep, and perhaps even amongst the shepherds. This is the glad tidings brought me by the Good Shepherd, for Whose sake I lay down my life for the sheep. I fear not for the little flock; for it is seen at a glance. I know my sheep and am known of mine. Such are they that know God and are known of God. My sheep hear my voice, which I have heard from the oracles of God, which I have been taught by the Holy Fathers, which I have taught alike on all occasions, not conforming myself to the fortune, and which I will never cease to teach; in which I was born, and in which I will depart.

XVI. These I call by name (for they are not nameless like the stars which are numbered and have names), and they follow me, for I rear them up beside the waters of rest; and they follow every such shepherd, whose voice they love to hear, as you see; but a stranger they will not follow, but will flee from him, because they have a habit of distinguishing the voice of their own from that of strangers. They will flee from Valentinus with his division of one into two, refusing to believe that the Creator is other than the Good. They will flee from Depth and Silence, and the mythical Aeons, that are verily worthy of Depth and Silence. They will flee from Marcion's God, compounded of elements and numbers; from Montanus' evil and feminine spirit; from the matter and darkness of Manes; from Novatus' boasting and wordy assumption of purity; from the analysis and confusion of Sabellius, and if I may use the expression, his absorption, contracting the Three into One, instead of defining the One in Three Personalities; from the difference of natures taught by Arius and his followers, and their new Judaism, confining the Godhead to the Unbegotten; from Photinus earthly Christ, who took his beginning from Mary. But they worship the Father and the Son and the Holy Ghost, One Godhead; God the Father, God the Son and (do not be angry) God the Holy Ghost, One Nature in

Three Personalities, intellectual, perfect, Self-existent, numerically separate, but not separate in Godhead.

XVII. These words let everyone who threatens me today concede to me; the rest let whoever will claim. The Father will not endure to be deprived of the Son, nor the Son of the Holy Ghost. Yet that must happen if They are confined to time, and are created Beings... for that which is created is not God. Neither will I bear to be deprived of my consecration; One Lord, One Faith, One Baptism. If this be canceled, from whom shall I get a second? What say you, you who destroy Baptism or repeat it? Can a man be spiritual without the Spirit? Has he a share in the Spirit who does not honor the Spirit? Can he honor Him who is baptized into a creature and a fellow- servant? It is not so; it is not so; for all your talk. I will not play Thee false, O Unoriginate Father, or Thee O Only-begotten Word, or Thee O Holy Ghost. I know Whom I have confessed, and whom I have renounced, and to Whom I have joined myself. I will not allow myself, after having been taught the words of the faithful, to learn also those of the unfaithful; to confess the truth, and then range myself with falsehood; to come down for consecration and to go back even less hallowed; having been baptized that I might live, to be killed by the water, like infants who die in the very birthpangs, and receive death simultaneously with birth. Why make me at once blessed and wretched, newly enlightened and unenlightened, Divine and godless, that I may make shipwreck even of the hope of regeneration? A few words will suffice. Remember your confession. Into what were you baptized? The Father? Good but Jewish still. The Son?... good... but not yet perfect. The Holy Ghost?... Very good... this is perfect. Now was it into these simply, or some common name of Them? The latter. And what was the common Name? Why, God. In this common Name believe, and ride on prosperously and reign, and pass on from hence into the Bliss of Heaven. And that is, as I think, the more distinct apprehension of These; to which may we all come, in the same Christ our God, to Whom be the glory and the might, with the Unoriginate Father, and the Lifegiving Spirit, now and for ever and to ages of ages. Amen.

On the arrival of the Egyptians

This Oration was preached at Constantinople in 380, under the following circumstances:

Peter, Patriarch of Alexandria, had sent a mission of five of his Suffragans to consecrate the impostor M aximus to the Throne occupied by **Gregory**. *This had led to much trouble, but in the end the intruder had been expelled and banished. Shortly afterwards an Egyptian fleet, probably the regular corn ships, had arrived at Constantinople, apparently on the day before a Festival. The crews of the ships, landing next day to go to Church, passed by the numerous Churches held by the Arians, and betook themselves to the little Anastasia. S. Gregory felt himself moved to congratulate them specially on such an act, after what had recently passed, and accordingly pronounced the following discourse.*

I. I Will address myself as is right to those who have come from Egypt; for they have come here eagerly, having overcome illwill by zeal, from that Egypt which is enriched by the River, raining out of the earth, and like the sea in its season, — if I too may follow in my small measure those who have so eloquently spoken of these matters; and which is also enriched by Christ my Lord, Who once was a fugitive into Egypt, and now is supplied by Egypt; the first, when He fled from Herod's massacre of the children; and now by the love of the fathers for their children, by Christ the new Food of those who hunger after good; the greatest alms of corn of which history speaks and men believe; the Bread which came down from heaven and giveth life to the world, that life which is indestructible and indissoluble, concerning Whom I now seem to hear the Father saying, Out of Egypt have I called My Son.

II. For from you hath sounded forth the Word to all men; healthfully believed and preached; and you are the best bringers of fruit of all men, specially of those who now hold the right faith, as far as I know, who am not only a lover of such food, but also its distributor, and not at home only but also abroad. For you indeed supply bodily food to peoples and cities so far as your lovingkindness reaches; and you supply spiritual food also, not to a particular people, nor to this or that city, circumscribed by narrow boundaries, though its people may think it very illustrious, but to almost the whole world. And you bring the remedy not for famine of bread or thirst of water, which is no very terrible famine — and to avoid it is easy; but to a famine of hearing the Word of the Lord, which it is most miserable to suffer, and a most laborious matter to cure at the present time, because iniquity hath abounded, and scarce anywhere do I find its genuine healers.

III. Such was Joseph your Superintendent of corn measures, whom I may call ours also; who by his surpassing wisdom was able both to foresee the famine and to cure it by decrees of government, healing the ill-favored and starving kine by means of the fair and fat. And indeed you may understand by Joseph which you will, either the great lover and creator and namesake of immortality or his successor in throne and word and hoary hair, our new Peter, not inferior in virtue or fame to him by whom the middle course was destroyed and crushed, though it still wriggles a little weakly, like the tail of a snake after it is cut off; the one of whom, after having departed this life in a good old age after many conflicts and wrestlings, looks upon us from above, I well know, and reaches a hand to those who are laboring for the right: and this the more, in proportion as he is freed from his bonds; and the other is hastening to the same end or dissolution of life, and is already drawing near the dwellers in heaven, but is still so far in the flesh as is needed to give the last aids to the Word, and to take his journey with richer provision.

IV. Of these great men and doctors and soldiers of the truth and victors, you are the nurslings and offspring; of these neither times nor tyrants, reason nor envy, nor fear, nor accuser, nor slanderer, whether waging open war against them, or plotting secretly; nor any who appeared to be of our side, nor any stranger, nor gold — that hidden tyrant, through which now almost everything is turned upside down and made to depend on the hazard of a die; nor flatteries nor threats, nor long and distant exiles (for they only could not be affected by confiscation, because of their great riches, which were — to possess nothing) nor anything else, whether absent or present or expected, could induce to take the worse part, and to be anywise traitor to the Trinity, or to suffer loss of the Godhead. On the contrary indeed, they grew strong by dangers, and became more zealous for true religion. For to suffer thus for Christ adds to one's love, and is as it were an earnest to high-souled men of further conflicts. These, O Egypt, are thy present tales and wonders.

V. Once thou didst praise me thy Mendesian Goats, and thy Memphite Apis, a fatted and fleshy calf, and the rites of Isis, and the mutilations of Osiris, and thy venerable Serapis, a log that was honored by myths and ages and the madness of its worshippers, as some unknown and heavenly matter, however it may have been aided by falsehood; and things yet more shameful than these, multiform images of monstrous beasts and creeping things, all of which Christ and the heralds of Christ have conquered, both the others who have been illustrious in their own times, and also the Fathers whom I have named just now; by whom, O admirable country, thou art more famous today than all others put together, whether in ancient or modern history.

VI. Wherefore I embrace and salute thee, O noblest of peoples and most Christian, and of warmest piety, and worthy of thy leaders; for I can find nothing greater to say of thee than this, nor anything by which better to welcome thee. And I greet thee, to a small extent with my tongue, but very heartily with the movements of my affections. O my people, for I call you mine, as of one mind and one faith, instructed by the same Fathers, and adoring the same Trinity. My people, for mine

187

thou art, though it seem not so to those who envy me. And that they who are in this case may be the deeper wounded, see, I give the right hand of fellowship before so many witnesses, seen and unseen. And I put away the old calumny by this new act of kindness. O my people, for mine thou art, though in saying so I, who am least of all men, am claiming for myself that which is greatest. For such is the grace of the Spirit that it makes of equal honor those who are of one mind. O my people, for mine thou art, though it be afar, because we are divinely joined together, and in a manner wholly different to the unions of carnal people; for bodies are united in place, but souls are fitted together by the Spirit. O my people, who didst formerly study how to suffer for Christ, but now if thou wilt hearken unto me, wilt study not to do aught, but to consider the power of doing to be a sufficient gain, and to deem that thou art offering a sacrifice to Christ, as in those days of thy endurance so in these of meekness. O people to whom the Lord hath prepared Himself to do good, as to do evil to thine enemies. O people, whom the Lord hath chosen to Himself out of all peoples; O people who art graven upon the hands of the Lord, to whom saith the Lord, Thou art My Will; and, Thy gates are carved work, and all the rest that is said to them that are being saved. O people; — nay, marvel not at my insatiability that I repeat your name so often; for I delight in this continual naming of you, like those who can never have enough of their enjoyment of certain spectacles or sounds.

VII. But, O people of God and mine, beautiful also was your yesterday's assembly, which you held upon the sea, and pleasant, if any sight ever was, to the eyes, when I saw the sea like a forest, and hidden by a cloud made with hands, and the beauty and speed of your ships, as though ordered for a procession, and the slight breeze astern, as though purposely escorting you, and wafting to the City your city of the Sea. Yet the present assembly which we now behold is more beautiful and more magnificent. For you have not hastened to mingle with the larger number, nor have you reckoned religion by numbers, nor endured to be a mere unorganized rabble, rather than a people purified by the Word of God; but having, as is right, rendered to Caesar the things that are Caesar's, ye have offered besides to God the things that are God's; to the former Custom, to the latter Fear; and after feeding the people with your cargoes, you yourselves have come to be fed by us. For we also distribute corn, and our distribution is perhaps not worth less than yours. Come eat of my Bread and drink of the Wine which I have mingled for you. I join with Wisdom in bidding you to my table. For I commend your good feeling, and I hasten to meet your ready mind, because ye came to us as to your own harbor, running to your like; and ye valued the kindred Faith, and thought it monstrous that, while they who insult higher things are in harmony with each other and think alike, and think to make good each man's individual falsehood by their common conspiracy, like ropes which get strength from being twisted together; yet you should not meet nor combine with those who are of the same mind, with whom it is more reasonable that you should associate, for we gather in the Godhead also. And that you may see that not in vain have you come to us, and that you have not brought up in a port among strangers and foreigners, but amongst your own people, and have been well guided by the Holy Ghost; we will discourse to you briefly concerning God; and do you recognize your own, like those who distinguish their kindred by the ensigns of their arms.

VIII. I find two highest differences in things that exist, viz.: — Rule, and Service; not such as among us either tyranny has cut or poverty has severed, but which nature has distinguished, if any like to use this word. For That which is First is also above nature. Of these the former is creative, and originating, and unchangeable; but the other is created, and subject and changing; or to speak yet more plainly, the one is above time, and the other subject to time. The Former is called God, and subsists in Three Greatest, namely, the Cause, the Creator, and the Perfecter; I mean the Father, the Son, and the Holy Ghost, who are neither so separated from one another as to be divided in nature, nor so contracted as to be circumscribed by a single person; the one alternative being that of the Arian madness, the other that of the Sabellian heresy; but they are on the one hand more single than what is altogether divided, and on the other more abundant than what is altogether singular. The other division is with us, and is called Creation, though one may be exalted above another according to the proportion of their nearness to God.

IX. This being so, if any be on the Lord's side let him come with us, and let us adore the One Godhead in the Three; not ascribing any name of humiliation to the unapproachable Glory, but having the exaltations of the Triune God continually in our mouth. For since we cannot properly describe even the greatness of Its Nature, on account of Its infinity and undefinableness, how can we assert of It humiliation? But if any one be estranged from God, and therefore divideth the One Supreme Substance into an inequality of Natures, it were marvelous if such an one were not Cut in sunder by the sword, and his portion appointed with the unbelievers, reaping any evil fruit of his evil thought both now and hereafter.

X. What must we say of the Father, Whom by common consent all who have been preoccupied with natural conceptions share, although He hath endured the beginnings of dishonor, having been first divided by ancient innovation into the Good and the Creator. And of the Son and of the Holy Ghost, see how simply and concisely we shall discourse. If any one could say of Either that He was mutable or subject to change; or that either in time, or place, or power, or energy He could be measured; or that He was not naturally good, or not Self-moved, or not a free agent, or a Minister, or a Hymnsinger; or that He feared, or was a recipient of freedom, or was not counted with God; let him prove this and we will acquiesce, and will be glorified by the Majesty of our Fellow Servants, though we lose our God. But if all that the Father has belongs likewise to the Son, except Causality; and all that is the Son's belongs also to the Spirit, except His Sonship, and whatsoever is spoken of Him as to Incarnation for me a man, and for my salvation, that, taking of mine, He may impart His own by this new commingling; then cease your babbling, though so late, O ye sophists of vain talk that falls at once to the ground; for why will ye die O House of Israel? — if I may mourn for you in the words of Scripture.

XI. For my part I revere also the Titles of the Word, which are so many, and so high and great, which even the demons respect. And I revere also the Equal Rank of the Holy Ghost; and I fear the threat pronounced against those who blaspheme Him. And blasphemy is not the reckoning Him God, but the severing Him from the Godhead. And here you must remark that That which is blasphemed is Lord, and That which is avenged is the Holy Ghost, evidently as Lord. I cannot bear to be unenlightened after my Enlightenment, by marking with a different stamp any of the Three into Whom I was baptized; and thus to be indeed buried in the water, and initiated not into Regeneration, but into death.

XII. I dare to utter something, O Trinity; and may pardon be granted to my folly, for the risk is to my soul. I too am an Image of God, of the Heavenly Glory, though I be placed on earth. I cannot believe that I am saved by one who is my equal. If the Holy Ghost is not God, let Him first be made God, and then let Him deify me His equal. But now what deceit this is on the part of grace, or rather of the givers of grace, to believe in God and to come away godless; by one set of questions and confessions leading to another set of conclusions. Alas for this fair fame, if after the Layer I am blackened, if I am to see those who are not yet cleansed brighter than myself; if I am cheated by the heresy of my Baptizer; if I seek for the stronger Spirit and find Him not. Give me a second Font before you think evil of the first. Why do you grudge me a complete regeneration? Why do you make me, who am the Temple of the Holy Ghost as of God, the habitation of a creature? Why do you honor part of what belongs to me, and dishonor part, judging falsely of the Godhead, to cut me off from the Gift, or rather to cut me in two by the gift? Either honor the Whole, or dishonor the Whole, O new Theologian, that, if you are wicked, you may at any rate be consistent with yourself, and not judge unequally of an equal nature.

XIII. To sum up my discourse: — Glorify Him with the Cherubim, who unite the Three Holies into One Lord, and so far indicate the Primal Substance as their wings open to the diligent. With David be enlightened, who said to the Light, In Thy Light shall we see Light, that is, in the Spirit we shall see the Son; and what can be of further reaching ray? With John thunder, sounding forth nothing that is low or earthly concerning God, but what is high and heavenly, Who is in the beginning, and is with God, and is God the Word, and true God of the true Father, and not a good fellow-servant honored only with the title of Son; and the Other Comforter (other, that is, from the Speaker, Who was the Word of God). And when you read, I and the Father are One, keep before your eyes the Unity of Substance; but when you see, "We will come to him, and make Our abode with

190

him," remember the distinction of Persons; and when you see the Names, Father, Son, and Holy Ghost, think of the Three Personalities.

XIV. With Luke be inspired as you study the Acts of the Apostles. Why do you range yourself with Ananias and Sapphira, those vain embezzlers (if indeed the theft of one's own property be a vain thing) and that by appropriating, not silver nor any other cheap and worthless thing, like a wedge of gold, or a didrachma, as did of old a rapacious soldier; but stealing the Godhead Itself, and lying, not to men but to God, as you have heard. What? Will you not reverence even the authority of the Spirit Who breathes upon whom, and when, and as He wills? He comes upon Cornelius and his companions before Baptism, to others after Baptism, by the hands of the Apostles; so that from both sides, both from the fact that He comes in the guise of a Master and not of a Servant, and from the fact of His being sought to make perfect, the Godhead of the Spirit is testified.

XV. Speak of God with Paul, who was caught up to the third Heaven, and who sometimes counts up the Three Persons, and that in varied order, not keeping the same order, but reckoning one and the same Person now first, now second, now third; and for what purpose? Why, to shew the equality of the Nature. And sometimes he mentions Three, sometimes Two or One, became That which is not mentioned is included. And sometimes he attributes the operation of God to the Spirit, as in no respect different from Him, and sometimes instead of the Spirit he brings in Christ; and at times he separates the Persons saying, "One God, of whom are all things, and we in Him; and one Lord Jesus Christ, by whom are all things, and we by Him;" at other times he brings together the one Godhead, "For of Him and through Him and in Him are all things;" that is, through the Holy Ghost, as is shown by many places in Scripture. To Him be glory for ever and ever. Amen.

On the Words of the Gospel, "When had Jesus finished these sayings," etc Matt 19:1

I. Jesus Who Chose The Fishermen, Himself also useth a net, and changeth place for place. Why? Not only that He may gain more of those who love God by His visitation; but also, as it seems to me, that He may hallow more places. To the Jews He becomes as a Jew that He may gain the Jews; to them that are under the Law as under the Law, that He may redeem them that are under the Law; to the weak as weak, that He may save the weak. He is made all things to all men that He may gain all. Why do I say, All things to all men? For even that which Paul could not endure to say of himself I find that the Savior suffered. For He is made not only a Jew, and not only doth He take to Himself all monstrous and vile names, but even that which is most monstrous of all, even very sin and very curse; not that He it such, but He is called so. For how can He be sin, Who setteth us free from sin; and how can He be a curse, Who redeemeth us from the curse of the Law? But it is in order that He may carry His display of humility even to this extent, and form us to that humility which is the producer of exaltation. As I said then, He is made a Fisherman; He condescendeth to all; He casteth the net; He endureth all things, that He may draw up the fish from the depths, that is, Man who is swimming in the unsettled and bitter waves of life.

II. Therefore now also, when He had finished these sayings He departed from Galilee and came into the coasts of Judea beyond Jordan; He dwelleth well in Galilee, in order that the people which sat in darkness may see great Light. He removeth to Judea in order that He may persuade people to rise up from the Letter and to follow the Spirit. He teacheth, now on a mountain; now He discourseth on a plain; now He passeth over into a ship; now He rebuketh the surges. And perhaps He goes to sleep, in order that He may bless sleep also; perhaps He is tired that He may hallow weariness also; perhaps He weeps that He may make tears blessed. He removeth from place to place, Who is not contained in any place; the timeless, the bodiless, the uncircumscript, the same Who was and is; Who was both above time, and came under time, and was invisible and is seen. He was in the beginning and was with God, and was God. The word Was occurs the third time to be confirmed by number. What He was He laid aside; what He was not He assumed; not that He became two, but He deigned to be One made out of the two. For both are God, that which assumed, and that which was assumed; two Natures meeting in One, not two Sons (let us not give a false account of the blending). He who is such and so great — but what has befallen me? I have fallen into human language. For how can So Great be said of the Absolute, and how can That which is without quantity be called Such? But pardon the word, for I am speaking of the greatest things with a limited instrument. And That great and long-suffering and formless and bodiless Nature will endure this, namely, my words as if of a body, and weaker than the truth. For if He condescended to Flesh, He will also endure such language.

III. And great multitudes followed Him, and He healed them there, where the multitude was greater. If He had abode upon His own eminence, if He had not condescended to infirmity, if He had remained what He was, keeping Himself unapproachable and incomprehensible, a few perhaps would have followed Him — perhaps not even a few, possibly only Moses — and He only so far as to see with difficulty the Back Parts of God. For He penetrated the cloud, either being placed outside the weight of the body or being withdrawn from his senses; for how could he have gazed upon the subtlety, or the incorporeity, or I know not how one should call it, of God, being incorporate and using material eyes? But inasmuch as He strips Himself for us, inasmuch as He comes down (and I speak of an exinanition, as it were, a laying aside and a diminution of His glory), He becomes by this comprehensible,

IV. And pardon me meanwhile that I again suffer a human affection. I am filled with indignation and grief for my Christ (and would that you might sympathize with me) when I see my Christ dishonored on this account on which He most merited honor. He on this account to be dishonored, tell me, that for you He was humble? Is He therefore a Creature, because He careth for the creature? Is He therefore subject to time, because He watches over those who are subject to time Nay, He beareth all things, He endureth all things. And what marvel? He put up with blows, He bore spittings, He tasted gall for my taste. And even now He bears to be stoned, not only by those who deal despite-fully with Him, but also by ourselves who seem to reverence Him. For to use corporeal names when discoursing of the incorporeal is perhaps the part of those who deal despitefully and stone Him; but pardon, I say again to our infirmity, for I do not willingly stone Him; but having no other words to use, we use what we have. Thou art called the Word, and Thou art above Word; Thou art above Light, yet art named Light; Thou art called Fire not as perceptible to sense, but because Thou purgest light and worthless matter; a Sword, because Thou severest the worse from the better; a Fan, because Thou purgest the threshing-floor, and blowest away all that is light and windy, and layest up in the garner above all that is weighty and full; an Axe, because Thou cuttest down the worthless fig-tree, after long patience, because Thou cuttest away the roots of wickedness; the Door, because Thou bringest in; the Way, because we go straight; the Sheep, because Thou art the Sacrifice; the High Priest, because Thou offerest the Body the Son, because Thou art of the Father. Again I stir men's tongues; again some men rave against Christ, or rather against me, who have been deemed worthy to be a herald of the Word. I am like John, The Voice of one crying in the wilderness — a wilderness that once was dry, but now is only too populous.

V. But, as I was saying, to return to my argument; for this reason great multitudes followed Him, because He condescended to our infirmities. What next? The Pharisees also, it says, came unto Him, tempting Him, and saying unto Him, is it lawful for a man to put away his wife for every cause? Again the Pharisees tempt

Him; again they who read the Law do not know the Law; again they who are expounders of the Law need others to teach them. It was not enough that Sadducees should tempt Him concerning the Resurrection, and Lawyers question Him about perfection, and the Herodians about the poll-tax, and others about authority; but some one must also ask about Marriage at Him who cannot be tempted, the Creator of wedlock, Him who from the First Cause made this whole race of mankind. And He answered and said unto them, Have ye not read that He which made them at the beginning made them male and female? He knoweth how to solve some of their questions and to bridle others. When He is asked, By what authority doest thou these things? He Himself, because of the utter ignorance of those who asked Him, replies with another question; The baptism of John, was it from Heaven or of men? He on both sides entangles His questioners, so that we also are able, following the example of Christ, sometimes to check those who argue with us over-officiously, and with still more absurd questions to solve the absurdity of their questions. For we too are wise in vanity at times, if I may boast of the things of folly. But when He sees a question that calls for reasoning, then He does not deem His questioners unworthy of prudent answers.

VI. The question which you have put seems to me to do honor to chastity, and to demand a kind reply. Chastity, in respect of which I see that the majority of men are ill-disposed, and that their laws are unequal and irregular. For what was the reason why they restrained the woman, but indulged the man, and that a woman who practices evil against her husband's bed is an adulteress, and the penalties of the law for this are very severe; but if the husband commits fornication against his wife, he has no account to give? I do not accept this legislation; I do not approve this custom. They who made the Law were men, and therefore their legislation is hard on women, since they have placed children also under the authority of their fathers, while leaving the weaker sex uncared for. God doth not so; but saith Honor thy father and thy mother, which is the first commandment with promise; that it may be well with thee; and, He that curseth father or mother, let him die the death. Similarly He gave honor to good and punishment to evil. And, The blessing of a father strengtheneth the houses of children, but the curse of a mother uprooteth the foundations. See the equality of the legislation. There is one Maker of man and woman; one debt is owed by children to both their parents.

VII. How then dost thou demand Chastity, while thou dost not thyself observe it? How dost thou demand that which thou dost not give? How, though thou art equally a body, dost thou legislate unequally? If thou enquire into the worse — The Woman Sinned, and so did Adam. The serpent deceived them both; and one was not found to be the stronger and the other the weaker. But dost thou consider the better? Christ saves both by His Passion. Was He made flesh for the Man? So He was also for the woman. Did He die for the Man? The Woman also is saved by His death. He is called of the seed of David; and so perhaps you think the Man is honored; but He is born of a Virgin, and this is on the Woman's side. They two,

He says, shall be one Flesh; so let the one flesh have equal honor." And Paul legislates for chastity by His example. How, and in what way? This Sacrament is great, he says, But I speak concerning Christ and the Church. It is well for the wife to reverence Christ through her husband: and it is well for the husband not to dishonor the Church through his wife. Let the wife, he says, see that she reverence her husband, for so she does Christ; but also he bids the husband cherish his wife, for so Christ does the Church. Let us, then, give further consideration to this saying.

VIII. Churn milk and it will be butter; examine this and perhaps you may find something more nourishing in it. For I think that the Word here seems to deprecate second marriage. For, if there were two Christs, there may be two husbands or two wives; but if Christ is One, one Head of the Church, let there be also one flesh, and let a second be rejected; and if it hinder the second what is to be said for a third? The first is law, the second is indulgence, the third is transgression, and anything beyond this is swinish, such as has not even many examples of its wickedness. Now the Law grants divorce for every cause; but Christ not for every cause; but He allows only separation from the whore; and in all other things He commands patience. He allows to put away the fornicatress, because she corrupts the offspring; but in all other matters let us be patient and endure; or rather be ye enduring and patient, as many as have received the yoke of matrimony. If you see lines or marks upon her, take away her ornaments; if a hasty tongue, restrain it; if a meretricious laugh, make it modest; if immoderate expenditure or drink, reduce it; if unseasonable going out, shackle it; if a lofty eye, chastise it. It is uncertain which is in danger, the separator or the separated. Let thy fountain of water, it says, be only thine own, and let no stranger share it with thee; and, let the colt of thy favors and the stag of thy love company with thee; do thou then take care not to be a strange river, nor to please others better than thine own wife. But if thou be carried elsewhere, then thou makest a law of lewdness for thy partner also. Thus saith the Savior.

IX. But what of the Pharisees? To them this word seems harsh. Yes, for they are also displeased at other noble words — both the older Pharisees, and the Pharisees of the present day. For it is not only race, but disposition also that makes a Pharisee. Thus also I reckon as an Assyrian or an Egyptian him who is ranged among these by his character. What then say the Pharisees? If the case of the man be so with his wife, it is not good to marry. Is it only now, O Pharisee, that thou understandest this, It is not good to marry? Didst thou not know it before when thou sawest widowhoods, and orphanhoods, and untimely deaths, and mourning succeeding to shouting, and funerals coming upon weddings, and childlessness, and all the comedy or tragedy that is connected with this? Either is most appropriate language. It is good to marry; I too admit it, for marriage is honorable in all, and the bed undefiled. It is good for the temperate, not for those who are insatiable, and who desire to give more than due honor to the flesh. When marriage is only marriage and conjunction and the desire for a succession of children, marriage is honorable, for it brings into the world more to please God. But when it kindles matter, and surrounds us with thorns, and as it were discovers the way of vice, then I too say, It is not good to marry.

X. Marriage is honorable; but I cannot say that it is more lofty than virginity; for virginity were no great thing if it were not better than a good thing. Do not however be angry, ye women that are subject to the yoke. We must obey God rather than man. But be ye bound together, both virgins and wives, and be one in the Lord, and each others' adornment. There would be no celibate if there were no marriage. For whence would the virgin have passed into this life? Marriage would not have been venerable unless it had borne virgin fruit to God and to life. Honor thou also thy mother, of whom thou wast born. Honor thou also her who is of a mother and is a mother. A mother she is not, but a Bride of Christ she is. The visible beauty is not hidden, but that which is unseen is visible to God. All the glory of the King's Daughter is within, clothed with golden fringes, embroidered whether by actions or by contemplation. And she who is under the yoke, let her also in some degree be Christ's; and the virgin altogether Christ's. Let the one be not entirely chained to the world, and let the other not belong to the world at all. For that which is a part to the yoked, is to the virgin all in all. Hast thou chosen the life of Angels? Art thou ranked among the unyoked? Sink not down to the flesh; sink not down to matter; be not wedded to matter, while otherwise thou remainest unwedded. A lascivious eye guardeth not virginity; a meretricious tongue mingles with the Evil One; feet that walk disorderly accuse of disease or danger. Let the mind also be virgin; let it not rove about; let it not wander; let it not carry in itself forms of evil things (for the form is a part of harlotry); let it not make idols in its soul of hateful things.

XI. But He said unto them, All men cannot receive this saying, save they to whom it is given. Do you see the sublimity of the matter? It is found to be nearly incomprehensible. For surely it is more than carnal that that which is born of flesh should not beget to the flesh. Surely it is Angelic that she who is bound to flesh should live not according to flesh, but be loftier than her nature. The flesh bound her to the world, but reason led her up to God. The flesh weighed her down, but reason gave her wings; the flesh bound her, but desire loosed her. With thy whole soul, O Virgin, be intent upon God (I give this same injunction to men and to women); and do not take the same view in other respects of what is honorable as the mass of men do; of family, of wealth, of throne, of dynasty, of that beauty which shews itself in complexion and composition of members, the plaything of time and disease. If thou hast poured out upon God the whole of thy love; if thou hast not two objects of desire, both the passing and the abiding, both the visible and the invisible, then thou hast been so pierced by the arrow of election, and hast so learned the beauty of the Bridegroom, that thou too canst say with the bridal drama and song, thou art sweetness and altogether loveliness.

XII. You see how streams confined in lead pipes, through being much compressed and carried to one point, often so far depart from the nature of water that that which is pushed from behind will often flow constantly upwards. So if thou confine thy desire, and be wholly joined to God, thou wilt not fall downward; thou wilt not be dissipated; thou wilt remain entirely Christ's, until thou see Christ thy Bridegroom. Keep thyself unapproachable, both in word and work and life, and thought and action. From all sides the Evil One interferes with thee; he spies thee everywhere, where he may strike, where wound thee; let him not find anything bared and ready to his stroke. The purer he sees thee, the more he strives to stain thee, for the stains on a shining garment are more conspicuous. Let not eye draw eye, nor laughter, nor familiarity night, lest night bring destruction. For that which is gradually drawn away and stolen, works a mischief which is unperceived at the time, but yet attains to the consummation of wickedness.

XIII. All men, He saith, cannot receive this saying, but they to whom it is given. When you hear this, It is given, do not understand it in a heretical fashion, and bring in differences of nature, the earthly and the spiritual and the mixed. For there are people so evilly disposed as to think that some men are of an utterly ruined nature, and some of a nature which is saved, and that others are of such a disposition as their will may lead them to, either to the better, or to the worse. For that men may have a certain aptitude, one more, another less, I too admit; but not that this aptitude alone suffices for perfection, but that it is reason which calls this out, that nature may proceed to action, just as fire is produced when a flint is struck with iron. When you hear To whom it is given, add, And it is given to those who are called and to those who incline that way. For when you hear, Not of him that willeth, nor of him that runneth, but of God that sheweth mercy, I counsel you to think the same. For since there are some who are so proud of their successes that they attribute all to themselves and nothing to Him that made them and gave them wisdom and supplied them with good; such are taught by this word that even to wish well needs help from God; or rather that even to choose what is right is divine and a gift of the mercy of God. For it is necessary both that we should be our own masters and also that our salvation should be of God. This is why He saith not of him that willeth; that is, not of him that willeth only, nor of him that runneth only, but also of God. That sheweth mercy. Next; since to will also is from God, he has attributed the whole to God with reason. However much you may run, however much you may wrestle, yet you need one to give the crown. Except the Lord build the house, they labored in vain that built it: Except the Lord keep the city, in vain they watched that keep it. I know, He says, that the race is not to the swift, nor the battle to the strong, nor the victory to the fighters, nor the harbors to the good sailors; but to God it belongs both to work victory, and to bring the baroque safe to port.

XIV. In another place it is also said and understood, and perhaps it is necessary that I should add it as follows to what has already been said, in order that I may impart to you also my wealth. The Mother of the Sons of Zebedee, in an impulse of parental affection, asked a thing in ignorance of the measure of what she was asking, but pardonably, through the excess of her love and of the kindness due to her children. For there is nothing more affectionate than a Mother, — and I speak of this that I may lay down a law for honoring Mothers. Their mother, then, asked Jesus that they might sit, the one on His right hand, the other on his left. But what saith the Savior? He first asks if they can drink the Cup Which He Himself was about to drink; and when this was professed, and the Savior accepted the profession (for He knew that they were being perfected by the same, or rather that they would be perfected thereby); what saith He? "They shall drink the cup; but to sit on My right hand and on My left — it is not Mine, He saith, to give this, but to whom it hath been given." Is then the ruling mind nothing? Nothing the labor? Nothing the reasoning? Nothing the philosophy? Nothing the fasting? Nothing the vigils, the sleeping on the ground, the shedding floods of tears? Is it for nothing of these, but in accordance with some election by lot, that a Jeremias is sanctified, and others are estranged from the womb?

XV. I fear lest some monstrous reasoning may come in, as of the soul having lived elsewhere, and then having been bound to this body, and that it is from that other life that some receive the gift of prophecy, and others are condemned, namely, those who lived badly. But since such a conception is too absurd, and contrary to the traditions of the Church (others if they like may play with such doctrines, but it is unsafe for us to play with them); we must in this place too add to the words "To whom it hath been given," this, "who are worthy;" who have not only received this character from the Father, but have given it to themselves.

XVI. For there are eunuchs which were made eunuchs from their mother' s womb, etc. I should very much like to be able to say something bold about eunuchs. Be not proud, ye who are eunuchs by nature. For, in point of self-restraint, this is perhaps unwilling. For it has not come to the test, nor has your self-restraint been proved by trial. For the good which is by nature is not a subject of merit; that which is the result of purpose is laudable. What merit has fire for burning, for it is its nature to burn? What merit has water for falling, a property given to it by its Maker? What thanks does the snow get for its coldness, or the sun for its shining? — It shines even if it does not wish. Claim merit if you please by willing the better things. You will claim it if, being carnal, you make yourself spiritual; if, while drawn down by the leaden flesh, you receive wings from reason; if though lowly born, you are found to be heavenly; if while chained down to the flesh, you shew yourself superior to the flesh.

XVII. Since then, natural chastity is not meritorious, I demand something else from the eunuchs. Do not go a whoring in respect of the Godhead. Having been wedded to Christ, do not dishonor Christ. Being perfected by the spirit, do not make the Spirit your own equal. If I yet pleased men, says Paul, I should not be the servant of

Christ. If I worshipped a creature, I should not be called a Christian. For why is Christianity precious? Is it not that Christ is God, unless my mingling with Him in love is a mere human passion? And yet I honor Peter, but I am not called a Petrine; and Paul, but have never been called a Pauline. I cannot allow myself to be named after a man, who am born of God. So then, if it is because you believe Him to be God that you are called a Christian, may you ever be so called, and may you remain in both the name and the thing; but if you are called from Christ only because you have an affection for Him, you attribute no more to him than other names which are given from some practice or fact.

XVIII. Consider those men who are devoted to horse racing. They are named after the colors and the sides on which they have placed themselves. You know the names without my mentioning them. If it is thus that you have got the name of Christian, the mere title is a very small thing even though you pride yourself upon it. But if it is because you believe Him to be God, shew your faith by your works. If the Son is a creature, even now also you are worshipping the creature instead of the Creator. If the Holy Ghost is a creature, you are baptized in vain, and are only sound on two sides, or rather not even on them; but on one you are altogether in danger. Imagine the Trinity to be a single pearl, alike on all sides and equally glistening. If any part of the pearl be injured; the whole beauty of the stone is gone. So when you dishonor the Son in order to honor the Father, He does not accept your honor. The Father doth not glory in the dishonor of the Son. If a wise Son maketh a glad Father, how much more doth the honor of the Son become that of the Father! And if you also accept this saying, My Son, glory not in the dishonor of thy Father, similarly the Father doth not glory in the Son's dishonor. If you dishonor the Holy Ghost, the Son receiveth not your honor. For though He be not of the Father in the same way as the Son, yet He is of the same Father. Either honor the whole or dishonor the whole, so as to have a consistent mind. I cannot accept your half piety. I would have you altogether pious, but in the way that I desire. Pardon my affection: I am grieved even for those who hate me. You were one of my members, even though you are now cut off: perhaps you will again become a member; and therefore I speak kindly. Thus much for the sake of the Eunuchs, that they may be chaste in respect of the Godhead.

XIX. For it is not only bodily sin which is called fornication and adultery, but any sin you have committed, and especially transgression against that which is divine. Perhaps you ask how we can prove this: — They went a whoring, it says, with their own inventions. Do you see an impudent act of fornication? And again, They committed adultery in the wood. See you a kind of adulterous religion? Do not then commit spiritual adultery, while keeping your bodies chaste. Do not shew that it is unwillingly you are chaste in body, by not being chaste where you can commit fornication. Why have you done your impiety? Why are you hurried to vice, so that it is all one to call a man a Eunuch or a villain? Place yourselves on the side of men, and, even though so late, have some manly thoughts. Avoid the women's apartments; do not let the disgrace of proclamation be added to the disgrace of the name. Would you have us persevere a little longer in this discourse, or are you tired with what we have said? Nay, by what follows let even the eunuchs be honored. For the word is one of praise.

XX. There are, He says, some eunuchs which were so born from their mother's womb; and there are some eunuchs which were made eunuchs of men; and there be eunuchs which have made themselves eunuchs for the Kingdom of Heaven's sake. He that is able to receive it, let him receive it. I think that the discourse would sever itself from the body, and represent higher things by bodily figures; for to stop the meaning at bodily eunuchs would be small and very weak, and unworthy of the Word; and we must understand in addition something worthy of the Spirit. Some, then, seem by nature to incline to good. And when I speak of nature, I am not slighting free will, but supposing both — an aptitude for good, and that which brings the natural aptitude to effect. And there are others whom reason cleanses, by cutting them off from the passions. These I imagine to be meant by those whom men have made Eunuchs, when the word of teaching distinguishing the better from the worse and rejecting the one and commanding the other (like the verse, Depart from evil and do good), works spiritual chastity. This sort of making eunuchs I approve; and I highly praise both teachers and taught, that the one have nobly effected, and the other still more nobly endured, the cutting off.

XXI. And there be eunuchs which have made themselves eunuchs for the Kingdom of Heaven's sake. Others, too, who have not met with teachers, have been laudable teachers to themselves. No father nor mother, no Priest or Bishop, nor any of those commissioned to teach, taught you your duty; but by moving reason in yourself and by kindling the spark of good by your free will, you made yourself a eunuch, and acquired such a habit of virtue that impulse to vice became almost an impossibility to you. Therefore I praise this kind of Eunuch-making also, and perhaps even above the others. He that is able to receive it let him receive it. Choose which part you will; either follow the Teacher or be your own teacher. One thing alone is shameful — that the passions be not extirpated. It matters not how they are extirpated. The teacher is God's creature; and you also have the same origin; and whether the teacher grasp this grace, or the good be your own — it is equally good.

XXII. Only let us cut ourselves off from passion, test any root of bitterness springing up trouble us; only let us follow the image; only let us reverence our Archetype. Cut off the bodily passions; cut off also the spiritual. For by how much the soul is more precious than the body, by so much more precious is it to cleanse the soul than the body. And if cleansing of the body be a praiseworthy act, see, I pray you, how much greater and higher is that of the soul. Cut away the Arian impiety; cut away the false opinion of Sabellius; do not join more than is right, or wrongly sever; do not either confuse the Three Persons into One, or make Three diversities of Nature. The One is praiseworthy if rightly understood; and the Three when rightly divided, when the division is of Persons, not of Godhead.

XXIII. I enact this for Laymen too, and I enjoin it also upon all Priests, and upon those commissioned to rule. Come to the aid of the Word, all of you to whom God has given power to aid. It is a great thing to check murder, to punish adultery, to chastise theft; much more to establish piety by law, and to bestow sound doctrine. My word will not be able to do as much in fighting for the Holy Trinity as your Edict, if you will bridle the ill disposed, if you will help the persecuted, if you will check the slayers, and prevent people from being slain. I am speaking not merely of bodily but of spiritual slaughter. For all sin is the death of the soul. Here let my discourse end.

XXIV. But it remains that I speak a prayer for those who are assembled. Husbands alike and wives, rulers and ruled, old men, and young men, and maidens, every sort of age, bear ye every loss whether of money or of body, but one thing alone do not endure — to lose the Godhead. I adore the Father, I adore the Son, I adore the Holy Ghost; or rather We adore them; I, who am speaking, before all and after all and with all, in the same Christ our Lord, to whom be the glory and the might for ever. Amen.

Introduction to the Theophany

The Title of this Oration has given rise to a doubt whether it was preached on Dec. 25, 380, or on Jan. 6, 381. The word Theophania is well known as a name for the Epiphany; which, however, according to Schaff, was originally a celebration both of the Nativity and the Baptism of our Lord. The two words seem both to have been used in the simplest sense of the Manifestation of God, and certainly were applied to Christmas Day. Thus Suidas, "The Epiphany is the Incarnation of the Savior;" and Epiphanius (Haer., 53), "The Day of the Epiphany is the day on which Christ was born according to the flesh." But S. Jerome applies the word to the Baptism of Christ; "The day of the Epiphany is still venerable; not, as some think, on account of His Birth in the flesh; for then He was hidden, not manifested; but it agrees with the time at which it was said, This is My beloved Son (In Ezech. I.). There is also a Sermon, attributed to S. Chrysostom, "On the Baptism of Christ," in which it is expressly denied that the name Theophany applies to Christmas. The Oration itself, however, contains evidence to shew that the Festival of our Lord's Birth was kept at the earlier date; for in c. 16 the Preacher says, "A little later you shall see Jesus submitting to be purified in the river Jordan for my purification." And another piece of evidence occurs in the oration In Sancta Lumina, c. 14, "At His Birth we duly kept festival, both I the leader of the feast, and you. Now we are come to another action of Christ and another Mystery."

The Oration is thus analyzed by Abbe Benoe it:

"After an exordium which is full of the enthusiasm and joy which such a subject naturally inspires the Orator recommends his hearers to celebrate the Festival by a pious gladness, and by hearing the Word of God; and not as the heathen celebrated their feasts, by profane amusements and all kinds of excess. He will try to satisfy their desires by speaking to them of God. God is infinite, ineffable, eternal, the Sovereign Good. He created the Angels in the beginning out of goodness. The fall of the Angels was followed by the creation of the material world. Man too fell, and God shewed His mercy even in the punishment. He used various means to raise him again; and at length He came Himself. Then the speaker forcibly argues against those who misuse the infinite condescension of the Word to contest His Godhead; he rapidly traces the principal features of His Life at once human and Divine; and ends with a recommendation to his hearers to imitate in all things the Life of Christ, so that they may have a share in His Kingdom in Heaven."

It is considered one of the best of Gregory's discourses. "By the grandeur of the plan," says Benoit, "the elevation of the ideas, and the rich fund of doctrine, this discourse is incontestably one of S. Gregory's most remarkable efforts."

On the Theophany or Birthday of Christ

I. Christ Is Born , glorify ye Him. Christ from heaven, go ye out to meet Him. Christ on earth; be ye exalted. Sing unto the Lord all the whole earth; and that I may join both in one word, Let the heavens rejoice, and let the earth be glad, for Him Who is of heaven and then of earth. Christ in the flesh, rejoice with trembling and with joy; with trembling because of your sins, with joy because of your hope. Christ of a Virgin; O ye Matrons live as Virgins, that ye may be Mothers of Christ. Who doth not worship Him That is from the beginning? Who doth not glorify Him That is the Last?

II. Again the darkness is past; again Light is made; again Egypt is punished with darkness; again Israel is enlightened by a pillar. The people that sat in the darkness of ignorance, let it see the Great Light of full knowledge. Old things are passed away, behold all things are become new. The letter gives way, the Spirit comes to the front. The shadows flee away, the Truth comes in upon them. Melchisedec is concluded. He that was without Mother becomes without Father (without Mother of His former state, without Father of His second). The laws of nature are upset; the world above must be filled. Christ commands it, let us not set ourselves against Him. O clap your hands together all ye people, because unto us a Child is born, and a Son given unto us, Whose Government is upon His shoulder (for with the Cross it is raised up), and His Name is called The Angel of the Great Counsel of the Father. Let John cry, Prepare ye the way of the Lord: I too will cry the power of this Day. He Who is not carnal is Incarnate; the Son of God becomes the Son of Man, Jesus Christ the Same yesterday, and today, and for ever. Let the Jews be offended, let the Greeks deride; let heretics talk till their tongues ache. Then shall they believe, when they see Him ascending up into heaven; and if not then, yet when they see Him coming out of heaven and sitting as Judge.

III. Of these on a future occasion; for the present the Festival is the Theophany or Birth-day, for it is called both, two titles being given to the one thing. For God was manifested to man by birth. On the one hand Being, and eternally Being, of the Eternal Being, above cause and word, for there was no word before The Word; and on the other hand for our sakes also Becoming, that He Who gives us our being might also give us our Well-being, or rather might restore us by His Incarnation, when we had by wickedness fallen from well-being. The name Theophany is given to it in reference to the Manifestation, and that of Birthday in respect of His Birth.

IV. This is our present Festival; it is this which we are celebrating today, the Coming of God to Man, that we might go forth, or rather (for this is the more proper expression) that we might go back to God — that putting off the old man, we might put on the New; and that as we died in Adam, so we might live in Christ, being born with Christ and crucified with Him and buried with Him and rising with Him. For I must undergo the beautiful conversion, and as the painful succeeded the more blissful, so must the more blissful come out of the painful. For where sin abounded Grace did much more abound; and if a taste condemned us, how much more doth the Passion of Christ justify us? Therefore let us keep the Feast, not after the manner of a heathen festival, but after a godly sort; not after the way of the world, but in a fashion above the world; not as our own but as belonging to Him Who is ours, or rather as our Master's; not as of weakness, but as of healing; not as of creation, but of re-creation.

V. And how shall this be? Let us not adorn our porches, nor arrange dances, nor decorate the streets; let us not feast the eye, nor enchant the ear with music, nor enervate the nostrils with perfume, nor prostitute the taste, nor indulge the touch, those roads that are so prone to evil and entrances for sin; let us not be effeminate in clothing soft and flowing, whose beauty consists in its uselessness, nor with the glittering of gems or the sheen of gold or the tricks of color, belying the beauty of nature, and invented to do despite unto the image of God; Not in rioting and drunkenness, with which are mingled, I know well, chambering and wantonness, since the lessons which evil teachers give are evil; or rather the harvests of worthless seeds are worthless. Let us not set up high beds of leaves, making tabernacles for the belly of what belongs to debauchery. Let us not appraise the bouquet of wines, the kickshaws of cooks, the great expense of unguents. Let not sea and land bring us as a gift their precious dung, for it is thus that I have learnt to estimate luxury; and let us not strive to outdo each other in intemperance (for to my mind every superfluity is intemperance, and all which is beyond absolute need), — and this while others are hungry and in want, who are made of the same clay and in the same manner.

VI. Let us leave all these to the Greeks and to the pomps and festivals of the Greeks, who call by the name of gods beings who rejoice in the reek of sacrifices, and who consistently worship with their belly; evil inventors and worshippers of evil demons. But we, the Object of whose adoration is the Word, if we must in some way have luxury, let us seek it in word, and in the Divine Law, and in histories; especially such as are the origin of this Feast; that our luxury may be akin to and not far removed from Him Who hath called us together. Or do you desire (for today I am your entertainer) that I should set before you, my good Guests, the story of these things as abundantly and as nobly as I can, that ye may know how a foreigner can feed the natives of the land, and a rustic the people of the town, and one who cares not for luxury those who delight in it, and one who is poor and homeless those who are eminent for wealth? We will begin from this point; and let me ask of you who delight in such matters to cleanse you mind and your ears and your thoughts, since our discourse is to be of God and Divine; that when you depart, you may have had the enjoyment of delights that really fade not away. And this same discourse shall be at once both very full and very concise, that you may neither be displeased at its deficiencies, nor find it unpleasant through satiety.

VII. God always was, and always is, and always will be. Or rather, God always Isaiah For Was and Will be are fragments of our time, and of changeable nature, but He is Eternal Being. And this is the Name that He gives to Himself when giving the Oracle to Moses in the Mount. For in Himself He sums up and contains all Being, having neither beginning in the past nor end in the future; like some great Sea of Being, limitless and unbounded, transcending all conception of time and nature, only adumbrated by the mind, and that very dimly and scantily… not by His Essentials, but by His Environment; one image being got from one source and another from another, and combined into some sort of presentation of the truth, which escapes us before we have caught it, and takes to flight before we have conceived it, blazing forth upon our Master-part, even when that is cleansed, as the lightning flash which will not stay its course, does upon our sight… in order as I conceive by that part of it which we can comprehend to draw us to itself (for that which is altogether incomprehensible is outside the bounds of hope, and not within the compass of endeavor), and by that part of It which we cannot comprehend to move our wonder, and as an object of wonder to become more an object of desire, and being desired to purify, and by purifying to make us like God; so that when we have thus become like Himself, God may, to use a bold expression, hold converse with us as Gods, being united to us, and that perhaps to the same extent as He already knows those who are known to Him. The Divine Nature then is boundless and hard to understand; and all that we can comprehend of Him is His boundlessness; even though one may conceive that because He is of a simple nature He is therefore either wholly incomprehensible, or perfectly comprehensible. For let us further enquire what is implied by "is of a simple nature." For it is quite certain that this simplicity is not itself its nature, just as composition is not by itself the essence of compound beings.

VIII. And when Infinity is considered from two points of view, beginning and end (for that which is beyond these and not limited by them is Infinity), when the mind looks to the depth above, not having where to stand, and leans upon phenomena to form an idea of God, it calls the Infinite and Unapproachable which it finds there by the name of Unoriginate. And when it looks into the depths below, and at the future, it calls Him Undying and Imperishable. And when it draws a conclusion from the whole it calls Him Eternal (oc'icovioc;). For Eternity (aicov is neither time nor part of time; for it cannot be measured. But what time, measured by the course of the sun, is to us, that Eternity is to the Everlasting, namely, a sort of time-like movement and interval co-extensive with their existence. This, however, is all I must now say about God; for the present is not a suitable time, as my present subject is not the doctrine of God, but that of the Incarnation. But when I say God, I mean Father, Son, and Holy Ghost. For Godhead is neither diffused beyond these, so as to bring in a mob of gods; nor yet is it bounded by a smaller compass than these, so as to condemn us for a poverty-stricken conception of Deity; either Judaizing to save the Monarchia, or failing into heathenism by the multitude of our gods. For the evil on either side is the same, though found in contrary directions.

This then is the Holy of Holies, which is hidden even from the Seraphim, and is glorified with a thrice repeated Holy, meeting in one ascription of the Title Lord and God, as one of our predecessors has most beautifully and loftily pointed out.

IX. But since this movement of self-contemplation alone could not satisfy Goodness, but Good must be poured out and go forth beyond Itself to multiply the objects of Its beneficence, for this was essential to the highest Goodness, He first conceived the Heavenly and Angelic Powers. And this conception was a work fulfilled by His Word, and perfected by His Spirit. And so the secondary Splendors came into being, as the Ministers of the Primary Splendor; whether we are to conceive of them as intelligent Spirits, or as Fire of an immaterial and incorruptible kind, or as some other nature approaching this as near as may be. I should like to say that they were incapable of movement in the direction of evil, and susceptible only of the movement of good, as being about God, and illumined with the first rays from God — for earthly beings have but the second illumination; but I am obliged to stop short of saying that, and to conceive and speak of them only as difficult to move because of him, who for his splendor was called Lucifer, but became and is called Darkness through his pride; and the apostate hosts who are subject to him, creators of evil by their revolt against good and our inciters.

X. Thus, then, and for these reasons, He gave being to the world of thought, as far as I can reason upon these matters, and estimate great things in my own poor language. Then when His first creation was in good order, He conceives a second world, material and visible; and this a system and compound of earth and sky, and all that is in the midst of them — an admirable creation indeed, when we look at the fair form of every part, but yet more worthy of admiration when we consider the harmony and the unison of the whole, and how each part fits in with every other, in fair order, and all with the whole, tending to the perfect completion of the world as a Unit. This was to shew that He could call into being, not only a Nature akin to Himself, but also one altogether alien to Himself. For akin to Deity are those natures which are intellectual, and only to be comprehended by mind; but all of which sense can take cognizance are utterly alien to It; and of these the furthest removed are all those which are entirely destitute of soul and of power of motion. But perhaps some one of those who are too festive and impetuous may say, What has all this to do with us? Spur your horse to the goal. Talk to us about the Festival, and the reasons for our being here today. Yes, this is what I am about to do, although I have begun at a somewhat previous point, being compelled to do so by love, and by the needs of my argument.

XI. Mind, then, and sense, thus distinguished from each other, had remained within their own boundaries, and bore in themselves the magnificence of the Creator- Word, silent praisers and thrilling heralds of His mighty work. Not yet was there any mingling of both, nor any mixtures of these opposites, tokens of a greater Wisdom and Generosity in the creation of natures; nor as yet were the whole riches of Goodness made known. Now the Creator- Word, determining to exhibit this, and to produce a single living being out of both — the visible and the invisible creations, I mean — fashions Man; and taking a body from already existing matter, and placing in it a Breath taken from Himself which the Word knew to be an intelligent soul and the Image of God, as a sort of second world. He placed him, great in littleness on the earth; a new Angel, a mingled worshipper, fully initiated into the visible creation, but only partially into the intellectual; King of all upon earth, but subject to the King above; earthly and heavenly; temporal and yet immortal; visible and yet intellectual; half-way between greatness and lowliness; in one person combining spirit and flesh; spirit, because of the favor bestowed on him; flesh, because of the height to which he had been raised; the one that he might continue to live and praise his Benefactor, the other that he might suffer, and by suffering be put in remembrance, and corrected if he became proud of his greatness. A living creature trained here, and then moved elsewhere; and, to complete the mystery, deified by its inclination to God. For to this, I think, tends that Light of Truth which we here possess but in measure, that we should both see and experience the Splendor of God, which is worthy of Him Who made us, and will remake us again after a loftier fashion.

XII. This being He placed in Paradise, whatever the Paradise may have been, having honored him with the gift of Free Will (in order that God might belong to him as the result of his choice, no less than to Him who had implanted the seeds of it), to till the immortal plants, by which is meant perhaps the Divine Conceptions, both the simpler and the more perfect; naked in his simplicity and in-artificial life, and without any covering or screen; for it was fitting that he who was from the beginning should be such. Also He gave him a Law, as a material for his Free Will to act upon. This Law was a Commandment as to what plants he might partake of, and which one he might not touch. This latter was the Tree of Knowledge; not, however, because it was evil from the beginning when planted; nor was it forbidden because God grudged it to us... Let not the enemies of God wag their tongues in that direction, or imitate the Serpent... But it would have been good if partaken of at the proper time, for the tree was, according to my theory, Contemplation, upon which it is only safe for those who have reached maturity of habit to enter; but which is not good for those who are still somewhat simple and greedy in their habit; just as solid food is not good for those who are yet tender, and have need of milk. But when through the Devil's malice and the woman's caprice, to which she succumbed as the more tender, and which she brought to bear upon the man, as she was the more apt to persuade, alas for my weakness! (for that of my first father was mine), he forgot the Commandment which had been given to him; he yielded to the baleful fruit; and for his sin he was banished, at once from the Tree of Life, and from Paradise, and from God; and put on the coats of skins... that is, perhaps, the coarser flesh, both mortal and contradictory. This was the first thing that he learnt — his own shame; and he hid himself from God. Yet here too he makes a gain, namely death, and the cutting off of sin, in order that evil may not be immortal. Thus his punishment is changed into a mercy; for it is in mercy, I am persuaded, that God inflicts punishment.

XIII. And having been first chastened by many means (because his sins were many, whose root of evil sprang up through divers causes and at sundry tithes), by word, by law, by prophets, by benefits, by threats, by plagues, by waters, by fires, by wars, by victories, by defeats, by signs in heaven and signs in the air and in the earth and in the sea, by unexpected changes of men, of cities, of nations (the object of which was the destruction of wickedness), at last he needed a stronger remedy, for his diseases were growing worse; mutual slaughters, adulteries, perjuries, unnatural crimes, and that first and last of all evils, idolatry and the transfer of worship from the Creator to the Creatures. As these required a greater aid, so also they obtained a greater. And that was that the Word of God Himself — Who is before all worlds, the Invisible, the Incomprehensible, the Bodiless, Beginning of Beginning, the Light of Light, the Source of Life and Immortality, the Image of the Archetypal Beauty, the immovable Seal, the unchangeable Image, the Father's Definition and Word, came to His own Image, and took on Him flesh for the sake of our flesh, and mingled Himself with an intelligent soul for my soul's sake, purifying like by like; and in all points except sin was made man. Conceived by the Virgin, who first in body and soul was purified by the Holy Ghost (for it was needful both that Childbearing should be honored, and that Virginity should receive a higher honor), He came forth then as God with that which He had assumed, One Person in two Natures, Flesh and Spirit, of which the latter deified the former. O new commingling; O strange conjunction; the Self-Existent comes into being, the Uncreate is created, That which cannot be contained is contained, by the intervention of an intellectual soul, mediating between the Deity and the corporeity of the flesh. And He Who gives riches becomes poor, for He assumes the poverty of my flesh, that I may assume the richness of His Godhead. He that is full empties Himself, for He empties Himself of His glory for a short while, that I may have a share in His Fullness. What is the riches of His Goodness? What is this mystery that is around me? I had a share in the image; I did not keep it; He partakes of my flesh that He may both save the image and make the flesh immortal. He communicates a second Communion far more marvelous than the first, inasmuch as then He imparted the better Nature, whereas now Himself partakes of the worse. This is more godlike than the former action, this is loftier in the eyes of all men of understanding.

XIV. To this what have those cavilers to say, those bitter reasoners about Godhead, those detractors of all that is praiseworthy, those darkeners of light, uncultured in respect of wisdom, for whom Christ died in vain, those unthankful creatures, the work of the Evil One? Do you turn this benefit into a reproach to God? Wilt thou deem Him little on this account, that He humbled Himself for thee; because the Good Shepherd, He who lays down His life for His sheep, came to seek for that which had strayed upon the mountains and the hills, on which thou wast then sacrificing, and found the wanderer; and having found it, took it upon His shoulders — on which He also took the Wood of the Cross; and having taken it, brought it back to the higher life; and having carried it back, numbered it amongst those who had never strayed. Because He lighted a candle — His own Flesh — and swept the house, cleansing the world from sin; and sought the piece of money, the Royal Image that was covered up by passions. And He calls together His Angel friends on the finding of the coin, and makes them sharers in His joy, whom He had made to share also the secret of the Incarnation? Because on the candle of the Forerunner there follows the light that exceeds in brightness; and to the Voice the Word succeeds; and to the Bridegroom's friend the Bridegroom; to him that prepared for the Lord a peculiar people, cleansing them by water in preparation for the Spirit? Dost thou reproach God with all this? Dost thou on this account deem Him lessened, because He girds Himself with a towel and washes His disciples' feet, and shows that humiliation is the best road to exaltation? Because for the soul that was bent to the ground He humbles Himself, that He may raise up with Himself the soul that was tottering to a fall under a weight of sin? Why dost thou not also charge upon Him as a crime the fact that He eats with Publicans and at Publicans' tables, and that He makes disciples of Publicans, that He too may gain somewhat... and what?... the salvation of sinners. If so, we must blame the physician for stooping over sufferings, and enduring evil odors that he may give health to the sick; or one who as the Law commands bent down into a ditch to save a beast that had fallen into it.

XV. He was sent, but as man, for He was of a twofold Nature; for He was wearied, and hungered, and was thirsty, and was in an agony, and shed tears, according to the nature of a corporeal being. And if the expression be also used of Him as God, the meaning is that the Father's good pleasure is to be considered a Mission, for to this He refers all that concerns Himself; both that He may honor the Eternal Principle, and because He will not be taken to be an antagonistic God. And whereas it is written both that He was betrayed, and also that He gave Himself up and that He was raised up by the Father, and taken up into heaven; and on the other hand, that He raised Himself and went up; the former statement of each pair refers to the good pleasure of the Father, the latter to His own Power. Are you then to be allowed to dwell upon all that humiliates Him, while passing over all that exalts Him, and to count on your side the fact that He suffered, but to leave out of the account the fact that it was of His own will? See what even now the Word has to suffer. By one set He is honored as God, but is confused with the Father, by another He is dishonored as mere flesh and severed from the Godhead. With which of them will He be most angry, or rather, which shall He forgive, those who injuriously confound Him or those who divide Him? For the former ought to have distinguished, and the latter to have united Him; the one in number, the other in Godhead. Stumblest Thou at His flesh? So did the Jews. Or dost thou call Him a Samaritan, and... I will not say the rest. Dost thou disbelieve in His Godhead? This did not even the demons, O thou who art less believing than demons and more stupid than Jews. Those did perceive that the name of Son implies equality of rank; these did know that He who drove them out was God, for they were convinced of it by their own experience. But you will admit neither the equality nor the Godhead. It would have been better for you to have been either a Jew or a demoniac (if I may utter an absurdity), than in uncircumcision and m sound health to be so wicked and ungodly in your attitude of mind.

XVI. A little later on you will see Jesus submitting to be purified in the River Jordan for my Purification, or rather, sanctifying the waters by His Purification (for indeed He had no need of purification Who taketh away the sin of the world) and the heavens cleft asunder, and witness borne to him by the Spirit That is of one nature with Him; you shall see Him tempted and conquering and served by Angels, and healing every sickness and every disease, and giving life to the dead (O that He would give life to you who are dead because of your heresy), and driving out demons, sometimes Himself, sometimes by his disciples; and feeding vast multitudes with a few loaves; and walking dryshod upon seas; and being betrayed and crucified, and crucifying with Himself my sin; offered as a Lamb, and offering as a Priest; as a Man buried in the grave, and as God rising again; and then ascending, and to come again in His own glory. Why what a multitude of high festivals there are in each of the mysteries of the Christ; all of which have one completion, namely, my perfection and return to the first condition of Adam. XVII. Now then I pray you accept His Conception, and leap before Him; if not like John from the womb, yet like David, because of the resting of the Ark. Revere the enrollment on account of which thou wast written in heaven, and adore the Birth by which thou wast loosed from the chains of thy birth, and honor little Bethlehem, which hath led thee back to Paradise; and worship the manger through which thou, being without sense, wast fed by the Word. Know as Isaiah bids thee, thine Owner, like the ox, and like the ass thy Master's crib; if thou be one of those who are pure and lawful food, and who chew the cud of the word and are fit for sacrifice. Or if thou art one of those who are as yet unclean and uneatable and unfit for sacrifice, and of the gentile portion, run with the Star, and bear thy Gifts with the Magi, gold and frankincense and myrrh, as to a King, and to God, and to One Who is dead for thee. With Shepherds glorify Him; with Angels join in chorus; with Archangels sing hymns. Let this Festival be common to the powers in heaven and to the powers upon earth. For I am persuaded that the Heavenly Hosts join in our exultation and keep high Festival with us today... because they love men, and they love God just like those whom David introduces after the Passion ascending with Christ and coming to meet Him, and bidding one another to lift up the gates.

XVIII. One thing connected with the Birth of Christ I would have you hate... the murder of the infants by Herod. Or rather you must venerate this too, the Sacrifice of the same age as Christ, slain before the Offering of the New Victim. If He flees into Egypt, joyfully become a companion of His exile. It is a grand thing to share the exile of the persecuted Christ. If He tarry long in Egypt, call Him out of Egypt by a reverent worship of Him there. Travel without fault through every stage and faculty of the Life of Christ. Be purified; be circumcised; strip off the veil which has covered thee from thy birth. After this teach in the Temple, and drive out the sacrilegious traders. Submit to be stoned if need be, for well I wot thou shalt be hidden from those who cast the stones; thou shalt escape even through the midst of them, like God. If thou be brought before Herod, answer not for the most part. He will respect thy silence more than most people's long speeches. If thou be scourged, ask for what they leave out. Taste gall for the taste's sake; drink vinegar; seek for spittings; accept blows, be crowned with thorns, that is, with the hardness of the godly life; put on the purple robe, take the reed in hand, and receive mock worship from those who mock at the truth; lastly, be crucified with Him, and share His Death and Burial gladly, that thou mayest rise with Him, and be glorified with Him and reign with Him. Look at and be looked at by the Great God, Who in Trinity is worshipped and glorified, and Whom we declare to be now set forth as clearly before you as the chains of our flesh allow, in Jesus Christ our Lord, to Whom be the glory for ever. Amen.

Introduction to the Orations on the Holy Lights and on Holy Baptism.

The Oration on the Holy Lights was preached on the Festival of the Epiphany 381, and was followed the next day by that on Baptism. In the Eastern Church this Festival is regarded as more particularly the commemoration of our Lord's Baptism, and is accordingly one of the great days for the solemn ministration of the Sacrament. It is generally called Theophania, and the Gospel in the Liturgy is S. Matthew 3:13-17. The Sunday in the Octave is called \xexa xa (pekoe (After The Lights), pointing to a time when the Feast was known as the "Holy Lights," as seems to have been the case in S. Gregory's day. This name is derived from Baptism, which was often in ancient days called Illumination, in reference to which name (derived from the spiritual grace of the Sacrament) lighted torches or candles were carried by the neophytes. It would appear that the solemnities of the Festival lasted two days, of which the second was devoted to the solemn conferring of the Sacrament. Accordingly we find two Orations belonging to the Festival. In the first, delivered on the Day itself he dwells more especially on the Feast and the Mystery of our Lord's Baptism therein commemorated; and proceeds to speak of the different kinds of Baptism, of which he enumerates Five, —

1. The figurative Baptism of Israel by Moses in the cloud and in the Sea.

2. The preparatory Baptism of repentance ministered by S. John the Baptist.

3. The spiritual Baptism of water and the Holy Ghost given us by our Lord.

4. The glorious Baptism of Martyrdom.

5. The painful Baptism of Penance.

In speaking of this last he takes occasion to refute the extreme rigorism of the followers of Novatus, who denied absolution to certain classes of sins committed after Baptism. In the second Oration, delivered next day, he dwells on the Sacrament of Baptism and its spiritual effects; and takes occasion to reprove the then still prevalent practice of deferring Baptism till the near approach of death. He likewise dwells on the truth that the validity and spiritual effect of the Sacrament is wholly independent of the rank or worthiness of the Priest who may minister it; and he concludes with a sketch of the obligations which its reception involves, with a very valuable exposition of the Creed, and of the Ceremonies which accompanied the administration of the Sacrament.

Oration on the Holy Lights

I. Again My Jesus, and again a mystery; not deceitful nor disorderly, nor belonging to Greek error or drunkenness (for so I call their solemnities, and so I think will every man of sound sense); but a mystery lofty and divine, and allied to the Glory above. For the Holy Day of the Lights, to which we have come, and which we are celebrating today, has for its origin the Baptism of my Christ, the True Light That lighteneth every man that cometh into the world, and effecteth my purification, and assists that light which we received from the beginning from Him from above, but which we darkened and confused by sin.

II. Therefore listen to the Voice of God, which sounds so exceeding clearly to me, who am both disciple and master of these mysteries, as would to God it may sound to you ; I Am TheLightOfThe World. Therefore approach ye to Him and be enlightened, and let not your faces be ashamed, being signed with the true Light. It is a season of new birth, let us be born again. It is a time of reformation, let us receive again the first Adam. Let us not remain what we are, but let us become whatwe once were. The Light Shineth In Darkness, in this life and in the flesh, and is chased by the darkness, but is not overtaken by it: — I mean the adverse power leaping up in its shamelessness against the visible Adam, but encountering God and being defeated; — in order that we, putting away the darkness, may draw near to the Light, and may then become perfect Light, the children of perfect Light. See the grace of this Day; see the power of this mystery. Are you not lifted up from the earth? Are you not clearly placed on high, being exalted by our voice and meditation? and you will be placed much higher when the Word shall have prospered the course of my words.

III. Is there any such among the shadowy purifications of the Law, aiding as it did with temporary sprinklings, and the ashes of an heifer sprinkling the unclean; or do the gentiles celebrate any such thing in their mysteries, every ceremony and mystery of which to me is nonsense, and a dark invention of demons, and a figment of an unhappy mind, aided by time, and hidden by fable? For what they worship as true, they veil as mythical. But if these things are true, they ought not to be called myths, but to be proved not to be shameful; and if they are false, they ought not to be objects of wonder; nor ought people so inconsiderately to hold the most contrary opinions about the same thing, as if they were playing in the market-place with boys or really ill-disposed men, not engaged in discussion with men of sense, and worshippers of the Word, though despisers of this artificial plausibility.

IV. We are not concerned in these mysteries with birth of Zeus and thefts of the Cretan Tyrant (though the Greeks may be displeased at such a title for him), nor with the name of Curetes, and the armed dances, which were to hide the wailings of a weeping God, that he might escape from his father's hate. For indeed it would be a strange thing that he who was swallowed as a stone should be made to weep as a child. Nor are we concerned with Phrygian mutilations and flutes and Corybantes, and all the ravings of men concerning Rhea, consecrating people to the mother of the gods, and being initiated into such ceremonies as befit the mother of such gods as these. Nor have we any carrying away of the Maiden, nor wandering of Demeter, nor her intimacy with Celei and Triptolemi and Dragons; nor her doings and sufferings... for I am ashamed to bring into daylight that ceremony of the night, and to make a sacred mystery of obscenity. Eleusis knows these things, and so do those who are eyewitnesses of what is there guarded by silence, and well worthy of it. Nor is our commemoration one of Dionysus, and the thigh that travailed with an incomplete birth, as before a head had travailed with another; nor of the hermaphrodite God, nor a chorus of the drunken and enervated host; nor of the folly of the Thebans which honors him; nor the thunderbolt of Semele which they adore. Nor is it the harlot mysteries of Aphrodite, who, as they themselves admit, was basely born and basely honored; nor have we here Phalli and Ithyphalli, shameful both in form and action; nor Taurian massacres of strangers; nor blood of Laconian youths shed upon the altars, as they scourged themselves with the whips; and in this case alone use their courage badly, who honor a goddess, and her a virgin. For these same people both honor effeminacy, and worship boldness.

V. And where will you place the butchery of Pelops, which feasted hungry gods, that bitter and inhuman hospitality? Where the horrible and dark specters of Hecate, and the underground puerilities and sorceries of Trophonius, or the babblings of the Dodonaean Oak, or the trickeries of the Delphian tripod, or the prophetic draught of Castalia, which could prophesy anything, except their own being brought to silence? Nor is it the sacrificial art of Magi, and their entrail forebodings, nor the Chaldaean astronomy and horoscopes, comparing our lives with the movements of the heavenly bodies, which cannot know even what they are themselves, or shall be. Nor are these Thracian orgies, from which the word Worship (GpnaKeioc) is said to be derived; nor rites and mysteries of Orpheus, whom the Greeks admired so much for his wisdom that they devised for him a lyre which draws all things by its music. Nor the tortures of Mithras which it is just that those who can endure to be initiated into such things should suffer; nor the manglings of Osiris, another calamity honored by the Egyptians; nor the ill-fortunes of Isis and the goats more venerable than the Mendesians, and the stall of Apis, the calf that luxuriated in the folly of the Memphites, nor all those honors with which they outrage the Nile, while themselves proclaiming it in song to be the Giver of fruits and corn, and the measurer of happiness by its cubits.

VI. I pass over the honors they pay to reptiles, and their worship of vile things, each of which has its peculiar cultus and festival, and all share in a common devilishness; so that, if they were absolutely bound to be ungodly, and to fall away from honoring God, and to be led astray to idols and works of art and things made with hands, men of sense could not imprecate anything worse upon themselves than that they might worship just such things, and honor them in just such a way; that, as

Paul says, they might receive in themselves that recompense of their error which was meet, in the very objects of their worship; not so much honoring them as suffering dishonor by them; abominable because of their error, and yet more abominable from the vileness of the objects of their adoration and worship; so that they should be even more without understanding than the objects of their worship; being as excessively foolish as the latter are vile.

VII. Well, let these things be the amusement of the children of the Greeks and of the demons to whom their folly is due, who turn aside the honor of God to themselves, and divide men in various ways in pursuit of shameful thoughts and fancies, ever since they drove us away from the Tree of Life, by means of the Tree of Knowledge unseasonably and improperly imparted to us, and then assailed us as now weaker than before; carrying clean away the mind, which is the ruling power in us, and opening a door to the passions. For, being of a nature envious and man-hating, or rather having become so by their own wickedness, they could neither endure that we who were below should attain to that which is above, having themselves fallen from above upon the earth; nor that such a change in their glory and their first natures should have taken place. This is the meaning of their persecution of the creature. For this God's Image was outraged; and as we did not like to keep the Commandments, we were given over to the independence of our error. And as we erred we were disgraced by the objects of our worship. For there was not only this calamity, that we who were made for good works to the glory and praise of our Maker, and to imitate God as far as might be, were turned into a den of all sorts of passions, which cruelly devour and consume the inner man; but there was this further evil, that man actually made gods the advocates of his passions, so that sin might be reckoned not only irresponsible, but even divine, taking refuge in the objects of his worship as his apology.

VIII. But since to us grace has been given to flee from superstitious error and to be joined to the truth and to serve the living and true God, and to rise above creation, passing by all that is subject to time and to first motion; let us look at and reason upon God and things divine in a manner corresponding to this Grace given us. But let us begin our discussion of them from the most fitting point. And the most fitting is, as Solomon laid down for us; us; The beginning of wisdom, he says, is to get wisdom. And what this is he tells us; the beginning of wisdom is fear. For we must not begin with contemplation and leave off with fear (for an unbridled contemplation would perhaps push us over a precipice), but we must be grounded and purified and so to say made light by fear, and thus be raised to the height. For where fear is there is keeping of commandments; and where there is keeping of commandments there is purifying of the flesh, that cloud which covers the soul and suffers it not to see the Divine Ray. And where them is purifying there is Illumination; and Illumination is the satisfying of desire to those who long for the greatest things, or the Greatest Thing, or That Which surpasses all greatness.

IX. Wherefore we must purify ourselves first, and then approach this converse with the Pure; unless we would have the same experience as Israel, who could not endure the glory of the face of Moses, and therefore asked for a veil; or else would feel and say with Manoah "We are undone O wife, we have seen God," although it was God only in his fancy; or like Peter would send Jesus out of the boat, as being ourselves unworthy of such a visit; and when I say Peter, I am speaking of the man who walked upon the waves; or like Paul would be stricken in eyes, as he was before he was cleansed from the guilt of his persecution, when he conversed with Him Whom he was persecuting — or rather with a short flash of That great Light; or like the Centurion would seek for healing, but would not, through a praiseworthy fear, receive the Healer into his house. Let each one of us also speak so, as long as he is still uncleansed, and is a Centurion still, commanding many in wickedness, and serving in the army of Caesar, the World-ruler of those who are being dragged down; "I am not worthy that thou shouldest come under my roof." But when he shall have looked upon Jesus, though he be little of stature like Zaccheus of old, and climb up on the top of the sycamore tree by mortifying his members which are upon the earth, and having risen above the body of humiliation, then he shall receive the Word, and it shall be said to him, This day is salvation come to this house. Then let him lay hold on the salvation, and bring forth fruit more perfectly, scattering and pouring forth rightly that which as a publican he wrongly gathered.

X. For the same Word is on the one hand terrible through its nature to those who are unworthy, and on the other through its loving kindness can be received by those who are thus prepared, who have driven out the unclean and worldly spirit from their souls, and have swept and adorned their own souls by self-examination, and have not left them idle or without employment, so as again to be occupied with greater armament by the seven spirits of wickedness... the same number as are reckoned of virtue (for that which is hardest to fight against calls for the sternest efforts)... but besides fleeing from evil, practice virtue, making Christ entirely, or at any rate to the greatest extent possible, to dwell within them, so that the power of evil cannot meet with any empty place to fill it again with himself, and make the last state of that man worse than the first, by the greater energy of his assault, and the greater strength and impregnability of the fortress. But when, having guarded our soul with every care, and having appointed goings up in our heart, and broken up our fallow ground, and sown unto righteousness, as David and Solomon and Jeremiah bid us, let us enlighten ourselves with the light of knowledge, and then let us speak of the Wisdom of God that hath been hid in a mystery, and enlighten others. Meanwhile let us purify ourselves, and receive the elementary initiation of the Word, that we may do ourselves the utmost good, making ourselves godlike, and receiving the Word at His coming; and not only so, but holding Him fast and shewing Him to others.

XI. And now, having purified the theater by what has been said, let us discourse a little about the Festival, and join in celebrating this Feast with festal and pious

216

souls. And, since the chief point of the Festival is the remembrance of God, let us call God to mind. For I think that the sound of those who keep Festival There, where is the dwelling of all the Blissful, is nothing else than this, the hymns and praises of God, sung by all who are counted worthy of that City. Let none be astonished if what I have to say contains some things that I have said before; for not only will I utter the same words, but I shall speak of the same subjects, trembling both in tongue and mind and thought when I speak of God for you too, that you may share this laudable and blessed feeling. And when I speak of God you must be illumined at once by one flash of light and by three. Three in Individualities or Hypostases, if any prefer so to call them, or persons, for we will not quarrel about names so long as the syllables amount to the same meaning; but One in respect of the Substance — that is, the Godhead. For they are divided without division, if I may so say; and they are united in division. For the Godhead is one in three, and the three are one, in whom the Godhead is, or to speak more accurately, Who are the Godhead. Excesses and defects we will omit, neither making the Unity a confusion, nor the division a separation. We would keep equally far from the confusion of Sabellius and from the division of Arius, which are evils diametrically opposed, yet equal in their wickedness. For what need is there heretically to fuse God together, or to cut Him up into inequality?

XII. For to us there is but One God, the Father, of Whom are all things, and One Lord Jesus Christ, by Whom are all things; and One Holy Ghost, in Whom are all things; yet these words, of, by, in, whom, do not denote a difference of nature (for if this were the case, the three prepositions, or the order of the three names would never be altered), but they characterize the personalities of a nature which is one and unconfused. And this is proved by the fact that They are again collected into one, if you will read — not carelessly — this other passage of the same Apostle, "Of Him and through Him and to Him are all things; to Him be glory forever, Amen." The Father is Father, and is Unoriginate, for He is of no one; the Son is Son, and is not unoriginate, for He is of the Father. But if you take the word Origin in a temporal sense, He too is Unoriginate, for He is the Maker of Time, and is not subject to Time. The Holy Ghost is truly Spirit, coming forth from the Father indeed, but not after the manner of the Son, for it is not by Generation but by Procession (since I must coin a word for the sake of clearness); for neither did the Father cease to be Unbegotten because of His begetting something, nor the Son to be begotten because He is of the Unbegotten (how could that be?), nor is the Spirit changed into Father or Son because He proceeds, or because He is God — though the ungodly do not believe it. For Personality is unchangeable; else how could Personality remain, if it were changeable, and could be removed from one to another? But they who make "Unbegotten" and "Begotten" natures of equivocal gods would perhaps make Adam and Seth differ in nature, since the former was not born of flesh (for he was created), but the latter was born of Adam and Eve. There is then One God in Three, and These Three are One, as we have said.

XIII. Since then these things are so, or rather since This is so; and His Adoration ought not to be rendered only by Beings above, but there ought to be also worshippers on earth, that all things may be filled with the glory of God (forasmuch as they are filled with God Himself); therefore man was created and honored with the hand and Image of God. But to despise man, when by the envy of the Devil and the bitter taste of sin he was pitiably severed from God his Maker — this was not in the Nature of God. What then was done, and what is the great Mystery that concerns us? An innovation is made upon nature, and God is made Man. "He that rideth upon the Heaven of Heavens in the East" of His own glory and Majesty, is glorified in the West of our meanness and lowliness. And the Son of God deigns to become and to be called Son of Man; not changing what He was (for It is unchangeable); but assuming what He was not (for He is full of love to man), that the Incomprehensible might be comprehended, conversing with us through the mediation of the Flesh as through a veil; since it was not possible for that nature which is subject to birth and decay to endure His unveiled Godhead. Therefore the Unmingled is mingled; and not only is God mingled with birth and Spirit with flesh, and the Eternal with time, and the Uncircumscribed with measure; but also Generation with Virginity, and dishonor with Him who is higher than all honor; He who is impassible with Suffering, and the Immortal with the corruptible. For since that Deceiver thought that he was unconquerable in his malice, after he had cheated us with the hope of becoming gods, he was himself cheated by God's assumption of our nature; so that in attacking Adam as he thought, he should really meet with God, and thus the new Adam should save the old, and the condemnation of the flesh should be abolished, death being slain by flesh.

XIV. At His birth we duly kept Festival, both I, the leader of the Feast, and you, and all that is in the world and above the world. With the Star we ran, and with the Magi we worshipped, and with the Shepherds we were illuminated, and with the Angels we glorified Him, and with Simeon we took Him up in our arms, and with Anna the aged and chaste we made our responsive confession. And thanks be to Him who came to His own in the guise of a stranger, because He glorified the stranger. Now, we come to another action of Christ, and another mystery. I cannot restrain my pleasure; I am rapt into God. Almost like John I proclaim good tidings; for though I be not a Forerunner, yet am I from the desert. Christ is illumined, let us shine forth with Him. Christ is baptized, let us descend with Him that we may also ascend with Him. Jesus is baptized; but we must attentively consider not only this but also some other points. Who is He, and by whom is He baptized, and at what time? He is the All-pure; and He is baptized by John; and the time is the beginning of His miracles. What are we to learn and to be taught by this? To purify ourselves first; to be lowly minded; and to preach only in maturity both of spiritual and bodily stature. The first has a word especially for those who rush to Baptism off hand, and without due preparation, or providing for the stability of the Baptismal Grace by the disposition of their minds to good. For since Grace contains remission of the past (for it is a grace), it is on that account more worthy of reverence, that we return not to the same vomit again. The second speaks to those who rebel against the Stewards of this Mystery, if they are their superiors in rank. The third is for those who are confident in their youth, and think that any time is the right one to teach or to preside. Jesus is purified, and dost thou despise purification?... and by John, and dost thou rise up against thy herald?... and at thirty years of age, and dost thou before thy beard has grown presume to teach the aged, or believe that thou teachest them, though thou be not reverend on account of thine age, or even perhaps for thy character? But here it may be said, Daniel, and this or that other, were judges in their youth, and examples are on your tongues; for every wrongdoer is prepared to defend himself. But I reply that that which is rare is not the law of the Church. For one swallow does not make a summer, nor one line a geometrician, nor one voyage a sailor.

XV. But John baptizes, Jesus comes to Him... perhaps to sanctify the Baptist himself, but certainly to bury the whole of the old Adam in the water; and before this and for the sake of this, to sanctify Jordan; for as He is Spirit and Flesh, so He consecrates us by Spirit and water. John will not receive Him; Jesus contends. "I have need to be baptized of Thee" says the Voice to the Word, the Friend to the Bridegroom; he that is above all among them that are born of women, to Him Who is the Firstborn of every creature; he that leaped in the womb, to Him Who was adored in the womb; he who was and is to be the Forerunner to Him Who was and is to be manifested. "I have need to be baptized of Thee;" add to this "and for Thee;" for he knew that he would be baptized by Martyrdom, or, like Peter, that he would be cleansed not only as to his feet. "And comest Thou to me?" This also was prophetic; for he knew that after Herod would come the madness of Pilate, and so that when he had gone before Christ would follow him. But what saith Jesus? "Suffer it to be so now," for this is the time of His Incarnation; for He knew that yet a little while and He should baptize the Baptist. And what is the "Fan?" The Purification. And what is the "Fire?" The consuming of the chaff, and the heat of the Spirit. And what the "Axe?" The excision of the soul which is incurable even after the dung. And what the Sword? The cutting of the Word, which separates the worse from the better, and makes a division between the faithful and the unbeliever; and stirs up the son and the daughter and the bride against the father and the mother and the mother in law, the young and fresh against the old and shadowy. And what is the Latchet of the shoe, which thou John who baptizest Jesus mayest not loose? thou who art of the desert, and hast no food, the new Elias, the more than Prophet, inasmuch as thou sawest Him of Whom thou didst prophesy, thou Mediator of the Old and New Testaments. What is this? Perhaps the Message of the Advent, and the Incarnation, of which not the least point may be loosed, I say not by those who are yet carnal and babes in Christ, but not even by those who are like John in spirit.

XVI. But further — Jesus goeth up out of the water... for with Himself He car ties up the world... and sees the heaven opened which Adam had shut against himself and all his posterity, as the gates of Paradise by the flaming sword. And the Spirit bears witness to His Godhead, for he descends upon One that is like Him, as does the Voice from Heaven (for He to Whom the witness is borne came from thence), and like a Dove, for He honors the Body (for this also was God, through its union with God) by being seen in a bodily form; and moreover, the Dove has from distant ages been wont to proclaim the end of the Deluge. But if you are to judge of Godhead by bulk and weight, and the Spirit seems to you a small thing because He came in the form of a Dove, O man of contemptible littleness of thought concerning the greatest of things, you must also to be consistent despise the Kingdom of Heaven, because it is compared to a grain of mustard seed; and you must exalt the adversary above the Majesty of Jesus, because he is called a great Mountain, and Leviathan and King of that which lives in the water, whereas Christ is called the Lamb, and the Pearl, and the Drop and similar names.

XVII. Now, since our Festival is of Baptism, and we must endure a little hardness with Him Who for our sake took form, and was baptized, and was crucified; let us speak about the different kinds of Baptism, that we may come out thence purified. Moses baptized but it was in water, and before that in the cloud and in the sea. This was typical as Paul saith; the Sea of the water, and the Cloud of the Spirit; the Manna, of the Bread of Life; the Drink, of the Divine Drink. John also baptized; but this was not like the baptism of the Jews, for it was not only in water, but also "unto repentance." Still it was not wholly spiritual, for he does not add "And in the Spirit." Jesus also baptized, but in the Spirit. This is the perfect Baptism. And how is He not God, if I may digress a little, by whom you too are made God? I know also a Fourth Baptism — that by Martyrdom and blood, which also Christ himself underwent: — and this one is far more august than all the others, inasmuch as it cannot be defiled by after-stains. Yes, and I know of a Fifth also, which is that of tears, and is much more laborious, received by him who washes his bed every night and his couch with tears; whose bruises stink through his wickedness; and who goeth mourning and of a sad countenance; who imitates the repentance of Manasseh and the humiliation of the Ninerites upon which God had mercy; who utters the words of the Publican in the Temple, and is justified rather than the stiff-necked Pharisee; who like the Canaanite woman bends down and asks for mercy and crumbs, the food of a dog that is very hungry.

XVIII. I, however, for I confess myself to be a man, — that is to say, an animal shifty and of a changeable nature, — both eagerly receive this Baptism, and worship Him Who has given it me, and impart it to others; and by shewing mercy make provision for mercy. For I know that I too am compassed with infirmity, and that with what measure I mete it shall be measured to me again. But what sayest thou, O new Pharisee pure in title but not in intention, who dischargest upon us the sentiments of Novatus, though thou sharest the same infirmities? Wilt thou not give any place to weeping? Wilt thou shed no tear? Mayest thou not meet with a Judge like thyself? Art thou not ashamed by the mercy of Jesus, Who took our infirmities and bare our sicknesses; Who came not to call the righteous but sinners to repentance; Who will have mercy rather than sacrifice; who forgiveth sins till seventy times seven. How blessed would your exaltation be if it really were purity, not pride, making laws above the reach of men, and destroying improvement by despair. For both are alike evil, indulgence not regulated by prudence, and condemnation that will never forgive; the one because it relaxes all reins, the other because it strangles by its severity. Shew me your purity, and I will approve your boldness. But as it is, I fear that being full of sores you will render them incurable. Will you not admit even David's repentance, to whom his penitence preserved even the gift of prophecy? nor the great Peter himself, who fell into human weakness at the Passion of our Savior? Yet Jesus received him, and by the threefold question and confession healed the threefold denial. Or will you even refuse to admit that he was made perfect by blood (for your folly goes even as far as that)? Or the transgressor at Corinth? But Paul confirmed love towards him when he saw his amendment, and gives the reason, "that such an one be not swallowed up by overmuch sorrow," being overwhelmed by the excess of the punishment. And will you refuse to grant liberty of marriage to young widows on account of the liability of their age to fall? Paul ventured to do so; but of course you can teach him; for you have been caught up to the Fourth heaven, and to another Paradise, and have heard words more unspeakable, and comprehend a larger circle in your Gospel.

XIX. But these sins were not after Baptism, you will say. Where is your proof? Either prove it — or refrain from condemning; and if there be any doubt, let charity prevail. But Novatus, you say, would not receive those who lapsed in the persecution. What do you mean by this? If they were unrepentant he was right; I too would refuse to receive those who either would not stoop at all or not sufficiently, and who would refuse to make their amendment counterbalance their sin; and when I do receive them, I will assign them their proper place; but if he refused those who wore themselves away with weeping, I will not imitate him. And why should Novatus's want of charity be a rule for me? He never punished covetousness, which is a second idolatry; but he condemned fornication as though he himself were not flesh and body. What say you? Are we convincing you by these words? Come and stand here on our side, that is, on the side of humanity. Let us magnify the Lord together. Let none of you, even though he has much confidence in himself, dare to say, Touch me not for I am pure, and who is so pure as I? Give us too a share in your brightness. But perhaps we are not convincing you? Then we will weep for you. Let these men then if they will, follow our way, which is Christ's way; but if they will not, let them go their own. Perhaps in it they will be baptized with Fire, in that last Baptism which is more painful and longer, which devours wood like grass, and consumes the stubble of every evil.

XX But let us venerate today the Baptism of Christ; and let us keep the feast well, not in pampering the belly, but rejoicing in spirit And how shall we luxuriate? "Wash you, make you clean" If ye be scarlet with sin and less bloody, be made

221

white as snow; if ye be red, and men bathed in blood, yet be ye brought to the whiteness of wool Anyhow be purified, and you shall be clean (for God rejoices in nothing so much as in the amendment and salvation of man, on whose behalf is every discourse and every Sacrament), that you may be like lights in the world, a quickening force to all other men; that you may stand as perfect lights beside That great Light, and may learn the mystery of the illumination of Heaven, enlightened by the Trinity more purely and clearly, of Which even now you are receiving in a measure the One Ray from the One Godhead in Christ Jesus our Lord; to Whom be the glory and the might for ever and ever Amen.

The Oration on Holy Baptism

Preached at Constantinople Jan. 6, 381, being the day following the delivery of that on the Holy Lights.

I. Yesterday we kept high Festival on the illustrious Day of the Holy Lights; for it was fitting that rejoicings should be kept for our Salvation, and that far more than for weddings and birthdays, and namedays, and house-warmings, and registrations of children, and anniversaries, and all the other festivities that men observe for their earthly friends. And now today let us discourse briefly con-concerning Baptism, and the benefits which accrue to us therefrom, even though our discourse yesterday spoke of it cursorily; partly because the time pressed us hard, and partly because the sermon had to avoid tediousness. For too great length in a sermon is as much an enemy to people's ears, as too much food is to their bodies. It will be worth your while to apply your minds to what we say, and to receive our discourse on so important a subject not perfunctorily, but with ready mind, since to know the power of this Sacrament is itself Enlightenment.

II. The Word recognizes three Births for us; namely, the natural birth, that of Baptism, and that of the Resurrection. Of these the first is by night, and is servile, and involves passion; but the second is by day, and is destructive of passion, cutting off all the veil that is derived from birth, and leading on to the higher life; and the third is more terrible and shorter, bringing together in a moment all mankind, to stand before its Creator, and to give an account of its service and conversation here; whether it has followed the flesh, or whether it has mounted up with the spirit, and worshipped the grace of its new creation. My Lord Jesus Christ has showed that He honored all these births in His own Person; the first, by that first and quickening Inbreathing; the second by His Incarnation and the Baptism wherewith He Himself was baptized; and the third by the Resurrection of which He was the Firstfruits; condescending, as He became the Firstborn among many brethren, so also to become the Firstborn from the dead.

III. Concerning two of these births, the first and the last, we have not to speak on the present occasion. Let us discourse upon the second, which is now necessary for us, and which gives its name to the Feast of the Lights. Illumination is the splendor of souls, the conversion of the life, the question put to the Godward conscience. It is the aid to our weakness, the renunciation of the flesh, the following of the Spirit, the fellowship of the Word, the improvement of the creature, the overwhelming of sin, the participation of light, the dissolution of darkness. It is the carriage to God, the dying with Christ, the perfecting of the mind, the bulwark of Faith, the key of the Kingdom of heaven, the change of life, the removal of slavery, the loosing of chains, the remodeling of the whole man. Why should I go into further detail? Illumination is the greatest and most magnificent of the Gifts of God. For just as we speak of the Holy of Holies, and the Song of Songs, as more comprehensive and

223

more excellent than others, so is this called Illumination, as being more holy than any other illumination which we possess.

IV. And as Christ the Giver of it is called by many various names, so too is this Gift, whether it is from the exceeding gladness of its nature (as those who are very fond of a thing take pleasure in using its name), or that the great variety of its benefits has reacted for us upon its names. We call it, the Gift, the Grace, Baptism, Unction, Illumination, the Clothing of Immortality, the Laver of Regeneration, the Seal, and everything that is honorable. We call it the Gift, because it is given to us in return for nothing on our part; Grace, because it is conferred even on debtors; Baptism, because sin is buried with it in the water; Unction, as Priestly and Royal, for such were they who were anointed; Illumination, because of its splendor; Clothing, because it hides our shame; the Laver, because it washes us; the Seal because it preserves us, and is moreover the indication of Dominion. In it the heavens rejoice; it is glorified by Angels, because of its kindred splendor. It is the image of the heavenly bliss. We long indeed to sing out its praises, but we cannot worthily do so.

V. God is Light: the highest, the unapproachable, the ineffable, That can neither be conceived in the mind nor uttered with the lips, That giveth life to every reasoning creature. He is in the world of thought, what the sun is in the world of sense; presenting Himself to our minds in proportion as we are cleansed; and loved in proportion as He is presented to our mind; and again, conceived in proportion as we love Him; Himself contemplating and comprehending Himself, and pouring Himself out upon what is external to Him. That Light, I mean, which is contemplated in the Father and the Son and the Holy Ghost, Whose riches is Their unity of nature, and the one outleaping of Their brightness. A second Light is the Angel, a kind of outflow or communication of that first Light, drawing its illumination from its inclination and obedience thereto; anti I know not whether its illumination is distributed according to the order of its state, or whether its order is due to the respective measures of its illumination. A third Light is man; a light which is visible to external objects. For they call man light, because of the faculty of speech in us. And the name is applied again to those of us who are more like God, and who approach God more nearly than others. I also acknowledge another Light, by which the primeval darkness was driven away or pierced. It was the first of all the visible creation to be called into existence; and it irradiates the whole universe, the circling orbit of the stars, and all the heavenly beacon fires.

VI. Light was also the firstborn commandment given to the firstborn man (for the commandment of the Law is a lamp and a light; and again, Because Thy judgments are a light upon the earth); although the envious darkness crept in and wrought wickedness. And a Light typical and proportionate to those who were its subjects was the written law, adumbrating the truth and the sacrament of the great Light, for Moses' face was made glorious by it. And, to mention more Lights — it was

224

Light that appeared out of Fire to Moses, when it burned the bush indeed, but did not consume it. to shew its nature and to declare the power that was in it. And it was Light that was in the pillar of fire that led Israel and tamed the wilderness. It was Light that carried up Elias in the car of fire, and yet did not burn him as it carried him. It was Light that shone round the Shepherds when the Eternal Light was mingled with the temporal. It was Light that was the beauty of the Star that went before to Bethlehem to guide the Wise Men's way, and to be the escort of the Light That is above us, when He came amongst us. Light was That Godhead Which was shewn upon the Mount to the disciples — and a little too strong for their eyes. Light was That Vision which blazed out upon Paul, and by wounding his eyes healed the darkness of his soul. Light is also the brilliancy of heaven to those who have been purified here, when the righteous shall shine forth as the Sun, and God shall stand in the midst of them, gods and kings, deciding and distinguishing the ranks of the Blessedness of heaven. Light beside these in a special sense is the illumination of Baptism of which we are now speaking; for it contains a great and marvelous sacrament of our salvation.

VII. For since to be utterly sinless belongs to God, and to the first and uncompounded nature (for simplicity is peaceful, and not subject to dissension), and I venture to say also that it belongs to the Angelic nature too; or at least, I would affirm that nature to be very nearly sinless, because of its nearness to God; but to sin is human and belongs to the Compound on earth (for composition is the beginning of separation); therefore the master did not think it right to leave His creature unaided, or to neglect its danger of separation from Himself; but on the contrary, just as He gave existence to that which did not exist, so He gave new creation to that which did exist, a diviner creation and a loftier than the first, which is to those who are beginning life a Seal, and to those who are more mature in age both a gift and a restoration of the image which had fallen through sin, that we may not, by becoming worse through despair, and ever being borne downward to that which is more evil, fall altogether from good and from virtue, through despondency; and having fallen into a depth of evil (as it is said) despise Him; but that like those who in the course of a long journey make a brief rest from labor at an inn, we should be enabled to accomplish the rest of the road fresh and full of courage. Such is the grace and power of baptism; not an overwhelming of the world as of old, but a purification of the sins of each individual, and a complete cleansing from all the bruises and stains of sin.

VIII. And since we are double-made, I mean of body and soul, and the one part is visible, the other invisible, so the cleansing also is twofold, by water and the spirit; the one received visibly in the body, the other concurring with it invisibly and apart from the body; the one typical, the other real and cleansing the depths. And this which comes to the aid of our first birth, makes us new instead of old, and like God instead of what we now are; recasting us without fire, and creating us anew without breaking us up, For, to say it all in one word, the virtue of Baptism is to be understood as a covenant with God for a second life and a purer conversation. And indeed all need to fear this very much, and to watch our own souls, each one of us, with all care, that we do not become liars in respect of this profession. For if God is called upon as a Mediator to ratify human professions, how great is the danger if we be found transgressors of the covenant which we have made with God Himself; and if we be found guilty before the Truth Himself of that lie, besides our other transgressions... and that when there is no second regeneration, or recreation, or restoration to our former state, even though we seek it with all our might, and with many sighs and tears, by which it is cicatrized over (with great difficulty in my opinion, though we all believe that it may be cicatrized). Yet if we might wipe away even the scars I should be glad, since I too have need of mercy. But it is better not to stand in need of a second cleansing, but to stop at the first, which is, I know, common to all, and involves no labor, and is of equal price to slaves, to masters, to poor, to rich, to humble, to exalted, to gentle, to simple, to debtors, to those who are free from debt; like the breathing of the air, and the pouring forth of the light, and the changes of the seasons, and the sight of creation, that great delight which we all share alike, and the equal distribution of the faith.

IX. For it is a strange thing to substitute for a painless remedy one which is more painful; to cast away the grace of mercy, and owe a debt of punishment; and to measure our amendment against sin. For how many tears must we contribute before they can equal the fount of baptism; and who will be surety for us that death shall wait for our cure, and that the judgment seat shall not summon us while still debtors, and needing the fire of the other world? You perhaps, as a good and pitiful husbandman, will entreat the Master still to spare the fig tree, and not yet to cut it down, though accused of unfruitfulness; but to allow you to put dung about it in the shape of tears, sighs, invocations, sleepings on the ground, vigils, mortifications of soul and body, and correction by confession and a life of humiliation. But it is uncertain if the Master will spare it, inasmuch as it cumbers the ground of another asking for mercy, and becoming deteriorated by the longsuffering shewn to this one. Let us then be buried with Christ by Baptism? that we may also rise with Him; let us descend with Him, that we may also be exalted with Him; let us ascend with Him, that we may also be glorified together.

X. If after baptism the persecutor and tempter of the light assail you (for he assailed even the Word my God through the veil, the hidden Light through that which was manifested), you have the means to conquer him. Fear not the conflict; defend yourself with the Water; defend yourself with the Spirit, by Which all the fiery darts of the wicked shall be quenched. It is Spirit, but That Spirit which rent the Mountains. It is Water, but that which quenches fire. If he assail you by your want (as he dared to assail Christ), and asks that stones should be made bread, do not be ignorant of his devices. Teach him what he has not learnt. Defend yourself with the Word of life, Who is the Bread sent down from heaven, and giving life to the world. If he plot against you with vain glory (as he did against Christ when he led

Him up to the pinnacle of the temple and said to Him, Cast Thyself down as a proof of Thy Godhead), be not overborne by elation. If you be taken by this he will not stop here. For he is insatiable, he grasps at every thing. He fawns upon you with fair pretenses, but he ends in evil; this is the manner of his fighting. Yes, and the robber is skilled in Scripture. On the one side was that It is written about the Bread, and on the other that it Is written about the Angels. It is written, quoth he, He shall give His Angels charge concerning thee, and they shall bear thee in their hands. O vile sophist! how was it that thou didst suppress the words that follow, for I know it well, even if thou passest it by in silence? I will make thee to go upon the asp and basilisk, and I will tread upon serpents and scorpions, being fenced by the Trinity. If he wrestle against thee to a fall through avarice, shewing thee all the Kingdoms at one instant and in the twinkling of an eye, as belonging to himself, and demand thy worship, despise him as a beggar. Say to him relying on the Seal, "I am myself the Image of God; I have not yet been east down from the heavenly Glory, as thou wast through thy pride; I have put on Christ; I have been transformed into Christ by Baptism; worship thou me." Well do I know that he will depart, defeated and put to shame by this; as he did from Christ the first Light, so he will from those who are illumined by Christ. Such blessings does the layer bestow on those who apprehend it; such is the rich feast which it provides for those who hunger aright.

XI. Let us then be baptized that we may win the victory; let us partake of the cleansing waters, more purifying than hyssop, purer than the legal blood, more sacred than the ashes of the heifer sprinkling the unclean, and providing a temporary cleansing of the body, but not a complete taking away of sin; for if once purged, why should they need further purification? Let us be baptized today, that we suffer not violence tomorrow; and let us not put off the blessing as if it were an injury, nor wait till we get more wicked that more may be forgiven us; and let us not become sellers and traffickers of Christ, lest we become more heavily burdened than we are able to bear, that we be not sunk with all hands and make shipwreck of the Gift, and lose all because we expected too much. While thou art still master of thy thoughts run to the Gift. While thou art not yet sick in body or in mind, nor seemest so to those who are with thee (though thou art really of sound mind); while thy good is not yet in the power of others, but thou thyself art still master of it; while thy tongue is not stammering or parched, or (to say no more) deprived of the power of pronouncing the sacramental words; while thou canst still be made one of the faithful, not conjecturally but confessedly; and canst still receive not pity but congratulation; while the Gift is still clear to thee, and there is no doubt about it; while the grace can reach the depth of thy soul, and it is not merely thy body that is washed for burial; and before tears surround thee announcing thy decease — and even these restrained perhaps for thy sake — and thy wife and children would delay thy departure, and are listening for thy dying words; before the physician is powerless to help thee, and is giving thee but hours to live — hours which are not his to give — and is balancing thy salvation with the nod of his head, and discoursing learnedly on thy disease after thou art dead, or making his charges heavier by withdrawals, or hinting at despair; before there is a struggle between the man who would baptize thee and the man who seeks thy money, the one striving that thou mayest receive thy Viaticum, the other that he may be inscribed in thy Will as heir — and there is no time for both.

XII. Why wait for a fever to bring you this blessing, and refuse it from God? Why will you have it through lapse of time, and not through reason? Why will you owe it to a plotting friend, and not to a saving desire? Why will you receive it of force and not of free will; of necessity rather than of liberty? Why must you hear of your death from another, rather than think of it as even now present? Why do you seek for drugs which will do no good, or the sweat of the crisis, when the sweat of death is perhaps upon you? Heal yourself before your extremity; have pity upon yourself the only true healer of your disease; apply to yourself the really saving medicine; while you are still sailing with a favoring breeze fear shipwreck, and you will be in less danger of it, if you make use of your terror as a helper. Give yourself occasion to celebrate the Gift with feasting, not with mourning; let the talent be cultivated, not buried in the ground; let some time intervene between the grace and death, that not only may the account of sins be wiped out, but something better may be written in its place; that you may have not only the Gift, but also the Reward; that you may not only escape the fire, but may also inherit the glory, which is bestowed by cultivation of the Gift. For to men of little soul it is a great thing to escape torment; but men of great soul aim also at attaining reward.

XIII. I know of three classes among the saved; the slaves, the hired servants, the sons. If you are a slave, be afraid of the whip; if you are a hired servant, look only to receive your hire; if you are more than this, a son, revere Him as a Father, and work that which is good, because it is good to obey a Father; and even though no reward should come of it for you, this is itself a reward, that you please your Father. Let us then take care not to despise these things. How absurd it would be to grasp at money and throw away health; and to be lavish of the cleansing of the body, but economical over the cleansing of the soul; and to seek for freedom from earthly slavery, but not to care about heavenly freedom; and to make every effort to be splendidly housed and dressed, but to have never a thought how you yourself may become really very precious; and to be zealous to do good to others, without any desire to do good to yourself. And if good could be bought, you would spare no money; but if mercy is freely at your feet, you despise it for its cheapness. Every time is suitable for your ablution, since any time may be your death. With Paul I shout to you with that loud voice, "Behold now is the accepted time; behold Now is the day of salvation;" and that Now does not point to any one time, but is every present moment. And again "Awake, thou that sleepest, and Christ shall give thee light," dispelling the darkness of sin. For as Isaiah says, In the night hope is evil, and it is more profitable to be received in the morning.

XIV. Sow in good season, and gather together, and open thy barns when it is the time to do so; and plant in season, and let the clusters be cut when they are ripe, and launch boldly in spring, and draw thy ship on shore again at the beginning of winter, when the sea begins to rage. And let there be to thee also a time for war and a time for peace; a time to marry, and a time to abstain from marrying; a time for friendship, and a time for discord, if this be needed; and in short a time for everything, if you will follow Solomon's advice. And it is best to do so, for the advice is profitable. But the work of your salvation is one upon which you should be engaged at all times; and let every time be to you the definite one for Baptism. If you are always passing over today and waiting for tomorrow, by your little procrastinations you will be cheated without knowing it by the Evil One, as his manner is. Give to me, he says, the present, and to God the future; to me your youth, and to God old age; to me your pleasures, and to Him your uselessness. How great is the danger that surrounds you. How many the unexpected mischances. War has expended you; or an earthquake overwhelmed you; or the sea swallowed you up; or a wild beast carried you off; or a sickness killed you; or a crumb going the wrong way (a most insignificant thing, but what is easier than for a man to die, though you are so proud of the divine image); or a too freely indulged drinking bout; or a wind knocked you down; or a horse ran away with you; or a drug maliciously scheming against you, or perhaps found to be deleterious when meant to be wholesome; or an inhuman judge; or an inexorable executioner; or any of the things which make the change swiftest and beyond the power of human aid.

XV. But if you would fortify yourself beforehand with the Seal, and secure yourself for the future with the best and strongest of all aids, being signed both in body and in soul with the unction, as Israel was of old with that blood and unction of the firstborn at night that guarded him, what then can happen to you, and what has been wrought out for you? Listen to the Proverbs. "If thou sittest, he says, thou shalt be without fear; and if thou sleepest, thy sleep shall be sweet." And listen to David giving thee the good news, "Thou shalt not be afraid for the terror by night, for mischance or noonday demon." This, even while you live, will greatly contribute to your sense of safety (for a sheep that is sealed is not easily snared, but that which is unmarked is an easy prey to thieves), and at your death a fortunate shroud, more precious than gold, more magnificent than a sepulcher, more reverent than fruitless libations, more seasonable than ripe firstfruits, which the dead bestow on the dead, making a law out of custom. Nay, if all things forsake thee, or be taken violently away from thee; money, possessions, thrones, distinctions, and everything that belongs to this early turmoil, yet you will be able to lay down your life in safety, having suffered no loss of the helps which God gave you unto salvation.

XVI. But are you afraid lest you should destroy the Gift, and do you therefore put off your cleansing, because you cannot have it a second time? What? Would you not be afraid of danger in time of persecution, and of losing the most precious

Thing you have — Christ? Would you then on this account avoid becoming a Christian? Perish the thought. Such a fear is not for a sane man; such an argument argues insanity. O incautious caution, if I may so. O trick of the Evil One! Truly he is darkness and pretends to be light; and when he can no longer prevail in open war, he lays snares in secret, and gives advice, apparently good, really evil, if by some trick at least he may prevail, and we find no escape from his plotting. And this is clearly what he is aiming at in this instance. For, being unable to persuade you to despise Baptism, he inflicts loss upon you through a fictitious security; that in consequence of your fear you may suffer unconsciously the very thing you are afraid of; and because you fear to destroy the Gift, you may for this very reason fail of the Gift altogether. This is his character; and he will never cease his duplicity as long as he sees us pressing onwards towards heaven from which he has fallen. Wherefore, O man of God, do thou recognize the plots of thine adversary; for the battle is against him that hath, and it is concerned with the most important interests. Take not thine enemy to be thy counselor; despise not to be and to be called Faithful. As long as you are a Catechumen you are but in the porch of Religion; you must come inside, and cross the court, and observe the Holy Things, and look into the Holy of Holies, and be in company with the Trinity. Great are the interests for which you are fighting, great too the stability which you need. Protect yourself with the shield of faith. He fears you, if you fight armed with this weapon, and therefore he would strip you of the Gift, that he may the more easily overcome you unarmed and defenseless. He assails every age, and every form of life; he must be repelled by all.

XVII. Art thou young? stand against thy passions; be numbered with the alliance in the army of God: do valiantly against Goliath. Take your thousands or your myriads; thus enjoy your manhood; but do not allow your youth to be withered, being killed by the imperfection of your faith. Are you old and near the predestined necessity? Aid your few remaining days. Entrust the purification to your old age. Why do you fear youthful passion in deep old age and at your last breath? Or will you wait to be washed till you are dead, and not so much the object of pity as of dislike? Are you regretting the dregs of pleasure, being yourself in the dregs of life? It is a shameful thing to be past indeed the flower of your age, but not past your wickedness; but either to be involved in it still, or at least to seem so by delaying your purification. Have you an infant child? Do not let sin get any opportunity, but let him be sanctified from his childhood; from his very tenderest age let him be consecrated by the Spirit. Fearest thou the Seal on account of the weakness of nature? O what a small-souled mother, and of how little faith! Why, Anna even before Samuel was born promised him to God, and after his birth consecrated him at once, and brought him up in the priestly habit, not fearing anything in human nature, but trusting in God. You have no need of amulets or incantations, with which the Devil also comes in, stealing worship from God for himself in the minds of vainer men. Give your child the Trinity, that great and noble Guard.

XVIII. What more? Are you living in Virginity? Be sealed by this purification; make this the sharer and companion of your life. Let this direct your life, your words, every member, every movement, every sense. Honor it, that it may honor you; that it may give to your head a crown of graces, and with a crown of delights may shield you. Art thou bound by wedlock? Be bound also by the Seal; make it dwell with you as a guardian of your continence, safer than any number of eunuchs or of doorkeepers. Art thou not yet wedded to flesh? Fear not this consecration; thou art pure even after marriage. I will take the risk of that. I will join you in wedlock. I will dress the bride. We do not dishonor marriage because we give a higher honor to virginity. I will imitate Christ, the pure Grooms-man and Bridegroom, as He both wrought a miracle at a wedding, and honors wedlock with His Presence. Only let marriage be pure and unmingled with filthy lusts. This only I ask; receive safety from the Gift, and give to the Gift the oblation of chastity in its due season, when the fixed time of prayer comes round, and that which is more precious than business. And do this by common consent and approval. For we do not command, we exhort; and we would receive something of you for your own profit, and the common security of you both. And in one word, there is no state of life and no occupation to which Baptism is not profitable. You who are a free man, be curbed by it; you who are in slavery, be made of equal rank; you who are in grief, receive comfort; let the gladsome be disciplined; the poor receive riches that cannot be taken away; the rich be made capable of being good stewards of their possessions. Do not play tricks or lay plots against your own salvation. For even if we can delude others we cannot delude ourselves. And so to play against oneself is very dangerous and foolish.

XIX. But you have to live in the midst of public affairs, and are stained by them; and it would be a terrible thing to waste this mercy. The answer is simple. Flee, if you can, even from the forum, along with the good company, making yourself the wings of an eagle, or, to speak more suitably, of a dove... for what have you to do with Caesar or the things of Caesar?... until you can rest where there is no sin, and no blackening, and no biting snake in the way to hinder your godly steps. Snatch your soul away from the world; flee from Sodom; flee from the burning; travel on without turning back, lest you should be fixed as a pillar of salt. Escape to the Mountain lest you be destroyed with the plain. But if you are already bound and constrained by the chain of necessity, reason thus with yourself; or rather let me reason thus with you. It is better both to attain the good and to keep the purification. But if it be impossible to do both it is surely better to be a little stained with your public affairs than to fall altogether short of grace; just as I think it better to undergo a slight punishment from father or master than to be put out of doors; and to be a little beamed upon than to be left in total darkness. And it is the part of wise men to choose, as in good things the greater and more perfect, so in evils the lesser and lighter. Wherefore do not overmuch dread the purification. For our success is always judged by comparison with our place in life by our just and merciful Judge; and often one who is in public life and has had small success has had a greater reward than one who in the enjoyment of liberty has not completely succeeded; as I think it more marvelous for a man to advance a little in fetters, than for one to run who is not carrying any weight; or to be only a little spattered in walking through mud, than to be perfectly clean when the road is clean. To give you a proof of what I have said: — Rahab the harlot was justified by one thing alone, her hospitality, though she receives no praise for the rest of her conduct; and the Publican was exalted by one thing, his humility, though he received no testimony for anything else; so that you may learn not easily to despair concerning yourself.

XX. But some will say, What shall I gain, if, when I am preoccupied by baptism, and have cut off myself by my haste from the pleasures of life, when it was in my power to give the reins to pleasure, and then to obtain grace? For the laborers in the vineyard who had worked the longest time gained nothing thereby, for equal wages were given to the very last. You have delivered me from some trouble, whoever you are who say this, because you have at last with much difficulty told the secret of your delay; and though I cannot applaud your shiftiness, I do applaud your confession. But come hither and listen to the interpretation of the parable, that you may not be injured by Scripture for want of information. First of all, there is no question here of baptism, but of those who believe at different times and enter the good vineyard of the Church. For from the day and hour at which each believed, from that day and hour he is required to work. And then, although they who entered first contributed more to the measure of the labor yet they did not contribute more to the measure of the purpose; nay perhaps even more was due to the last in respect of this, though the statement may seem paradoxical. For the cause of their later entrance was their later call to the work of the vineyard. In all other respects let us see how different they are. The first did not believe or enter till they had agreed on their hire; but the others came forward to do the work without an agreement, which is a proof of greater faith. And the first were found to be of an envious and murmuring nature, but no such charge is brought against the others. And to the first, that which was given was wages, though they were worthless fellows; to the last it was the free gift. So that the first were convicted of folly, and with reason deprived of the greater reward. Let us see what would have happened to them if they had been late. Why, the equal pay, evidently. How then can they blame the employer as unjust because of their equality? For all these things take away the merit of their labor froth the first, although they were at work first; and therefore it turns out that the distribution of equal pay was just, if you measure the good will against the labor.

XXI. But supposing that the Parable does sketch the power of the font according to your interpretation, what would prevent you, if you entered first, and bore the heat, from avoiding envy of the last, that by this very lovingkindness you might obtain more, and receive the reward, not as of grace but as of debt? And next, the workmen who receive the wages are those who have entered, not those who have missed, the vineyard; which last is like to be your case. So that if it were certain that you would obtain the Gift, though you are of such a mind, and maliciously keep back some of the labor, you might be forgiven for taking refuge in such arguments, and desiring to make unlawful gain out of the kindness of the master; though I might assure you that the very fact of being able to labor is a greater reward to any who is not altogether of a huckstering mind. But since there is a risk of your being altogether shut out of the vineyard through your bargaining, and losing the capital through stopping to pick up little gains, do let yourselves be persuaded by my words to forsake the false interpretations and contradictions, and to come forward without arguing to receive the Gift, lest you should be snatched away before you realize your hopes, and should find out that it was to your own loss that you devised these sophistries.

XXII. But then, you say, is not God merciful, and since He knows our thoughts and searches out our desires, will He not take the desire of Baptism instead of Baptism? You are speaking in riddles, if what you mean is that because of God's mercy the unenlightened is enlightened in His sight; and he is within the kingdom of heaven who merely desires to attain to it, but refrains from doing that which pertains to the kingdom. I will, however, speak out boldly my opinion on these matters; and I think that all other sensible men will range themselves on my side. Of those who have received the gift, some were altogether alien from God and from salvation, both addicted to all manner of sin, and desirous to be bad; others were semivicious, and in a kind of mean state between good and bad; others again, while they did that which was evil, yet did not approve their own action, just as men in a fever are not pleased with their own sickness. And others even before they were illuminated were worthy of praise; partly by nature, and partly by the care with which they prepared themselves for Baptism. These after their initiation became evidently better, and less liable to fall; in the one case with a view to procuring good, and in the other in order to preserve it. And amongst these, those who gave in to same evil are better than those who were altogether bad; and better still than those who yielded a little, are those who were more zealous, and broke up their fallow ground before Baptism; they have the advantage over the others of having already labored; for the font does not do away with good deeds as it does with sins. But better even than these are they who are also cultivating the Gift, and are polishing themselves to the utmost possible beauty.

XXIII. And so also in those who fail to receive the Gift, some are altogether animal or bestial, according as they are either foolish or wicked; and this, I think, has to be added to their other sins, that they have no reverence at all for this Gift, but look upon it as a mere gift — to be acquiesced in if given them, and if not given them, then to be neglected. Others know and honor the Gift, but put it off; some through laziness, some through greediness. Others are not in a position to receive it, perhaps on account of infancy, or some perfectly involuntary circumstance through which they are prevented from receiving it, even if they wish. As then in the former case we found much difference, so too in this. They who altogether despise it are worse than they who neglect it through greed or carelessness. These are worse than they who have lost the Gift through ignorance or tyranny, for tyranny is nothing but an involuntary error. And I think that the first will have to suffer punishment, as for all their sins, so for their contempt of baptism; and that the second will also have to suffer, but less, because it was not so much through wickedness as through folly that they wrought their failure; and that the third will be neither glorified nor punished by the righteous Judge, as unsealed and yet not wicked, but persons who have suffered rather than done wrong. For not every one who is not bad enough to be punished is good enough to be honored; just as not every one who is not good enough to be honored is bad enough to be punished. And I look upon it as well from another point of view. If you judge the murderously disposed man by his will alone, apart from the act of murder, then you may reckon as baptized him who desired baptism apart from the reception of baptism. But if you cannot do the one how can you do the other? I cannot see it. Or, if you like, we will put it thus If desire in your opinion has equal power with actual baptism, then judge in the same way in regard to glory, and you may be content with longing for it, as if that were itself glory. And what harm is done you by your not attaining the actual glory, as long as you have the desire for it?

XXIV. Therefore since you have heard these words, come forward to it, and be enlightened, and your faces shall not be ashamed through missing the Grace. Receive then the Enlightenment in due season, that darkness pursue you not, and catch you, and sever you from the Illumining. The night cometh when no man can work after our departure hence. The one is the voice of David, the other of the True Light which lighteth every man that cometh into the world. And consider how Solomon reproves you who are too idle or lethargic, saying, How long wilt thou sleep, O sluggard, and when wilt thou arise out of thy sleep? You rely upon this or that, and "pretend pretenses in sins;" I am waiting for Epiphany; I prefer Easter; I will wait for Pentecost. It is better to be baptized with Christ, to rise with Christ on the Day of His Resurrection, to honor the Manifestation of the Spirit. And what then? The end will come suddenly in a day for which thou lookest not, and in an hour that thou art not aware of; and then you will have for a companion lack of grace; and you will be famished in the midst of all those riches of goodness, though you ought to reap the opposite fruit from the opposite course, a harvest by diligence, and refreshment from the font, like the thirsty hart that runs in haste to the spring, and quenches the labor of his race by water; and not to be in Ishmael's case, dried up for want of water, or as the fable has it, punished by thirst in the midst of a spring. It is a sad thing to let the market day go by and then to seek for work. It is a sad thing to let the Manna pass and then to long for food. It is a sad thing to take a counsel too late, and to become sensible of the loss only when it is impossible to repair it; that is, after our departure hence, and the bitter closing of the acts of each man's life, and the punishment of sinners, and the glory of the purified. Therefore do not delay in coming to grace, but hasten, lest the robber outstrip you, lest the adulterer pass you by, lest the insatiate be satisfied before you, lest the murderer seize the blessing first, or the publican or the fornicator, or any of these violent ones who take the Kingdom of heaven by force. For it suffers violence willingly, and is tyrannized over through goodness.

XXV. Take my advice, my friend, and be slow to do evil, but swift to your salvation; for readiness to evil and tardiness to good are equally bad. If you are invited to a revel, be not swift to go; if to apostasy, leap away; if a company of evildoers say to you, "Come with us, share our bloodguiltiness, let us hide in the earth a righteous man unjustly," do not lend them even your ears. Thus you will make two very great gains; you will make known to the other his sin, and you will deliver yourself from evil company. But if David the Great say unto you, Come and let us rejoice in the Lord; or another Prophet, Come and let us ascend into the Mountain of the Lord; or our Savior Himself, Come unto me all ye that labor and are heavy laden, and I will give you rest; or, Arise, let us go hence, shining brightly, glittering above snow, whiter than milk, shining above the sapphire stone; let us not resist or delay. Let us be like Peter and John, and let us hasten; as they did to the Sepulcher and the Resurrection, so we to the Font; running together, racing against each other, striving to be first to obtain this Blessing. And say not, "Go away, and come again, and tomorrow I will be baptized," when you may have the blessing today. "I will have with me father, mother, brothers, wife, children, friends, and all whom I value, and then I will be saved; but it is not yet the fitting time for me to be made bright;" for if you say so, there is reason to fear lest you should have as sharers of your sorrow those whom you hoped to have as sharers of your joy. If they will be with you, well; — but do not wait for them. For it is base to say, "But where is my offering for my baptism, and where is my baptismal robe, in which I shall be made bright, and where is what is wanted for the entertainment of my baptizers, that in these too I may become worthy of notice? For, as you see, all these things are necessary, and on account of this the Grace will be lessened." Do not thus trifle with great things, or allow yourself to think so basely. The Sacrament is greater than the visible environment. Offer yourself; clothe yourself with Christ, feast me with your conduct; I rejoice to be thus affectionately treated, and God Who gives these great gifts rejoices thus. Nothing is great in the sight of God, but what the poor may give, so that the poor may not here also be outrun, for they cannot contend with the rich. In other matters there is a distinction between poor and rich, but here the more willing is the richer.

XXVI. Let nothing hinder you from going on, nor draw you away from your readiness. While your desire is still vehement, seize upon that which you desire. While the iron is hot, let it be tempered by the cold water, lest anything should happen in the interval, and put an end to your desire. I am Philip; do you be Candace's Eunuch. Do you also say, "See, here is water, what doth hinder me to be baptized?" Seize the opportunity; rejoice greatly in the blessing; and having spoken be baptized; and having been baptized be saved; and though you be an Ethiopian body, be made white in soul. Do not say, "A Bishop shall baptize me, — and he a Metropolitan, — and he of Jerusalem (for the Grace does not come of a place, but of the Spirit), — and he of noble birth, for it would be a sad thing for my nobility to be insulted by being baptized by a man of no family." Do not say, "I do not mind a mere Priest, if he is a celibate, and a religious, and of angelic life; for it would be a sad thing for me to be defiled even in the moment of my cleansing." Do not ask for credentials of the preacher or the baptizer. For another is his judge, and the examiner of what thou canst not see. For man looketh on the outward appearance, but the Lord looketh on the heart. But to thee let every one be trustworthy for purification, so only he is one of those who have been approved, not of those who are openly condemned, and not a stranger to the Church. Do not judge your judges, you who need healing; and do not make nice distinctions about the rank of those who shall cleanse you, or be critical about your spiritual fathers. One may be higher or lower than another, but all are higher than you. Look at it this way. One may be golden, another iron, but both are rings and have engraved on them the same royal image; and thus when they impress the wax, what difference is there between the seal of the one and that of the other? None. Detect the material in the wax, if you are so very clever. Tell me which is the impression of the iron ring, and which of the golden. And how do they come to be one? The difference is in the material and not in the seal. And so anyone can be your baptizer; for though one may excel another in his life, yet the grace of baptism is the same, and any one may be your consecrator who is formed in the same faith.

XXVII. Do not disdain to be baptized with a poor man, if you are rich; or if you are noble, with one who is lowborn; or if you are a master, with one who is up to the present time your slave. Not even so will you be humbling yourself as Christ, unto Whom you are baptized today, Who for your sake took upon Himself even the form of a slave. From the day of your new birth all the old marks were effaced, and Christ was put upon all in one form. Do not disdain to confess your sins, knowing how John baptized, that by present shame you may escape from future shame (for this too is a part of the future punishment); and prove that you really hate sin by making a shew of it openly, and triumphing over it as worthy of contempt. Do not reject the medicine of exorcism, nor refuse it because of its length. This too is a touchstone of your right disposition for grace. What labor have you to do compared with that of the Queen of Ethiopia, who arose and came from the utmost part of the earth to see the wisdom of Solomon? And behold a Greater than Solomon is here in the judgment of those who reason maturely. Do not hesitate either at length of journey, or distance by sea; or fire, if this too lies before you; or of any other, small or great, of the hindrances that you may attain to the gift. But if without any labor and trouble at all you may obtain that which you desire, what folly it is to put off the gift: "Ho, every one that thirsteth, come ye to the waters," Esaias invites you, "and he that hath no money, come buy wine and milk, without money and without price." O swiftness of His mercy: O easiness of the Covenant: This blessing may be bought by you merely for willing it; He accepts the very desire as a great price; He thirsts to be thirsted for; He gives to drink to all who desire to drink; He takes it as a kindness to be asked for the kindness; He is ready and liberal; He gives with more pleasure than others receive. Only let us not be condemned for frivolity by asking for little, and for what is unworthy of the Giver. Blessed is he from whom Jesus asks drink, as He did from that Samaritan woman, and gives a well of water springing up unto eternal life. Blessed is he that soweth beside all waters, and upon every soul, tomorrow to be ploughed and watered, which today the ox and the ass tread, while it is dry and without water, and oppressed with unreason. And blessed is he who, though he be a "valley of rushes," is watered out of the House of the Lord; for he is made fruitbearing instead of rushbearing, and produces that which is for the food of man, not that which is rough and unprofitable. And for the sake of this we must be very careful not to miss the Grace.

XXVIII. Be it so, some will say, in the case of those who ask for Baptism; what have you to say about those who are still children, and conscious neither of the loss nor of the grace? Are we to baptize them too? Certainly, if any danger presses. For it is better that they should be unconsciously sanctified than that they should depart unsealed and uninitiated. A proof of this is found in the Circumcision on the eighth day, which was a sort of typical seal, and was conferred on children before they had the use of reason. And so is the anointing of the doorposts, which preserved the firstborn, though applied to things which had no consciousness. But in respect of others I give my advice to wait till the end of the third year, or a little more or less, when they may be able to listen and to answer something about the Sacrament; that, even though they do not perfectly understand it, yet at any rate they may know the outlines; and then to sanctify them in soul and body with the great sacrament of our consecration. For this is how the matter stands; at that time they begin to be responsible for their lives, when reason is matured, and they learn the mystery of life (for of sins of ignorance owing to their tender years they have no account to give), and it is far more profitable on all accounts to be fortified by the Font, because of the sudden assaults of danger that befall us, stronger than our helpers.

XXIX. But, one says, Christ was thirty years old when He was baptized, and that although He was God; and do you bid us hurry our Baptism? — You have solved the difficulty when you say He was God. For He was absolute cleansing; He had no need of cleansing; but it was for you that He was purified, just as it was for you that, though He had not flesh, yet He is clothed with flesh. Nor was there any danger to Him from putting off Baptism, for He had the ordering of His own Passion as of His own Birth. But in your case the danger is to no small interests, if you were to depart after a birth to corruption alone, and without being clothed with incorruption. And there is this further point for me to consider, that that particular time of baptism was a necessity for Him, but your case is not the same. He manifested Himself in the thirtieth year after His birth and not before; first, in order that He might not appear ostentatious, which is a condition belonging to vulgar minds; and next, because that age tests virtue thoroughly, and is the right time to teach. And since it was needful for Him to undergo the passion which saves the world, it was needful also that all things which belong to the passion should fit into the passion; the Manifestation, the Baptism, the Witness from Heaven, the Proclamation, the concourse of the multitude, the Miracles; and that they should be as it were one body, not torn asunder, nor broken apart by intervals. For out of the Baptism and Proclamation arose that earthquake of people coming together, for so Scripture calls that time; and out of the multitude arose the shewing of the signs and the miracles that lead up to the Gospel. And out of these came the jealousy, and from this the hatred, and out of the hatred the circumstance of the plot against Him, and the betrayal; and out of these the Cross, and the other events by which our Salvation has been effected. Such are the reasons in the case of Christ so far as we can attain to them. And perhaps another more secret reason might be found.

XXX. But for you, what necessity is there that by following the examples which are far above you, you should do a thing so ill-advised for yourself? For there are many other details of the Gospel History which are quite different to what happens nowadays, and the seasons of which do not correspond. For instance Christ fasted a little before His temptation, we before Easter. As far as the fasting days are concerned it is the same, but the difference in the seasons is no little one. He armed Himself with them against temptation; but to us this fast is symbolical of dying with Christ, and it is a purification in preparation for the festival. And He fasted absolutely for forty days, for He was God; but we measure our fasting by our power, even though some are led by zeal to rush beyond their strength. Again, He gave the Sacrament of the Passover to His Disciples in an upper chamber, and after supper, and one day before He suffered; but we celebrate it in Houses of Prayer, and before food, and after His resurrection. He rose again the third day; our resurrection is not till after a long time. But matters which have to do with Him are neither abruptly separated from us, nor yet yoked together with those which concern us in point of time; but they were handed down to us just so far as to be patterns of what we should do, and then they carefully avoided an entire and exact resemblance.

XXXI. If then you will listen to me, you will bid a long farewell to all such arguments, and you will jump at this Blessing, and begin to struggle in a twofold conflict; first, to prepare yourself for baptism by purifying yourself; and next, to preserve the baptismal gift; for it is a matter of equal difficulty to obtain a blessing which we have not, and to keep it when we have gained it. For often what zeal has acquired sloth has destroyed; and what hesitation has lost diligence has regained. A great assistance to the attainment of what you desire are vigils, fasts, sleeping on the ground, prayers, tears, pity of and almsgiving to those who are in need. And let these be your thanksgiving for what you have received, and at the same time your safeguard of them. You have the benefit to remind you of many commandments; so do not transgress them. Does a poor man approach you? Remember how poor you once were, and how rich you were made. One in want of bread or of drink, perhaps another Lazarus, is cast at your gate; respect the Sacramental Table to which you have approached, the Bread of Which you have partaken, the Cup in Which you have communicated, being consecrated by the Sufferings of Christ. If a stranger fall at your feet, homeless and a foreigner, welcome in him Him who for your sake was a stranger, and that among His own, and who came to dwell in you by His grace, and who drew you towards the heavenly dwelling place. Be a Zaccheus, who yesterday was a Publican, and is today of liberal soul; offer all to the coming in of Christ, that though small in bodily stature you may show yourself great, nobly contemplating Christ. A sick or a wounded man lies before you; respect your own health, and the wounds from which Christ delivered you. If you see one naked clothe him, in honor of your own garment of incorruption, which is Christ, for as many as were baptized into Christ have put on Christ. If you find a debtor falling at your feet, tear up every document, whether just or unjust. Remember the ten thousand talents which Christ forgave you, and be not a harsh exactor of a smaller debt — and that from whom? From your fellow servant, you who were forgiven so much more by the Master. Otherwise you will have to give satisfaction to His mercy, which you would not imitate and take as your copy.

XXXII. Let the layer be not for your body only, but also for the image of God in you; not merely a washing away of sins in you, but also a correction of your temper; let it not only wash away the old filth, but let it purify the fountainhead. Let it not only move you to honorable acquisition, but let it teach you also honorably to lose possession; or, which is more easy, to make restitution of what you have wrongfully acquired. For what profit is it that your sin should have been forgiven you, but the loss which you have inflicted should not be repaired to him whom you have injured? Two sins are on your conscience, the one that you made a dishonest gain, the other that you retained the gains; you received forgiveness for the one, but in respect of the other you are still in sin, for you have still possession of what belongs to another; and your sin has not been put to an end, but only divided by the time which has elapsed. Part of it was perpetrated before your Baptism, but part remains after your Baptism; for Baptism carries forgiveness of Past, not of Present sins; and its purification must not be played with, but be genuinely impressed upon you; you must be made perfectly bright, and not be merely colored; you must receive the gift, not of a mere covering of your sins, but of a taking them clean away. Blessed are they whose iniquities are forgiven... this is done by the complete cleansing... and whose sins are hidden... this belongs to those who are not yet healed in their deepest soul. Blessed is the man to whom the Lord will not impute sin.... This is a third class of sinners, whose actions are not praiseworthy, but who are innocent of intention.

XXXIII. What say I then, and what is my argument? Yesterday you were a Canaanite soul bent together by sin; today you have been made straight by the

Word. Do not be bent gain, and condemned to the earth, as if weighed down by the Devil with a wooden collar, nor get an incurable curvature. Yesterday you were being dried up by an abundant hemorrhage, for you were pouring out crimson sin; today stanched and flourishing again, for you have touched the hem of Christ and your issue has been stayed. Guard, I pray you, the cleansing lest you should again have a hemorrhage, and not be able to lay hold of Christ to steal salvation; for Christ does not like to be stolen from often, though He is very merciful. Yesterday you were flung upon a bed, exhausted and paralyzed, and you had no one when the water should be troubled to put you into the pool. Today you have Him Who is in one Person Man and God, or rather God and Man. You were raised up from your bed, or rather you took up your bed, and publicly acknowledged the benefit. Do not again be thrown upon your bed by sinning, in the evil rest of a body paralyzed by its pleasures. But as you now are, so walk, mindful of the command, Behold thou art made whole; sin no more lest a worse thing happen unto thee if thou prove thyself bad after the blessing thou hast received. You have heard the loud voice, Lazarus, come forth, as you lay in the tomb; not, however, after four days, but after many days; and you were loosed from the bonds of your graveclothes. Do not again become dead, nor live with those who dwell in the tombs; nor bind yourself with the bonds of your own sins; for it is uncertain whether you will rise again from the tomb till the last and universal resurrection, which will bring every work into judgment, not to be healed, but to be judged, and to give account of all which for good or evil it has treasured up.

XXXIV. If you were full of leprosy, that shapeless evil, yet you scraped off the evil matter, and received again the Image whole. Shew your cleansing to me your Priest, that I may recognize how much more precious it is than the legal one. Do not range yourself with the nine unthankful men, but imitate the tenth. For although he was a Samaritan, yet he was Of better mind than the others. Make certain that you will not break out again with evil ulcers, and find the indisposition of your body hard to heal. Yesterday meanness and avarice were withering your hand; today let liberality and kindness stretch it out. It is a noble cure for a weak hand to disperse abroad, to give to the poor, to pour out the things which we possess abundantly, till we reach the very bottom; and perhaps this will gush forth food for you, as for the woman of Sarepta, and especially if you happen to be feeding an Elias, to recognize that it is a good abundance to be needy for the sake of Christ, Who for our sakes became poor. If you were deaf and dumb, let the Word sound in your ears, or rather keep there Him Who hath sounded. Do not shut your ears to the Instruction of the Lord, and to His Counsel, like the adder to charms. If you are blind and unenlightened, lighten your eyes that you sleep not in death. In God's Light see light, and in the Spirit of God be enlightened by the Son, That Threefold and Undivided Light. If you receive all the Word, you will bring therewith upon your own soul all the healing powers of Christ, with which separately these individuals were healed. Only be not ignorant of the measure of grace; only let not the enemy, while you sleep, maliciously sow tares. Only take care that as by your cleansing you have become an object of enmity to the Evil One, you do not again make yourself an object of pity by sin. Only be careful lest, while rejoicing and lifted up above measure by the blessing, you fall again through pride. Only be diligent as to your cleansing, "setting ascensions in your heart," and keep with all diligence the remission which you have received as a gift, in order that, while the remission comes from God, the preservation of it may come from yourself also.

XXXV. How shall this be? Remember always the parable, and so will you best and most perfectly help yourself. The unclean and malignant spirit is gone out of you, being chased by baptism. He will not submit to the expulsion, he will not resign himself to be houseless and homeless: He goes through waterless places, dry of the Divine Stream, and there he desires to abide. He wanders, seeking rest; he finds none. He lights on baptized souls, whose sins the font has washed away. He fears the water; he is choked with the cleansing, as the Legion were in the sea. Again he returns to the house whence he came out. He is shameless, he is contentious, he makes a fresh assault upon it, he makes a new attempt. If he finds that Christ has taken up His abode there, and has filled the place which he had vacated, he is driven back again, and goes off without success and is become an object of pity in his wandering state. But if he finds in you a place, swept and garnished indeed, but empty and idle, equally ready to take in this or that which shall first occupy it, he makes a leap into it, he takes up his abode there with a larger train; and the last state is worse than the first, inasmuch as then there was a hope of amendment and safety, but now the evil is rampant, and drags in sin by its flight from good, and therefore the possession is more secure to him who dwells there.

XXXVI. I will remind you again about Illuminations, and that often, and will reckon them up from Holy Scripture. For I myself shall be happier for remembering them (for what is sweeter than light to those who have tasted light?) and I will dazzle you with my words. There is sprung up a light for the righteous, and its partner joyful gladness. And, The light of the righteous is everlasting; and Thou art shining wondrously from the everlasting mountains, is said to God, I think of the Angelic powers which aid our efforts after good. And you have heard David's words; The Lord is my Light and my Salvation, whom then shall I fear? And now he asks that the Light and the Truth may be sent forth for him, now giving thanks that he has a share in it, in that the Light of God is marked upon him; that is, that the signs of the illumination given are impressed upon him and recognized. One light alone let us shun — that which is the offspring of the baleful fire; let us not walk in the light of our fire, and in the flame which we have kindled. For I know a cleansing fire which Christ came to send upon the earth, and He Himself is anagogically called a Fire. This Fire takes away whatsoever is material and of evil habit; and this He desires to kindle with all speed, for He longs for speed in doing us good, since He gives us even coals of fire to help us. I know also a fire which is not cleansing, but avenging; either that fire of Sodom which He pours down on all sinners, mingled with brimstone and storms, or that which is prepared for the Devil and his Angels or that which proceeds from the face of the Lord, and shall burn up his enemies round about; and one even more fearful still than these, the unquenchable fire which is ranged with the worm that dieth not but is eternal for the wicked. For all these belong to the destroying power; though some may prefer even in this place to take a more merciful view of this fire, worthily of Him That chastises.

XXXVII. And as I know of two kinds of fire, so also do I of light. The one is the light of our ruling power directing our steps according to the will of God; the other is a deceitful and meddling one, quite contrary to the true light, though pretending to be that light, that it may cheat us by its appearance. This really is darkness, yet has the appearance of noonday, the high perfection of light. And so I read that passage of those who continually flee in darkness at noonday; for this is really night, and yet is thought to be bright light by those who have been ruined by luxury. For what saith David? "Night was around me and I knew it not, for I thought that my luxury was enlightenment." But such are they, and in this condition; but let us kindle for ourselves the light of knowledge. This will be done by sowing unto righteousness, and reaping the fruit of life, for action is the patron of contemplation, that amongst other things we may learn also what is the true light, and what the false, and be saved from falling unawares into evil wearing the guise of good. Let us be made light, as it was said to the disciples by the Great Light, ye are the light of the world. Let us be made lights in the world, holding forth the Word of Life; that is, let us be made a quickening power to others. Let us lay hold of the Godhead; let us lay hold of the First and Brightest Light. Let us walk towards Him shining, before our feet stumble upon dark and hostile mountains. While it is day let us walk honestly as in the day, not in rioting and drunkenness, not in chambering and wantonness, which are the dishonesties of the night.

XXXVIII. Let us cleanse every member, Brethren, let us purify every sense; let nothing in us be imperfect or of our first birth; let us leave nothing unilluminated. Let us enlighten our eyes, that we may look straight on, and not bear in ourselves any harlot idol through curious and busy sight; for even though we might not worship lust, yet our soul would be defiled. If there be beam or mote, let us purge it away, that we may be able to see those of others also. Let us be enlightened in our ears; let us be enlightened in our tongue, that we may hearken what the Lord God will speak, and that He may cause us to hear His lovingkindness in the morning, and that we may be made to hear of joy and gladness, spoken into godly ears, that we may not be a sharp sword, nor a whetted razor, nor turn under our tongue labor and toil, but that we may speak the Wisdom of God in a mystery, even the hidden Wisdom, reverencing the fiery tongues. Let us be healed also in the smell, that we be not effeminate; and be sprinkled with dust instead of sweet perfumes, but may smell the Ointment that was poured out for us, spiritually receiving it; and so formed and transformed by it, that from us too a sweet odor may be smelled. Let us

242

cleanse our touch, our taste, our throat, not touching them over gently, nor delighting in smooth things, but handling them as is worthy of Him, the Word That was made flesh for us; and so far following the example of Thomas, not pampering them with dainties and sauces, those brethren of a more baleful pampering, but tasting and learning that the Lord is good, with the better and abiding taste; and not for a short while refreshing that baneful and thankless dust, which lets pass and does not hold that which is given to it; but delighting it with the words which are sweeter than honey.

XXXIX. And in addition to what has been said, it is good with our head cleansed, as the head which is the workshop of the senses is cleansed, to hold fast the Head of Christ, from which the whole body is fitly joined together and compacted; and to cast down our sin that exalted itself, when it would exalt us above our better part. It is good also for the shoulder to be sanctified and purified that it may be able to take up the Cross of Christ, which not everyone can easily do. It is good for the hands to be consecrated, and the feet; the one that they may in every place be lifted up holy; and that they may lay hold of the discipline of Christ, lest the Lord at any time be angered; and that the Word may gain credence by action, as was the case with that which was given in the hand of a prophet; the other, that they be not swift to shed blood, nor to run to evil, but that they be prompt to run to the Gospel and the Prize of the high Calling, and to receive Christ Who washes and cleanses them. And if there be also a cleansing of that belly which receiveth and digesteth the food of the Word, it were good also; not to make it a God by luxury and the meat that perisheth, but rather to give it all possible cleansing, and to make it more spare, that it may receive the Word of God at the very heart, and grieve honorably over the sins of Israel. I find also the heart and inward parts deemed worthy of honor. David convinces me of this, when he prays that a clean heart may be created in him, and a right spirit renewed in his inward parts; meaning, I think, the mind and its movements or thoughts.

XL. And what of the loins, or reins, for we must not pass these over? Let the purification take hold of these also. Let our loins be girded about and kept in check by continence, as the Law bade Israel of old when partaking of the Passover. For none comes out of Egypt purely, or escapes the Destroyer, except he who has disciplined these. And let the reins be changed by that good conversion by which they transfer all the affections to God, so that they can say, Lord, all my desire is before Thee, and the day of man have I not desired; for you must be a man of desires, but they must be those of the spirit. For thus you would destroy the dragon that carries the greater part of his strength upon his navel and his loins, by slaying the power that comes to him from these. Do not be surprised at my giving a more abundant honor to our uncomely parts, mortifying them and making them chaste by my speech, and standing up against the flesh. Let us give to God all our members which are upon the earth; let us consecrate them all; not the lobe of the liver or the kidneys with the fat, nor some part of our bodies now this now that

243

(why should we despise the rest?); but let us bring ourselves entire, let us be reasonable holocausts, perfect sacrifices; and let us not make only the shoulder or the breast a portion for the Priest to take away, for that would be a small thing, but let us give ourselves entire, that we may receive back ourselves entire; for this is to receive entirely, when we give ourselves to God and offer as a sacrifice our own salvation.

XLI. Besides all this and before all, keep I pray you the good deposit, by which I live and work, and which I desire to have as the companion of my departure; with which I endure all that is so distressful, and despise all delights; the confession of the Father and the Son and the Holy Ghost. This I commit unto you today; with this I will baptize you and make you grow. This I give you to share, and to defend all your life, the One Godhead and Power, found in the Three in Unity, and comprising the Three separately, not unequal, in substances or natures, neither increased nor diminished by superiorities or inferiorities; in every respect equal, in every respect the same; just as the beauty and the greatness of the heavens is one; the infinite conjunction of Three Infinite Ones, Each God when considered in Himself; as the Father so the Son, as the Son so the Holy Ghost; the Three One God when contemplated together; Each God because Consubstantial; One God because of the Monarchia. No sooner do I conceive of the One than I am illumined by the Splendor of the Three; no sooner do I distinguish Them than I am carried back to the One. When I think of any One of the Three I think of Him as the Whole, and my eyes are filled, and the greater part of what I am thinking of escapes me. I cannot grasp the greatness of That One so as to attribute a greater greatness to the Rest. When I contemplate the Three together, I see but one torch, and cannot divide or measure out the Undivided Light.

XLII. Do you fear to speak of Generation lest you should attribute aught of passion to the impassible God? I on the other hand fear to speak of Creation, lest I should destroy God by the insult and the untrue division, either cutting the Son away from the Father, or from the Son the Substance of the Spirit. For this paradox is involved, that not only is a created Life foisted into the Godhead by those who measure Godhead badly; but even this created life is divided against itself. For as these low earthly minds make the Son subject to the Father, so again is the rank of the Spirit made inferior to that of the Son, until both God and created life are insulted by the new Theology. No, my friends, there is nothing servile in the Trinity, nothing created, nothing accidental, as I have heard one of the wise say. If I yet pleased men I should not be the servant of Christ, says the Apostle; and if I yet worshipped a creature, or were baptized into a creature, I should not be made divine, nor have changed my first birth. What shall I say to those who worship Astarte or Chemosh, the abomination of the Sidonians, or the likeness of a star, a God a little above them to these idolaters, but yet a creature and a piece of workmanship, when I myself either do not worship Two of Those into Whose united Name I am baptized, or else worship my fellow-servants, for they are fellow-servants, even if a little higher in the scale; for differences must exist among fellow-servants.

XLIII. I should like to call the Father the greater, because from him flows both the Equality and the Being of the Equals (this will be granted on all hands), but I am afraid to use the word Origin, lest I should make Him the Origin of Inferiors, and thus insult Him by precedencies of honor. For the lowering of those Who are from Him is no glory to the Source. Moreover, I look with suspicion at your insatiate desire, for fear you should take hold of this word Greater, and divide the Nature, using the word Greater in all senses, whereas it does not apply to the Nature, but only to Origination. For in the Consubstantial Persons there is nothing greater or less in point of Substance. I would honor the Son as Son before the Spirit, but Baptism consecrating me through the Spirit does not allow of this. But are you afraid of being reproached with Tritheism? Do you take possession of this good thing, the Unity in the Three, and leave me to fight the battle. Let me be the shipbuilder, and do you use the ship; or if another is the builder of the ship, take me for the architect of the house, and do you live in it with safety, though you spent no labor upon it. You shall not have a less prosperous voyage, or a less safe habitation than I who built them, because you have not labored upon them. See how great is my indulgence; see the goodness of the Spirit; the war shall be mine, yours the achievement; I will be under fire, and you shall live in peace; but join with your defender in prayer, and give me your hand by the Faith. I have three stones which I will sling at the Philistine; I have three inspirations against the son of the Sareptan, with which I will quicken the slain; I have three floods against the faggots with which I will consecrate the Sacrifice with water, raising the most unexpected fire; and I will throw down the prophets of shame by the power of the Sacrament.

XLIV. What need have I any more of speech? It is the time for teaching, not for controversy. I protest before God and the elect Angels, be thou baptized in this faith. If thy heart is written upon in some other way than as my teaching demands, come and have the writing changed; I am no unskilled calligrapher of these truths. I write that which is written upon my own heart; and I teach that which I have been taught, and have kept from the beginning up to these hoar hairs. Mine is the risk; be mine also the reward of being the Director of your soul, and consecrating you by Baptism. But if you are already rightly disposed, and marked with the good inscription, see that you keep what is written, and remain unchanged in a changing time concerning an unchanging Thing. Follow Pilate's example in the better sense; you who are rightly written on, imitate him who wrote wrongfully. Say to those who would persuade you differently, what I have written, I have written. For indeed I should be ashamed if, while that which was wrong remained inflexible, that which is right should be so easily bent aside; whereas we ought to be easily bent to that which is better from that which is worse, but immovable from the better to the worse. If it be thus, and according to this teaching that you come to Baptism, lo

I will not refrain my lips, lo I lend my hands to the Spirit; let us hasten your salvation. The Spirit is eager, the Consecrator is ready, the Gift is prepared. But if you still halt and will not receive the perfectness of the Godhead, go and look for someone else to baptize — or rather to drown you: I have no time to cut the Godhead, and to make you dead in the moment of your regeneration, that you should have neither the Gift nor the Hope of Grace, but should in so short a time make shipwreck of your salvation. For whatever you may subtract from the Deity of the Three, you will have overthrown the whole, and destroyed your own being made perfect.

XLV. But not yet perhaps is there formed upon your soul any writing good or bad; and you want to be written upon today, and formed by us unto perfection. Let us go within the cloud. Give me the tables of your heart; I will be your Moses, though this be a bold thing to say; I will write on them with the finger of God a new Decalogue. I will write on them a shorter method of salvation. And if there be any heretical or unreasoning beast, let him remain below, or he will run the risk of being stoned by the Word of truth. I will baptize you and make you a disciple in the Name of the Father and of the Son and of the Holy Ghost; and These Three have One common name, the Godhead. And you shall know, both by appearances and by words that you reject all ungodliness, and are united to all the Godhead. Believe that all that is in the world, both all that is seen and all that is unseen, was made out of nothing by God, and is governed by the Providence of its Creator, and will receive a change to a better state. Believe that evil has no substance or kingdom, either unoriginate or self-existent or created by God; but that it is our work, and the evil one's, and came upon us through our heedlessness, but not from our Creator. Believe that the Son of God, the Eternal Word, Who was begotten of the Father before all time and without body, was in these latter days for your sake made also Son of Man, born of the Virgin Mary ineffably and stainlessly (for nothing can be stained where God is, and by which salvation comes), in His own Person at once entire Man and perfect God, for the sake of the entire sufferer, that He may bestow salvation on your whole being, having destroyed the whole condemnation of your sins: impassible in His Godhead, passible in that which He assumed; as much Man for your sake as you are made God for His. Believe that for us sinners He was led to death; was crucified and buried, so far as to taste of death; and that He rose again the third day, and ascended into heaven, that He might take you with Him who were lying low; and that He will come again with His glorious Presence to judge the quick and the dead; no longer flesh, nor yet without a body, according to the laws which He alone knows of a more godlike body, that He may be seen by those who pierced Him, and on the other hand may remain as God without carnality. Receive besides this the Resurrection, the Judgment and the Reward according to the righteous scales of God; and believe that this will be Light to those whose mind is purified (that is, God — seen and known) proportionate to their degree of purity, which we call the Kingdom of heaven; but to those who suffer from blindness of their ruling faculty, darkness, that is estrangement from God,

246

proportionate to their blindness here. Then, in the tenth place, work that which is good upon this foundation of dogma; for faith without works is dead, even as are works apart from faith. This is all that may be divulged of the Sacrament, and that is not forbidden to the ear of the many. The rest you shall learn within the Church by the grace of the Holy Trinity; and those matters you shall conceal within yourself, sealed and secure.

XLVI. But one thing more I preach unto you. The Station in which you shall presently stand after your Baptism before the Great Sanctuary is a foretype of the future glory. The Psalmody with which you will be received is a prelude to the Psalmody of Heaven; the lamps which you will kindle are a Sacrament of the illumination there with which we shall meet the Bridegroom, shining and virgin souls, with the lamps of our faith shining, not sleeping through our carelessness, that we may not miss Him that we look for if He come unexpectedly; nor yet unfed, and without oil, and destitute of good works, that we be not cast out of the Bridechamber. For I see how pitiable is such a case. He will come when the cry demands the meeting, and they who are prudent shall meet Him, with their light shining and its food abundant, but the others seeking for oil too late from those who possess it. And He will come with speed, and the former shall go in with Him, but the latter shall be shut out, having wasted in preparations the time of entrance; and they shall weep sore when all too late they learn the penalty of their slothfulness, when the Bride-chamber can no longer be entered by them for all their entreaties, for they have shut it against themselves by their sin, following in another fashion the example of those who missed the Wedding feast with which the good Father feasts the good Bridegroom; one on account of a newly wedded wife; another of a newly purchased field; another of a yoke of oxen; which he and they acquired to their misfortune, since for the sake of the little they lose the great. For none are there of the disdain fill, nor of the slothful, nor of those who are clothed in filthy rags and not in the Wedding garment even though here they may have thought themselves worthy of wearing the bright robe there, and secretly intruded themselves, deceiving themselves with vain hopes. And then, What? When we have entered, then the Bridegroom knows what He will teach us, and how He will converse with the souls that have come in with Him. He will converse with them, I think in teaching things more perfect and more pure. Of which may we all, both Teachers and Taught, have share, in the Same Christ our Lord, to Whom be the Glory and the Empire, for ever and ever. Amen.

Introduction to the Oration of Pentecost

It is uncertain to what year the following Oration belongs. It was, however, certainly delivered at Constantinople; the Benedictine Editors think in the year 381, in which case the day would be May 16. An indication tending to establish this date is found in c. 14, in the expression of apprehension of personal danger to himself for his boldness in setting forth the true faith. In fact, in the earlier part of this year, after the Emperor Theodosius had put him in possession of the Patriarchal Throne, vacant By the expulsion and deposition of the Arian Demophilus, he had narrowly escaped assassination at the hands of the Arians.

The Oration deals again with the subject of the Fifth Theological Oration, the question of the Deity of the Holy Ghost, but proceeds to establish the point by quite a different set of arguments from those adopted in the former discourse, none of whose points are here repeated.

The Preacher begins by commenting on the various ways in which Festivals are kept by Jews, by Heathen and by Christians. Then he remarked on the mystical significance of the number Seven, which he illustrates by several instances; and next proceeds with his principal Subject.

God the Holy Ghost, he says, completes the work of Christ. Those who regard Him as a Created Being, as did the followers of Macedonius, are thereby guilty of blasphemy and impiety. The true Faith recognizes Him as God; and this belief is necessary to salvation; yet some reserve must be employed in applying that Name to Him. We must indeed insist on the recognition of His possession of all the attributes of Godhead; and we must at any rate bear with those who, like the Orator himself, also give Him the Name of God, which he hopes all his hearers will receive from the Holy Ghost grace to do. Then he proceeds to shew from Holy Scripture that in fact all the Attributes of Deity do belong to the Holy Spirit; and that His distinctive Personal Mark is that He is neither Unbegotten like the Father, nor Begotten like the Son. He does not touch on the question of the double Procession. It would seem from some expressions in c. 8 that this Discourse was not delivered to his usual audience, but to an Assembly of "Religious." The Title of the Oration varies in different MSS. Thus some have it "Of The Same On Pentecost," to which one adds "And On The Holy Spirit;" and another puts it "Of The Same, a Homily on Pentecost." The printed Editions before the Benedictine have "On The Holy Pentecost."

On Pentecost

I. Let us reason a little about the Festival, that we may keep it spiritually. For different persons have different ways of keeping Festival; but to the worshipper of the Word a discourse seems best; and of discourses, that which is best adapted to the occasion. And of all beautiful things none gives so much joy to the lover of the beautiful, as that the lover of festivals should keep them spiritually. Let us look into the matter thus. The Jew keeps festival as well as we, but only in the letter. For while following after the bodily Law, he has not attained to the spiritual Law. The Greek too keeps festival, but only in the body, and in honor of his own gods and demons, some of whom are creators of passion by their own admission, and others were honored out of passion. Therefore even their manner of keeping festival is passionate, as though their very sin were an honor to God, in Whom their passion takes refuge as a thing to be proud of. We too keep festival, but we keep it as is pleasing to the Spirit. And it is pleasing to Him that we should keep it by discharging some duty, either of action or speech. This then is our manner of keeping festival, to treasure up in our soul some of those things which are permanent and will cleave 'to it, not of those which will forsake us and be destroyed, and which only tickle our senses for a little while; whereas they are for the most part, m my judgment at least, harmful and ruinous. For sufficient unto the body is the evil thereof. What need has that fire of further fuel, or that beast of more plentiful food, to make it more uncontrollable, and too violent for reason?

II. Wherefore we must keep the feast spiritually. And this is the beginning of our discourse; for we must speak, even if our speech do seem a little too discursive; and we must be diligent for the sake of those who love learning, that we may as it were mix up some seasoning with our solemn festival. The children of the Hebrews do honor to the number Seven, according to the legislation of Moses (as did the Pythagoreans in later days to the number Four, by which indeed they were in the habit of swearing as the Simonians and Marcionites do by the number Eight and the number Thirty, inasmuch as they have given names to and reverence a system of Aeons of these numbers); I cannot say by what rules of analogy, or in consequence of what power of this number; anyhow they do honor to it. One thing indeed is evident, that God, having in six days created matter, and given it form, and having arranged it in all kinds of shapes and mixtures, and having made this present visible world, on the seventh day rested from all His works, as is shewn by the very name of the Sabbath, which in Hebrew means Rest. If there be, however, any more lofty reason than this, let others discuss it. But this honor which they pay to it is not confined to days alone, but also extends to years. That belonging to days the Sabbath proves, because it is continually observed among them; and in accordance with this the removal of leaven is for that number of days. And that belonging to years is shewn by the seventh year, the year of Release; and it consists not only of Hebdomads, but of Hebdomads of Hebdomads, alike in days and years. The Hebdomads of days give birth to Pentecost, a day called holy among them; and those of years to what they call the Jubilee, which also has a release of land, and a manumission of slaves, and a release of possessions bought. For this nation consecrates to God, not only the firstfruits of offspring, or of firstborn, but also those of days and years. Thus the veneration paid to the number Seven gave rise also to the veneration of Pentecost. For seven being multiplied by seven generates fifty all but one day, which we borrow from the world to come, at once the Eighth and the first, or rather one and indestructible. For the present sabbatism of our souls can find its cessation there, that a portion may be given to seven and also to eight (so some of our predecessors have interpreted this passage of Solomon).

III. As to the honor paid to Seven there are many testimonies, but we will be content with a few out of the many. For instance, seven precious spirits are named; for I think Isaiah loves to call the activities of the Spirit spirits; and the Oracles of the Lord are purified seven times according to David, and the just is delivered from six troubles and in the seventh is not smitten. But the sinner is pardoned not seven times, but seventy times seven. And we may see it by the contrary also (for the punishment of wickedness is to be praised), Cain being avenged seven times, that is, punishment being exacted from him for his fratricide, and Lamech seventy times seven, because he was a murderer after the law and the condemnation. And wicked neighbors receive sevenfold into their bosom; and the House of Wisdom rests on seven pillars and the Stone of Zerubbabel is adorned with seven eyes; and God is praised seven times a day. And again the barren beareth seven, the perfect number, she who is contrasted with her who is imperfect in her children."

IV. And if we must also look at ancient history, I perceive that Enoch, the seventh among our ancestors, was honored by translation. I perceive also that the twenty-first, Abraham, was given the glory of the Patriarchate, by the addition of a greater mystery. For the Hebdomad thrice repeated brings out this number. And one who is very bold might venture even to come to the New Adam, my God and Lord Jesus Christ, Who is counted the Seventy- seventh from the old Adam who fell under sin, in the backward genealogy according to Luke. And I think of the seven trumpets of Jesus, the son of Nave, and the same number of circuits and days and priests, by which the walls of Jericho were shaken down. And so too the seven compassings of the City; in the same way as there is a mystery in the threefold breathings of Elias, the Prophet, by which he breathed life into the son of the Sareptan widow, and the same number of his floodings of the wood, when he consumed the sacrifice with fire sent from God, and condemned the prophets of shame who could not do the like at his challenge. And the sevenfold looking for the cloud imposed upon the young servant; and Elissaaeus stretching himself that number of times upon the child of the Shunammite, by which stretching the breath of life was restored. To the same doctrine belongs, I think (if I may omit the seven-stemmed and seven-lamped candlestick of the Temple) that the ceremony of the Priests' consecration lasted seven days; and seven that of the purifying of a leper, and that of the Dedication of the Temples the same number, and that in the seventieth year the people returned from the Captivity; that whatever is in Units may appear also in Decads, and the mystery of the Hebdomad be reverenced in a more perfect number. But why do I speak of the distant past? Jesus Himself who is pure perfection, could in the desert and with five loaves feed five thousand, and again with seven loaves four thousand. And the leavings after they were satisfied were in the first case twelve baskets full, and in the other seven baskets; neither, I imagine, without a reason or unworthy of the Spirit. And if you read for yourself you may take note of many numbers which contain a meaning deeper than appears on the surface. But to come to an instance which is most useful to us on the present occasion, not that for these reasons or others very similar or yet more divine, the Hebrews honor the Day of Pentecost, mad we also honor it; just as there are other rites of the Hebrews which we observe… they were typically observed by them, and by us they are sacramentally reinstated. And now having said so much by way of preface about the Day, let us proceed to what we have to say further.

V. We are keeping the feast of Pentecost and of the Coming of the Spirit, and the appointed time of the Promise, and the fulfillment of our hope. And how great, how august, is the Mystery. The dispensations of the Body of Christ are ended; or rather, what belongs to His Bodily Advent (for I hesitate to say the Dispensation of His Body, as long as no discourse persuades me that it is better to have put off the body), and that of the Spirit is beginning. And what were the things pertaining to the Christ? The Virgin, the Birth, the Manger, the Swaddling, the Angels glorifying Him, the Shepherds running to Him, the course of the Star, the Magi worshipping Him and bringing Gifts, Herod's murder of the children, the Flight of Jesus into Egypt, the Return from Egypt, the Circumcision, the Baptism, the Witness from Heaven, the Temptation, the Stoning for our sake (because He had to be given as an Example to us of enduring affliction for the Word), the Betrayal, the Nailing, the Burial, the Resurrection, the Ascension; and of these even now He suffers many dishonors at the hands of the enemies of Christ; and He bears them, for He is long suffering. But from those who love Him He receives all that is honorable. And He defers, as in the former case His wrath, so in ours His kindness; in their case perhaps to give them the grace of repentance, and in ours to test our love; whether we do not faint in our tribulations and conflicts for the true Religion, as was from of old the order of His Divine Economy, and of his unsearchable judgments, with which He orders wisely all that concerns us. Such are the mysteries of Christ. And what follows we shall see to be more glorious; and may we too be seen. As to the things of the Spirit, may the Spirit be with me, and grant me speech as much as I desire; or if not that, yet as is in due proportion to the season. Anyhow He will be with me as my Lord; not in servile guise, nor awaiting a command, as some think. For He bloweth where He wills and on whom He wills, and to what extent He wills. Thus we are inspired both to think and to speak of the Spirit.

VI. They who reduce the Holy Spirit to the rank of a creature are blasphemers and wicked servants, and worst of the wicked. For it is the part of wicked servants to despise Lordship, and to rebel against dominion, and to make That which is free their fellow-servant. But they who deem Him God are inspired by God and are illustrious in their mind; and they who go further and call Him so, if to well disposed hearers are exalted; if to the low, are not reserved enough, for they commit pearls to clay, and the noise of thunder to weak ears, and the sun to feeble eyes, and solid food to those who are still using milk; whereas they ought to lead them little by little up to what lies beyond them, and to bring them up to the higher truth; adding light to light, and supplying truth upon truth. Therefore we will leave the more mature discourse, for which the time has not yet come, and will speak with them as follows.

VII. If, my friends, you will not acknowledge the Holy Spirit to be uncreated, nor yet eternal; clearly such a state of mind is due to the contrary spirit — forgive me, if in my zeal I speak somewhat over boldly. If, however, you are sound enough to escape this evident impiety, and to place outside of slavery Him Who gives freedom to yourselves, then see for yourselves with the help of the Holy Ghost and of us what follows. For I am persuaded that you are to some extent partakers of Him, so that I will go into the question with you as kindred souls. Either shew me some mean between lordship and servitude, that I may there place the rank of the Spirit; or, if you shrink from imputing servitude to Him, there is no doubt of the rank in which you must place the object of your search. But you are dissatisfied with the syllables, and you stumble at the word, and it is to you a stone of stumbling and a rock of offense; for so is Christ to some minds. It is only human after all. Let us meet one another in a spiritual manner; let us be full rather of brotherly than of self love. Grant us the Power of the Godhead, and we will give up to you the use of the Name. Confess the Nature in other words for which you have greater reverence, and we will heal you as infirm people, filching from you some matters in which you delight. For it is shameful, yes, shameful and utterly illogical, when you are sound in soul, to draw petty distinctions about the sound, and to hide the Treasure, as if you envied it to others, or were afraid lest you should sanctify your own tongue too. But it is even more shameful for us to be in the state of which we accuse you, and, while condemning your petty distinctions of words to make petty distinctions of letters.

VIII. Confess, my friends, the Trinity to be of One Godhead; or if you will, of One Nature; and we will pray the Spirit to give you this word God. He will give it to you, I well know, inasmuch as He has already granted you the first portion and the second; and especially if that about which we are contending is some spiritual cowardice, and not the devil's objection. Yet more clearly and concisely, let me say, do not you call us to account for our loftier word (for envy has nothing to do with this ascent), and we will not find fault with what you have been able to attain, until by another road you are brought up to the same resting place. For we are not seeking victory, but to gain brethren, by whose separation from us we are torn. This we concede to you in whom we do find something of vital truth, who are sound as to the Son. We admire your life, but we do not altogether approve your doctrine. Ye who have the things of the Spirit, receive Himself in addition, that ye may not only strive, but strive lawfully, which is the condition of your crown. May this reward of your conversation be granted you, that you may confess the Spirit perfectly and proclaim with us, aye and before us, all that is His due. Yes, and I will venture even more on your behalf; I will even utter the Apostle's wish. So much do I cling to you, and so much do I revere your array, and the color of your continence, and those sacred assemblies, and the august Virginity, and purification, and the Psalmody that lasts all night and your love of the poor, and of the brethren, and of strangers, that I could consent to be Anathema from Christ, and even to suffer something as one condemned, if only you might stand beside us, and we might glorify the Trinity together. For of the others why should I speak, seeing they are clearly dead (and it is the part of Christ alone to raise them, Who quickeneth the dead by His own Power), and are unhappily separated in place as they are bound together by their doctrine; and who quarrel among themselves as much as a pair of squinting eyes in looking at the same object, and differ with one another, not in sight but in position — if indeed we may charge them only with squinting, and not with utter blindness. And now that I have to some extent laid down your position, come, let us return again to the subject of the Spirit, and I think you will follow me now.

IX. The Holy Ghost, then, always existed, and exists, and always will exist. He neither had a beginning, nor will He have an end; but He was everlastingly ranged with and numbered with the Father and the Son. For it was not ever fitting that either the Son should be wanting to the Father, or the Spirit to the Son. For then Deity would be shorn of Its Glory in its greatest respect, for It would seem to have arrived at the consummation of perfection as if by an afterthought. Therefore He was ever being partaken, but not partaking; perfecting, not being perfected; sanctifying, not being sanctified; deifying, not being deified; Himself ever the same with Himself, and with Those with Whom He is ranged; invisible, eternal, incomprehensible, unchangeable, without quality, without quantity, without form, impalpable, self-moving, eternally moving, with free-will, self-powerful, All-powerful (even though all that is of the Spirit is referable to the First Cause, just as is all that is of the Only -begotten); Life and Lifegiver; Light and Lightgiver; absolute Good, and Spring of Goodness; the Right, the Princely Spirit; the Lord, the Sender, the Separator; Builder of His own Temple; leading, working as He wills; distributing His own Gifts; the Spirit of Adoption, of Truth, of Wisdom, of Understanding, of Knowledge, of Godliness, of Counsel, of Fear (which are ascribed to Him) by Whom the Father is known and the Son is glorified; and by Whom alone He is known; one class, one service, worship, power, perfection, sanctification. Why make a long discourse of it? All that the Father hath the Son hath also, except the being Unbegotten; and all that the Son hath the Spirit hath also, except the Generation. And these two matters do not divide the Substance, as I understand it, but rather are divisions within the Substance.

X. Are you laboring to bring forth objections? Well, so am I to get on with my discourse. Honor the Day of the Spirit; restrain your tongue if you can a little. It is the time to speak of other tongues — reverence them or fear them, when you see that they are of fire. To-day let us teach dogmatically; tomorrow we may discuss. To-day let us keep the feast; tomorrow will be time enough to behave ourselves unseemly — the first mystically, the second theatrically; the one in the Churches, the other in the marketplace; the one among the sober, the other among the drunken; the one as befits those who vehemently desire, the other, as among those who make a joke of the Spirit. Having then put an end to the element that is foreign to us, let us now thoroughly furnish our own friends.

XI. He wrought first in the heavenly and angelic powers, and such as are first after God and around God. For from no other source flows their perfection and their brightness, and the difficulty or impossibility of moving them to sin, but from the Holy Ghost. And next, in the Patriarchs and Prophets, of whom the former saw Visions of God, or knew Him, and the latter also foreknew the future, having their master part molded by the Spirit, and being associated with events that were yet future as if present, for such is the power of the Spirit. And next in the Disciples of Christ (for I omit to mention Christ Himself, in Whom He dwelt, not as energizing, but as accompanying His Equal), and that in three ways, as they were able to receive Him, and on three occasions; before Christ was glorified by the Passion, and after He was glorified by the Resurrection; and after His Ascension, or Restoration, or whatever we ought to call it, to Heaven. Now the first of these manifests Him — the healing of the sick and casting out of evil spirits, which could not be apart from the Spirit; and so does that breathing upon them after the Resurrection, which was clearly a divine inspiration; and so too the present distribution of the fiery tongues, which we are now commemorating. But the first manifested Him indistinctly, the second more expressly, this present one more perfectly, since He is no longer present only in energy, but as we may say, substantially, associating with us, and dwelling in us. For it was fitting that as the Son had lived with us in bodily form — so the Spirit too should appear in bodily form; and that after Christ had returned to His own place, He should have come down to us — Coming because He is the Lord; Sent, because He is not a rival God. For such words no less manifest the Unanimity than they mark the separate Individuality.

XII. And therefore He came after Christ, that a Comforter should not be lacking unto us; but Another Comforter, that you might acknowledge His co-equality. For this word Another marks an Alter Ego, a name of equal Lordship, not of inequality. For Another is not said, I know, of different kinds, but of things consubstantial. And He came in the form of Tongues because of His close relation to the Word. And they were of Fire, perhaps because of His purifying Power (for our Scripture knows of a purifying fire, as any one who wishes can find out), or else because of His Substance. For our God is a consuming Fire, and a Fire burning up the ungodly; though you may again pick a quarrel over these words, being brought into difficulty by the Con substantiality. And the tongues were cloven, because of the diversity of Gifts; and they sat to signify His Royalty and Rest among the Saints, and because the Cherubim are the Throne of God. And it took place in an Upper Chamber (I hope I am not seeming to any one over tedious), because those who should receive it were to ascend and be raised above the earth; for also certain upper chambers are covered with Divine Waters, by which the praise of God are sung. And Jesus Himself in an Upper Chamber gave the Communion of the Sacrament to those who were being initiated into the higher Mysteries, that thereby might be shewn on the one hand that God must come down to us, as I know He did of old to Moses; and on the other that we must go up to Him, and that so there should come to pass a Communion of God with men, by a coalescing of the dignity. For as long as either remains on its own footing, the One in His Glory the other in his lowliness, so long the Goodness of God cannot mingle with us, and His lovingkindness is incommunicable, and there is a great gulf between, which cannot be crossed; and which separates not only the Rich Man from Lazarus and Abraham's Bosom which he longs for, but also the created and changing natures from that which is eternal and immutable.

XIII. This was proclaimed by the Prophets in such passages as the following: — The Spirit of the Lord is upon me; and, There shall rest upon Him Seven Spirits; and The Spirit of the Lord descended and led them; and The spirit of Knowledge filling Bezaleel, the Master-builder of the Tabernacle; and, The Spirit provoking to anger; and the Spirit carrying away Elias in a chariot, and sought in double measure by Elissaeus; and David led and strengthened by the Good and Princely Spirit. And He was promised by the mouth of Joel first, who said, And it shall be in the last days that I will pour out of My Spirit upon all flesh (that is, upon all that believe), and upon your sons and upon your daughters, and the rest; and then afterwards by Jesus, being glorified by Him, and giving back glory to Him, as He was glorified by and glorified the Father. And how abundant was this Promise. He shall abide for ever, and shall remain with you, whether now with those who in the sphere of time are worthy, or hereafter with those who are counted worthy of that world, when we have kept Him altogether by our life here, and not rejected Him in so far as we sin.

XIV. This Spirit shares with the Son in working both the Creation and the Resurrection, as you may be shewn by this Scripture; By the Word of the Lord were the heavens made, and all the power of them by the breath of His Mouth; and this, The Spirit of God that made me, and the Breath of the Almighty that teacheth me; and again, Thou shalt send forth Thy Spirit and they shall be created, and Thou shalt renew the face of the earth. And He is the Author of spiritual regeneration. Here is your proof: — None can see or enter into the Kingdom, except he be born again of the Spirit, and be cleansed from the first birth, which is a mystery of the night, by a remolding of the day and of the Light, by which every one singly is created anew. This Spirit, for He is most wise and most loving, if He takes possession of a shepherd makes him a Psalmist, subduing evil spirits by his song, and proclaims him King; if he possess a goatherd and scraper of sycamore fruit, He makes him a Prophet. Call to mind David and Amos. If He possess a goodly youth, He makes him a Judge of Elders, even beyond his years, as Daniel testifies, who conquered the lions in their den. If He takes possession of Fishermen, He makes them catch the whole world in the nets of Christ, taking them up in the meshes of the Word. Look at Peter and Andrew and the Sons of Thunder, thundering the things of the Spirit. If of Publicans, He makes gain of them for discipleship, and makes them merchants of souls; witness Matthew, yesterday a Publican, today an Evangelist. If of zealous persecutors, He changes the current of their zeal, and makes them Pauls instead of Sauls, and as full of piety as He found them of wickedness. And He is the Spirit of Meekness, and yet is provoked by those who sin. Let us therefore make proof of Him as gentle, not as wrathful, by confessing His Dignity; and let us not desire to see Him implacably wrathful. He too it is who has made me today a bold herald to you; — if without rest to myself, God be thanked; but if with risk, thanks to Him nevertheless; in the one case, that He may spare those that hate us; in the other, that He may consecrate us, in receiving this reward of our preaching of the Gospel, to be made perfect by blood.

XV. They spoke with strange tongues, and not those of their native land; and the wonder was great, a language spoken by those who had not learnt it. And the sign is to them that believe not, and not to them that believe, that it may be an accusation of the unbelievers, as it is written, With other tongues and other lips will I speak unto this people, and not even so will they listen to Me saith the Lord. But they heard. Here stop a little and raise a question, how you are to divide the words. For the expression has an ambiguity, which is to be determined by the punctuation. Did they each hear in their own dialect so that if I may so say, one sound was uttered, but many were heard; the air being thus beaten and, so to speak, sounds being produced more clear than the original sound; or are we to put the stop after "they Heard," and then to add "them speaking in their own languages" to what follows, so that it would be speaking in languages their own to the hearers, which would be foreign to the speakers? I prefer to put it this latter way; for on the other plan the miracle would be rather of the hearers than of the speakers; whereas in this it would be on the speakers' side; and it was they who were reproached for drunkenness, evidently because they by the Spirit wrought a miracle in the matter of the tongues.

XVI. But as the old Confusion of tongues was laudable, when men who were of one language in wickedness and impiety, even as some now venture to be, were building the Tower; for by the confusion of their language the unity of their intention was broken up, and their undertaking destroyed; so much more worthy of praise is the present miraculous one. For being poured from One Spirit upon many men, it brings them again into harmony. And there is a diversity of Gifts, which stands in need of yet another Gift to discern which is the best, where all are praiseworthy. And that division also might be called noble of which David says, Drown O Lord and divide their tongues. Why? Because they loved all words of drowning, the deceitful tongue. Where he all but expressly arraigns the tongues of the present day which sever the Godhead. Thus much upon this point.

XVII. Next, since it was to inhabitants of Jerusalem, most devout Jews, Parthians, Medes, and Elamites, Egyptians, and Libyans, Cretans too, and Arabians, and Mesopotamians, and my own Cappadocians, that the tongues spake, and to Jews (if any one prefer so to understand it), out of every nation under heaven thither collected; it is worth while to see who these were and of what captivity. For the captivity in Egypt and Babylon was circumscribed, and moreover had long since been brought to an end by the Return; and that under the Romans, which was exacted for their audacity against our Savior, was not yet come to pass, though it was in the near future. It remains then to understand it of the captivity under Antiochus, which happened not so very long before this time. But if any does not accept this explanation, as being too elaborate, seeing that this captivity was neither ancient nor widespread over the world, and is looking for a more reliable — perhaps the best way to take it would be as follows. The nation was removed many times, as Esdras related; and some of the Tribes were recovered, and some were left behind; of whom probably (dispersed as they were among the nations) some would have been present and shared the miracle.

XVIII. These questions have been examined before by the studious, and perhaps not without occasion; and whatever else any one may contribute at the present day, he will be joined with us. But now it is our duty to dissolve this Assembly, for enough has been said. But the Festival is never to be put an end to; but kept now indeed with our bodies; but a little later on altogether spiritually there, where we shall see the reasons of these things more purely and clearly, in the Word Himself, and God, and our Lord Jesus Christ, the True Festival and Rejoicing of the Saved — to Whom be the glory and the worship, with the Father and the Holy Ghost, now and for ever. Amen.

Introduction to Oration 42

The Last Farewell

This Oration was delivered during the Second Oecumenical Council, held at Constantinople A.D. 381. Historical as well as personal motives render the occasion of the deepest interest. The audience consisted of the one hundred and fifty Bishops of the Eastern Church who took part in the Council, and of the speaker's own flock, the orthodox Christians of Constantinople. He had by his own exertions gathered that flock together, after it had been ravaged by heretical teachers. He had won the admiration and affection of its members, by his courageous championship of the Faith, his lucid teaching, and his fatherly care for their spiritual needs. He had been, against his will, enthroned with acclamation in the highest ecclesiastical position in the Eastern Church, and called to preside over the Synod of its assembled Bishops. Finding himself unable to guide the deliberations of the Council in regard to a question of the highest importance, and perceiving that he himself and his position were made by some of the Bishops a fresh cause of dissension, he felt bound to resign his high office, and endeavor by this personal sacrifice to restore peace to the Church. His language is worthy of the occasion. Obliged to deal with the topics which had caused dissension, he handles them with gentle and discriminating tact; he speaks with great self-restraint in his own defense; he sets forth with tenderest feeling the common experiences of himself and his flock: he gives with dignity and clearness his last public exposition of the Faith; and finally, in language of exquisite beauty, spoken with the quivering tones of an aged man, he bids a tender farewell to his flock, his cathedral, and his throne, with all their affecting associations. It was an occasion whose pathos is unsurpassed in history. Orator and audience were alike deeply moved, and the emotion has been renewed in all those who have read his words, and realized the scene of their delivery. The Last Farewell in the presence of the One Hundred and Fifty Bishops

1. What think ye of our affairs, dear shepherds and fellow-shepherds: whose feet are beautiful, for you bring glad tidings of peace and of the good things with which ye have come; beautiful again in our eyes, to whom ye have come in season, not to convert a wandering sheep, but to converse with a pilgrim shepherd? What.think ye of this our pilgrimage? And of its fruit, or rather of that of the Spirit within us, by Whom we are ever moved, and specially have now been moved, desiring to have, and perhaps having, nothing of our own? Do you of yourselves understand and perceive — and are you kindly critics of our actions? Or must we, like those from whom a reckoning is demanded as to their military command, or civil government, or administration of the exchequer, publicly and in person submit to you the accounts of our administration? Not indeed that we are ashamed of being judged, for we are ourselves judges in turn, and both with the same charity. But the law is an ancient one: for even Paul communicated to the Apostles his Gospel: not for the sake of ostentation, for the Spirit is far removed from all ostentation, but in order to establish his success and correct his failure, if indeed there were any such in his

words or actions, as he declares when writing of himself. Since even the Spirits of the Prophets are subject to the prophets, according to the order of the Spirit who regulates and divides all things well. And do not wonder that, while he rendered his account privately and to some, I do so publicly, and to all. For my need is greater than his, of being aided by the freedom of my censors, if I am proved to have failed in my duty, lest I should run, or have run, in vain. And the only possible mode of self-defense is speech in the presence of men who know the facts.

2. What then is my defense? If it be false, you must convict me, but if true, you on behalf of whom and in whose presence I speak, must bear witness to it. For you are my defense, my witnesses, and my crown of rejoicing, if I also may venture to boast myself a little in the Apostle's language. This flock was, when it was small and poor, as far as appearances went, nay, not even a flock, but a slight trace and relic of a flock, without order, or shepherd, or bounds, with neither right to pasturage, nor the defense of a fold, wandering upon the mountains and in caves and dens of the earth, scattered and dispersed hither and thither as each one could find shelter or pasture, or could gratefully secure its own safety; like that flock which was harassed by lions, dispersed by tempest, or scattered in darkness, the lamentation of prophets who compared it to the misfortunes of Israel, given up to the Gentiles; over which we also lamented, so long as our lot was worthy of lamentation. For in very deed we also were thrust out and cast off, and scattered upon every mountain and hill, from the need of a shepherd: and a dreadful storm fell upon the Church, and fearful beasts assailed her, who do not even now, after the calm, spare us, but without being ashamed of themselves, wield a greater power than the time should allow; while a gloomy darkness, far more oppressive than the ninth plague of Egypt, the darkness which might be felt, enveloped and concealed everything, so that we could scarcely even see one another.

3. To speak in a more feeling strain, trusting in Him Who then forsook me, as in a Father, "Abraham has been ignorant of us, Israel has acknowledged us not, but Thou art our Father, and unto Thee do we look; beside Thee we know none else, we make mention of Thy name." Therefore, says Jeremiah, I will plead with Thee, I will reason the cause with Thee. We are become as at the beginning, when Thou barest not rule over us, and Thou hast forgotten Thy holy covenant, and shut up Thy mercies from us. Therefore we, the worshippers of the Trinity, the perfect suppliants of the perfect Deity, became a reproach to Thy Beloved, neither daring to bring down to our own level any of the things above us, nor in such wise to rise up against the godless tongues which fought against God, as to make His Majesty a fellow servant with ourselves; but, as is plain, we were delivered up on account of our other sins, and because our conduct had been unworthy of Thy commandments, and we had walked after our own evil mind. For what other reason can there be for our being delivered up to the most unrighteous and wicked men of all the dwellers upon the earth? First Nebuchadnezzar afflicted us, possessed during the Christian era with an anti-Christian rage, hating Christ just because he

had through Him gained salvation, and having bartered the sacred books for sacrifices to those who are no gods. He devoured me, he tore me in pieces, a slight darkness enveloped me, if I may even in my lamentation keep to the language of Scripture. If the Lord had not helped me, and righteously delivered him to the hands of the lawless, by casting him off (such are the judgments of God) to the Persians, by whom his blood was righteously shed for his unholy sheddings of blood, since in this case alone justice could not afford even to be long suffering, my soul had shortly dwelt in the grave. The second no more kindly, if he were not even more grievous still, for while he bore the name of Christ, he was a false Christ, and at once a burden and a reproach to the Christians, for, while to obey him was ungodly, to suffer at his hands was inglorious, since they did not even seem to be wronged, nor to gain by their sufferings the glorious title of martyr, inasmuch as the truth was in this case perverted, for while they suffered as Christians, they were supposed to be punished as heretics. Alas! how rich we were in misfortunes, for the fire consumed the beauties of the world. That which the palmerworm left did the locust eat, and that which the locust left did the caterpillar eat: then came the cankerworm, then, what next I know not, one evil springing up after another. But for what purpose should I give a tragic description of the evils of the time, and of the penalty exacted from us, or, if I must rather call it so, the testing and refining we endured? At any rate, we went through fire and water, and have attained a place of refreshment by the good pleasure of God our Savior.

4. To return to my original startingpoint. This was my field, when it was small and poor, unworthy not only of God, Who has been, and is cultivating the whole world with the fair seeds and doctrines of piety, but, apparently, even of any poor and needy man of slender means. Nay it did not deserve to be called a field, requiring neither barn nor threshing-floor, and not even worthy of the sickle; with neither heap nor sheaves, or small and untimely sheaves, like those on the housetop, which do not fill the hand of the reaper, nor call forth a blessing from them which go by. Such was my field, such my harvest; great and well-eared and fat in the eyes of Him Who beholdeth hidden things, and becoming such a husbandman, its abundance springing from the valleys of souls well tilled with the Word: unrecognized however in public, and not collected together, but gathered in fragments, as an ear gleaned in the stubble, as gleaning-grapes in the vintage, where there is no cluster left. I think I may add, only too appropriately, I found Israel like a figtree in the wilderness, and like one or two ripe grapes in an unripe cluster, preserved as a blessing from the Lord, and a consecrated firstfruit, though small as yet and scanty, and not filling the mouth of the eater: and as an ensign on a hill, and as a beacon on a mountain, or any other solitary thing visible only to few. Such was its former poverty and dejection.

5. But since God, Who maketh poor and maketh rich, Who killeth and maketh alive; Who maketh and transformeth all things; Who turneth night into day, winter into spring, storm into calm, drought into abundance of rain; and often for the sake

260

of the prayers of one righteous man sorely persecuted; Who lifteth up the meek on high, and bringeth the ungodly down to the ground; since God said to Himself, I have surely seen the affliction of Israel; and they shall no longer be further vexed with clay and brick-making; and when He spake He visited, and in His visitation He saved, and led forth His people with a mighty hand and outstretched arm, by the hand of Moses and Aaron, His chosen — what is the result, and what wonders have been wrought? Those which books and monuments contain. For besides all the wonders by the way, and that mighty roar, to speak most concisely, Joseph came into Egypt alone and soon after six hundred thousand depart from Egypt. What more marvelous than this? What greater proof of the generosity of God, when from men without means He wills to supply the means for public affairs? And the land of promise is distributed through one who was hated, and he who was sold dispossesses nations, and is himself made a great nation, and that small offshoot becomes a luxuriant vine, so great that it reaches to the river, and is stretched out to the sea, and spreads from border to border, and hides the mountains with the height of its glory and is exalted above the cedars, even the cedars of God, whatever we are to take these mountains and cedars to be.

6. Such then was once this flock, and such it is now, so healthy and well grown, and if it be not yet in perfection, it is advancing towards it by constant increase, and I prophesy that it will advance. This is foretold me by the Holy Spirit, if I have any prophetic instinct and insight into the future. And from what has preceded I am able to be confident, and recognize this by reasoning, being the nursling of reason. For it was much more improbable that, from that condition, it should reach its present development, than that, as it now is, it should attain to the height of renown. For ever since it began to be gathered together, by Him Who quickeneth the dead, bone to its bone, joint to joint, and the Spirit of life and regeneration was given to it in their dryness, its entire resurrection has been, I know well, sure to be fulfilled: so that the rebellious should not exalt themselves, and that those who grasp at a shadow, or at a dream when one awaketh, or at the dispersing breezes, or at the traces of a ship in the water, should not think that they have anything. Howl, firtree, for the cedar is fallen! Let them be instructed by the misfortunes of others, and learn that the poor shall not alway be forgotten, and that the Deity will not refrain, as Habakkuk says, from striking through the heads of the mighty ones in His fury — the Deity, Who has been struck through and impiously divided into Ruler and Ruled, in order to insult the Deity in the highest degree by degrading It, and oppress a creature by equality with Deity.

7. I seem indeed to hear that voice, from Him Who gathers together those who are broken, and welcomes the oppressed: Enlarge thy cords, break forth on the right hand and on the left, drive in thy stakes, spare not thy curtains. I have given thee up, and I will help thee. In a little wrath I smote thee, but with everlasting mercy I will glorify thee. The measure of His kindness exceeds the measure of His discipline. The former things were owing to our wickedness, the present things to

the adorable Trinity: the former for our cleansing, the present for My glory, Who will glorify them that glorify Me, and I will move to jealousy them that move Me to jealousy. Behold this is sealed up with Me, and this is the indissoluble law of recompense. But thou didst surround thyself with walls and tablets and richly set stones, and long porticos and galleries, and didst shine and sparkle with gold, which thou didst, in part pour forth like water, in part treasure up like sand; not knowing that better is faith, with no other roof but the sky to cover it, than impiety rolling in wealth, and that three gathered together in the Name of the Lord count for more with God than tens of thousands of those who deny the Godhead. Would you prefer the whole of the Canaanites to Abraham alone? or the men of Sodom to Lot? or the Midianites to Moses, when each of these was a pilgrim and a stranger? How do the three hundred men with Gideon, who bravely lapped, compare with the thousands who were put to flight? Or the servants of Abraham, who scarcely exceeded them in number, with the many kings and the army of tens of thousands whom, few as they were, they overtook and defeated? Or how do you understand the passage that though the number of the children of Israel be as the sand of the sea, a remnant shall be saved? And again, I have left me seven thousand men, who have not bowed the knee to Baal? This is not the case; it is not? God has not taken pleasure in numbers.

8. Thou countest tens of thousands, God counts those who are in a state of salvation; thou countest the dust which is without number, I the vessels of election. For nothing is so magnificent in God's sight as pure doctrine, and a soul perfect in all the dogmas of the truth. — For there is nothing worthy of Him Who made all things, of Him by Whom are all things, and for Whom are all things, so that it can be given or offered to God: not merely the handiwork or means of any individual, but even if we wished to honor Him, by uniting together all the property and handiwork of all mankind. Do not I fill heaven and earth? saith the Lord! and what house will ye build Me? or what is the place of My rest? But, since man must needs fall short of what is worthy, I ask of you, as approaching it most nearly, piety, the wealth which is common to all and equal in My eyes, wherein the poorest may, if he be nobleminded, surpass the most illustrious. For this kind of glory depends upon purpose, not upon affluence. These things be well assured, I will accept at your hands. To tread My courts ye shall not proceed, but the feet of the meek shall tread them, who have duly and sincerely acknowledged Me, and My only-begotten Word, and the Holy Spirit. How long will ye inherit My holy Mountain? How long shall My ark be among the heathen? Now for a little longer ye indulge yourselves in that which belongs to others, and gratify your desires. For as ye have devised to reject Me, so will I also reject you, saith the Lord Almighty.

9. This I seemed to hear Him say, and to see Him do, and besides, to hear Him shouting to His people, which once were few and scattered and miserable, and have now become many, and compact enough and enviable, Go through My gates and be ye enlarged. Must you always be in trouble and dwell in tents, while those who

262

vex you rejoice exceedingly? And to. the presiding Angels, for I believe, as John teaches me in his Revelation, that each Church has its guardian, Prepare ye the way of My people, and cast away the stones from the way, that there may be no stumblingblock or hindrance for the people in the divine road and entrance, now, to the temples made with hands, but soon after, to Jerusalem above, and the Holy of holies there, which will, I know, be the end of suffering and struggle to those who here bravely travel on the way. Among whom are ye also called to be Saints, a people of possession, a royal priesthood, the most excellent portion of the Lord, a whole river from a drop, a heavenly lamp from a spark, a tree from a grain of mustard seed, on which the birds come and lodge.

10. These we present to you, dear shepherds, these we offer to you, with these we welcome our friends, and guests, and fellow pilgrims. We have nothing fairer or more splendid to offer to you, for we have selected the greatest of all our possessions, that you may see that, strangers as we are, we are not in want, but though poor are making many rich. If these things are small and unworthy of notice, I would fain learn what is greater and of more account. For, if it be no great thing to have established and strengthened with wholesome doctrines a city which is the eye of the universe, in its exceeding strength by sea and land, which is, as it were, the link between the Eastern and Western shores, in which the extremities of the world from every side meet together, and from which, as the common mart of the faith, they take their rise, a city borne hither and thither on the eddying currents of so many tongues, it will be long ere anything be considered great or worthy of esteem. But if it be indeed a subject for praise, allow to us some glory on this account, since we have contributed in some portion to these results which ye see.

11. Lift up thine eyes round about, and see, thou critic of my words! See the crown which has been platted in return for the hirelings of Ephraim and the crown of insolence; see the assembly of the presbyters, honored for years and wisdom, the fair order of the deacons, who are not far from the same Spirit, the good conduct of the readers, the people's eagerness for teaching, both of men and women, who are equally renowned for virtue: the men, whether philosophers or simple folk, being alike wise in divine things, whether rulers or ruled, being all in this respect duly under rule; whether soldiers or nobles, students or men of letters, being all soldiers of God, though in all other respects meek, ready to fight for the Spirit, all reverencing the assembly above, to which we obtain an entrance, not by the mere letter, but by the quickening Spirit, all in very deed being men of reason, and worshippers of Him Who is in truth the Word: the women, if married, being united by a Divine rather than by a carnal bond; if unwedded and free, being entirely dedicated to God; whether young or old, some honorably advancing towards old age, others eagerly striving to remain immortal, being renewed by the best of hopes.

12. To those who platted this crown — that which I speak, I speak it not after the Lord, nevertheless I will say it — I also have given assistance. Some of them are the result of my words, not of those which we have uttered at random, but of those which we have loved — nor again of those which are meretricious, though the language and manners of the harlot have been slanderously attributed to me, but of those which are most grave. Some of them are the offspring and fruit of my Spirit, as the Spirit can beget those who rise superior to the body. To this I have no doubt that those who are kindly among you, nay all of you, will testify, since I have been the husbandman of all: and my sole reward is your confession. For we neither have, nor have had, any other object. For virtue, that it may remain virtue, is without reward, its eyes fixed alone on that which is good.

13. Would you have me say something still more venturesome? Do you see the tongues of the enemy made gentle, and those who made war upon the Godhead against me tranquilized? This also is the result of our Spirit, of our husbandry. For we are not undisciplined in our exercise of discipline, nor do we hurl insults, as many do, who assail not the argument but the speaker, and sometimes strive by their invective to hide the weakness of their reasoning; as the cuttlefish are said to cast forth ink before them, in order to escape from their pursuers, or themselves to hunt others when unperceived. But we show that our warfare is in behalf of Christ by fighting as Christ, the peaceable and meek, Who has borne our infirmities, fought. Though peaceable, we do not injure, the word of truth, by yielding a jot, to gain a reputation for reasonableness; for we do not pursue that which is good by means of ill: and we are peaceable by the legitimate character of our warfare, confined as it is to our own limits, and the rules of the Spirit. Upon these points, this is my decision, and I lay down the law for all stewards of souls and dispensers of the Word: neither to exasperate others by their harshness, nor to render them arrogant by submissiveness: but to be of good words in treating of the Word, and in neither direction to overstep the mean.

14. But you are perhaps longing for me to give an exposition of the faith, in so far as I am able. For I shall myself be sanctified by the effort of memory, and the people also will be benefited, by its special delight in such discussions, and you will fully acknowledge it — unless we are the objects of groundless envy, as the rivals, in the manifestation of the truth, of those whom we do not excel. For as, of deep waters, some in the depths are utterly hidden, some foam against any obstruction, and hesitate a while before breaking (as they promise to our ears), some do actually break; so also, of those who are professors of the Divine philosophy — setting aside the utterly misguided — some keep their piety entirely secret and hidden within themselves, some are not far from the birth pangs, avoiding impiety, yet not speaking out their piety, either from cautious reserve in their teaching, or under pressure of fear, being themselves sound, as they say, in mind, but not making sound their people, as if they had been en-trusted with the government of their own souls, but not of those of others; while there are some who make public their

treasure, unable to restrain themselves from giving birth to their piety, and not considering that to be salvation which saves themselves alone, without bestowing upon others the overflow of their blessings. Among these would I range myself, and all who by my side have nobly dared to confess the truth.

15. One concise proclamation of our teaching, an inscription intelligible to all, is this people, which so sincerely worships the Trinity, that it would sooner sever anyone from this life, than sever one of the three from the Godhead: of one mind, of equal zeal, and united to one another, to us and to the Trinity by unity of doctrine. Briefly to run over its details: That which is without beginning, and is the beginning, and is with the beginning, is one God. For the nature of that which is without beginning does not consist in being without beginning or being unbegotten, for the nature of anything lies, not in what it is not but in what it is. It is the assertion of what is, not the denial of what is not. And the Beginning is not, because it is a beginning, separated from that which has no beginning. For its beginning is not its nature, any more than the being without beginning is the nature of the other. For these are the accompaniments of the nature, not the nature itself. That again which is with that which has no beginning, and with the beginning, is not anything else than what they are. Now, the name of that which has no beginning is the Father, and of the Beginning the Son, and of that which is with the Beginning, the Holy Ghost, and the three have one Nature — God. And the union is the Father from Whom and to Whom the order of Persons runs its course, not so as to be confounded, but so as to be possessed, without distinction of time, of will, or of power. For these things in our case produce a plurality of individuals, since each of them is separate both from every other quality, and from every other individual possession of the same quality. But to Those who have a simple nature, and whose essence is the same, the term One belongs in its highest sense.

16. Let us then bid farewell to all contentious shiftings and balancings of the truth on either side, neither, like the Sabellians, assailing the Trinity in the interest of the Unity, and so destroying the distinction by a wicked confusion; nor, like the Arians, assailing the Unity in the interest of the Trinity, and by an impious distinction overthrowing the Oneness. For our object is not to exchange one evil for another, but to ensure our attainment of that which is good. These are the playthings of the Wicked One, who is ever swaying our fortunes towards the evil. But we, walking along the royal road which lies between the two extremes, which is the seat of the virtues, as the authorities say, believe in the Father, the Son and the Holy Ghost, of one Substance and glory; in Whom also baptism has its perfection, both nominally and really (thou knowest who hast been initiated!); being a denial of atheism and a confession of Godhead; and thus we are regenerated, acknowledging the Unity in the Essence and in the undivided worship, and the Trinity in the Hypostases or Persons (which term some prefer.) And let not those who are contentious on these points utter their scandalous taunts, as if our faith

depended on terms and not on realities. For what do you mean who assert the three Hypostases? Do you imply three Essences by the term? I am assured that you would loudly shout against those who do so. For you teach that the Essence of the Three is One and the same. What do you mean, who assert the Three Persons? Do you imagine a single compound sort of being, with three faces, or of an entirely human form? Perish the thought! You too will loudly reply that he who thinks thus, will never see the face of God, whatever it may be. What is the meaning of the Hypostases of the one party, of the Persons of the other, to ask this further question? That They are three, Who are distinguished not by natures, but by properties. Excellent. How could men agree and harmonize better than you do, even if there be a difference between the syllables you use? You see what a reconciler I am, bringing you back from the letter to the sense, as we do with the Old and New Testaments.

17. But, to resume: let us speak of the Unbegotten, the Begotten, and the Proceeding, if anyone likes to create names: for we shall have no fear of bodily conceptions attaching to Those who are not embodied, as the calumniators of the Godhead think. For the creature must be called God's, and this is for us a great thing, but God never. Otherwise I shall admit that God is a creature, if I become God, in the strict sense of the term. For this is the truth. If God, He is not a creature; for the creature ranks with us who are not Gods. And if a creature, he is not God, for he had a beginning in time. And there was a time when he who had a beginning was not. And that of which non-existence was its prior condition, has not being in the strict sense of the term. And how can that, which strictly has not being, be God? Not one single one, then, of the Three is a creature, nor, what is worse, came into being for my sake; for in that case he would be not only a creature, but inferior in honor to us. For, if I am for the glory of God, and he is for my sake, as the tongs for the wagon, the saw for the door, I am his superior in causality. For in whatever degree God is superior to creatures, in the same degree is he, who came into being for my sake, inferior to me who exist for God's sake.

18. Moreover, the Moabites and Ammonites must not even be allowed to enter into the Church of God, I mean those sophistical, mischievous arguments which enquire curiously into the generation and inexpressible procession of God, and rashly set themselves in array against the Godhead: as if it were necessary that those things which it is beyond the power of language to set forth, must either be accessible to them alone, or else have no existence because they have not comprehended them. We however, following the Divine Scriptures, and removing out of the way of the blind the stumbling blocks contained in them, will cling to salvation, daring any and every thing rather than arrogance against God. As for the evidences, we leave them to others, since they have been set forth by many, and by ourselves also with no little care. And indeed, it would be a very shameful thing for me at this time to be gathering together proofs for what has all along been believed. For it is not the best order of things, first to teach and then to learn, even in matters

which are small and of no consequence, and much more in those which are Divine and of such great importance. Nor, again, is it proper to the present occasion to explain and disentangle the difficulties of Scripture, a task requiring fuller and more careful consideration than our present purpose will allow. Such then, to sum up, is our teaching. I have entered into these details, with no intention of contending against the adversaries: for I have already often, even if it be imperfectly, fought out the question with them: but in order that I might exhibit to you the character of my teaching, that you might see whether I have not a share in the defense of your own, and do not take my stand on the same side, and opposed to the same enemies as yourselves.

19. You have now, my friends, heard the defense of my presence here: if it be deserving of praise, thanks are due for it to God, and to you who called me; if it has fallen below your expectation, I give thanks even on this behalf. For I am assured that it has not been altogether deserving of censure, and am confident that you also admit this. Have we at all made a gain of this people? Have we consulted at all our own interests, as I see is most often the case? Have we caused any vexation to the Church? To others possibly, with whose idea that they had gained judgment against us by default, we have joined issue in our argument; but in no wise, as far as I am aware, to you. I have taken no ox of yours, says the great Samuel, in his contention against Israel on the subject of the king, nor any propitiation for your souls, the Lord is witness among you, nor this, nor that, proceeding at greater length, that I may not count up every particular; but I have kept the priesthood pure and unalloyed. And if I have loved power, or the height of a throne, or to tread Kings' courts, may I never possess any distinction, or if I gain it, may I be hurled from it.

20. What then do I mean? I am no proficient in virtue without reward, having not attained to so high a degree of virtue. Give me the reward of my labors. What reward? Not that which some, prone to any suspicion would suppose, but that which it is safe for me to seek. Give me a respite from my long labors; give honor to my foreign service; elect another in my place, the one who is being eagerly sought on your behalf, someone who is clean of hands, someone who is not unskilled in voice, someone who is able to gratify you on all points, and share with you the ecclesiastical cares; for this is especially the time for such. But behold, I pray you, the condition of this body, so drained by time, by disease, by toil. What need have you of a timid and unmanly old man, who is, so to speak, dying day by day, not only in body, but even in powers of mind, who finds it difficult to enter into these details before you? Disobey not the voice of your teacher: for indeed you have never yet disobeyed it. I am weary of being charged with my gentleness. I am weary of being assailed in words and in envy by enemies, and by our own. Some aim at my breast, and are less successful in their effort, for an open enemy can be guarded against. Others lie in wait for my back, and give greater pain, for the unsuspected blow is the more fatal. If again I have been a pilot, I have been one of the most skillful; the sea has been boisterous around us, boiling about the ship, and there has

been considerable uproar among the passengers, who have always been fighting about something or another, and roaring against one another and the waves. What a struggle I have had, seated at the helm, contending alike with the sea and the passengers, to bring the vessel safe to land through this double storm? Had they in every way supported me, safety would have been hardly won, and when they were opposed to me, how has it been possible to avoid making shipwreck?

21. What more need be said? But how can I bear this holy war? For there has been said to be a holy, as well as a Persian, war. How shall I unite and join together the hostile occupants of sees, and hostile pastors, and the people broken up along with, and opposed to them, as if by some chasms caused by earthquakes between neighboring and adjoining places; or as, in pestilential diseases, befalls servants and members of the family, when the sickness readily attacks in succession one after another; and besides the very quarters of the globe are affected by the spirit of faction, so that East and West are arrayed on opposite sides, and bid fair to be severed in opinion no less than in position. How long are parties to be mine and yours, the old and the new, the more rational and the more spiritual, the more noble and the more ignoble, the more and the less numerous? I am ashamed of my old age, when, after being saved by Christ, I am called by the name of others.

22. 1 cannot bear your horse races and theatres, and this rage for rivalry in expense and party spirit. We unharness, and harness ourselves on the other side, we neigh against each other, we almost beat the air, as they do, and fling the dust towards heaven, like those which are excited; and under other masks satisfy our own rivalry, and become evil arbiters of emulation, and senseless judges of affairs. To-day sharing the same thrones and opinions, if our leaders thus carry us along; tomorrow hostile alike in position and opinion, if the wind blows in the contrary direction. Amid the variations of friendship and hatred, our names also vary: and what is most terrible, we are not ashamed to set forth contrary doctrines to the same audience; nor are we constant to the same objects, being rendered different at different times by our contentiousness. They are like the ebb and flow of some narrow strait. For as when the children are at play in the midst of the market place, it would be most disgraceful and unbecoming for us to leave our household business, and join them; for children's toys are not becoming for old age: so, when others are contending, even if I am better informed than the majority, I could not allow myself to be one of them, rather than, as I now do, enjoy the freedom of obscurity. For, besides all this, my feeling is that I do not, on most points, agree with the majority, and cannot bear to walk in the same way. Rash and stupid though it may be, such is my feeling. That which is pleasant to others causes pain to me, and I am pleased with what is painful to others. So that I should not be surprised if I were even imprisoned as a disagreeable man, and thought by most men to be out of my senses, as is said to have been the case with one of the Greek philosophers, whose moderation exposed him to the charge of madness, because he laughed at everything, since he saw that the objects of the eager pursuit of the majority were

ridiculous; or even be thought full of new wine as were in later days the disciples of Christ, because they spoke with tongues, since men knew not that it was the power of the Spirit, and not a distraction of mind.

23. Now, consider the charges laid against us. You have been ruler of the church, it is said, for so long, and favored by the course of time, and the influence of the sovereign, a most important matter. What change have we been able to notice? How many men have in days gone by used us outrageously? What sufferings have we failed to undergo? Ill-usage? Threats? Banishment? Plunder? Confiscation? The burning of priests at sea? The desecration of temples by the blood of the saints, till, instead of temples, they became charnel-houses? The public slaughter of aged Bishops, to speak more accurately, of Patriarchs? The denial of access to every place in the case of the godly alone? In fact any kind of suffering which could be mentioned? And for which of these have we requited the wrongdoers? For the wheel of fortune gave us the power of rightly treating those who so treated us, and our persecutors ought to have received a lesson. Apart from all other things, speaking only of our experiences, not to mention your own, have we not been persecuted, maltreated, driven from churches, houses, and, most terrible of all, even from the deserts? Have we not had to endure an enraged people, insolent governors, the disregard of Emperors and their decrees? What was the result? We became stronger, and our persecutors took to flight. That was actually the case. The power to requite them seemed to me a sufficient vengeance on those who had wronged us. These men thought otherwise; for they are exceedingly exact and just in requiting: and accordingly they demand what the state of things permits. What governor, they say, has been fined? What populace chastised? What ringleaders of the populace? What fear of ourselves have we been able to inspire for the future?

24. Perhaps we may be reproached, as we have been before, with the exquisite character of our table, the splendor of our apparel, the officers who precede us, our haughtiness to those who meet us. I was not aware that we ought to rival the consuls, the governors, the most illustrious generals, who have no opportunity of lavishing their incomes; or that our belly ought to hunger for the enjoyment of the goods of the poor, and to expend their necessaries on superfluities, and belch forth over the altars. I did not know that we ought to ride on splendid horses, and drive in magnificent carriages, and be preceded by a procession and surrounded by applause, and have everyone make way for us, as if we were wild beasts, and open out a passage so that our approach might be seen afar. If these sufferings have been endured, they have now passed away: Forgive me this wrong. Elect another who will please the majority: and give me my desert, my country life, and my God, Whom alone I may have to please, and shall please by my simple life. It is a painful thing to be deprived of speeches and conferences, and public gatherings, and applause like that which now lends wings to my thoughts, and relatives, and friends and honors, and the beauty and grandeur of the city, and its brilliancy which dazzles those who look at the surface without investigating the inner nature of

things; but yet not so painful as being clamored against and besmirched amid public disturbances and agitations, which trim their sails to the popular breeze. For they seek not for priests, but for orators, not for stewards of souls, but for treasurers of money, not for pure offerers of the sacrifice, but for powerful patrons. I will say a word in their defense: we have thus trained them, by becoming all things to all men, whether to save or destroy all, I know not.

25. What say you? Are you persuaded, have you been overcome by my words? Or must I use stronger terms in order to persuade you? Yea by the Trinity Itself, Whom you and I alike worship, by our common hope, and for the sake of the unity of this people, grant me this favor; dismiss me with your prayers; let this be the proclamation of my contest; give me my certificate of retirement, as sovereigns do to their soldiers; and, if you will, with a favorable testimony, that I may enjoy the honor of it; if not, just as you please; this will make no difference to me, until God sees what my case really is. What successor then shall we elect? God will provide Himself a shepherd for the office, as He once provided a lamb for a burnt-offering. I only make this further request, — let him be one who is the object of envy, not the object of pity; not one who yields everything to all, but one who can on some points offer resistance for the sake of what is best: for though the one is most pleasant, the other is most profitable. So do you prepare for me your addresses of dismissal: I will now bid you farewell.

26. Farewell my Anastasia, whose name is redolent of piety: for thou hast raised up for us the doctrine which was in contempt: farewell, scene of our common victory, modern Shiloh, where the tabernacle was first fixed, after being carried about in its wanderings for forty years in the wilderness. Farewell likewise, grand and renowned temple, our new inheritance, whose greatness is now due to the Word, which once wast a Jebus, and hast now been made by us a Jerusalem. Farewell, all ye others, inferior only to this in beauty, scattered through the various parts of the city, like so many links, uniting together each your own neighborhood, which have been filled with worshippers of whose existence we had despaired, not by me, in my weakness, but by the grace which was with me. Farewell, ye Apostles, noble settlers here, my masters in the strife; if I have not often kept festival with you, it has been possibly due to the Satan which I, like S. Paul, who was one of you, carry about in my body for my own profit, and which is the cause of my now leaving you. Farewell, my throne, envied and perilous height; farewell assembly of high priests, honored by the dignity and age of its priests, and all ye others ministers of God round the holy table, drawing nigh to the God Who draws nigh to you. Farewell, choirs of Nazarites, harmonies of the Psalter, night-long stations, venerable virgins, decorous matrons, gatherings of widows and orphans, and ye eyes of the poor, turned towards God and towards me. Farewell, hospitable and Christ-loved dwellings, helpers of my infirmity. Farewell, ye lovers of my discourses, in your eagerness and concourse, ye pencils seen and unseen, and thou balustrade, pressed upon by those who thrust themselves forward to hear the word. Farewell, Emperors, and palace,

and ministers and household of the Emperor, whether faithful or not to him, I know not, but for the most part, unfaithful to God. Clap your hands, shout aloud, extol your orator to the skies. This pestilent and garrulous tongue has ceased to speak to you. Though it will not utterly cease to speak: for it will fight with hand and ink: but for the present we have ceased to speak.

27. Farewell, mighty Christ-loving city. I will testify to the truth, though thy zeal be not according to knowledge. Our separation renders us more kindly. Approach the truth: be converted at this late hour. Honor God more than you have been wont to do. It is no disgrace to change, while it is fatal to cling to evil. Farewell, East and West, for whom and against whom I have had to fight; He is witness, Who will give you peace, if but a few would imitate my retirement. For those who resign their thrones will not also lose God, but will have the seat on high, which is far more exalted and secure. Last of all, and most of all, I will cry, — farewell ye Angels, guardians of this church, and of my presence and pilgrimage, since our affairs are in the hands of God. Farewell, O Trinity, my meditation, and my glory. Mayest Thou be preserved by those who are here, and preserve them, my people: for they are mine, even if I have my place assigned elsewhere; and may I learn that Thou art ever extolled and glorified in word and conduct. My children, keep, I pray you, that which is committed to your trust. Remember my stonings. The grace of our Lord Jesus Christ be with you all. Amen.

Introduction to Oration 43 The Pangyric on S Basil

S. Basil died January 1, A.D. 379. A serious illness, in addition to other causes, prevented S. Gregory from being present at his funeral (Epist. 79). Benoit holds that an expression (Epitaph, cxix. 38) in which S. Gregory says that his "lips are fettered" proves that he was still in retirement at Seleucia. This is an unwarranted deduction. In this Oration, 2, the Saint, alluding to his illness in disparaging terms, alleges his labors at Constantinople as a more pressing reason for his absence: and says that he undertook the task according to the judgment of S. Basil. This implies that S. Gregory went to Constantinople before the death of S. Basil, or that he had then been influenced by his friend's advice and was on the point of setting out — more probably the former, as we may be sure that, if S. Gregory had been still at Seleucia, no reason but physical incapacity would have kept him from his friend's side. His pressing duties at Constantinople and the difficulties of the long journey were the "other causes" of his letter to S. Gregory of Nyssa: and we know that he suffered from serious illness at Constantinople (Carm. xi. 887. Orat. xxiii. 1). S. Gregory left Constantinople in June, A.D. 381, and Tillemont places the date of this Oration soon after his return to Nazianzus. Benoit thinks that it was probably delivered on the anniversary of S. Basil's death. The Oration, as all critics are agreed, is one of great power and beauty. Its length (62 pages folio), the physical weakness of the speaker, and the limits of the endurance of even an interested audience, incline us to suppose that it was not spoken in its present form. We cannot well set aside expressions which clearly point to actual delivery, but it may have been amplified later.

Funeral Oration on the great S Basil, Bishop of Caesarea in Cappadocia

1. It has then been ordained that the great Basil, who used so constantly to furnish me with subjects for my discourses, of which he was quite as proud as any other man of his own, should himself now furnish me with the grandest subject which has ever fallen to the lot of an orator. For I think that if anyone desired, in making trial of his powers of eloquence, to test them by the standard of that one of all his subjects which he preferred (as painters do with epoch-making pictures), he would choose that which stood first of all others, but would set aside this as beyond the powers of human eloquence. So great a task is the praise of such a man, not only to me, who have long ago laid aside all thought of emulation, but even to those who live for eloquence, and whose sole object is the gaining of glory by subjects like this. Such is my opinion, and, as I persuade myself, with perfect justice. But I know not what subject I can treat with eloquence, if not this; or what greater favor I can do to myself, to the admirers of virtue, or to eloquence itself, than express our admiration for this man. To me it is the discharge of a most sacred debt. And our speech is a debt beyond all others due to those who have been gifted, in particular, with powers of speech. To the admirers of virtue a discourse is at once a pleasure and an incentive to virtue. For when I have learned the praises of men, I have a distinct idea of their progress: now, there is none of us all, within whose power it is not to

272

attain to any point whatsoever in that progress. As for eloquence itself, in either case, all must go well with it. For, if the discourse be almost worthy of its subject — eloquence will have given an exhibition of its power: if it fall far short of it, as must be the case when the praises of Basil are being set forth, by an actual demonstration of its incapacity, it will have declared the superiority of the excellences of its subject to all expression in words.

2. These are the reasons which have urged me to speak, and to address myself to this contest. And at my late appearance, long after his praises have been set forth by so many, who have publicly and privately done him honor, let no one be surprised. Yea, may I be pardoned by that divine soul, the object of my constant reverence! And as, when he was amongst us, he constantly corrected me in many points, according to the rights of a friend and the still higher law; for I am not ashamed to say this, for he was a standard of virtue to us all; so now, looking down upon me from above, he will treat me with indulgence. I ask pardon too of any here who are among his warmest admirers, if indeed anyone can be warmer than another, and we are not all abreast in our zeal for his good fame. For it is not contempt which has caused me to fall short of what might have been expected of me: nor have I been so regardless of the claims of virtue or of friendship; nor have I thought that to praise him befitted any other more than me. No! any first reason was, that I shrunk from this task, for I will say the truth, as priests do, who approach their sacred duties before being cleansed both in voice and mind. In the second place, I remind you, though you know it well, of the task in which I was engaged on behalf of the true doctrine, which had been properly forced upon me, and had carried me from home, according, as I suppose, to the will of God, and certainly according to the judgment of our noble champion of the truth, the breath of whose life was pious doctrine alone, such as promotes the salvation of the whole world. As for my bodily health, I ought not, perhaps, to dare to mention it, when my subject is a man so doughty in his conquest of the body, even before his removal hence, and who maintained that no powers of the soul should suffer hindrance from this our fetter. So much for my defense. I do not think I need labor it further, in speaking of him to you who know so clearly my affairs. I must now proceed with my eulogy, commending myself to his God, in order that my commendations may not prove an insult to the man, and that I may not lag far behind all others; even though we all equally fall as far short of his due, as those who look upon the heavens or the rays of the Sun.

3. Had I seen him to be proud of his birth, and the rights of birth, or any of those infinitely little objects of those whose eyes are on the ground, we should have had to inspect a new catalogue of the Heroes. What details as to his ancestors might I not have laid under contribution! Nor would even history have had any advantage over me, since I claim this advantage, that his celebrity depends, not upon fiction or legend, but upon actual facts attested by many witnesses. On his father's side Pontus offers to me many details, in no wise inferior to its wonders of old time, of

which all history and poesy are full; there are many others concerned with this my native land, of illustrious men of Cappadocia, renowned for its youthful progeny, no less than for its horses. Accordingly we match with his father's family that of his mother. What family owns more numerous, or more illustrious generals and governors, or court officials, or again, men of wealth, and lofty thrones, and public honors, and oratorical renown? If it were permitted me to wish to mention them, I would make nothing of the Pelopidae and Cecropidae, the Alcmaeonids, the Aeacidae, and Heracleidae, and other most noble families: inasmuch as they, in default of public merit in their house, betake themselves to the region of uncertainty, claiming demigods and divinities, merely mythical personages, as the glory of their ancestors, whose most vaunted details are incredible, and those which we can believe are an infamy.

4. But since our subject is a man who has maintained that each man's nobility is to be judged of according to his own worth, and that, as forms and colors, and likewise our most celebrated and most infamous horses, are tested by their own properties, so we too ought not to be depicted in borrowed plumes; after mentioning one or two traits, which, though inherited from his ancestors, he made his own by his life, and which are specially likely to give pleasure to my hearers, I will then proceed to deal with the man himself. Different families and individuals have different points of distinction and interest, great or small, which, like a patrimony of longer or shorter descent, come down to posterity: the distinction of his family on either side was piety, which I now proceed to display.

5. There was a persecution, the most frightful and severe of all; I mean, as you know, the persecution of Maximinus, which, following closely upon those which immediately preceded it, made them all seem gentle, by its excessive audacity, and by its eagerness to win the crown of violence in impiety. It was overcome by many of our champions, who wrestled with it to the death, or well-nigh to the death, with only life enough left in them to survive their victory, and not pass away in the midst of the struggle; remaining to be trainers in virtue, living witnesses, breathing trophies, silent exhortations, among whose numerous ranks were found Basil's paternal ancestors, upon whom, in their practice of every form of piety, that period bestowed many a fair garland. So prepared and determined were they to bear readily all those things on account of which Christ crowns those who have imitated His struggle on our behalf.

6. But since their strife must needs be lawful, and the law of martyrdom alike forbids us voluntarily to go to meet it (in consideration for the persecutors, and for the weak) or to shrink from it if it comes upon us; for the former shows foolhardiness, the latter cowardice; in this respect they paid due honor to the Lawgiver; but what was their device, or rather, to what were they led by the Providence which guided them in all things? They betook themselves to a thicket on the mountains of Pontus, of which there are many deep ones of considerable

extent, with very few comrades of their flight, or attendants upon their needs. Let others marvel at the length of time, for their flight was exceedingly prolonged, to about seven years, or a little more, and their mode of life, delicately nurtured as they were, was straitened and unusual, as may be imagined, with the discomfort of its exposure to frost and heat and rain: and the wilderness allowed no fellowship or converse with friends: a great trial to men accustomed to the attendance and honor of a numerous retinue. But I will proceed to speak of what is still greater and more extraordinary: nor will anyone fail to credit it, save those who, in their feeble and dangerous judgment, think little of persecutions and dangers for Christ's sake.

7. These noble men, suffering from the lapse of time, and feeling a distaste for ordinary food, felt a longing for something more appetizing. They did not indeed speak as Israel did, for they were not murmurers like them, in their afflictions in the desert, after the escape from Egypt — that Egypt would have been better for them than the wilderness, in the bountiful supply of its flesh-pots, and other dainties which they had left behind them there, for the brickmaking and the clay seemed nothing to them then in their folly — but in a more pious and faithful manner. For why, said they, is it incredible that the God of wonders, who bountifully fed in the wilderness his homeless and fugitive people, raining bread upon them, and abounding in quails, nourishing them not only with necessaries, but even with luxuries: that He, Who divided the sea, and stayed the sun, and parted the river, with all the other things that He has done; for under such circumstances the mind is wont to recur to history, and sing the praises of God's many wonders: that He, they went on, should feed us champions of piety with dainties today? Many animals which have escaped the tables of the rich, have their lairs in these mountains, and many eatable birds fly over our longing heads, any of which can surely be caught at the mere fiat of Thy will! At these words, their quarry lay before them, with food come of its own accord, a complete banquet prepared without effort, stags appearing all at once from some place in the hills. How splendid they were! how fat! how ready for the slaughter! It might almost be imagined that they were annoyed at not having been summoned earlier. Some of them made signs to draw others after them, the rest followed their lead. Who pursued and drove them? No one. What riders? What kind of dogs, what barking, or cry, or young men who had occupied the exits according to the rules of the chase? They were the prisoners of prayer and righteous petition. Who has known such a hunt among men of this, or any day?

8. O what a wonder! They were themselves stewards of the chase; what they would, was caught by the mere will to do so; what was left, they sent away to the thickets, for another meal. The cooks were extemporized, the dinner exquisite, the guests were grateful for this wonderful foretaste of their hopes. And hence they grew more earnest in their struggle, in return for which they had received this blessing. Such is my history. And do thou, my persecutor, in thy admiration for legends, tell of thy huntresses, and Orions, and Actaeons, those ill-fated hunters, and the hind substituted for the maiden, if any such thing rouses thee to emulation, and if we

grant that this story is no legend. The sequel of the tale is too disgraceful. For what is the benefit of the exchange, if a maiden is saved to be taught to murder her guests, and learn to requite humanity with inhumanity? Let this one instance, such as it is, chosen out of many, represent the rest, as far as I am concerned. I have not related it to contribute to his reputation: for neither does the sea stand in need of the rivers which flow into it, many and great though they be, nor does the present subject of my praises need any contributions to his fair fame. No! my object is to exhibit the character of his ancestors, and the example before his eyes, which he so far excelled. For if other men find it a great additional advantage to receive somewhat of their honor from their forefathers, it is a greater thing for him to have made such an addition to the original stock that the stream seems to have run uphill.

9. The union of his parents, cemented as it was by a community of virtue, no less than by cohabitation, was notable for many reasons, especially for generosity to the poor, for hospitality, for purity of soul as the result of self-discipline, for the dedication to God of a portion of their property, a matter not as yet so much cared for by most men, as it now has grown to be, in consequence of such previous examples, as have given distinction to it, and for all those other points, which have been published throughout Pontus and Cappadocia, to the satisfaction of many: in my opinion, however, their greatest claim to distinction is the excellence of their children. Legend indeed has its instances of men whose children were many and beautiful, but it is practical experience which has presented to us these parents, whose own character, apart from that of their children, was sufficient for their fair fame, while the character of their children would have made them, even without their own eminence in virtue, to surpass all men by the excellence of their children. For the attainment of distinction by one or two of their offspring might be ascribed to their nature; but when all are eminent, the honor is clearly due to those who brought them up. This is proved by the blessed roll of priests and virgins, and of those who, married, have allowed nothing in their union to hinder them from attaining an equal repute, and so have made the distinction between them to consist in the condition, rather than in the mode of their life.

10. Who has not known Basil, our archbishop's father, a great name to everyone, who attained a father's prayer, if anyone, I will not say as no one, ever did? For he surpassed all in virtue, and was only prevented by his son from gaining the first prize. Who has not known Emmelia, whose name was a forecast of what she became, or else whose life was an exemplification of her name? For she had a right to the name which implies gracefulness, and occupied, to speak concisely, the same place among women, as her husband among men. So that, when it was decided that he, in whose honor we are met, should be given to men to submit to the bondage of nature, as anyone of old has been given by God for the common advantage, it was neither fitting that he should be born of other parents, nor that they should possess another son: and so the two things suitably concurred. I have now, in

obedience to the Divine law which bids us to pay all honor to parents, bestowed the firstfruits of my praises upon those whom I have commemorated, and proceed to treat of Basil himself, premising this, which I think will seem true to all who knew him, that we only need his own voice to pronounce his eulogium. For he is at once a brilliant subject for praise, and the only one whose powers of speech make him worthy of treating it. Beauty indeed and strength and size, in which I see that most men rejoice, I concede to anyone who will — not that even in these points he was inferior to any of those men of small minds who busy themselves about the body, while he was still young, and had not yet reduced the flesh by austerity — but that I may avoid the fate of unskillful athletes, who waste their strength in vain efforts after minor objects, and so are worsted in the crucial struggle, whose results are victory and the distinction of the crown. The praise, then, which I shall claim for him is based upon grounds which no one, I think, will consider superfluous, or beyond the scope of my oration.

11. I take it as admitted by men of sense, that the first of our advantages is education; and not only this our more noble form of it, which disregards rhetorical ornaments and glory, and holds to salvation, and beauty in the objects of our contemplation: but even that external culture which many Christians ill-judgingly abhor, as treacherous and dangerous, and keeping us afar from God. For as we ought not to neglect the heavens, and earth, and air, and all such things, because some have wrongly seized upon them, and honor God's works instead of God: but to reap what advantage we can from them for our life and enjoyment, while we avoid their dangers; not raising creation, as foolish men do, in revolt against the Creator, but from the works of nature apprehending the Worker, and, as the divine apostle says, bringing into captivity every thought to Christ: and again, as we know that neither fire, nor food, nor iron, nor any other of the elements, is of itself most useful, or most harmful, except according to the will of those who use it; and as we have compounded healthful drugs from certain of the reptiles; so from secular literature we have received principles of enquiry and speculation, while we have rejected their idolatry, terror, and pit of destruction. Nay, even these have aided us in our religion, by our perception of the contrast between what is worse and what is better, and by gaining strength for our doctrine from the weakness of theirs. We must not then dishonor education, because some men are pleased to do so, but rather suppose such men to be boorish and uneducated, desiring all men to be as they themselves are, in order to hide themselves in the general, and escape the detection of their want of culture. But come now, and, after this sketch of our subject and these admissions, let us contemplate the life of Basil.

12. In his earliest years he was swathed and fashioned, in that best and purest fashioning which the Divine David speaks of as proceeding day by day, in contrast with that of the night, under his great father, acknowledged in those days by Pontus, as its common teacher of virtue. Under him then, as life and reason grew and rose together, our illustrious friend was educated: not boasting of a Thessalian

mountain cave, as the workshop of his virtue, nor of some braggart Centaur, the tutor of the heroes of his day: nor was he taught under such tuition to shoot hares, and run down fawns, or hunt stags, or excel in war, or in breaking colts, using the same person as teacher and horse at once; nor nourished on the fabulous marrows of stags and lions, but he was trained in general education, and practiced in the worship of God, and, to speak concisely, led on by elementary instructions to his future perfection. For those who are successful in life or in letters only, while deficient in the other, seem to me to differ in nothing from one-eyed men, whose loss is great, but their deformity greater, both in their own eyes, and in those of others. While those who attain eminence in both alike, and are ambidextrous, both possess perfection, and pass their life with the blessedness of heaven. This is what befell him, who had at home a model of virtue in well-doing, the very sight of which made him excellent from the first. As we see foals and calves skipping beside their mothers from their birth, so he too, running close beside his father in foal-like wantonness, without being left far behind in his lofty impulses toward virtue, or, if you will, sketching out and showing traces of the future beauty of his virtue, and drawing the outlines of perfection before the time of perfection arrived.

13. When sufficiently trained at home, as he ought to fall short in no form of excellence, and not be surpassed by the busy bee, which gathers what is most useful from every flower, he set out for the city of Caesarea, to take his place in the schools there, I mean this illustrious city of ours, for it was the guide and mistress of my studies, the metropolis of letters, no less than of the cities which she excels and reigns over: and if any one were to deprive her of her literary power, he would rob her of her fairest and special distinction. Other cities take pride in other ornaments, of ancient or of recent date, that they may have something to be described or to be seen. Letters form our distinction here, and are our badge, as if upon the field of arms or on the stage. His subsequent life let those detail who trained him, or enjoyed his training, as to what he was to his masters, what he was to his classmates, equaling the former, surpassing the latter in every form of culture, what renown he won in a short time from all, both of the common people, and of the leaders of the state; by showing both a culture beyond his years, and a steadfastness of character beyond his culture. An orator among orators, even before the chair of the rhetoricians, a philosopher among philosophers, even before the doctrines of philosophers: highest of all a priest among Christians even before the priesthood. So much deference was paid to him in every respect by all. Eloquence was his by-work, from which he culled enough to make it an assistance to him in Christian philosophy, since power of this kind is needed to set forth the objects of our contemplation. For a mind which cannot express itself is like the motion of a man in a lethargy. His pursuit was philosophy, and breaking from the world, and fellowship with God, by concerning himself, amid things below, with things above, and winning, where all is unstable and fluctuating, the things which are stable and remain.

14. Thence to Byzantium, the imperial city of the East, for it was distinguished by the eminence of its rhetorical and philosophic teachers, whose most valuable lessons he soon assimilated by the quickness and force of his powers: thence he was sent by God, and by his generous craving for culture, to Athens the home of letters. Athens, which has been to me, if to any one, a city truly of gold, and the patroness of all that is good. For it brought me to know Basil more perfectly, though he had not been unknown to me before; and in my pursuit of letters, I attained to happiness; and in another fashion had the same experience as Saul, who, seeking his father's asses, found a kingdom, and gained incidentally what was of more importance than the object which he had in view. Hitherto my course has been clear, leading me in my encomiums along a level and easy, in fact, a king's highway: henceforth I know not how to speak or whither to turn: for my task is becoming arduous. For here I am anxious, and seize this opportunity to add from my own experience somewhat to my speech, and to dwell a little upon the recital of the causes and circumstances which originated our friendship, or to speak more strictly, our unity of life and nature. For as our eyes are not ready to turn from attractive objects, and, if we violently tear them away, are wont to return to them again; so do we linger in our description of what is most sweet to us. I am afraid of the difficulty of the undertaking. I will try, however, to use all possible moderation. And if I am at all overpowered by my regret, pardon this most righteous of all feelings, the absence of which would be a great loss, in the eyes of men of feeling.

15. We were contained by Athens, like two branches of some river-stream, for after leaving the common fountain of our fatherland, we had been separated in our varying pursuit of culture, and were now again united by the impulsion of God no less than by our own agreement. I preceded him by a little, but he soon followed me, to be welcomed with great and brilliant hope. For he was versed in many languages, before his arrival, and it was a great thing for either of us to outstrip the other in the attainment of some object of our study. And I may well add, as a seasoning to any speech, a short narrative, which will be a reminder to those who know it, a source of information to those who do not. Most of the young men at Athens in their folly are mad after rhetorical skill — not only those who are ignobly born and unknown, but even the noble and illustrious, in the general mass of young men difficult to keep under control. They are just like men devoted to horses and exhibitions, as we see, at the horse-races; they leap, they shout, raise clouds of dust, they drive in their seats, they beat the air, (instead of the horses) with their fingers as whips, they yoke and unyoke the horses, though they are none of theirs: they readily exchange with one another drivers, horses, positions, leaders: and who are they who do this? Often poor and needy fellows, without the means of support for a single day. This is just how the students feel in regard to their own tutors, and their rivals, in their eagerness to increase their own numbers and thereby enrich them. The matter is absolutely absurd and silly. Cities, roads, harbors, mountain tops, coastlines, are seized upon — in short, every part of Attica, or of the rest of

Greece, with most of the inhabitants; for even these they have divided between the rival parties.

16. Whenever any newcomer arrives, and falls into the hands of those who seize upon him, either by force or willingly, they observe this Attic law, of combined jest and earnest. He is first conducted to the house of one of those who were the first to receive him, or of his friends, or kinsmen, or countrymen, or of those who are eminent in debating power, and purveyors of arguments, and therefore especially honored among them; and their reward consists in the gain of adherents. He is next subjected to the raillery of any one who will, with the intention I suppose, of checking the conceit of the newcomers, and reducing them to subjection at once. The raillery is of a more insolent or argumentative kind, according to the boorishness or refinement of the railer: and the performance, which seems very fearful and brutal to those who do not know it, is to those who have experienced it very pleasant and humane: for its threats are feigned rather than real. Next, he is conducted in procession through the market place to the bath. The procession is formed by those who are charged with it in the young man's honor, who arrange themselves in two ranks separated by an interval, and precede him to the bath. But when they have approached it, they shout and leap wildly, as if possessed, shouting that they must not advance, but stay, since the bath will not admit them; and at the same time frighten the youth by furiously knocking at the doors: then allowing him to enter, they now present him with his freedom, and receive him after the bath as an equal, and one of themselves. This they consider the most pleasant part of the ceremony, as being a speedy exchange and relief from annoyances. On this occasion I not only refused to put to shame my friend the great Basil, out of respect for the gravity of his character, and the ripeness of his reasoning powers, but also persuaded all the rest of the students to treat him likewise, who happened not to know him. For he was from the first respected by most of them, his reputation having preceded him. The result was that he was the only one to escape the general rule, and be accorded a greater honor than belongs to a freshman's position.

17. This was the prelude of our friendship. This was the kindling spark of our union: thus we felt the wound of mutual love. Then something of this kind happened, for I think it right not to omit even this. I find the Armenians to be not a simple race, but very crafty and cunning. At this time some of his special comrades and friends, who had been intimate with him even in the early days of his father's instruction, for they were members of his school, came up to him under the guise of friendship, but with envious, and not kindly intent, and put to him questions of a disputations rather than rational kind, trying to overwhelm him at the first onset, having known his original natural endowments, and unable to brook the honor he had then received. For they thought it a strange thing that they who had put on their gowns, and been exercised in shouting, should not get the better of one who was a stranger and a novice. I also, in my vain love for Athens, and trusting to their professions without perceiving their envy, when they were giving

way, and turning their backs, since I was indignant that in their persons the reputation of Athens should be destroyed, and so speedily put to shame, supported the young men, and restored the argument; and by the aid of my additional weight, for in such cases a small addition makes all the difference, and, as the poet says, "made equal their heads in the fray." But, when I perceived the secret motive of the dispute, which could no longer be kept under, and was at last clearly exposed, I at once drew back, and retired from their ranks, to range myself on his side, and made the victory decisive. He was at once delighted at what had happened, for his sagacity was remarkable, and being filled with zeal, to describe him fully in Homer's language, he pursued in confusion with argument those valiant youths, and, smiting them with syllogisms, only ceased when they were utterly routed, and he had distinctly won the honors due to his power. Thus was kindled again, no longer a spark, but a manifest and conspicuous blaze of friendship.

18. Their efforts having thus proved fruitless, while they severely blamed their own rashness, they cherished such annoyance against me that it broke out into open hostility, and a charge of treachery, not only to them, but to Athens herself: inasmuch as they had been confuted and put to shame at the first onset, by a single student, who had not even had time to gain confidence. He moreover, according to that human feeling, which makes us, when we have all at once attained to the high hopes which we have cherished, look upon their results as inferior to our expectation, he, I say, was displeased and annoyed, and could take no delight in his arrival. He was seeking for what he had expected, and called Athens an empty happiness. I however tried to remove his annoyance, both by argumentative encounter, and by the enchantments of reasoning; alleging, as is true, that the disposition of a man cannot at once be detected, without a long time and more constant association, and that culture likewise is not made known to those who make trial of her, after a few efforts and in a short time. In this way I restored his cheerfulness, and by this mutual experience, he was the more closely united to me.

19. And when, as time went on, we acknowledged our mutual affection, and that philosophy was our aim, we were all in all to one another, housemates, messmates, intimates, with one object in life, or an affection for each other ever growing warmer and stronger. Love for bodily attractions, since its objects are fleeting, is as fleeting as the flowers of spring. For the flame cannot survive, when the fuel is exhausted, and departs along with that which kindles it, nor does desire abide, when its incentive wastes away. But love which is godly and under restraint, since its object is stable, not only is more lasting, but, the fuller its vision of beauty grows, the more closely does it bind to itself and to one another the hearts of those whose love has one and the same object. This is the law of our superhuman love. I feel that I am being unduly borne away, and I know not how to enter upon this point, yet I cannot restrain myself from describing it. For if I have omitted anything, it seems, immediately afterwards, of pressing importance, and of more consequence than what I had preferred to mention. And if any one would carry me tyrannically

forward, I become like the polyps, which when they are being dragged from their holes, cling with their suckers to the rocks, and cannot be detached, until the last of these has had exerted upon it its necessary share of force. If then you give me leave, I have my request, if not I must take it from myself.

20. Such were our feelings for each other, when we had thus supported, us Pindar has it, our "well-built chamber with pillars of gold," as we advanced under the united influences of God's grace and our own affection. Oh! how can I mention these things without tears. We were impelled by equal hopes, in a pursuit especially obnoxious to envy, that of letters. Yet envy we knew not, and emulation was of service to us. We struggled, not each to gain the first place for himself, but to yield it to the other; for we made each other's reputation to be our own. We seemed to have one soul, inhabiting two bodies. And if we must not believe those whose doctrine is "All things are in all;" yet in our case it was worthy of belief, so did we live in and with each other. The sole business of both of us was virtue, and living for the hopes to come, having retired from this world, before our actual departure hence. With a view to this, were directed all our life and actions, under the guidance of the commandment, as we sharpened upon each other our weapons of virtue; and if this is not a great thing for me to say, being a rule and standard to each other, for the distinction between what was right and what was not. Our associates were not the most dissolute, but the most sober of our comrades; not the most pugnacious, but the most peaceable, whose intimacy was most profitable: knowing that it is more easy to be tainted with vice, than to impart virtue; just as we can more readily be infected with a disease, than bestow health. Our most cherished studies were not the most pleasant, but the most excellent; this being one means of forming young minds in a virtuous or vicious mold.

21. Two ways were known to us, the first of greater value, the second of smaller consequence: the one leading to our sacred buildings and the teachers there, the other to secular instructors. All others we left to those who would pursue them — to feasts, theatres, meetings, banquets. For nothing is in my opinion of value, save that which leads to virtue and to the improvement of its devotees. Different men have different names, derived from their fathers, their families, their pursuits, their exploits: we had but one great business and name — to be and to be called Christians of which we thought more than Gyges of the turning of his ring, if this is not a legend, on which depended his Lydian sovereignty: or than Midas did of the gold through which he perished, in answer to his prayer that all he had might turn to gold — another Phrygian legend. For why should I speak of the arrow of the Hyperborean Abaris, or of the Argive Pegasas, to whom flight through the air was not of such consequence as was to us our rising to God, through the help of, and with each other? Hurtful as Athens was to others in spiritual things, and this is of no slight consequence to the pious, for the city is richer in those evil riches — idols — than the rest of Greece, and it is hard to avoid being carried along with their devotees and adherents, yet we, our minds being closed up and fortified

against this, suffered no injury. On the contrary, strange as it may seem, we were thus the more confirmed in the faith, from our perception of their trickery and unreality, which led us to despise these divinities in the very home of their worship. And if there is, or is believed to be, a river flowing with fresh water through the sea, or an animal which can dance in fire, the consumer of all things, such were we among all our comrades.

22. And, best of all, we were surrounded by a far from ignoble band, under his instruction and guidance, and delighting in the same objects, as we ran on foot beside that Lydian car, his own course and disposition: and so we became famous, not only among our own teachers and comrades, but even throughout Greece, and especially in the eyes of its most distinguished men. We even passed beyond its boundaries, as was made clear by the evidence of many. For our instructors were known to all who knew Athens, and all who knew them, knew us, as the subject of conversation, being actually looked upon, or heard of by report, as an illustrious pair. Orestes and Pylades were in their eyes nothing to us, or the sons of Molione, the wonders of the Homeric scroll, celebrated for their union in misfortune, and their splendid driving, as they shared in reins and whip alike. But I have been unawares betrayed into praising myself, in a manner I would not have allowed in another. And it is no wonder that I gained here in some advantage from his friendship, and that, as in life he aided me in virtue, so since his departure he has contributed to my renown. But I must return to my proper course.

23. Who possessed such a degree of the prudence of old age, even before his hair was gray? Since it is by this that Solomon defines old age. Who was so respectful to both old and young, not only of our contemporaries, but even of those who long preceded him? Who, owing to his character, was less in need of education? Yet who, even with his character, was so imbued with learning? What branch of learning did he not traverse; and that with unexampled success, passing through all, as no one else passed through any one of them: and attaining such eminence in each, as if it had been his sole study? The two great sources of power in the arts and sciences, ability and application, were in him equally combined. For, because of the pains he took, he had but little need of natural quickness, and his natural quickness made it unnecessary for him to take pains; and such was the cooperation and unity of both, that it was hard to see for which of the two he was more remarkable. Who had such power in Rhetoric, which breathes with the might of fire, different as his disposition was from that of rhetoricians? Who in Grammar, which perfects our tongues in Greek and compiles history, and presides over meters and legislates for poems? Who in Philosophy, that really lofty and high reaching science, whether practical and speculative, or in that part of it whose oppositions and struggles are concerned with logical demonstrations; which is called Dialectic, and in which it was more difficult to elude his verbal toils, if need required, than to escape from the Labyrinths? Of Astronomy, Geometry, and numerical proportion he had such a grasp, that he could not be baffled by those who are clever in such sciences:

283

excessive application to them he despised, as useless to those whose desire is godliness: so that it is possible to admire what he chose more than what he neglected, or what he neglected more than what he chose. Medicine, the result of philosophy and laboriousness, was rendered necessary for him by his physical delicacy, and his care of the sick. From these beginnings he attained to a mastery of the art, not only in its empirical and practical branches, but also in its theory and principles. But what are these, illustrious though they be, compared with the moral discipline of the man? To those who have had experience of him, Minos and Rhadamanthus were mere trifles, whom the Greeks thought worthy of the meadows of Asphodel and the Elysian plains, which are their representations of our Paradise, derived from those books of Moses which are also ours, for though their terms are different, this is what they refer to under other names.

24. Such was the case, and his galleon was laden with all the learning attainable by the nature of man; for beyond Cadiz there is no passage. There was left no other need but that of rising to a more perfect life, and grasping those hopes upon which we were agreed. The day of our departure was at hand, with its attendant speeches of farewell, and of escort, its invitations to return, its lamentations, embraces and tears. For there is nothing so painful to any one, as is separation from Athens and one another, to those who have been comrades there. On that occasion was seen a piteous spectacle, worthy of record. Around us were grouped our fellow students and classmates and some of our teachers, protesting amid entreaties, violence, and persuasion, that, whatever happened, they would not let us go; saying and doing everything that men in distress could do. And here I will bring an accusation against myself, and also, daring though it be, against that divine and irreproachable soul. For he, by detailing the reasons of his anxiety to return home, was able to prevail over their desire to retain him, and they were compelled, though with reluctance, to agree to his departure. But I was left behind at Athens, partly, to say the truth, because I had been prevailed on — partly because he had betrayed me, having been persuaded to forsake and hand over to his captors one who refused to forsake him. A thing incredible, before it happened. For it was like cutting one body into two, to the destruction of either part, or the severance of two bullocks who have shared the same manger and the same yoke, amid pitiable bellowings after one another in protest against the separation. However, my loss was not of long duration, for I could not long bear to be seen in piteous plight, nor to have to account to every one for our separation: so, after a brief stay at Athens, my longing desire made me, like the horse in Homer, to burst the bonds of those who restrained me, and prancing o'er the plains, rush to my mate.

25. Upon our return, after a slight indulgence to the world and the stage, sufficient to gratify the general desire, not from any inclination to theatrical display, we soon became independent, and, after being promoted from the rank of beardless boys to that of men, made bold advances along the road of philosophy, for though no longer together, since envy would not allow this, we were united by our eager

desire. The city of Caesarea took possession of him, as a second founder and patron, but in course of time he was occasionally absent, as a matter of necessity due to our separation, and with a view to our determined course of philosophy. Dutiful attendance on my aged parents, and a succession of misfortunes kept me apart from him, perhaps without right or justice, but so it was. And to this cause I am inclined to ascribe all the inconsistency and difficulty which have befallen my life, and the hindrances in the way of philosophy, which have been unworthy of my desire and purpose. But as for my fate, let it lead whither God pleases, only may its course be the better for his intercessions. As regards himself, the manifold love of God toward man, and His providential care for our race did, after shewing forth his merits under many intervening circumstances with ever greater brilliancy, set him up as a conspicuous and celebrated light for the Church, by advancing him to the holy thrones of the priesthood, to blaze forth, through the single city of Caesarea, to the whole world. And in what manner? Not by precipitate advancement, nor by at once cleansing and making him wise, as is the wont of many present candidates for preferment: but bestowing upon him the honor in the due order of spiritual advancement.

26. For I do not praise the disorder and irregularity which sometimes exist among us, even in those who preside over the sanctuary. I do not venture, nor is it just, to accuse them all. I approve the nautical custom, which first gives the oar to the future steersman, and afterward leads him to the stern, and entrusts him with the command, and seats him at the helm, only after a long course of striking the sea and observing the winds. As is the case again in military affairs: private, captain, general. This order is the best and most advantageous for their subordinates. And if it were so in our case, it would be of great service. But, as it is, there is a danger of the holiest of all offices being the most ridiculous among us. For promotion depends not upon virtue, but upon villainy; and the sacred thrones fall not to the most Worthy, but to the most powerful. Samuel, the seer into futurity, is among the prophets: but Saul, the rejected one, is also there. Rehoboam, the son of Solomon, is among the kings, but so also is Jeroboam, the slave and apostate. And there is not a physician, or a painter who has not first studied the nature of diseases, or mixed many colors, or practiced drawing: but a prelate is easily found, without laborious training, with a reputation of recent date, being sown and springing up in a moment, as the legend of the giants goes. We manufacture those who are holy in a day, and bid those to be wise, who have had no instruction, and have contributed nothing before to their dignity, except the will. So one man is content with an inferior position, and abides in his low estate, who is worthy of a lofty one, and has meditated much on the inspired words, and has reduced the flesh by many laws into subjection to the spirit: while the other haughtily takes precedence, and raises his eyebrow over his betters, and does not tremble at his position, nor is he appalled at the sight, seeing the disciplined man beneath him; and wrongly supposes himself to be his superior in wisdom as well as in rank, having lost his senses under the influence of his position.

27. Not so our great and illustrious Basil. In this grace, as in all others, he was a public example. For he first read to the people the sacred books, while already able to expound them, nor did he deem himself worthy of this rank in the sanctuary, and thus proceeded to praise the Lord in the seat of the Presbyters, and next in that of the Bishops, attaining the office neither by stealth nor by violence, instead of seeking for the honor, being sought for by it, and receiving it not as a human favor, but as from God and divine. The account of his bishopric must be deferred: over his subordinate ministry let us linger a while, for indeed it had almost escaped me, in the midst of my discourse.

28. There arose a disagreement between him and his predecessor in the rule over this Church: its source and character it is best to pass over in silence, yet it arose. He was a man in other respects far from ignoble, and admirable for his piety, as was proved by the persecution of that time, and the opposition to him, yet his feeling against Basil was one to which men are liable. For Momus seizes not only upon the common herd, but on the best of men, so that it belongs to God alone to be utterly uninfluenced by and proof against such feelings. All the more eminent and wise portion of the Church was roused against him, if those are wiser than the majority who have separated themselves from the world and consecrated their life to God. I mean the Nazarites of our day, and those who devote themselves to such pursuits. They were annoyed that their chief should be neglected, insulted, and rejected, and they ventured upon a most dangerous proceeding. They determined to revolt and break off from the body of the Church, which admits of no faction, severing along with themselves no small fraction of the people, both of the lower ranks, and of those of position. This was most easy, owing to three very strong reasons. In the first place, the man was held in repute, beyond any other, I think, of the philosophers of our time, and able, if he wished, to inspire with courage the conspirators. Next, his opponent was suspected by the city, in consequence of the tumult which accompanied his institution, of having obtained his preferment in an arbitrary manner, not according to the laws and canons. Also there were present some of the bishops of the West, drawing to themselves all the orthodox members of the Church.

29. What then did our noble friend, the disciple of the Peaceable One? It was not his habit to resist his traducers or partisans, nor was it his part to fight, or rend the body of the Church, which was from other reasons the subject of attack, and hardly bestead, from the great power of the heretics. With my advice and earnest encouragement on the point, he set out from the place with me into Pontus, and presided over the abodes of contemplation there. He himself too founded one worthy of mention, as he welcomed the desert together with Elijah and John, those professors of austerity; thinking this to be more profitable for him than to form any design in reference to the present juncture unworthy of his philosophy, and to ruin in a time of storm the straight course which he was making, where the surges of

disputation were lulled to a calm. Yet wonderfully philosophic though his retirement was, we shall find his return still more wonderful. For thus it was.

30. While we were thus engaged, there suddenly arose a cloud full of hail, with destructive roar, overwhelming every Church upon which it burst and seized: an Emperor, most fond of gold and most hostile to Christ, infected with these two most serious diseases, insatiate avarice and blasphemy; a persecutor in succession to the persecutor, and, in succession to the apostate, not indeed an apostate, though no better to Christians, or rather, to the more devout and pure party of Christians, who worship the Trinity, which I call the only true devotion and saving doctrine. For we do not measure out the Godhead into portions, nor banish from Itself by unnatural estrangements the one and unapproachable Nature; nor cure one evil by another, destroying the godless confusion of Sabellius by a more impious severance and division; which was the error of Arius, whose name declares his madness, the disturber and destroyer of a great part of the Church. For he did not honor the Father, by dishonoring His offspring with his unequal degrees Of Godhead. But we recognize one glory of the Father, the equality of the Only-begotten; and one glory of the Son, that of the Spirit. And we hold that, to subordinate any of the Three, is to destroy the whole. For we worship and acknowledge Them as Three in their properties, but One in their Godhead. He however had no such idea, being unable to look up, but being debased by those who led him, he dared to debase along with himself even the Nature of the Godhead, and became a wicked creature reducing Majesty to bondage, and aligning with creation the uncreated and timeless Nature.

31. Such was his mind, and with such impiety he took the field against us. For we must consider it to be nothing else than a barbaric inroad which, instead of destroying walls, cities and houses, and other things of little worth, made with hands and capable of restoration, spent its ravages upon men's souls. A worthy army joined in his assault, the evil rulers of the Churches, the bitter governors of his world-wide Empire. Some of the Churches they now held, some they were assaulting, others they' hoped to gain by the already exercised influence of the Emperor, and the violence which he threatened. But in their purpose of perverting our own, their confidence was specially based on the smallness of mind of those whom I have mentioned, the inexperience of our prelate, and the infirmities which prevailed among us. The struggle would be fierce: the zeal of numerous troops was far from ignoble, but their array was weak, from the want of a leader and strategist to contend for them with the might of the Word and of the Spirit. What then did this noble and magnanimous and truly Christ- loving soul? No need of many words to urge his presence and aid. At once when he saw me on my mission, for the struggle on behalf of the faith was common to us both, he yielded to my entreaty; and decided by a most excellent distinction, based on spiritual reasons, that the time for punctiliousness (if indeed we may give way to such feelings at all) is a time of security, but that forbearance is required in the hour of necessity. He immediately returned with me from Pontus, and as a zealous volunteer took his

place in the fight for the endangered truth, and devoted himself to the service of his mother, the Church.

32. Did then his actual efforts fall short of his preliminary zeal? Were they directed by courage, but not by prudence, or by skill, while he shrank from danger? Or, in spite of their unexampled perfection on all these points, was there left in him some trace of irritation? Far from it. He was at once completely reconciled, and took part in every plan and effort. He removed all the thorns and stumbling blocks which were in our way, upon which the enemy relied in their attack upon us. He took hold of one, grasped another, thrust away a third. He became to some a stout wall and rampart, to others an axe breaking the rock in pieces, or a fire among the thorns, as the divine Scripture says, easily destroying those fagots who were insulting the Godhead. And if his Barnabas, who speaks and records these things, was of service to Paul in the struggle, it is to Paul that thanks are due, for choosing and making him his comrade in the strife.

33. Thus the enemy failed, and, base men as they were, for the first time were then basely put to shame and worsted, learning not to be ready to despise the Cappadocians, of all men in the world, whose special qualities are firmness in the faith, and loyal devotion to the Trinity; to Whom is due their unity and strength, and from Whom they receive an even greater and stronger assistance than they are able to give. Basil's next business and purpose was to conciliate the prelate, to allay suspicion, to persuade all men that the irritation which had been felt was due to the temptation and effort of the Evil one, in his envy of virtuous concord: carefully complying with the laws of obedience and spiritual order. Accordingly he visited him, with instruction and advice. While obedient to his wishes, he was everything to him, a good counselor, a skillful assistant, an expounder of the Divine Will, a guide of conduct, a staff for his old age, a support of the faith, most trusty of those within, most practical of those without, in a word, as much inclined to goodwill, as he had been thought to hostility. And so the power of the Church came into his hands almost, if not quite, to an equal degree with the occupant of the see. For in return for his good-will, he was requited with authority. And their harmony and combination of power was wonderful. The one was the leader of the people, the other of their leader, like a lion-keeper, skillfully soothing the possessor of power. For, having been recently installed in the see, and still somewhat under the influence of the world, and not yet furnished with the things of the Spirit, in the midst of the eddying tide of enemies assaulting the Church, he was in need of some one to take him by the hand and support him. Accordingly he accepted the alliance, and imagined himself the conqueror of one who had conquered him.

34. Of his care for and protection of the Church, there are many other tokens; his boldness towards the governors and other most powerful men in the city: the decisions of disputes, accepted without hesitation, and made effective by his simple word, his inclination being held to be decisive: his support of the needy, most of

them in spiritual, not a few also in physical distress: for this also often influences the soul and reduces it to subjection by its kindness; the support of the poor, the entertainment of strangers, the care of maidens; legislation written and unwritten for the monastic life: arrangements of prayers, adornments of the sanctuary, and other ways in which the true man of God, working for God, would benefit the people: one being especially important and noteworthy. There was a famine, the most severe one ever recorded. The city was in distress, and there was no source of assistance, or relief for the calamity. For maritime cities are able to bear such times of need without difficulty, by an exchange of their own products for what is imported: but an inland city like ours can neither turn its superfluity to profit, nor supply its need, by either disposing of what we have, or importing what we have not: but the hardest part of all such distress is, the insensibility and insatiability of those who possess supplies. For they watch their opportunities, and turn the distress to profit, and thrive upon misfortune: heeding not that he who shows mercy to the poor, lendeth to the Lord, nor that he that withholdeth corn, the people shall curse him: nor any other of the promises to the philanthropic, and threats against the inhuman. But they are too insatiate, in their ill-judged policy; for while they shut up their bowels against their fellows, they shut up those of God against themselves, forgetting that their need of Him is greater than others' need of them. Such are the buyers and sellers of corn, who neither respect their fellows, nor are thankful to God, from Whom comes what they have, while others are straitened.

35. He indeed could neither rain bread from heaven by prayer, to nourish an escaped people in the wilderness, nor supply fountains of food without cost from the depth of vessels which are filled by being emptied, and so, by an amazing return for her hospitality, support one who supported him; nor feed thousands of men with five loaves whose very fragments were a further supply for many tables. These were the works of Moses and Elijah, and my God, from Whom they too derived their power. Perhaps also they were characteristic of their time and its circumstances: since signs are for unbelievers not for those who believe. But he did devise and execute with the same faith things which correspond to them, and tend in the same direction. For by his word and advice he opened the stores of those who possessed them, and so, according to the Scripture dealt food to the hungry, and satisfied the poor with bread, and fed them in the time of dearth, and filled the hungry souls with good things. And in what way? for this is no slight addition to his praise. He gathered together the victims of the famine with some who were but slightly recovering from it, men and women, infants, old men, every age which was in distress, and obtaining contributions of all sorts of food which can relieve famine, set before them basins of soup and such meat as was found preserved among us, on which the poor live. Then, imitating the ministry of Christ, Who, girded with a towel, did not disdain to wash the disciples' feet, using for this purpose the aid of his own servants, and also of his fellow servants, he attended to the bodies and souls of those who needed it, combining personal respect with the supply of their necessity, and so giving them a double relief.

36. Such was our young furnisher of corn, and second Joseph: though of him we can say somewhat more. For the one made a gain from the famine, and bought up Egypt in his philanthropy, by managing the time of plenty with a view to the time of famine, turning to account the dreams of others for that purpose. But the other's services were gratuitous, and his succor of the famine gained no profit, having only one object, to win kindly feelings by kindly treatment, and to gain by his rations of corn the heavenly blessings. Further he provided the nourishment of the Word, and that more perfect bounty and distribution, which is really heavenly and from on high — if the word be that bread of angels, wherewith souls are fed and given to drink, who are a hungered for God, and seek for a food which does not pass away or fail, but abides forever. This food he, who was the poorest and most needy man whom I have known, supplied in rich abundance to the relief not of a famine of bread, nor of a thirst for water, but a longing for that Word which is really life-giving and nourishing, and causes to grow to spiritual manhood him who is duly fed thereon.

37. After these and similar actions — why need I stay to mention them all? — when the prelate whose name betokened his godliness had passed away, having sweetly breathed his last in Basil's arms, he was raised to the lofty throne of a Bishop, not without difficulty or without the envious struggles of the prelates of his native land, on whose side were found the greatest scoundrels of the city. But the Holy Spirit must needs win the day — and indeed the victory was decisive. For He brought from a distance, to anoint him, men illustrious and zealous for godliness, and with them the new Abraham, our Patriarch, I mean my father, in regard to whom an extraordinary thing happened. For, failing as he was from the number of his years, and worn away almost to his last breath by disease, he ventured on the journey to give assistance by his vote, relying on the aid of the Spirit. In brief, he was placed in his litter, as a corpse is laid in its tomb, to return in the freshness and strength of youth, with head erect, having been strengthened by the imposition of hands and unction, and, it is not too much to say by the head of him who was anointed. This must be added to the instances of old time, which prove that labor bestows health, zealous purpose raises the dead, and old age leaps up when anointed by the Spirit.

38. Having thus been deemed worthy of the office of prelate, as it is seemly that men should who have lived such a life, and won such favor and consideration, he did not disgrace, by his subsequent conduct, either his own philosophy, or the hopes of those who had trusted him. But he ever so far surpassed himself as he has been shown hitherto to have surpassed others, his ideas on this point being most excellent and philosophic. For he held that, while it is virtuous in a private individual to avoid vice, and be to some extent good, it is a vice in a chief and ruler, especially in such an office, to fail to surpass by far the majority of men, and by constant progress to make his virtue correspond to his dignity and throne: for it is difficult for one in high position to attain the mean, and by his eminence in virtue

raise up his people to the golden mean. Or rather to treat this question more satisfactorily, I think that the result is the same as I see in the case of our Savior, and of every specially wise man, I fancy, when He was with us in that form which surpassed us and yet is ours. For He also, the gospel says, increased in wisdom and favor, as well as in stature, not that these qualities in Him were capable of growth: for how could that which was perfect from the first become more perfect, but that they were gradually disclosed and displayed? So I think that the virtue of Basil, without being itself increased, obtained at this time a wider exercise, since his power provided him with more abundant material.

39. He first of all made it plain that his office had been bestowed upon him, not by human favor, but by the gift of God. This will also be shown by my conduct. For in what philosophic research did he not, about that time, join with me? So every one thought that I should run to meet him after what had happened, and show my delight at it (as would, perhaps, have been the case with any one else) and claim a share in his authority, rather than rule beside him, according to the inferences they drew from our friendship. But, in my exceeding anxiety to avoid the annoyance and jealousy of the time, and specially since his position was still a painful and troubled one, I remained at home, and forcibly restrained my eager desire, while, though he blamed me, Basil accepted my excuse. And when, on my subsequent arrival, I refused, for the same reason the honor of this chair, and a dignified position among the Presbyters, he kindly refrained from blaming, nay he praised me, preferring to be charged with pride by a small clique, in their ignorance of our policy, rather than do anything contrary to reason and his own resolutions. And indeed, how could a man have better shown his soul to be superior to all fawning and flattery, and his single object to be the law of right, than by thus treating me, whom he acknowledged as among the first of his friends and associates?

40. His next task was to appease, and allay by magnanimous treatment, the opposition to himself: and that without any trace of flattery or servility, but in a most chivalrous and magnanimous way; with a view, not merely to present exigencies, but also to the fostering of future obedience. For, seeing that, while tenderness leads to laxity and slackness, severity gives rise to stubbornness and self-will, he was able to avoid the dangers of each course by a combination of both, blending his correction with consideration, and gentleness with firmness, influencing men in most cases principally by his conduct rather than by argument: not enslaving them by art, but winning them by good nature, and attracting them by the sparing use, rather than by the constant exercise, of his power. And, most important of all, they were brought to recognize the superiority of his intellect and the inaccessibility of his virtue, to consider their only safety to consist in being on his side and under his command, their sole danger to be in opposition to him, and to think that to differ from him involved estrangement from God. Thus they willingly yielded and surrendered, submitting themselves, as if in a thunder-clap, and hastening to anticipate each other with their excuses, and exchange the

intensity of their hostility for an equal intensity of goodwill, and advance in virtue, which they found to be the one really effective defense. The few exceptions to this conduct were passed by and neglected, because their ill-nature was incurable, and they expended their powers in wearing out themselves, as rust consumes itself together with the iron on which it feeds.

41. Affairs at home being now settled to his mind, in a way that faithless men who did not know him would have thought impossible, his designs became greater and took a loftier range. For, while all others had their eyes on the ground before them, and directed attention to their own immediate concerns, and, if these were safe, troubled themselves no further, being incapable of any great and chivalrous design or undertaking; he, moderate as he was in all other respects, could not be moderate in this, but with head erect, casting his mental eye about him, took in the whole world over which the word of salvation has made its way. And when he saw the great heritage of God, purchased by His own words and laws and sufferings, the holy nation, the royal priesthood, in such evil plight that it was torn asunder into ten thousand opinions and errors: and the vine brought out of Egypt and transplanted, the Egypt of impious and dark ignorance, which had grown to such beauty and boundless size that the whole earth was covered with the shadow of it, while it overtopped mountains and cedars, now being ravaged by that wicked wild boar, the devil, he could not content himself with quietly lamenting the misfortune, and merely lifting up his hands to God, and seeking from Him the dispersion of the pressing misfortunes, while he himself was asleep, but felt bound to come to her aid at some expense to himself.

42. For what could be more distressing than this calamity, or call more loudly on one whose eyes were raised aloft for exertions on behalf of the common weal? The good or ill success of an individual is of no consequence to the community, but that of the community involves of necessity the like condition of the individual. With this idea and purpose, he who was the guardian and patron of the community (and, as Solomon says with truth, a perceptive heart is a moth to the bones, unsensitiveness is cheerily confident, while a sympathetic disposition is a source of pain, and constant consideration wastes away the heart), he, I say, was consequently in agony and distress from many wounds; like Jonah and David, he wished in himself to die and gave not sleep to his eyes, nor slumber to his eyelids, he expended what was left of his flesh upon his reflections, until he discovered a remedy for the evil: and sought for aid from God and man, to stay the general conflagration, and dissipate the gloom which was lowering over us.

43. One of his devices was of the greatest service. After a period of such recollection as was possible, and private spiritual conference, in which, after considering all human arguments, and penetrating into all the deep things of the Scriptures, he drew up a sketch of pious doctrine, and by wrestling with and attacking their opposition he beat off the daring assaults of the heretics: overthrowing in hand to

hand struggles by word of mouth those who came to close quarters, and striking those at a distance by arrows winged with ink, which is in no wise inferior to inscriptions on tablets; not giving directions for one small nation only like that of the Jews, concerning meats and drinks, temporary sacrifices, and purifications of the flesh; but for every nation and part of the world, concerning the Word of truth, the source of our salvation. Again, since unreasoning action and unpractical reasoning are alike ineffectual, he added to his reasoning the succor which comes from action; he paid visits, sent messages, gave interviews, instructed, reproved, rebuked, threatened, reproached, undertook the defense of nations, cities and individuals, devising every kind of succor, and procuring from every source specifics for disease: a second Bezaleel, an architect of the Divine tabernacle, applying every material and art to the work, and combining all in a harmonious and surpassing beauty.

44. Why need I enter into further detail? We were assailed again by the Anti-Christian Emperor, that tyrant of the faith, with more abundant impiety and a hotter onset, inasmuch as the dispute must be with a stronger antagonist, like that unclean and evil spirit, who when sent forth upon his wanderings from man, returns to take up his abode in him again with a greater number of spirits, as we have heard in the Gospels. This spirit he imitated, both in renewing the contest in which he had formerly been worsted, and in adding to his original efforts. He thought that it was a strange and insufferable thing that he, who ruled over so many nations and had won so much renown, and reduced under the power of impiety all those round about him, and overcome every adversary, should be publicly worsted by a single man, and a single city, and so incur the ridicule not only of those patrons of ungodliness by whom he was led, but also, as he supposed, of all men.

45. It is said that the King of Persia, on his expedition into Greece, was not only urged to immoderate threats, by elation at the numbers of every race of men which in his wrath and pride he was leading against them: but thought to terrify them the more, by making them afraid of him, in consequence of his novel treatment of the elements. A strange land and sea were heard of, the work of the new creator; and an army which sailed over the dry land, and marched over the ocean, while islands were carried off, and the sea was scourged, and all the other mad proceedings of that army and expedition, which, though they struck terror into the ignoble, were ridiculous in the eyes of men of brave and steadfast hearts. There was no need of anything of this kind in the expedition against us, but what was still worse and more harmful, this was what the Emperor was reported to say and do. He stretched forth his mouth unto heaven, speaking blasphemy against the most High, and his tongue went through the world. Excellently did the inspired David before our days thus describe him who made heaven to stoop to earth, and reckoned with the creation that supermundane nature, which the creation cannot even contain, even though in kindness to man it did to some extent come among us, in order to draw to itself us who were lying upon the ground.

46. Furious indeed were his first acts of wantonness, more furious still his final efforts against us. What shall I speak of first? Exiles, banishments, confiscations, open and secret plots, persuasion, where time allowed, violence, where persuasion was impossible. Those who clung to the orthodox faith, as we did, were extruded from their churches; others were intruded, who agreed with the Imperial soul-destroying doctrines, and begged for testimonials of impiety, and subscribed to statements still harder than these. Burnings of Presbyters at sea, impious generals, not those who conquered the Persians, or subdued the Scythians, or reduced any other barbaric nation, but those who assailed churches, and danced in triumph upon altars, and defiled the unbloody sacrifices with the blood of man and victims, and offered insult to the modesty of virgins. With what object? The extrusion of the Patriarch Jacob, and the intrusion in his place of Esau, who was hated, even before his birth. This is the description of his first acts of wantonness, the mere recollection and mention of which even now, rouses the tears of most of us.

47. Accordingly, when, after passing through all quarters, he made his attack in order to enslave this impregnable and formidable mother of the Churches, the only still remaining unquenched spark of the truth, he discovered that he had been for the first time ill advised. For he was driven back like a missile which strikes upon some stronger body, and recoiled like a broken hawser. Such was the prelate of the Church that he met with, such was the bulwark by which his efforts were broken and dissipated. Other particulars may be heard from those who tell and recount them, from their own experience — and none of those who recount them is destitute of this full experience. But all must be filled with admiration who are aware of the struggles of that time, the assaults, the promises, the threats, the commissioners sent before him to try to prevail upon us, men of judicial and military rank, men from the harem, who are men among women, women among men, whose only manliness consisted in their impiety, and being incapable of natural licentiousness, commit fornication in the only way they can, with their tongues; the chief cook Nebuzaradan, who threatened us with the weapons of his art, and was despatched by his own fire. But what especially excites my wonder, and what I could not, even if I would, pass by, I will describe as concisely as possible.

48. Who has not heard of the prefect of those days, who, for his own part, treated us with such excessive arrogance, having himself been admitted, or perhaps committed, to baptism by the other party; and strove by exceeding the letter of his instructions, and gratifying his master in every particular, to guarantee and preserve his own possession of power. Though he raged against the Church, and assumed a lion-like aspect, and roared like a lion till most men dared not approach him, yet our noble prelate was brought into or rather entered his court, as if bidden to a feast, instead of to a trial. How can I fitly describe, either the arrogance of the prefect or the prudence with which it was met by the Saint. "What is the meaning, Sir Basil," he said, addressing him by name, and not as yet deigning to term him Bishop, "of your daring, as no other dares, to resist and oppose so great a

potentate?" "In what respect?" said our noble champion, "and in what does my rashness consist? For this I have yet to learn." "In refusing to respect the religion of your Sovereign, when all others have yielded and submitted themselves?" "Because," said he, "this is not the will of my real Sovereign; nor can I, who am the creature of God, and bidden myself to be God, submit to worship any creature." "And what do we," said the prefect, "seem to you to be? Are we, who give you this injunction, nothing at all? What do you say to this? Is it not a great thing to be ranged with us as your associates?" "You are, I will not deny it," said he, "a prefect, and an illustrious one, yet not of more honor than God. And to be associated with you is a great thing, certainly; for you are yourself the creature of God; but so it is to be associated with any other of my subjects. For faith, and not personal importance, is the distinctive mark of Christianity."

49. Then indeed the prefect became excited, and rose from his seat, boiling with rage, and making use of harsher language. "What?" said he, "have you no fear of my authority? "Fear of what?" said Basil, "How could it affect me? "Of what? Of any one of the resources of my power." "What are these? "said Basil, "pray, inform me." "Confiscation, banishment, torture, death." "Have you no other threat?" said he, "for none of these can reach me." "How indeed is that?" said the prefect. "Because," he replied, "a man who has nothing, is beyond the reach of confiscation; unless you demand my tattered rags, and the few books, which are my only possessions. Banishment is impossible for me, who am confined by no limit of place, counting my own neither the land where I now dwell, nor all of that into which I may be hurled; or, rather, counting it all God's, whose guest and dependent I am. As for tortures, what hold can they have upon one whose body has ceased to be? Unless you mean the first stroke, for this alone is in your power. Death is my benefactor, for it will send me the sooner to God, for Whom I live, and exist, and have all but died, and to Whom I have long been hastening."

50. Amazed at this language, the prefect said, "No one has ever yet spoken thus, and with such boldness, to Modestus." "Why, perhaps," said Basil, "you have not met with a Bishop, or in his defense of such interests he would have used precisely the same language. For we are modest in general, and submissive to every one, according to the precept of our law. We may not treat with haughtiness even any ordinary person, to say nothing of so great a potentate. But where the interests of God are at stake, we care for nothing else, and make these our sole object. Fire and sword and wild beasts, and rakes which tear the flesh, we revel in, and fear them not. You may further insult and threaten us, and do whatever you will, to the full extent of your power. The Emperor himself may hear this — that neither by violence nor persuasion will you bring us to make common cause with impiety, not even though your threats become still more terrible."

51. At the close of this colloquy, the prefect, having been convinced by the attitude of Basil, that he was absolutely impervious to threats and influence, dismissed him

from the court, his former threatening manner being replaced by somewhat of respect and deference. He himself with all speed obtained an audience of the Emperor, and said: "We have been worsted, Sire, by the prelate of this Church. He is superior to threats, invincible in argument, uninfluenced by persuasion. We must make trial of some more feeble character; and in this case resort to open violence, or submit to the disregard of our threatenings." Hereupon the Emperor, forced by the praises of Basil to condemn his own conduct (for even an enemy can admire a man's excellence), would not allow violence to be used against him: and, like iron, which is softened by fire, yet still remains iron, though turned from threatening to admiration, would not enter into communion with him, being prevented by shame from changing his course, but sought to justify his conduct by the most plausible excuse he could, as the sequel will show.

52. For he entered the Church attended by the whole of his train; it was the festival of the Epiphany, and the Church was crowded, and, by taking his place among the people, he made a profession of unity. The occurrence is not to be lightly passed over. Upon his entrance he was struck by the thundering roll of the Psalms, by the sea of heads of the congregation, and by the angelic rather than human order which pervaded the sanctuary and its precincts: while Basil presided over his people, standing erect, as the Scripture says of Samuel, with body and eyes and mind undisturbed, as if nothing new had happened, but fixed upon God and the sanctuary, as if, so to say, he had been a statue, while his ministers stood around him in fear and reverence. At this sight, and it was indeed a sight unparalleled, overcome by human weakness, his eyes were affected with dimness and giddiness, his mind with dread. This was as yet unnoticed by most people. But when he had to offer the gifts at the Table of God, which he must needs do himself, since no one would, as usual, assist him, because it was uncertain whether Basil would admit him, his feelings were revealed. For he was staggering, and had not some one in the sanctuary reached out a hand to steady his tottering steps, he would have sunk to the ground in a lamentable fall. So much for this.

53. As for the wisdom of his conference with the Emperor, who, in his quasi-communion with us entered within the veil to see and speak to him, as he had long desired to do, what else can I say but that they were inspired words, which were heard by the courtiers and by us who had entered with them? This was the beginning and first establishment of the Emperor's kindly feeling towards us; the impression produced by this reception put an end to the greater part of the persecution which assailed us like a river.

54. Another incident is not of less importance than those I have mentioned. The wicked were victorious, and the decree for his banishment was signed, to the full satisfaction of those who furthered it. The night had come, the chariot was ready, our haters were exultant, the pious in despair, we surrounded the zealous traveler, to whose honorable disgrace nothing was wanting. What next? It was undone by

God. For He Who smote the first-born of Egypt, for its harshness towards Israel, also struck the son of the Emperor with disease. How great was the speed! There was the sentence of banishment, here the decree of sickness: the hand of the wicked scribe was restrained, and the saint was preserved, and the man of piety presented to us, by the fever which brought to reason the arrogance of the Emperor. What could be more just or more speedy than this? This was the series of events: the Emperor's child was sick and in bodily pain. The father was pained for it, for what can the father do? On all sides he sought for aid in his distress, he summoned the best physicians, he betook himself to intercessions with the greatest fervor, and flung himself upon the ground. Affliction humbles even emperors, and no wonder, for the like sufferings of David in the case of his child are recorded for us. But as no cure for the evil could anywhere be found, he applied to the faith of Basil, not personally summoning him, in shame for his recent ill treatment, but entrusting the mission to others of his nearest and dearest friends. On his arrival, without the delay or reluctance which any one else might have shown, at once the disease relaxed, and the father cherished better hopes; and had he not blended salt water with the fresh, by trusting to the heterodox at the same time that he summoned Basil, the child would have recovered his health and been preserved for his father's arms. This indeed was the conviction of those who were present at the time, and shared in the distress.

55. The same mischance is said to have befallen the prefect. He also was obliged by sickness to bow beneath the hands of the Saint, and, in reality, to men of sense a visitation brings instruction, and affliction is often better than prosperity. He fell sick, was in tears, and in pain, he sent for Basil, and en-treated him, crying out, "I own that you were in the right; only save me!" His request was granted, as he himself acknowledged, and convinced many who had known nothing of it; for he never ceased to wonder at and describe the powers of the prelate. Such was his conduct in these cases, such its result. Did he then treat others in a different way, and engage in petty disputes about trifles, or fail to rise to the heights of philosophy in a course of action which merits no praise and is best passed over in silence? By no means. He who once stirred up the wicked Hadad against Israel, stirred up against him the prefect of the province of Pontus; nominally, from annoyance connected with some poor creature of a woman, but in reality as a part of the struggle of impiety against the truth. I pass by all his other insults against Basil, or, for it is the same thing, against God; for it is against Him and on His behalf that the contest was waged. One instance of it, however, which brought special disgrace upon the assailant, and exalted his adversary, if philosophy and eminence for it be a great and lofty thing, I will describe at length.

56. The assessor of a judge was attempting to force into a distasteful marriage a lady of high birth whose husband was but recently dead. At a loss to escape from this high-handed treatment, she resorted to a device no less prudent than daring. She fled to the holy table, and placed herself under the protection of God against

outrage. What, in the Name of the Trinity Itself, if I may introduce into my panegyric somewhat of the forensic style, ought to have been done, I do not say, by the great Basil, who laid down the law for us all in such matters, but by any one who, though far inferior to him, was a priest? Ought he not to have allowed her claim, to have taken charge of, and cared for, her; to have raised his hand in defense of the kindness of God and the law which gives honor to the altar? Ought he not to have been willing to do and suffer anything, rather than take part in any inhuman design against her, and outrage at once the holy table, and the faith in which she had taken sanctuary? No! said the baffled judge, all ought to yield to my authority, and Christians should betray their own laws. The suppliant whom he demanded, was at all hazards retained. Accordingly, in his rage, he at last sent some of the magistrates to search the saint's bedchamber, with the purpose of dishonoring him, rather than from any necessity. What! Search the house of a man so free from passion, whom the angels revere, at whom women do not venture even to look? And, not content with this, he summoned him, and put him on his defense; and that, in no gentle or kindly manner, but as if he were a convict. Upon Basil's appearance, standing, like my Jesus, before the judgment seat of Pilate, he presided at the trial, full of wrath and pride. Yet the thunderbolts did not fall, and the sword of God still glittered, and waited, while His bow, though bent, was restrained. Such indeed is the custom of God.

57. Consider another struggle between our champion and his persecutor. His ragged pallium having been ordered to be torn away, "I will also, if you wish it, strip off my coat," said he. His fleshless form was threatened with blows, and he offered to submit to be torn with combs, and he said, "By such laceration you will cure my liver, which, as you see, is wearing me away." Such was their argument. But when the city perceived the outrage and the common danger of all — for each one considered this insolence a danger to himself, it became all on fire with rage; and, like a hive roused by smoke, one after another was stirred and arose, every race' and every age, but especially the men from the- small- arms factory and from the imperial weaving-sheds. For men at work in these trades are specially hot-tempered and daring, because of the liberty allowed them. Each man was armed with the tool he was using, or with whatever else came to hand at the moment. Torch in hand, amid showers of stones, with cudgel's ready, all ran and shouted together in their united zeal. Anger makes a terrible soldier or general. Nor were the women weaponless, when roused by such an occasion. Their pins were their spears, and no longer remaining women, they were by the strength of their eagerness endowed with masculine courage. It is a short story. They thought that they would share among themselves the piety of destroying him, and held him to be most pious who first laid hands on one who had dared such deeds. What then was the conduct of this haughty and daring judge? He begged for mercy in a pitiable state of distress, cringing before them to an unparalleled extent, until the arrival of the martyr without bloodshed, who had won his crown without blows, and now restrained the people by the force of his personal influence, and delivered the man who had

insulted him and now sought his protection. This was the doing of the God of Saints, Who worketh and changeth all things for the best, who resisteth the proud, but giveth grace to the humble. And why should not He, Who divided the sea and stayed the river, and ruled the elements, and by stretching out set up a trophy, to save His exiled people, why should not He have also rescued this man from his perils?

58. This was the end and fortunate dose, in the Providence of God, of the war with the world, a close worthy of his faith. But here at once is the beginning of the war with the Bishops, and their allies, which involved great disgrace, and still greater injury to their subjects. For who could persuade others to be temperate, when such was the conduct of their prelates? For a long time they had been unkindly disposed towards him, on three grounds. They neither agreed with him in the matter of the faith, except in so far as they were absolutely obliged to yield to the majority of the faithful. Nor had they altogether laid aside the grudge they owed him for his election. And, what was most grievous of all to them, though they would have been most ashamed to own it — he so far outshone them in reputation. There was also a further cause of dissension which stirred up again the others. When our country had been divided into two provinces and metro-political sees, and a great part of the former was being added to the new one, this again roused their factious spirit. The one thought it right that the ecclesiastical boundaries should be settled by the civil ones: and therefore claimed those newly added, as belonging to him, and severed from their former metropolitan. The other clung to the ancient custom, and to the division which had come down from our fathers. Many painful results either actually followed, or were struggling in the womb of the future. Synods were wrongfully gathered by the new metropolitan, and revenues seized upon. Some of the presbyters of the churches refused obedience, others were won over. In consequence the affairs of the churches fell into a sad state of dissension and division. Novelty indeed has a certain charm for men, and they readily turn events to their own advantage, and it is easier to overthrow something which is already established, than to restore it when overthrown. What however enraged him most was, that the revenues of the Taurus, which passed along before his eyes, accrued to his rival, as also the offerings at Saint Orestes', of which he was greatly desirous to reap the fruits. He even went so far as, on one occasion when Basil was riding along his own road, to seize his mules by the bridle and bar the passage with a robber band. And with how specious a pretext, the care of his spiritual children and of the souls entrusted to him, and the defense of the faith — pretexts which veiled that most common vice, insatiable avarice — and further, the wrongfulness of paying dues to heretics, a heretic being any one who had displeased him.

59. The holy man of God however, metropolitan as he was of the true Jerusalem above, was neither carried away with the failure of those who fell, nor allowed himself to overlook this conduct, nor did he desire any inadequate remedy for the evil. Let us see how great and wonderful it was, or, I would say, how worthy of his

soul. He made of the dissension a cause of increase to the Church, and the disaster, under his most able management, resulted in the multiplication of the Bishops of the country. From this ensued three most desirable consequences; a greater care for souls, the management by each city of its own affairs, and the cessation of the war in this quarter. I am afraid that I myself was treated as an appendage to this scheme. By no other term can I readily describe the position. Greatly as I admire his whole conduct, to an extent indeed beyond my powers of expression, of this single particular I find it impossible to approve, for I will acknowledge my feelings in regard to it, though these are from other sources not unknown to most of you. I mean the change and faithlessness of his treatment of myself, a cause of pain which even time has not obliterated. For this is the source of all the inconsistency and tangle of my life; it has robbed me of the practice, or at least the reputation, of philosophy; of small moment though the latter be. The defense, which you will perhaps allow me to make for him, is this; his ideas were superhuman, and having, before his death, become superior to worldly influences, his only interests were those of the Spirit: while his regard for friendship was in no wise lessened by his readiness then, and then only, to disregard its claims, when they were in conflict with his paramount duty to God, and when the end he had in view was of greater importance than the interests he was compelled to set aside.

60. I am afraid that, in avoiding the imputation of indifference at the hands of those who desire to know all that can be said about him, I shall incur a charge of prolixity from those whose ideal is the golden mean. For the latter Basil himself had the greatest respect, being specially devoted to the adage "In all things the mean is the best," and acting upon it throughout his life. Nevertheless, disregarding alike those who desire undue conciseness or excessive prolixity, I proceed thus with my speech. Different men attain success in different ways, some applying themselves to one alone of the many forms of excellence, but no one, of those hitherto known to me, arriving at the highest eminence in all respects; he being in my opinion the best, who has won his laurels on the widest field, or gained the highest possible renown in some single particular. Such however was the height of Basil's fame, that he became the pride of human kind. Let us consider the matter thus. Is any one devoted to poverty and a life devoid of property, and free from superfluity? What did he possess besides his body, and the necessary coverings of the flesh? His wealth was the having nothing, and he thought the cross, with which he lived, more precious than great riches. For no one, however much he may wish, can obtain possession of all things, but any one can learn to despise, and so prove himself superior to, all things. Such being his mind, and such his life, he had no need of an altar and of vainglory, nor of such a public announcement as "Crates sets Crates the Theban free." For his aim was ever to be, not to seem, most excellent. Nor did he dwell in a tub, and in the midst of the market-place, and so by luxuriating in publicity turn his poverty into riches: but was poor and unkempt, yet without ostentation: and taking cheerfully the casting overboard of all that he ever had, sailed lightly across the sea of life.

61. A wondrous thing is temperance, and fewness of wants, and freedom from the dominion of pleasures, and from the bondage of that cruel and degrading mistress, the belly. Who was so independent of food, and, without exaggeration, more free from the flesh? For he flung away all satiety and surfeit to creatures destitute of reason, whose life is slavish and debasing. He paid little attention to such things as, next to the appetite, are of equal rank, but, as far as possible, lived on the merest necessaries, his only luxury being to prove himself not luxurious, and not, in consequence, to have greater needs: but he looked to the lilies and the birds, whose beauty is artless, and their food casual, according to the important advice of my Christ, who made Himself poor in the flesh for our sakes, that we might enjoy the riches of His Godhead. Hence came his single coat and well worn cloak, and his bed on the bare ground, his vigils, his unwashedness (such were his decorations) and his most sweet food and relish, bread, and salt, his new dainty, and the sober and plentiful drink, with which fountains supply those who are free from trouble. The result, or the accompaniment, of these things were the attendance on the sick and practice of medicine, our common intellectual pursuit. For, though inferior to him in all other respects, I must needs be his equal in distress.

62. A great thing is virginity, and celibacy, and being ranked with the angels, and with the single nature; for I shrink from calling it Christ's, Who, though He willed to be born for our sakes who are born, by being born of a Virgin, enacted the law of virginity, to lead us away from this life, and cut short the power of the world, or rather, to transmit one world to another, the present to the future. Who then paid more honor to virginity, or had more control of the flesh, not only by his personal example, but in those under his care? Whose are the convents, and the written regulations, by which he subdued every sense, and regulated every member, and won to the real practice of virginity, turning inward the view of beauty, from the visible to the invisible; and by wasting away the external, and withdrawing fuel from the flame, and revealing the secrets of the heart to God, Who is the only bridegroom of pure souls, and takes in with himself the watchful souls, if they go to meet him with lamps burning and a plentiful supply of oil? Moreover he reconciled most excellently and united the solitary and the community life. These had been in many respects at variance and dissension, while neither of them was in absolute and unalloyed possession of good or evil: the one being more calm and settled, tending to union with God, yet not free from pride, inasmuch as its virtue lies beyond the means of testing or comparison; the other, which is of more practical service, being not free from the tendency to turbulence. He founded cells for ascetics and hermits, but at no great distance from his cenobitic communities, and, instead of distinguishing and separating the one from the other, as if by some intervening wall, he brought them together and united them, in order that the contemplative spirit might not be cut off from society, nor the active life be uninfluenced by the contemplative, but that, like sea and land, by an interchange of their several gifts, they might unite in promoting the one object, the glory of God.

63. What more? A noble thing is philanthropy, and the support of the poor, and the assistance of human weakness. Go forth a little way from the city, and behold the new city, the storehouse of piety, the common treasury of the wealthy, in which the superfluities of their wealth, aye, and even their necessaries, are stored, in consequence of his exhortations, freed from the power of the moth, no longer gladdening the eyes of the thief, and escaping both the emulation of envy, and the corruption of time: where disease is regarded in a religious light, and disaster is thought a blessing, and sympathy is put to the test. Why should I compare with this work Thebes of the seen portals, and the Egyptian Thebes, and the walls of Babylon, and the Carian tomb of Mausolus, and the Pyramids, and the bronze without weight of the Colossus, or the size and beauty of shrines that are no more, and all the other objects of men's wonder, and historic record, from which their founders gained no advantage, except a slight need of fame. My subject is the most wonderful of all, the short road to salvation, the easiest ascent to heaven. There is no longer before our eyes that terrible and piteous spectacle of men who are living corpses, the greater part of whose limbs have mortified, driven away from their cities and homes and public places and fountains, aye, and from their own dearest ones, recognizable by their names rather than by their features: they are no longer brought before us at our gatherings and meetings, in our common intercourse and union, no longer the objects of hatred, instead of pity on account of their disease; composers of piteous songs, if any of them have their voice still left to them. Why should I try to express in tragic style all our experiences, when no language can be adequate to their hard lot? He however it was, who took the lead in pressing upon those who were men, that they ought not to despise their fellowmen, nor to dishonor Christ, the one Head of all, by their inhuman treatment of them; but to use the misfortunes of others as an opportunity of firmly establishing their own lot, and to lend to God that mercy of which they stand in need at His hands. He did not therefore disdain to honor with his lips this disease, noble and of noble ancestry and brilliant reputation though he was, but saluted them as brethren, not, as some might suppose, from vainglory, (for who was so far removed from this feeling?) but taking the lead in approaching to tend them, as a consequence of his philosophy, and so giving not only a speaking, but also a silent, instruction. The effect produced is to be seen not only in the city, but in the country and beyond, and even the leaders of society have vied with one another in their philanthropy and magnanimity towards them. Others have had their cooks, and splendid tables, and the devices and dainties of confectioners, and exquisite carriages, and soft, flowing robes; Basil's care was for the sick, and the relief of their wounds, and the imitation of Christ, by cleansing leprosy, not by a word, but in deed.

64. As to all this, what will be said by those who charge him with pride and haughtiness? Severe critics they are of such conduct, applying to him, whose life was a standard, those who were not standards at all. Is it possible that he who kissed the lepers, and humiliated himself to such a degree, could treat haughtily those who were in health: and, while wasting his flesh by abstinence, puff out his soul with

302

empty arrogance? Is it possible to condemn the Pharisee, and expound the debasing effect of haughtiness, to know Christ, Who condescended to the form of a slave, and ate with publicans, and washed the disciples' feet, and did not disdain the cross, in order to nail my sin to it: and, more incredible still, to see God crucified, aye, along with robbers also, and derided by the passers by, impassable, and beyond the reach of suffering as He is; and yet, as his slanderers imagine, soar himself above the clouds, and think that nothing can be on an equality with him. Nay, what they term pride is, I fancy, the firmness and steadfastness and stability of his character. Such persons would readily, it seems to me, call bravery rashness, and the circumspect a coward, and the temperate misanthropic, and the just illiberal. For indeed this philosophic axiom is excellent, which says that the vices are settled close to the virtues, and are, in some sense, their next-door neighbors: and it is most easy, for those whose training in such subjects has been defective, to mistake a man for what he is not. For who honored virtue and castigated vice more than he, or showed himself more kind to the upright, more severe to the wrong doers? His very smile often amounted to praise, his silence to rebuke, racking the evil in the secret conscience. And if a man have not been a chatterer, and jester, and gossip, nor a general favorite, because of having pleased others by becoming all things to all men, what of that? Is he not in the eyes of sensible men worthy of praise rather than of blame? Unless it is a fault in the lion that he is terrible and royal, and does not look like an ape, and that his spring is noble, and is valued for its wonderfulness: while stage-players ought to win our admiration for their pleasant and philanthropic characters, because they please the vulgar, and raise a laugh by their sounding slaps in the face. And if this indeed be our object, who was so pleasant when you met him, as I know, who have had the longest experience? Who was more kindly in his stories, more refined in his wit, more tender in his rebukes? His reproofs gave rise to no arrogance, his relaxation to no dissipation, but avoiding excess in either, he made use of both in reason and season, according to the rules of Solomon, who assigns to every business a season.

65. But what are these to his renown for eloquence, and his powers of instruction, which have won the favor of the ends of the world? As yet we have been compassing the foot of the mountain, to the neglect of its summit, as yet we have been crossing a strait, paying no heed to the mighty and deep ocean. For I think that if any one ever has become, or can become, a trumpet, in his far sounding resonance, or a voice of God, embracing the universe, or an earthquake of the world, by some unheard of miracle, it is his voice and intellect which deserve these titles, for surpassing and excelling all men as much as we surpass the irrational creatures. Who, more than he, cleansed himself by the Spirit, and made himself worthy to set forth divine things? Who was more enlightened by the light of knowledge, and had a closer insight into the depths of the Spirit, and by the aid of God beheld the things of God? Whose language could better express intellectual truth, without, as most men do, limping on one foot, by either failing to express his ideas, or allowing his eloquence to outstrip his reasoning powers? In both respects he won a like

distinction, and showed himself to be his own equal, and absolutely perfect. To search all things, yea, the deep things of God is, according to the testimony of S. Paul, the office of the Spirit, not because He is ignorant of them, but because He takes delight in their contemplation. Now all the things of the Spirit Basil had fully investigated, and hence he drew his instructions for every kind of character, his lessons in the sublime, and his exhortations to quit things present, and adapt ourselves to things to come.

66. The sun is extolled by David for its beauty, its greatness, its swift course, and its power, splendid as a bridegroom, majestic as a giant; while, from the extent of its circuit, it has such power that it equally sheds its light from one end of heaven to the other, and the heat thereof is in no wise lessened by distance. Basil's beauty was virtue, his greatness theology, his course the perpetual motion reaching even to God by its ascents, and his power the sowing and distribution of the Word. So that I will not hesitate to say even this, his utterance went out into all lands, and the power of his words to the ends of the world: as S. Paul says of the Apostles, borrowing the words from David. What other charm is there in any gathering today? What pleasure in banquets, in the courts, in the churches? What delight in those in authority, and those beneath them? What in the hermits, or the cenobites? What in the leisured classes, or those busied in affairs? What in profane schools of philosophy or in our own? There is one, which runs through all, and is the greatest — his writings and labors. Nor do writers require any supply of matter besides his teaching or writings. All the laborious studies of old days in the Divine oracles are silent, while the new ones are in everybody's mouth, and he is the best teacher among us who has the deepest acquaintance with his works, and speaks of them and explains them in our ears. For he alone more than supplies the place of all others to those who are specially eager for instruction.

67. I will only say this of him. Whenever I handle his Hexaemeron, and take its words on my lips, I am brought into the presence of the Creator, and understand the words of creation, and admire the Creator more than before, using my teacher as my only means of sight. Whenever I take up his polemical works, I see the fire of Sodom, by which the wicked and rebellious tongues are reduced to ashes, or the tower of Chalane, impiously built, and righteously destroyed. Whenever I read his writings on the Spirit, I find the God Whom I possess, and grow bold in my utterance of the truth, from the support of his theology and contemplation. His other treatises, in which he gives explanations for those who are shortsighted, by a threefold inscription on the solid tablets of his heart, lead me on from a mere literal or symbolical interpretation to a still wider view, as I proceed from one depth to another, calling upon deep after deep, and finding light after light, until I attain the highest pinnacle. When I study his panegyrics on our athletes, I despise the body, and enjoy the society of those whom he is praising, and rouse myself to the struggle. His moral and practical discourses purify soul and body, making me a temple fit for God, and an instrument struck by the Spirit, to celebrate by its strains the glory and

power of God. In fact, he reduces me to harmony and order, and changes me by a Divine transformation.

68. Since I have mentioned theology, and his most sublime treatises in this science, I will make this addition to what I have already said. For it is of great service to the community, to save them from being injured by an unjustifiably low opinion of him. My remarks are directed against those evil disposed persons who shelter their own vices under cover of their calumnies against others. In his defense of orthodox teaching, and of the union and coequal divinity of the Holy Trinity, to use terms which are, I think, as exact and clear as possible, he would have eagerly welcomed as a gain, and not a danger, not only expulsion from his see, in which he had originally no desire to be enthroned, but even exile, and death, and its preliminary tortures. This is manifest from his actual conduct and sufferings. For when he had been sentenced to banishment on behalf of the truth, the only notice which he took of it was, to bid one of his servants to take his writing tablet and follow him. He held it necessary, according to the divine David's advice, to guide his words with discretion, and to endure for a while the time of war, and the ascendancy of the heretics, until it should be succeeded by a time of freedom and calm, which would admit of freedom of speech. The enemy were on the watch for the unqualified statement "the Spirit is God;" which, although it is true, they and the wicked patron of their impiety imagined to be impious; so that they might banish him and his power of theological instruction from the city, and themselves be able to seize upon the church, and make it the starting point and citadel, from which they could overrun with their evil doctrine the rest of the world. Accordingly, by the use of other terms, and by statements which unmistakably had the same meaning, and by arguments necessarily leading to this conclusion, he so overpowered his antagonists, that they were left without reply, and involved in their own admissions, — the greatest proof possible of dialectical power and skill. His treatise on this subject makes it further manifest, being evidently written by a pen borrowed from the Spirit's store. He postponed for the time the use of the exact term, begging as a favor from the Spirit Himself and his earnest champions, that they would not be annoyed at his economy, nor, by clinging to a single expression, ruin the whole cause, from an uncompromising temper, at a crisis when religion was in peril. He assured them that they would stiff er no injury from a slight change in their expressions, and from teaching the same truth in other terms. For our salvation is not so much a matter of words as of actions; for we would not reject the Jews, if they desired to unite with us, and yet for a while sought to use the term "Anointed" instead of "Christ:" while the community would suffer a very serious injury, if the church were seized upon by the heretics.

69. That he, no less than any other, acknowledged that the Spirit is God, is plain from his often having publicly preached this truth, whenever opportunity offered, and eagerly confessed it when questioned in private. But he made it more clear in his conversations with me, from whom he concealed nothing during our

conferences upon this subject. Not content with simply asserting it, he proceeded, as he had but very seldom done before, to imprecate upon himself that most terrible fate of separation from the Spirit, if he did not adore the Spirit as consubstantial and coequal with the Father and the Son. And if any one would accept me as having been his fellow laborer in this cause, I will set forth one point hitherto unknown to most men. Under the pressure of the difficulties of the period, he himself undertook the economy, while allowing freedom of speech to me, whom no one was likely to drag from obscurity to trial or banishment, in order that by our united efforts our Gospel might be firmly established. I mention this, not to defend his reputation, for the man is stronger than his assailants, if there are any such; but to prevent men from thinking that the terms found in his writings are the utmost limit of the truth, and so have their faith weakened, and consider that their own error is supported by his theology, which was the joint result of the influences of the time and of the Spirit, instead of considering the sense of his writings, and the object with which they were written, so as to be brought closer to the truth, and enabled to silence the partisans of impiety. At any rate let his theology be mine, and that of all dear to me! And so confident am I of his spotlessness in this respect, that I take him for my partner in this, as in all else: and may what is mine be attributed to him, what is his to me, both at the hands of God, and of the wisest of men! For we would not say that the Evangelists are at variance with one another, because some are more occupied with the human side of the Christ, and others pay attention to His Divinity; some having commenced their history with what is within our own experience, others with what is above us; and by thus sharing the substance of their message, they have procured the advantage of those who receive it, and followed the impressions of the Spirit Who was within them.

70. Come then, there have been many men of old days illustrious for piety, as lawgivers, generals, prophets, teachers, and men brave to the shedding of blood, Let us compare our prelate with them, and thus recognize his merit. Adam was honored by the hand of God, and the delights of Paradise, and the first legislation: but, unless I slander the reputation of our first parent, he kept not the command, Now Basil both received and observed it, and received no injury from the tree of knowledge, and escaped the flaming sword, and, as I am well assured, has attained to Paradise. Enos first ventured to call upon the Lord. Basil both called upon Him himself, and, what is far more excellent, preached Him to others. Enoch was translated, attaining to his translation as the reward of a little piety (for the faith was still in shadow) and escaped the peril of the remainder of life, but Basil's whole life was a translation, and he was completely tested in a complete life. Noah was entrusted with the ark, and the seeds of a new world committed to a small house of wood, in their preservation from the waters. Basil escaped the deluge of impiety and made of his own city an ark of safety, which sailed lightly over the heretics, and afterwards recovered the whole world.

71. Abraham was a great man, a patriarch, the offerer of the new sacrifice, by presenting to Him who had given it the promised seed, as a ready offering, eager for slaughter. But Basil's offering was no slight one, when he offered himself to God, without any equivalent being given in his stead, (for how could that have been possible?) so that his sacrifice was consummated. Isaac was promised even before his birth, Basil promised himself, and took for his spouse Rebekah, I mean the Church, not fetched from a distance by the mission of a servant, but bestowed upon and entrusted to him by God close at home: nor was he outwitted in the preference of his children, but bestowed upon each what was due to him, without any deception, according to the judgment of the Spirit. I extol the ladder of Jacob, and the pillar which he anointed to God, and his wrestling with Him, whatever it was; and, in my opinion, it was the contrast and opposition of the human stature to the height of God, resulting in the tokens of the defeat of his race. I extol also his clever devices and success in cattle-breeding, and his children, the twelve Patriarchs, and the distribution of his blessings, with their glorious prophecy of the future. But I still more extol Basil for the ladder which he did not merely see, but which he ascended by successive steps towards excellence, and the pillar which he did not anoint, but which he erected to God, by pillorying the teaching of the ungodly; and the wrestling with which he wrestled, not with God, but, on behalf of God, to the overthrow of the heretics; and his pastoral care, whereby he grew rich, through gaining for himself a number of marked sheep greater than that of the unmarked, and his illustrious fruitfulness in spiritual children, and the blessing with which he established many.

72. Joseph was a provider of corn, but in Egypt only, and not frequently, and of bodily food. Basil did so for all men, and at all times, and in spiritual food, and therefore, in my opinion, his was the more honorable function. Like Job, the man of Uz, he was both tempted, and overcame, and at the close of his struggles gained splendid honor, having been shaken by none of his many assailants, and having gained a decisive victory over the efforts of the tempter, and put to silence the unreason of his friends, who knew not the mysterious character of his affliction. "Moses and Aaron among His priests." Truly was Moses great, who inflicted the plagues upon Egypt, and delivered the people among many signs and wonders, and entered within the cloud, and sanctioned the double law, outward in the letter, and inward in the Spirit. Aaron was Moses' brother, both naturally and spiritually, and offered sacrifices and prayers for the people, as the hierophant of the great and holy tabernacle, which the Lord pitched, and not man. Of both of them Basil was a rival, for he tortured, not with bodily but with spiritual and mental plagues, the Egyptian race of heretics, and led to the land of promise the people of possession, zealous of good works; he inscribed laws, which are no longer obscure, but entirely spiritual, on tables which are not broken but are preserved; he entered the Holy of holies, not once a year, but often, I may say every day, and thence he revealed to us the Holy Trinity; and cleansed the people, not with temporary sprinklings, but with eternal purifications: What is the special excellence of Joshua? His generalship,

and the distribution of the inheritance, and the taking possession of the Holy Land. And was not Basil an Exarch? Was he not a general of those who are saved by faith? Did he not assign the different inheritances and abodes, according to the will of God, among his followers? So that he too could use the words, "The lot is fallen unto me in pleasant places; and "my fortunes are in Thy hands," fortunes more precious than those which come to us on earth, and can be snatched away.

73. Further, to run over the Judges, or the most illustrious of the Judges, there is "Samuel among those that call upon His Name," who was given to God before his birth, and sanctified immediately after his birth, and the anointer with his horn of kings and priests. But was not Basil as an infant to God from the womb, and offered with a coat at the altar, and was he not a seer of heavenly things, and anointed of the Lord, and the anointer of those who are perfected by the Spirit? Among the kings, David is celebrated, whose victories and trophies gained from the enemy are on record, but his most characteristic trait was his gentleness, and, before his kingly office, his power with the harp, able to soothe even the evil spirit. Solomon asked of God and obtained breadth of heart, making the furthest possible progress in wisdom and contemplation, so that he became the most famous man of his time. Basil, in my opinion, was in no wise, or but little inferior, to the one in gentleness, to the other in wisdom, so that he soothed the arrogance of infuriated sovereigns; and did not merely bring the queen of the south from the ends of the earth, or any other individual, to visit him because of his renown for wisdom, but made his wisdom known in all the ends of the world. I pass over the rest of Solomon's life. Even if we spare it, it is evident to all.

74. Do you praise the courage of Elijah in the presence of tyrants, and his fiery translation? Or the fair inheritance of Elisha, the sheepskin mantle, accompanied by the spirit of Elijah? You must also praise the life of Basil, spent in the fire. I mean in the multitude of temptations, and his escape through fire, which burnt, but did not consume, the mystery of "the bush," and the fair cloak of skin from on high, his indifference to the flesh. I pass by the rest, the three young men bedewed in the fire, the fugitive prophet praying in the whale's belly, and coming forth from the creature, as from a chamber; the just man in the den, restraining the lions' rage, and the struggle of the seven Maccabees, who were perfected with their father and mother in blood, and in all kinds of tortures. Their endurance he rivaled, and won their glory.

75. I now turn to the New Testament, and comparing his life with those who are here illustrious, I shall find in the teachers a source of honor for their disciple. Who was the forerunner of Jesus? John, the voice of the Word, the lamp of the Light, before Whom he even leaped in the womb, and Whom he preceded to Hades, whither he was despatched by the rage of Herod, to herald even there Him who was coming. And, if my language seems audacious to anyone, let me assure him beforehand, that in making this comparison, I neither prefer Basil, nor imply that

he is equal to him who surpasses all who are born of women, but only show that he was stirred to emulation, and possessed to some extent his striking features. For it is no slight thing for the earnest to imitate the greatest of men, even in a slight degree. Is it not indeed manifest that Basil was a copy of John's asceticism? He also lived in the wilderness, and wore in nightly watchings a ragged garb, during his shrinking retirement; he also loved a similar food, purifying himself for God by abstinence; he also was thought worthy to be a herald, if not a forerunner, of Christ, and there went out to him not only all the region round about, but also that which was beyond its borders; he also stood between the two covenants, abolishing the letter of the one by administering the spirit of the other, and bringing about the fulfillment of the hidden law through the dissolution of that which was apparent.

76. He emulated the zeal of Peter, the intensity of Paul, the faith of both these then of name and of surname, the lofty utterance of the sons of Zebedee, the frugality and simplicity of all the disciples. Therefore he was also entrusted with the keys of the heavens, and not only from Jerusalem and round about unto Illyricum but he embraces a wider circle in the Gospel; he is not named, but becomes, a Son of thunder; and lying upon the breast of Jesus, he draws thence the power of his word, and the depth of his thoughts. He was prevented from becoming a Stephen, eager though he was, since reverence stayed the hands of those who would have stoned him. I am able to sum up still more concisely, to avoid treating in detail on these points of each individual. In some respects he discovered, in some he emulated, in others he surpassed the good. In his many-sided virtues he excelled all men of this day. I have but one thing left to say, and in few words.

77. So great was his virtue, and the eminence of his fame, that many of his minor characteristics, nay, even his physical defects, have been assumed by others with a view to notoriety. For instance his paleness, his beard, his gait, his thoughtful, and generally meditative, hesitation in speaking, which, in the ill-judged, inconsiderate imitation of many, took the form of melancholy. And besides, the style of his dress, the shape of his bed, and his manner of eating, none of which was to him a matter of consequence, but simply the result of accident and chance. So you might see many Basils in outward semblance, among these statues in outline, for it would be too much to call them his distant echo. For an echo, though it is the dying away of a sound, at any rate represents it with great clearness, while these men fall too far short of him to satisfy even their desire to approach him. Nor was it a slight thing, but a matter with good reason held in the highest estimation, to chance to have met him or done him some service, or to carry away the souvenir of something which he had said or done in jest or in earnest: as I know that I have myself often taken pride in doing; for his improvisations were much more precious and brilliant than the labored efforts of other men.

78. But when, after he had finished his course, and kept the faith, he longed to depart, and the time for his crown was approaching, he did not hear the summons:

"Get thee up into the mountain and die," hut "Die and come up to us." And here again he wrought a wonder in no wise inferior to those mentioned before. For when he was almost dead, and breathless, and had lost the greater part of his powers; he grew stronger in his last words, so as to depart with the utterances of religion, and, by ordaining the most excellent of his attendants, bestowed upon them both his hand and the Spirit: so that his disciples, who had aided him in his priestly office, might not be defrauded of the priesthood. The remainder of my task I approach, but with reluctance, as it would fall more filly from the mouths of others than from my own. For cannot philosophize over my misfortune, even if greatly longed to do so, when I recollect that the loss is common to us all, and that the misfortune has befallen the whole world.

79. He lay, drawing his last breath, and awaited by the choir on high, towards which he had long directed his gaze. Around him poured the whole city, unable to bear his loss, inveighing against his departure, as if it had been an oppression, and clinging to his soul, as though it had been capable of restraint or compulsion at their bands or their prayers. Their suffering had driven them distracted, all were eager, were it possible, to add to his life a portion of their own. And when they failed, for it must needs be proved that he was a man, and, with his last words "Into thy Hands I commend my spirit," he had joyfully resigned his soul to the care of the angels who carried him away; not without having some religious instructions and injunctions for the benefit of those who were present — then occurred a wonder more remarkable than any which had happened before.

80. The saint was being carried out, lifted high by the hands of holy men, and everyone was eager, some to seize the hem of his garment, others only just to touch the shadow, or the bier which bore his holy remains (for what could be more holy or pure than that body), others to draw near to those who were carrying it, others only to enjoy the sight, as if even this were beneficial. Market places, porticos, houses of two or three stories were filled with people escorting, preceding, following, accompanying him, and trampling upon each other; tens of thousands of every race and age, beyond all previous experience. The psalmody was overborne by the lamentations, philosophic resignation sank beneath the misfortune. Our own people vied with strangers, Jews, Greeks, and foreigners, and they with us, for a greater share in the benefit, by means of a more abundant lamentation. To close my story, the calamity ended in danger; many souls departed along with him, from the violence of the pushing and confusion, who have been thought happy in their end, departing together with him, "funeral victims," perhaps some fervid orator might call them. The body having at last escaped froth those who would seize it, and made its way through those who went before it, was consigned to the tomb of his fathers, the high priest being added to the priests, the mighty voice which rings in my ears to the heralds, the martyr to the martyrs. And now he is in heaven, where, if I mistake not, he is offering sacrifices for us, and praying for the people, for though, he has left us, he bus not entirely left us. While I, Gregory, who am half

dead, and, cleft in twain, torn away from our great union, and dragging along a life of pain which runs not easily, as may be supposed, after separation from him, know not what is to be my end now that I have lost my guidance. And even now I am admonished and instructed in nightly visions, if ever I fall short of my duty. And my present object is not so much to mingle lamentations with my praises, or to portray the public life of the man, or publish a picture of virtue common to all time, and an example salutary to all churches, and to all souls, which we may keep in view, as a living law, and so rightly direct our lives as to counsel you, who have been completely initiated into his doctrine, to fix your eyes upon him, as one who sees you and is seen by you, and thus to be perfected by the Spirit.

81. Come hither then, and surround me, all ye members of his choir, both of the clergy and the laity, both of our own country and from abroad; aid me in my eulogy, by each supplying or demanding the account of some of his excellencies. Regard, ye occupants of the bench, the lawgiver; ye politicians, the statesman; ye men of the people, his orderliness; ye men of letters, the instructor; ye virgins, the leader of the bride; ye who are yoked in marriage, the restrainer; ye hermits, him who gave you wings; ye cenobites, the judge; ye simple men, the guide; ye contemplatives, the divine; ye cheerful ones, the bridle; ye unfortunate men, the consoler, the staff of boar hairs, the guide of youth, the relief of poverty, the steward of abundance. Widows also will, I imagine, praise their protector, orphans their father poor men their friend, strangers their entertainer, brothers the man of brotherly love, the sick their physician, whatever be their sickness and the healing they need, the healthy the preserver of health, and all men him who made himself all things to all that he might gain the majority, if not all.

82. This is my offering to thee, Basil, uttered by the tongue which once was the sweetest of all to thee, of him who was thy fellow in age and rank. If it have approached thy deserts, thanks are due to thee, for it was from confidence in thee that I undertook to speak of thee. But if it fall far short of thy expectations, what must be our feelings, who are worn out with age and disease and regret for thee? Yet God is pleased, when we do what we can. Yet mayest thou gaze upon us from above, thou divine and sacred person; either stay by thy entreaties our thorn in the flesh, given to us by God for oar discipline, or prevail upon us to bear it boldly, and guide all our life towards that which is most for our profit. And if we be translated, do thou receive us there also in thine own tabernacle, that, as we dwell together, and gaze together more clearly and more perfectly upon the holy and blessed Trinity, of Which we have now in some degree received the image, our longing may at last be satisfied, by gaining this recompense for all the battles we have fought and the assaults we have endured. Such are our words on thy behalf: who will there be to praise us, since we leave this life after thee, even if we offer any topic worthy of words or praise in Christ Jesus our Lord, to Whom be glory forever? Amen.

Introduction to the Second Oration on Easter

This Oration was not, as its title would perhaps lead us to suppose, delivered immediately after the first; but an interval of many years elapsed between them, and the two have no connection with each other. Chronologically they are the first and last of S. Gregory's Sermons. The Second was delivered in the Church of Arianzus, a village near Nazianzus, where he had inherited some property, to which he withdrew after resigning the Archbishopric of Constantinople, and then, finding the administration even of the little Bishopric of Nazianzus too much for his advancing years and declining strength, he retired to Arianzus about the end of A.D. 383, dying there in 389 or 390. "The exordium of this discourse is quite in the style of the Bible; the Orator here describes and puts words into the mouth of the Angel of the Resurrection. His object is to show the importance of the day's solemnities, and to explain allegorically all the circumstances of the ancient Passover, applying them to Christ and the Christian life. Two passages are borrowed verbatim from the discourse on the Nativity, preached at Constantinople" (Benoit). The Benedictine Editors profess themselves unable to determine whether this repetition is due to S. Gregory himself — or to the carelessness of some amanuensis.

The Second Oration of Easter

1. I will stand upon my watch, saith the venerable Habakkuk; and I will take my post beside him today on the authority and observation which was given me of the Spirit; and I will look forth, and will observe what shall be said to me. Well, I have taken my stand, and looked forth; and behold a man riding on the clouds and he is very high, and his countenance is as the countenance of Angel, and his vesture as the brightness of piercing lightning; and he lifts his hand toward the East, and cries with a loud voice. His voice is like the voice of a trumpet; and round about Him is as it were a multitude of the Heavenly Host; and he saith, Today is salvation come unto the world, to that which is visible, and to that which is invisible. Christ is risen from the dead, rise ye with Him. Christ is returned again to Himself, return ye. Christ is freed from the tomb, be ye freed from the bond of sin. The gates of hell are opened, and death is destroyed, and the old Adam is put aside, and the New is fulfilled; if any man be in Christ he is a new creature; be ye renewed. Thus he speaks; and the rest sing out, as they did before when Christ was manifested to us by His birth on earth, their glory to God in the highest, on earth, peace, goodwill among men. And with them I also utter the same words among you. And would that I might receive a voice that should rank with the Angel's, and should sound through all the ends of the earth.

II. The Lord's Passover, the Passover, and again I say the Passover to the honor of the Trinity. This is to us a Feast of feasts and a Solemnity of solemnities as far exalted above all others (not only those which are merely human and creep on the ground, but even those which are of Christ Himself, and are celebrated in His honor) as the Sun is above the stars. Beautiful indeed yesterday was our splendid array, and our illumination, in which both in public and private we associated ourselves, every kind of men, and almost every rank, illuminating the night with our crowded fires, formed after the fashion of that great light, both that with which the heaven above us lights its beacon fires, and that which is above the heavens, amid the angels (the first luminous nature, next to the first nature of all, because springing directly from it), and that which is in the Trinity, from which all light derives its being, parted from the undivided light and honored. But today's is more beautiful and more illustrious; inasmuch as yesterday's light was a forerunner of the rising of the Great Light, and as it were a kind of rejoicing in preparation for the Festival; but today we are celebrating the Resurrection itself, no longer as an object of expectation, but as having already come to pass, and gathering the whole world unto itself. Let then different persons bring forth different fruits and offer different offerings at this season, smaller or greater., such spiritual offerings as are dear to God., as each may have power. For scarcely Angels themselves could offer gifts worthy of its rank, those first and intellectual and pure beings, who are also eye-witnesses of the Glory That is on high; if even these can attain the full strain of praise. We will for our part offer a discourse, the best and most precious thing we have — especially as we are praising the Word for the blessing which He hath bestowed on the reasoning creation. I will begin from this point. For I cannot endure, when I am engaged in offering the sacrifice of the lips concerning the Great Sacrifice and the greatest of days, to fail to recur to God, and to take my beginning from Him. Therefore I pray you, cleanse your mind and ears and thoughts, all you who delight in such subjects, since the discourse will be concerning God, and will be divine; that you may depart filled with delights of a sort that do not pass away into nothingness. And it shall be at once very full and very concise, so as neither to distress you by its deficiencies, nor to displease you by satiety.

III. God always was and always is, and always will be; or rather, God always Is For Was and Will Be are fragments of our time, and of changeable nature. But He is Eternal Being; and this is the Name He gives Himself when giving the Oracles to Moses in the Mount. For in Himself He sums up and contains all Being, having neither beginning in the past nor end in the future... like some great Sea of Being, limitless and unbounded, transcending all conception of time and nature, only adumbrated by the mind, and that very dimly and scantily... not by His Essentials but by His Environment, one image being got from one source and another from another, and combined into some sort of presentation of the truth, which escapes us before we have caught it, and which takes to flight before we have conceived it, blazing forth upon our master-part, even when that is cleansed, as the lightning flash which will not stay its course does upon our sight... in order, as I conceive, by that part of it which we can comprehend to draw us to itself (for that which is altogether incomprehensible is outside the bounds of hope, and not within the compass of endeavor); and by that part of It which we cannot comprehend to move our wonder; and as an object of wonder to become more an object of desire; and being desired, to purify; and purifying to make us like God; so that, when we have become like Himself, God may, to use a bold expression, hold converse with us as God; being trailed to us, and known by us; and that perhaps to the same extent as He already knows those who are known to Him. The Divine Nature, then, is boundless and hard to understand, and all that we can comprehend of Him is His boundlessness; even though one may conceive that because He is of a simple Nature He is therefore either wholly incomprehensible or perfectly comprehensible. For let us farther enquire what is implied by "is of a simple Nature?" For it is quite certain that this simplicity is not itself its nature, just as composition is not by itself the essence of compound beings.

IV. And when Infinity is considered from two points of view, beginning and end (for that which is beyond these and not limited by them is Infinity), when the mind looks into the depths above, not having where to stand, and leans upon phenomena to form an idea of God it calls the Infinite and Unapproachable which it finds there by the name of Unoriginate. And when it looks into the depth below and at the future, it calls Him Undying and Imperishable. And when it draws a conclusion from the whole, it calls Him Eternal. For Eternity is neither time nor part of time; for it cannot be measured. But what time measured by the course of the sun is to as, that Eternity is to the Everlasting; namely a sort of timeline movement and interval, coextensive with Their Existence. This however is all that I must now say of God; for the present is not a suitable time, as my present subject is not the doctrine of God, but that of the Incarnation. And when I say God, I mean Father, Son, and Holy Ghost; for Godhead is neither diffused beyond These, so as to introduce a mob of gods, nor yet bounded by a smaller compass than These, so as to condemn us for a poverty stricken conception of Deity, either Judaizing to save the Monarchia, or falling into heathenism by the multitude of our gods. For the evil on either side is the same, though found in contrary directions. Thus then is the Holy of Holies, Which is hidden even from the Seraphim, and is glorified with a thrice-repeated Holy meeting in one ascription of the title Lord and God, as one of our predecessors has most beautifully and loftily reasoned out.

V. But since this movement of Self-contemplation alone could not satisfy Goodness, but Good must be poured out and go forth beyond Itself, to multiply the objects of Its beneficence (for this was essential to the highest Goodness), He first conceived the Angelic and Heavenly Powers. And this conception was a work fulfilled by His Word and perfected by His Spirit. And so the Secondary Splendors came into being, as the ministers of the Primary Splendor (whether we are to conceive of them as intelligent Spirits, or as Fire of an immaterial and incorporeal kind, or as some other nature approaching this as near as may be). I should like to say that they are incapable of movement in the direction of evil, and susceptible only of the movement of good, as being about God and illuminated with the first Rays from God (for earthly beings have but the second illumination), but I am obliged to stop short of saying that they are immovable, and to conceive and speak of them as only difficult to move, because of him who for His Splendor was called Lucifer, but became and is called Darkness through his pride; and the Apostate Hosts who are subject to him, creators of evil by their revolt against good, and our inciters.

VI. Thus then and for these reasons, He gave being to the world of thought, as far as I can reason on these matters, and estimate great things in my own poor language. Then, when His first Creation was in good order, He conceives a second world, material and visible; and this a system of earth and sky and all that is in the midst of them; an admirable creation indeed when we look at the fair form of every part, but yet more worthy of admiration when we consider the harmony and unison of the whole, and how each part fits in with every other in fair order, and all with the whole, tending to the perfect completion of the world as a Unit. This was to shew that He could call into being not only a nature akin to Himself, but also one altogether alien to Him. For akin to Deity are those natures which are intellectual, and only to be comprehended by mind; but all of which sense can take cognizance are utterly alien to It; and of these the furthest removed from it are all those which are entirely destitute of soul and power of motion.

VII. Mind then and sense, thus distinguished from each other, had remained within their own boundaries, and bore in themselves the magnificence of the Creator- Word, silent praisers and thrilling heralds of His mighty work. Not yet was there any mingling of both, nor any mixture of these opposites, tokens of a greater wisdom and generosity in the creation of natures; nor as yet were the whole riches of goodness made known. Now the Creator- Word, determining to exhibit this, and to produce a single living being out of both (the invisible and the visible creation, I mean) fashions Man; and taking a body from already existing matter, and placing in it a Breath taken from Himself (which the Word knew to be an intelligent soul, and the image of God), as a sort of second world, great in littleness, He placed him on the earth, a new Angel, a mingled worshipper, fully initiated into the visible creation, but only partially into the intellectual; king of all upon earth, but subject to the King above; earthly and heavenly; temporal and yet immortal; visible and yet intellectual; halfway between greatness and lowliness; in one person combining spirit and flesh; spirit because of the favor bestowed on him, flesh on account of the height to which he bad been raised; the one that he might continue to live and glorify his benefactor, the other that he might suffer, and by suffering be put in remembrance, and be corrected if he became proud in his greatness; a living creature, trained here and then moved elsewhere; and to complete the mystery, deified by its inclination to God for to this, I think, tends that light of Truth which here we possess but in measure; that we should both see and experience the Splendor of God, which is worthy of Him Who made us, and will dissolve us, and remake us after a loftier fashion.

315

VIII. This being He placed in paradise — whatever that paradise may have been (having honored him with the gift of free will, in order that good might belong to him as the result of his choice, no less than to Him Who had implanted the seeds of it) — to till the immortal plants, by which is perhaps meant the Divine conceptions, both the simpler and the more perfect; naked in his simplicity and inartificial life; and without any covering or screen; for it was fitting that he who was from the beginning should be such. And He gave Him a Law, as material for his free will to act upon. This Law was a commandment as to what plants he might partake of, and which one he might not touch. This latter was the Tree of Knowledge; not, however, because it was evil from the beginning when planted; nor was it forbidden because God grudged it to men — let not the enemies of God wag their tongues in that direction, or imitate the serpent. But it would have been good if partaken of at the proper time; for the Tree was, according to my theory, Contemplation, which it is only safe for those who have reached maturity of habit to enter upon; but which is not good for those who are still somewhat simple and greedy; just as neither is solid food good for those who are yet tender and have need of milk. But when through the devil's malice and the woman's caprice, to which she succumbed as the more tender, and which she brought to bear upon the man, as she was the more apt to persuade — alas for my weakness, for that of my first father was mine; he forgot the commandment which had been given him, and yielded to the baleful fruit; and for his sin was banished at once from the tree of life, and from paradise, and from God; and put on the coats of skins, that is, perhaps, the coarser flesh, both mortal and contradictory. And this was the first thing which he learnt — his own shame — and he hid himself from God. Yet here too he makes a gain, namely death and the cutting off of sin, in order that evil may not be immortal. Thus, his punishment is changed into a mercy, for it is in mercy, I am persuaded, that God inflicts punishment.

IX. And having first been chastened by many means because his sins were many, whose root of evil sprang up through divers causes and sundry times, by word, by law, by prophets, by benefits, by threats, by plagues, by waters, by fires, by wars, by victories, by defeats, by signs in heaven, and signs in the air, and in the earth, and in the sea; by unexpected changes of men, of cities, of nations (the object of which was the destruction of wickedness) at last he needed a stronger remedy, for his diseases were growing worse; mutual slaughters, adulteries, perjuries, unnatural crimes, and that first and last of all evils, idolatry, and the transfer of worship from the Creator to the creatures. As these required a greater aid, so they also obtained a greater. And that was that the Word of God Himself, Who is before all worlds, the Invisible, the Incomprehensible, the Bodiless, the Beginning of beginning, the Light of Light, the Source of Life and Immortality, the Image of the Archetype, the Immovable Seal, the Unchangeable Image, the Father's Definition and Word, came to His own Image, and took on Him Flesh for the sake of our flesh, and mingled Himself with an intelligent soul for my soul's sake, purifying like by like; and in all points except sin was made Man; conceived by the Virgin, who first in

316

body and soul was purified by the Holy Ghost, for it was needful both That Child-bearing should be honored and that Virginity should receive a higher honor. He came forth then, as God, with That which He had assumed; one Person in two natures, flesh and Spirit, of which the latter deified the former. O new commingling; O strange conjunction! the Self-existent comes into Being, the Uncreated is created, That which cannot be contained is contained by the intervention of an intellectual soul mediating between the Deity and the corporeity of the flesh. And He who gives riches becomes poor; for He assumes the poverty of my flesh, that I may assume the riches of His Godhead. He that is full empties Himself; for He empties Himself of His Glory for a short while, that I may have a share in His Fullness. What is the riches of His Goodness? What is this mystery that is around me? I had a share in the Image and I did not keep it; He partakes of my flesh that He may both save the Image and make the flesh immortal. He communicates a Second Communion, far more marvelous than the first, inasmuch as then He imparted the better nature, but now He Himself assumes the worse. This is more godlike than the former action; this is loftier in the eyes of all men of understanding.

X. But perhaps some one of those who are too impetuous and festive may say, "What has all this to do with us? Spur on your horse to the goal; talk to us about the Festival and the reasons for our being here today." Yes, this is what I am about to do, although I have begun at a somewhat previous point, being compelled to do so by the needs of my argument. There will be no harm in the eyes of scholars and lovers of the beautiful if we say a few words about the word Pascha itself, for such an addition will not be useless in their ears. This great and venerable Pascha is called Phaska by the Hebrews in their own language; and the word means Passing Over. Historically, from their flight and migration from Egypt into the Land of Canaan; spiritually, from the progress and ascent from things below to things above and to the Land of Promise. And we observe that a thing which we often find to have happened in Scripture, the change of certain nouns from an uncertain to a clearer sense, or from a coarser to a more refined, has taken place in this instance. For some people, supposing this to be a name of the Sacred Passion, and in consequence Grecizing the word by changing Phi and Kappa into Pi and Chi, called the Day Pascha. And custom took it up and confirmed the word, with the help of the ears of most people, to whom it had a more pious sound.

XI. But before our time the Holy Apostle declared that the Law was but a shadow of things to come, which are conceived by thought. And God too, who in still older times gave oracles to Moses, said when giving laws concerning these things, See thou make all things according to the pattern shewed thee in the Mount, when He shewed him the visible things as an adumbration of and design for the things that are invisible. And I am persuaded that none of these things has been ordered in vain, none without a reason, none in a groveling manner or unworthy of the legislation of God and the ministry of Moses, even though it be difficult in each type to find a theory descending to the most delicate details, to every point about the Tabernacle itself, and its measures and materials, and the Levites and Priests who carried them, and all the particulars which were enacted about the Sacrifices and the purifications and the Offerings; and though these are only to be understood by those who rank with Moses in virtue, or have made the nearest approach to his learning. For in that Mount itself God is seen by men; on the one hand through His own descent from His lofty abode, on the other through His drawing us up from our abasement on earth, that the Incomprehensible may be in some degree, and as far as is safe, comprehended by a mortal nature. For in no other way is it possible for the denseness of a material body and an imprisoned mind to come into consciousness of God, except by His assistance. Then therefore all men do not seem to have been deemed worthy of the same rank and position; but one of one place and one of another, each, I think, according to the measure of his own purification. Some have even been altogether driven away, and only permitted to hear the Voice from on high, namely those whose dispositions are altogether like wild beasts, and who are unworthy of divine mysteries.

XII. But we, standing midway between those whose minds are utterly dense on the one side, and on the other those who are very contemplative and exalted, that we may neither remain quite idle and immovable, nor yet be more busy than we ought, and fall short of and be estranged from our purpose — for the former course is Jewish and very low, and the latter is only fit for the dream- sooth- say er, and both alike are to be condemned — let us say our say upon these matters, so far as is within our reach, and not very absurd, or exposed to the ridicule of the multitude. Our belief is that since it was needful that we, who had fallen in consequence of the original sin, and had been led away by pleasure, even as far as idolatry and unlawful bloodshed, should be recalled and raised up again to our original position through the tender mercy of God our Father, Who could not endure that such a noble work of His own hands as Man should be lost to Him; the method of our new creation, and of what should be done, was this: — that all violent remedies were disapproved, as not likely to persuade us, and as quite possibly tending to add to the plague, through our chronic pride; but that God disposed things to our restoration by a gentle and kindly method of cure. For a crooked sapling will not bear a sudden bending the other way, or violence from the hand that would straighten it, but will be more quickly broken than straightened; and a horse of a hot temper and above a certain age will not endure the tyranny of the bit without some coaxing and encouragement. Therefore the Law is given to us as an assistance, like a boundary wall between God and idols, drawing us away from one and to the Other. And it concedes a little at first, that it may receive that which is greater. It concedes the Sacrifices for a time, that it may establish God in us, and then when the fitting time shall come may abolish the Sacrifices also; thus wisely changing our minds by gradual removals, and bringing us over to the Gospel when we have already been trained to a prompt obedience.

XIII. Thus then and for this cause the written Law came in, gathering us into Christ; and this is the account of the Sacrifices as I account for them. And that you may not be ignorant of the depth of His Wisdom and the riches of His unsearchable judgments, He did not leave even these unhallowed altogether, or useless, or with nothing in them but mere blood. But that great, and if I may say so, in Its first nature unsacrificeable Victim, was intermingled with the Sacrifices of the Law, and was a purification, not for a part of the world, nor for a short time, but for the whole world and for all time. For this reason a Lamb was chosen for its innocence, and its clothing of the original nakedness. For such is the Victim, That was offered for us, Who is both in Name and fact the Garment of incorruption. And He was a perfect Victim not only on account of His Godhead, than which nothing is more perfect; but also on account of that which He assumed having been anointed with Deity, and having become one with That which anointed It, and I am bold to say, made equal with God. A Male, because offered for Adam; or rather the Stronger for the strong, when the first Man had fallen under sin; and chiefly because there is in Him nothing feminine, nothing unmanly; but He burst from the bonds of thee Virgin-Mother' s womb with much power, and a Male was brought forth by the Prophetess, as Isaiah declares the good tidings. And of a year old, because He is the Sun of Righteousness setting out from heaven, and circumscribed by His visible Nature, and returning unto Himself. And "The blessed crown of Goodness," — being on every side equal to Himself and alike; and not only this, but also as giving life to all the circle of the virtues, gently commingled and intermixed with each other, according to the Law of Love and Order. And Immaculate and guileless, as being the Healer of faults, and of the defects and taints that come from sin. For though He both took on Him our sins and bare our diseases, yet He did not Himself suffer aught that needed healing. For He was tempted in all points like as we are yet without sin For he that persecuted the Light that shineth in darkness could not overtake Him.

XIV. What more? The First Month is introduced, or rather the beginning of months, whether it was so among the Hebrews from the beginning, or was made so later on this account, and became the first in consequence of the Mystery; and the tenth of the Month, for this is the most complete number, of units the first perfect unit, and the parent of perfection. And it is kept until the fifth day, perhaps because the Victim, of Whom I am speaking, purifies the five senses, from which comes falling into sin, and around which the war rages, inasmuch as they are open to the incitements to sin. And it was chosen, not only out of the lambs, but also out of the inferior species, which are placed on the left hand — the kids; because He is sacrificed not only for the righteous, but also for sinners; and perhaps even more for these, inasmuch as we have greater need of His mercy. And we need not be surprised that a lamb for a house should be required as the best course, but if that could not be, then one might be obtained by contributions (owing to poverty) for the houses of a family; because it is clearly best that each individual should suffice for his own perfecting, and should offer his own living sacrifice holy unto God

Who called him, being consecrated at all times and in every respect. But if that cannot be, then that those who are akin in virtue and of like disposition should be made use of as helpers. For I think this provision means that we should communicate of the Sacrifice to those who are nearest, if there be need.

XV. Then comes the Sacred Night, the Anniversary of the confused darkness of the present life, into which the primeval darkness is dissolved, and all things come into life and rank and form, and that which was chaos is reduced to order. Then we flee from Egypt, that is from sullen persecuting sin; and from Pharaoh the unseen tyrant, and the bitter taskmasters, changing our quarters to the world above; and are delivered from the clay and the brickmaking, and from the husks and dangers of this fleshly condition, which for most men is only not overpowered by mere husklike calculations. Then the Lamb is slain, and act and word are sealed with the Precious Blood; that is, habit and action, the sideposts of our doors; I mean, of course, of the movements of mind and opinion, which are rightly opened and closed by contemplation, since there is a limit even to thoughts. Then the last and gravest plague upon the persecutors, truly worthy of the night; and Egypt mourns the first-born of her own reasonings and actions which are also called in the Scripture the Seed of the Chaldeans removed, and the children of Babylon dashed against the rocks and destroyed; and the whole air is full of the cry and clamor of the Egyptians; and then the Destroyer of them shall withdraw from us in reverence of the Unction. Then the removal of leaven; that is, of the old and sour wickedness, not of that which is quickening and makes bread; for seven days, a number which is of all the most mystical, and is co-ordinate with this present world, that we may not lay in provision of any Egyptian dough, or relic of Pharisaic or ungodly teaching.

XVI. Well, let them lament; we will feed on the Lamb toward evening — for Christ's Passion was in the completion of the ages; because too He communicated His Disciples in the evening with His Sacrament, destroying the darkness of sin; and not sodden, but roast — that our word may have in it nothing that is unconsidered or watery, or easily made away with.; but may be entirely consistent and solid, and free from all that is impure and from all vanity. And let us be aided by the good coals, kindling and purifying our minds from Him That cometh to send fire on the earth, that shall destroy all evil habits, and to hasten its kindling. Whatsoever then there be, of solid and nourishing in the Word, shall be eaten with the inward parts and hidden things of the mind, and shall be consumed and given up to spiritual digestion; aye, from head to foot, that is, from the first contemplations of Godhead to the very last thoughts about the Incarnation. Neither let us carry aught of it abroad, nor leave it till the morning; because most of our Mysteries may not be carried out to them that are outside, nor is there beyond this night any further purification; and procrastination is not creditable to those who have a share in the Word. For just as it is good and well-pleasing to God not to let anger last through the day, but to get rid of it before sunset, whether you take this of time or in a mystical sense, for it is not safe for us that the Sun of

Righteousness should go down upon our wrath; so too we ought not to let such Food remain all night, nor to put it off till tomorrow. But whatever is of bony nature and not fit for food and hard for us even to understand, this must not be broken; that is, badly divined and misconceived (I need not say that in the history not a bone of Jesus was broken, even though His death was hastened by His crucifiers on account of the Sabbath); nor must it be stripped off and thrown away, lest that which is holy should be given to the dogs, that is, to the evil hearers of the Word; just as the glorious pearl of the Word is not to be cast before swine; but it shall be consumed with the fire with which the burnt offerings also are consumed, being refined and preserved by the Spirit That searcheth and knoweth all things, not destroyed in the waters, nor scattered abroad as the calf's head which was hastily made by Israel was by Moses, for a reproach for their hardness of heart.

XVII. Nor would it be right for us to pass over the manner of this eating either, for the Law does not do so, but carries its mystical labor even to this point in the literal enactment. Let us consume the Victim in haste, eating It with unleavened bread, with bitter herbs, and with our loins girded, and our shoes on our feet, and leaning on staves like old men; with haste, that we fall not into that fault which was forbidden to Lot by the commandment, that we look not around, nor stay in all that neighborhood, but that we escape to the mountain, that we be not overtaken by the strange fire of Sodom, nor be congealed into a pillar of salt in consequence of our turning back to wickedness; for this is the result of delay. With bitter herbs, for a life according to the Will of God is bitter and arduous, especially to beginners, and higher than pleasures. For although the new yoke is easy and the burden light, as you are told, yet this is on account of the hope and the reward, which is far more abundant than the hardships of this life. If it were not so, who would not say that the Gospel is more full of toil and trouble than the enactments of the Law? For, while the Law prohibits only the completed acts of sin, we are condemned for the causes also, almost as if they were acts. The Law says, Thou shalt not commit adultery, but you may not even desire, kindling passion by curious and earnest looks. Thou shalt not kill, says the Law; but you are not even to return a blow, but on the contrary are to offer yourself to the smiter. How much more ascetic is the Gospel than the Law! Thou shall not forswear thyself is the Law; but you are not to swear at all, either a greater or a lesser oath, for an oath is the parent of perjury. Thou shalt not join house to house, nor field to field, oppressing the poor, but you are to set aside willingly even your just possessions, and to be stripped for the poor, that without encumbrance you may take up the Cross and be enriched with the unseen riches.

XVIII. And let the loins of the unreasoning animals be unbound and loose, for they have not the gift of reason which can overcome pleasure (it is not needful to say that even they know the limit of natural movement). But let that part of your being which is the seat of passion, and which neighs, as Holy Scripture calls it, when sweeping away this shameful passion, be restrained by a girdle of continence, so that you may eat the Passover purely, having mortified your members which are upon the earth, and copying the girdle of John, the Hermit and Forerunner and great Herald of the Truth. Another girdle I know, the soldierly and manly one, I mean, from which the Euzoni of Syria and certain Monozoni take their name. And it is in respect of this too that God saith in an oracle to Job, "Nay, but gird up thy loins like a man, and give a manly answer." With this also holy David boasts that he is girded with strength from God, and speaks of God Himself as clothed with strength and girded about with power — against the ungodly of course — though perhaps some may prefer to see in this a declaration of the abundance of His power, and, as it were, its restraint, just as also He clothes Himself with Light as with a garment. For who shall endure His unrestrained power and light? Do I enquire what there is common to the loins and to truth? What then is the meaning to S. Paul of the expression, "Stand, therefore, having your loins girt about with truth?" Is it perhaps that contemplation is to restrain concupiscence, and not to allow it to be carried in another direction? For that which is disposed to love in a particular direction will not have the same power towards other pleasures.

XIX. And as to shoes, let him who is about to touch the Holy Land which the feet of God have trodden, put them off, as Moses did upon the Mount, that he may bring there nothing dead; nothing to come between Man and God. So too if any disciple is sent to preach the Gospel, let him go in a spirit of philosophy and without excess, inasmuch as he must, besides being without money and without staff and with but one coat, also be barefooted, that the feet of those who preach the Gospel of Peace and every other good may appear beautiful. But he who would flee from Egypt and the things of Egypt must put on shoes for safety's sake, especially in regard to the scorpions and snakes in which Egypt so abounds, so as not to be injured by those which watch the heel which also we are bidden to tread under foot. And concerning tire staff and the signification of it, my belief is as follows. There is one I know to lean upon, and another which belongs to Pastors and Teachers, and which corrects human sheep. Now the Law prescribes to you the staff to lean upon, that you may not break down in your mind when you hear of God's Blood, and His Passion, and His death; and that you may not be carried away to heresy in your defense of God; but without shame and without doubt may eat the Flesh and drink the Blood, if you are desirous of true life, neither disbelieving His words about His Flesh, nor offended at those about His Passion. Lean upon this, and stand firm and strong, in nothing shaken by the adversaries nor carried away by the plausibility of their arguments. Stand upon thy High Place; in the Courts of Jerusalem place thy feet; lean upon the Rock, that thy steps in God be not shaken.

XX. What sayest thou? Thus it hath pleased Him that thou shouldest come forth out of Egypt, the iron furnace; that thou shouldest leave behind the idolatry of that country, and be led by Moses and his lawgiving and martial rule. I give thee a piece of advice which is not my own, or rather which is very much my own, if thou consider the matter spiritually. Borrow from the Egyptians vessels of gold and silver; with these take thy journey; supply thyself for the road with the goods of strangers, or rather with thine own. There is money owing to thee, the wages of thy bondage and of thy brickmaking; be clever on thy side too in asking retribution; be an honest robber. Thou didst suffer wrong there whilst thou wast fighting with the clay (that is, this troublesome and filthy body) and wast building cities foreign and unsafe, whose memorial perishes with a cry. What then? Dost thou come out for nothing and without wages? But why wilt thou leave to the Egyptians and to the powers of thine adversaries that which they have gained by wickedness, and will spend with yet greater wickedness? It does not belong to them: they have ravished it, and have sacrilegiously taken it as plunder from Him who saith, The silver is Mine and the gold is Mine, and I give it to whom I will. Yesterday it was theirs, for it was permitted to be so; today the Master takes it and gives it to thee, that thou mayest make a good and saving use of it. Let us make to ourselves friends of the Mammon of unrighteousness, that when we fail, they may receive us in the time of judgment.

XXI. If you are a Rachel or a Leah, a patriarchal and great soul, steal whatever idols of your father you can find; not, however, that you may keep them, but that you may destroy them; and if you are a wise Israelite remove them to the Land of the Promise, and let the persecutor grieve over the loss of them, and learn through being outwitted that it was vain for him to tyrannize over and keep in bondage better men than himself. If thou doest this, and comest out of Egypt thus, I know well that thou shalt be guided by the pillar of fire and cloud by night and day. The wilderness shall be tamed for thee, and the Sea divided; Pharaoh shall be drowned; bread shall be rained down: the rock shall become a fountain; Amalek shall be conquered, not with arms alone, but with the hostile hand of the righteous forming both prayers and the invincible trophy of the Cross; the River shall be cut off; the sun shall stand still; and the moon be restrained; walls shall be overthrown even without engines; swarms of hornets shall go before thee to make a way for Israel, and to hold the Gentiles in check; and all the other events which are told in the history after these and with these (not to make a long story) shall be given thee of God. Such is the feast thou art keeping today; and in this manner I would have thee celebrate both the Birthday and the Burial of Him Who was born for thee and suffered for thee. Such is the Mystery of the Passover; such are the mysteries sketched by the Law and fulfilled by Christ, the Abolisher of the letter, the Perfecter of the Spirit, who by His Passion taught us how to suffer, and by His glorification grants us to be glorified with Him.

XXII. Now we are to examine another fact and dogma, neglected by most people, but in my judgment well worth enquiring into. To Whom was that Blood offered that was shed for us, and why was It shed? I mean the precious and famous Blood of our God and High priest and Sacrifice. We were detained in bondage by the Evil One, sold under sin, and receiving pleasure in exchange for wickedness. Now, since a ransom belongs only to him who holds in bondage, I ask to whom was this offered, and for what cause? If to the Evil One, lie upon the outrage! If the robber receives ransom, not only from God, but a ransom which consists of God Himself, and has such an illustrious payment for his tyranny, a payment for whose sake it would have been right for him to have left us alone altogether. But if to the Father, I ask first, how? For it was not by Him that we were being oppressed; and next, On what principle did the Blood of His Only begotten Son delight the Father, Who would not receive even Isaac, when he was being offered by his Father, but changed the sacrifice, putting a ram in the place of the human victim? Is it not evident that the Father accepts Him, but neither asked for Him nor demanded Him; but on account of the Incarnation, and because Humanity must be sanctified by the Humanity of God, that He might deliver us Himself, and overcome the tyrant, and draw us to Himself by the mediation of His Son, Who also arranged this to the honor of the Father, Whom it is manifest that He obeys in all things? So much we have said of Christ; the greater part of what we might say shall be reverenced with silence. But that brazen serpent was hung up as a remedy for the biting serpents, not as a type of Him that suffered for us, but as a contrast; and it saved those that looked upon it, not because they believed it to live, but because it was killed, and killed with it the powers that were subject to it, being destroyed as it deserved. And what is the fitting epitaph for it from us? "O death, where is thy sting? O grave, where is thy victory?" Thou art overthrown by the Cross; thou art slain by Him who is the Giver of life; thou art without breath, dead, without motion, even though thou keepest the form of a serpent lifted up on high on a pole.

XXIII. Now we will partake of a Passover which is still typical; though it is plainer than the old one. For that is ever new which is now becoming known. It is ours to learn what is that drinking and that enjoyment, and His to teach and communicate the Word to His disciples. For teaching is food, even to the Giver of food. Come hither then, and let us partake of the Law, but in a Gospel manner, not a literal one; perfectly, not imperfectly; eternally, not temporarily. Let us make our Head, not the earthly Jerusalem, but the heavenly City; not that which is now trodden under foot by armies, but that which is glorified by Angels. Let us sacrifice not young calves, nor lambs that put forth horns and hoofs, in which many parts are destitute of life and feeling; but let us sacrifice to God the sacrifice of praise upon the heavenly Altar, with the heavenly dances; let us hold aside the first veil; let us approach the second, and look into the Holy of Holies. Shall I say that which is a greater thing yet? Let us sacrifice ourselves to God; or rather let us go on sacrificing throughout every day and at every moment. Let us accept anything for the Word's sake. By sufferings let us imitate His Passion: by our blood let us reverence His Blood: let us gladly mount upon the Cross. Sweet are the nails, though they be very painful. For to suffer with Christ and for Christ is better than a life of ease with others.

XXIV. If you are a Simon of Cyrene, take up the Cross and follow. If you are crucified with Him as a robber, acknowledge God as a penitent robber. If even He was numbered among the transgressors for you and your sin, do you become law-abiding for His sake. Worship Him Who was hanged for you, even if you yourself are hanging; make some gain even from your wickedness; purchase salvation by your death; enter with Jesus into Paradise, so that you may learn from what you have fallen. Contemplate the glories that are there; let the murderer die outside with his blasphemies; and if you be a Joseph of Arimathaea, beg the Body from him that crucified Him, make thine own that which cleanses the world. If you be a Nicodemus, the worshipper of God by night, bury Him with spices. If you be a Mary, or another Mary, or a Salome, or a Joanna, weep in the early morning. Be first to see the stone taken away, and perhaps you will see the Angels and Jesus Himself. Say something; hear His Voice. If He say to you, Touch Me not, stand afar off; reverence the Word, but grieve not; for He knoweth those to whom He appeareth first. Keep the feast of the Resurrection; come to the aid of Eve who was first to fall, of Her who first embraced the Christ, and made Him known to the disciples. Be a Peter or a John; hasten to the Sepulcher, running together, running against one another, vying in the noble race. And even if you be beaten in speed, win the victory of zeal; not Looking into the tomb, but Going in. And if, like a Thomas, you were left out when the disciples were assembled to whom Christ shews Himself, when you do see Him be not faithless; and if you do not believe, then believe those who tell you; and if you cannot believe them either, then have confidence in the print of the nails. If He descend into Hell, descend with Him. Learn to know the mysteries of Christ there also, what is the providential purpose of the twofold descent, to save all men absolutely by His manifestation, or there too only them that believe.

XXV. And if He ascend up into Heaven, ascend with Him. Be one of those angels who escort Him, or one of those who receive Him. Bid the gates be lifted up, or be made higher, that they may receive Him, exalted after His Passion. Answer to those who are in doubt because He bears up with Him His body and the tokens of His Passion, which He had not when He came down, and who therefore inquire, "Who is this King of Glory?" that it is the Lord strong and mighty, as in all things that He hath done from time to time and does, so now in His battle and triumph for the sake of Mankind. And give to the doubting of the question the twofold answer. And if they marvel and say as in Isaiah's drama Who is this that cometh from Edom and from the things of earth? Or How are the garments red of Him that is without blood or body, as of one that treads in the full wine-press? Set forth the beauty of the array of the Body that suffered, adorned by the Passion, and made splendid by the Godhead, than which nothing can be more lovely or more beautiful.

XXVI. To this what will those cavilers say, those bitter reasoners about Godhead, those detractors of all things that are praiseworthy, those darkeners of Light, uncultured in respect of Wisdom, for whom Christ died in vain, unthankful creatures, the work of the Evil One. Do you turn this benefit into a reproach to God? Will you deem Him little on this account, that He humbled Himself for your sake, and because to seek for that which had wandered the Good Shepherd, He who layeth down His life for the sheep, came upon the mountains and hills upon which you used to sacrifice, and found the wandering one; and having formal it, took it upon His shoulders, on which He also bore the wood; and having borne it, brought it back to the life above; and having brought it back, numbered it among those who have never strayed. That He lit a candle, His own flesh, and swept the house, by cleansing away the sin of the world, and sought for the coin, the Royal Image that was all covered up with passions, and calls together His friends, the Angelic Powers, at the finding of the coin, and makes them sharers of His joy, as He had before made them sharers of the secret of His Incarnation? That the Light that is exceeding bright should follow the Candle — Forerunner, and the Word, the Voice, and the Bridegroom, the Bridegroom's friend, that prepared for the Lord a peculiar people and cleansed them by the water in preparation for the Spirit? Do you Reproach God with this? Do you conceive of Him as less because He girds Himself with a towel and washes His disciples, and shows that humiliation is the best road to exaltation; because He humbles Himself for the sake of the soul that is bent down to the ground, that He may even exalt with Himself that which is bent double under a weight of sin? How comes it that you do not also charge it upon Him as a crime that He eateth with Publicans and at Publicans' tables, and makes disciples of Publicans that He too may make some gain. And what gain? The salvation of sinners. If so, one must blame the physician for stooping over suffering and putting up with evil smells in order to give health to the sick; and him also who leans over the ditch, that he may, according to the Law, save the beast that has fallen into it.

XXVII. He was sent, but sent according to His Manhood (for He was of two Natures), since He was hungry and thirsty and weary, and was distressed and wept, according to the Laws of human nature. But even if He were sent also as God, what of that? Consider the Mission to be the good pleasure of the Father, to which He refers all that concerns Himself, both that He may honor the Eternal Principle, and that He may avoid the appearance of being a rival God. For He is said on the one hand to have been betrayed, and on the other it is written that He gave Himself up; and so too that He was raised and taken up by the Father, and also that of His own power He rose and ascended. The former belongs to the Good Pleasure, the latter to His own Authority; but you dwell upon all that diminishes Him, while you ignore all that exalts Him. For instance, you score that He suffered, but you do not add "of His own Will." Ah, what things has the Word even now to suffer! By some He is honored as God but confused with the Father; by others He is dishonored as Flesh, and is severed from God. With whom shall He be most angry — or rather which shall He forgive — those who falsely contract Him, or those who divide Him? For the former ought to have made a distinction, and the latter to have made a Union, the one in number, the other in Godhead. Do you stumble at His Flesh? So did the Jews. Do you call Him a Samaritan, and the rest which I will not utter? This did not even the demons, O man more unbelieving than demons, and more stupid than Jews. The Jews recognized the title Son as expressing equal rank; and the demons knew that He who drove them out was God, for they were persuaded by their own experience. But you will not either admit the equality or confess the Godhead. It would have been better for you to have been circumcised and a demoniac — to reduce the matter to an absurdity — than in uncircumcision and robust health to be thus ill and ungodly disposed. But for our war with such men, let it be brought to an end by their returning, however late, to a sound mind, if they will; or else if they will not, let it be postponed to another occasion, if they continue as they are. Anyhow, we will have no fear when contending for the Trinity with the help of the Trinity.

XXVIII. It is now needful for us to sum up our discourse as follows: We were created that we might be made happy. We were made happy when we were created. We were entrusted with Paradise that we might enjoy life. We received a Commandment that we might obtain a good repute by keeping it; not that God did not know what would take place, but because He had laid down the law of Free Will. We were deceived because we were the objects of envy. We were cast out because we transgressed. We fasted because we refused to fast, being overpowered by the Tree of Knowledge. For the Commandment was ancient, coeval with ourselves, and was a kind of education of our souls and curb of luxury, to which we were reasonably made subject, in order that we might recover by keeping it that which we had lost by not keeping it. We needed an Incarnate God, a God put to death, that we might live. We were put to death together with Him, that we might be cleansed; we rose again with Him because we were put to death with Him; we were glorified with Him, because we rose again with Him.

XXIX. Many indeed are the miracles of that time: God crucified; the sun darkened and again rekindled; for it was fitting that the creatures should suffer with their Creator; the veil rent; the Blood and Water shed from His Side; the one as from a man, the other as above man; the rocks rent for the Rock's sake; the dead raised for a pledge of the final Resurrection of all men; the Signs at the Sepulcher and after the Sepulcher, which none can worthily celebrate; and yet none of these equal to the Miracle of my salvation. A few drops of Blood recreate the whole world, and become to all men what rennet is to milk, drawing us together and compressing us into unity.

XXX. But, O Pascha, great and holy and purifier of all the world — for I will speak to thee as to a living person — O Word of God and Light and Life and Wisdom and Might — for I rejoice in all Thy names — O Offspring and Expression and Signet of the Great Mind; O Word conceived and Man contemplated, Who bearest all things, binding them by the Word of Thy power; receive this discourse, not now as firstfruits, but perhaps as the completion of my offerings, a thanksgiving, and at the same time a supplication, that we may suffer no evil beyond those necessary and sacred cares in which our life has been passed; and stay the tyranny of the body over us; (Thou seest, O Lord, how great it is and how it bows me down) or Thine own sentence, if we are to be condemned by Thee. But if we are to be released, in accordance with our desire, and be received into the Heavenly Tabernacle, there too it may be we shall offer Thee acceptable Sacrifices upon Thine Altar, to Father and Word and Holy Ghost; for to Thee belongeth all glory and honor and might, world without end. Amen.

Select Letters of Saint Gregory Nazianzen Archbishop of Constantinople

A Selection from the letters of Saint Gregory Nazianzen, sometime Archbishop of Constantinople

Section 1: Letters on the Apollinarian Controversy

Intoduction

The circumstances which called forth the two letters to Cledonius have already been described in the first section of the General Prolegomena, and it will not be necessary here to add much to what was there said. In the letter to Nectarius, his own successor on the throne of Constantinople, written about A.D. 383, and sometimes reckoned as Orat. XL VI., S. Gregory gives extracts from a work of Apollinarius himself, but without mentioning the rifle of the book. In this treatise the fundamental errors of the heresy (see Proleg. c. 1, p. 172) are laid down. Apollinarius, according to S. Gregory, declares that the Son of God was from all eternity clothed with a human body, and not from the time of His conception only by the Blessed Virgin; but that this humanity of God is without human mind, the place of which was supplied by the Godhead of the Only-begotten. And he goes even further and ascribes passibility and mortality to the very Godhead of Christ. Therefore S. Gregory earnestly protests against any toleration being granted to these heretics, or even permission to hold their assemblies; for, he says, toleration or permission would certainly be regarded by them as a condonation of their doctrinal position, and a condemnation of that of the Church. Dr. Ullman, however, thinks that while S. Gregory was certainly speaking the truth in saying that he had in his hands a pamphlet by Apollinarius, yet that he, perhaps unconsciously, exaggerated the heretical character of its contents, pushing its statements to consequences which Apollinarius would have repudiated. The one purpose of the latter was, in Dr. Ullman' s view, to safeguard the doctrine of the Unity of Christ; and he thought that the orthodox expression of Two Whole and Perfect Natures tended to a Nestorian division of the Person of Christ; and so he used language which certainly seemed to confound the natures, or at any rate to make the Incarnation imperfect, inasmuch as a Christ in Whom the human mind is absent, and its place filled up by the Godhead of the Son, cannot be said to be perfect Man. But while Epiphanius mentions these extravagances of the heresy, and does so with a lingering feeling of regret for the lapse of so good a man whose services in the past had been of so much value to the Church, yet, in the spirit common to Ecclesiastical authorities of the time, he would rather ascribe them to an expansion of Apollinarius' teaching by his younger disciples who did not really understand what Apollinarius himself meant.

Olympius, to whom the last of this series is addressed, was Governor of Cappadocia Secunda in A.D. 382. He was a man for whom S. Gregory had a very high esteem, and with whom he was upon terms of close friendship, as will be seen from other letters of

Gregory to him in another division of this Selection. The occasion of the present letter was the necessity to appeal to the secular power for aid to punish a sect of Apollinarians at Nazianzus, who had ventured to take advantage of S. Gregory's absence at the Baths of Xanxaris to procure the consecration of a Bishop of their own way of thinking. Technically the See was vacant, but the administration had been committed to Gregory by the Bishops of the Province, and though he, foreseeing some such attempt on the part of the heretics, had been very earnest in pressing upon the Metropolitan and his Comprovincials the necessity of filling this throne by a canonical election, yet he was by no means prepared to hand over the authority, with which he had been invested, to an irregularly elected and uncanonically consecrated heretic.

To Nectarius, Bishop of Constantinople (Letter 202)

The Care of God, which throughout the time before us guarded the Churches, seems to have utterly forsaken this present life. And my soul is immersed to such a degree by calamities that the private sufferings of my own life hardly seem to be worth reckoning among evils (though they are so numerous and great, that if they befell anyone else I should think them unbearable); but I can only look at the common sufferings of the Churches; for if at the present crisis some pains be not taken to find a remedy for them, things will gradually get into an altogether desperate condition. Those who follow the heresy of Arius or Eudoxius (I cannot say who stirred them up to this folly) are making a display of their disease, as if they had attained some degree of confidence by collecting congregations as if by permission. And they of the Macedonian party have reached such a pitch of folly that they are arrogating to themselves the name of Bishops, and are wandering about our districts babbling of Eleusius as to their ordinations. Our bosom evil, Eunomius, is no longer content with merely existing; but unless he can draw away everyone with him to his ruinous heresy, he thinks himself an injured man. All this, however, is endurable. The most grievous item of all in the woes of the Church is the boldness of the Apollinarians, whom your Holiness has overlooked, I know not how, when providing themselves with authority to hold meetings on an equality with myself. However, you being, as you are, thoroughly instructed by the grace of God in the Divine Mysteries on all points, are well informed, not only as to the advocacy of the true faith, but also as to all those arguments which have been devised by the heretics against the sound faith; and yet perhaps it will not be unseasonable that your Excellency should hear from my littleness that a pamphlet by Apollinarius has come into my hands, the contents of which surpass all heretical pravity. For he asserts that the Flesh which the Only-begotten Son assumed in the Incarnation for the remodeling of our nature was no new acquisition, but that that carnal nature was in the Son from the beginning. And he puts forward as a witness to this monstrous assertion a garbled quotation from the Gospels, namely, No man hath Ascended up into Heaven save He which came down from Heaven, even the Son of Man which is in Heaven. As though even before He came down He was the Son of Man, and when He came down He brought with Him that Flesh, which it appears He had in Heaven, as though it had existed before the ages, and been joined with His Essence. For he alleges another saying of an Apostle, which he cuts off from the whole body of its context, that The Second Man is the Lord from Heaven. Then he assumes that that Man who came down from above is without a mind, but that the Godhead of the Only -begotten fulfills the function of mind, and is the third part of this human composite, inasmuch as soul and body are in it on its human side, but not mind, the place of which is taken by God the Word. This is not yet the most serious part of it; that which is most terrible of all is that he declares that the Only -begotten God, the Judge of all, the Prince of Life, the Destroyer of Death, is mortal, and underwent the Passion in His proper Godhead; and that in the three days' death of His body, His Godhead also was put to death with His body, and thus was raised again from the dead by the Father. It would be tedious to go through all the other propositions which he adds to these monstrous absurdities. Now, if they who hold such views have authority to meet, your Wisdom approved in Christ must see that, inasmuch as we do not approve their views, any permission of assembly granted to them is nothing less than a declaration that their view is thought more true than ours. For if they are permitted to teach their view as godly men, and with all confidence to preach their doctrine, it is manifest that the doctrine of the Church has been condemned, as though the truth were on their side. For nature does not admit of two contrary doctrines on the same subject being both true. How then could your noble and lofty mind submit to suspend your usual courage in regard to the correction of so great an evil? But even though there is no precedent for such a course, let your inimitable perfection in virtue stand up at a crisis like the present, and teach our most pious Emperor, that no gain will come from his zeal for the Church on other points if he allows such an evil to gain strength from freedom of speech for the subversion of sound faith.

To Cledonius the priest against Apollinarius (Letter 101)

To our most reverend and God-Beloved brother and fellow-priest Clendonius, Gregory, Greeting in the Lord.

I desire to learn what is this fashion of innovation in things Concerning the Church, which allows anyone who likes, or the passerby, as the Bible says, to tear asunder the flock that has been well led, and to plunder it by larcenous attacks, or rather by piratical and fallacious teachings. For if our present assailants had any ground for condemning us in regard of the faith, it would not have been right for them, even in that case, to have ventured on such a course without giving us notice. They ought rather to have first persuaded us, or to have been willing to be persuaded by us (if at least any account is to be taken of us as fearing God, laboring for the faith, and helping the Church), and then, if at all, to innovate; but then perhaps there would be an excuse for their outrageous conduct. But since our faith has been proclaimed, both in writing and without writing, here and in distant parts, in times of danger and of safety, how comes it that some make such attempts, and that others keep silence?

The most grievous part of it is not (though this too is shocking) that the men instill their own heresy into simpler souls by means of those who are worse; but that they also tell lies about us and say that we share their opinions and sentiments; thus baiting their hooks, and by this cloak villainously fulfilling their will, and making our simplicity, which looked upon them as brothers and not as foes, into a support of their wickedness. And not only so, but they also assert, as I am told, that they have been received by the Western Synod, by which they were formerly condemned, as is well known to everyone. If, however, those who hold the views of Apollinarius have either now or formerly been received, let them prove it and we will be content. For it is evident that they can only have been so received as assenting to the Orthodox Faith, for this were an impossibility on any other terms. And they can surely prove it, either by the minutes of the Synod, or by Letters of Communion, for this is the regular custom of Synods. But if it is mere words, and an invention of their own, devised for the sake of appearances and to give them weight with the multitude through the credit of the persons, teach them to hold their tongues, and confute them; for we believe that such a task is well suited to your manner of life and orthodoxy. Do not let the men deceive themselves and others with the assertion that the "Man of the Lord," as they call Him, Who is rather our Lord and God, is without human mind. For we do not sever the Man from the Godhead, but we lay down as a dogma the Unity and Identity of Person, Who of old was not Man but God, and the Only Son before all ages, unmingled with body or anything corporeal; but Who in these last days has assumed Manhood also for our salvation; passible in His Flesh, impassible in His Godhead; circumscript in the body, uncircumscript in the Spirit; at once earthly and heavenly, tangible and intangible, comprehensible and incomprehensible; that by One and the Same Person, Who was perfect Man and also God, the entire humanity fallen through sin might be created anew.

If anyone does not believe that Holy Mary is the Mother of God, he is severed from the Godhead. If anyone should assert that He passed through the Virgin as through a channel, and was not at once divinely and humanly formed in her (divinely, because without the intervention of a man; humanly, because in accordance with the laws of gestation), he is in like manner godless. If any assert that the Manhood was formed and afterward was clothed with the Godhead, he too is to be condemned. For this were not a Generation of God, but a shirking of generation. If any introduce the notion of Two Sons, one of God the Father, the other of the Mother, and discredits the Unity and Identity, may he lose his part in the adoption promised to those who believe aright. For God and Man are two natures, as also soul and body are; but there are not two Sons or two Gods. For neither in this life are there two manhoods; though Paul speaks in some such language of the inner and outer man. And (if I am to speak concisely) the Savior is made of elements which are distinct from one another (for the invisible is not the same with the visible, nor the timeless with that which is subject to time), yet He is not two Persons. God forbid! For both natures are one by the combination, the Deity being made Man, and the Manhood deified or however one should express it. And I say different Elements, because it is the reverse of what is the case in the Trinity; for There we acknowledge different Persons so as not to confound the persons; but not different Elements, for the Three are One and the same in Godhead.

If any should say that it wrought in Him by grace as in a Prophet, but was not and is not united with Him in Essence — let him be empty of the Higher Energy, or rather full of the opposite. If any worship not the Crucified, let him be Anathema and be numbered among the Deicides. If any assert that He was made perfect by works, or that after His Baptism, or after His Resurrection from the dead, He was counted worthy of an adoptive Sonship, like those whom the Greeks interpolate as added to the ranks of the gods, let him be anathema. For that which has a beginning or a progress or is made perfect, is not God, although the expressions may be used of His gradual manifestation. If any assert that He has now put off His holy flesh, and that His Godhead is stripped of the body, and deny that He is now with His body and will come again with it, let him not see the glory of His Coming. For where is His body now, if not with Him Who assumed it? For it is not laid by in the sun, according to the babble of the Manichaeans, that it should be honored by a dishonor; nor was it poured forth into the air and dissolved, us is the nature of a voice or the flow of an odor, or the course of a lightning flash that never stands. Where in that case were His being handled after the Resurrection, or His being seen hereafter by them that pierced Him, for Godhead is in its nature invisible. Nay; He will come with His body — so I have learnt — such as He was seen by His Disciples in the Mount, or as he shewed Himself for a moment, when his Godhead overpowered the carnality. And as we say this to disarm suspicion, so we write the other to correct the novel teaching. If anyone assert that His flesh came down from heaven, and is not from hence, nor of us though above us, let him be anathema. For the words, The Second Man is the Lord from Heaven; and, As is the Heavenly, such are they that are Heavenly; and, No man hath ascended up into Heaven save He which came down from Heaven, even the Son of Man which is in Heaven; and the like, are to be understood as said on account of the Union with the heavenly; just as that All Things were made by Christ, and that Christ dwelleth in your hearts is said, not of the visible nature which belongs to God, but of what is perceived by the mind, the names being mingled like the natures, and flowing into one another, according to the law of their intimate union.

If anyone has put his trust in Him as a Man without a human mind, he is really bereft of mind, and quite unworthy of salvation. For that which He has not assumed He has not healed; but that which is united to His Godhead is also saved. If only half Adam fell, then that which Christ assumes and saves may be half also; but if the whole of his nature fell, it must be united to the whole nature of Him that was begotten, and so be saved as a whole. Let them not, then, begrudge us our complete salvation, or clothe the Savior only with bones and nerves and the portraiture of humanity. For if His Manhood is without soul, even the Arians admit this, that they may attribute His Passion to the Godhead, as that which gives motion to the body is also that which suffers. But if He has a soul, and yet is without a mind, how is He man, for man is not a mindless animal? And this would necessarily involve that while His form and tabernacle was human, His soul should be that of a horse or an ox, or some other of the brute creation. This, then, would be what He saves; and I have been deceived by the Truth, and led to boast of an honor which had been bestowed upon another. But if His Manhood is intellectual and not without mind, let them cease to be thus really mindless. But, says such an one, the Godhead took the place of the human intellect. How does this touch me? For Godhead joined to flesh alone is not man, nor to soul alone, nor to both apart from intellect, which is the most essential part of man. Keep then the whole man, and mingle Godhead therewith, that you may benefit me in my completeness. But, he asserts, He could not contain Two perfect Natures. Not if you only look at Him in a bodily fashion. For a bushel measure will not hold two bushels, nor will the space of one body hold two or more bodies. But if you will look at what is mental and incorporeal, remember that I in my one personality can contain soul and reason and mind and the Holy Spirit; and before me this world, by which I mean the system of things visible and invisible, contained Father, Son, and Holy Ghost. For such is the nature of intellectual Existences, that they can mingle with one another and with bodies, incorporeally and invisibly. For many sounds are comprehended by one ear; and the eyes of many are occupied by the same visible objects, and the smell by odors; nor are the senses narrowed by each other, or crowded out, nor the objects of sense diminished by the multitude of the perceptions. But where is there mind of man or angel so perfect in comparison of the Godhead that the presence of the greater must crowd out the other? The light is nothing compared with the sun, nor a little damp compared with a river, that we must first do away with the lesser, and take the light from a house, or the moisture from the earth, to enable it to contain the greater and more perfect. For how shall one thing contain two completenesses, either the house, the sunbeam and the sun, or the earth, the moisture and the river? Here is matter for inquiry; for indeed the question is worthy of much consideration. Do they not know, then, that what is perfect by comparison with one thing may be imperfect by comparison with another, as a hill compared with a mountain, or a grain of mustard seed with a bean or any other of the larger seeds, although it may be called larger than any of the same kind? Or, if you like, an Angel compared with God, or a man with an Angel. So our mind is perfect and commanding, but only in respect of soul and body; not absolutely perfect; and a servant and a subject of God, not a sharer of His Princedom and honor. So Moses was a God to Pharaoh, but a servant of God, as it is written; and the stars which illumine the night are hidden by the Sun, so much that you could not even know of their existence by daylight; and a little torch brought near a great blaze is neither destroyed, nor seen, nor extinguished; but is all one blaze, the bigger one prevailing over the other.

But, it may be said, our mind is subject to condemnation. What then of our flesh? Is that not subject to condemnation? You must therefore either set aside the latter on account of sin, or admit the former on account of salvation. If He assumed the worse that He might sanctify it by His incarnation, may He not assume the better that it may be sanctified by His becoming Man? If the clay was leavened and has become a new lump, O ye wise men, shall not the Image be leavened and mingled with God, being deified by His Godhead? And I will add this also: If the mind was utterly rejected, as prone to sin and subject to damnation, and for this reason He assumed a body but left out the mind, then there is an excuse for them who sin with the mind; for the witness of God — according to you — has shewn the impossibility of healing it. Let me state the greater results. You, my good sir, dishonor my mind (you a Sarcolater, if I am an Anthropolater that you may tie God down to the Flesh, since He cannot be otherwise tied; and therefore you take away the wall of partition. But what is my theory, who am but an ignorant man, and no Philosopher. Mind is mingled with mind, as nearer and more closely related, and through it with flesh, being a Mediator between God and carnality.

Further let us see what is their account of the assumption of Manhood, or the assumption of Flesh, as they call it. If it was in order that God, otherwise incomprehensible, might be comprehended, and might converse with men through His Flesh as through a veil, their mask and the drama which they represent is a pretty one, not to say that it was open to Him to converse with us in other ways, as of old, in the burning bush and in the appearance of a man. But if it was that He might destroy the condemnation by sanctifying like by like, then as He needed flesh for the sake of the flesh which had incurred condemnation, and soul for the sake of our soul, so, too, He needed mind for the sake of mind, which not only fell in Adam, but was the first to be affected, as the doctors say of illnesses. For that which received the command was that which failed to keep the command, and that which failed to keep it was that also which dared to transgress; and that which transgressed was that which stood most in need of salvation; and that which needed salvation was that which also He took upon Him. Therefore, Mind was taken upon Him. This has now been demonstrated, whether they like it or no, by, to use their own expression, geometrical and necessary proofs. But you are acting as if, when a man's eye had been injured and his foot had been injured in consequence, you were to attend to the foot and leave the eye uncared for; or as if, when a painter had drown something badly, you were to alter the picture, but to pass over the artist as if he had succeeded. But if they, overwhelmed by these arguments, take refuge in the proposition that it is possible for God to save man even apart from mind, why, I suppose that it would be possible for Him to do so also apart from flesh by a mere act of will, just as He works all other things, and has wrought them without body. Take away, then, the flesh as well as the mind, that your monstrous folly may be complete. But they are deceived by the latter, and, therefore, they run to the flesh, because they do not know the custom of Scripture. We will teach them this also.

For what need is there even to mention to those who know it, the fact that everywhere in Scripture he is called Man, and the Son of Man?

If, however, they rely on the passage, The Word was made Flesh and dwelt among us, and because of this erase the noblest part of Man (as cobblers do the thicker part of skins) that they may join together God and Flesh, it is time for them to say that God is God only of flesh, and not of souls, because it is written, "As Thou hast given Him power over all Flesh," and "Unto Thee shall all Flesh come;" and "Let all Flesh bless His holy Name," meaning every Man. Or, again, they must suppose that our fathers went down into Egypt without bodies and invisible, and that only the Soul of Joseph was imprisoned by Pharaoh, because it is written, " They went down into Egypt with threescore and fifteen Souls," and "The iron entered into his Soul," a thing which could not be bound. They who argue thus do not know that such expressions are used by Synecdoche, declaring the whole by the part, as when Scripture says that the young ravens call upon God, to indicate the whole feathered race; or Pleiades, Hesperus, and Arcturus are mentioned, instead of all the Stars and His Providence over them.

Moreover, in no other way was it possible for the Love of God toward us to be manifested than by making mention of our flesh, and that for our sake He descended even to our lower part. For that flesh is less precious than soul, everyone who has a spark of sense will acknowledge. And so the passage, The Word was made Flesh, seems to me to be equivalent to that in which it is said that He was made sin, or a curse for us; not that the Lord was transformed into either of these, how could He be? But because by taking them upon Him He took away our sins and bore our iniquities. This, then, is sufficient to say at the present time for the sake of clearness and of being understood by the many. And I write it, not with any desire to compose a treatise, but only to check the progress of deceit; and if it is thought well, I will give a fuller account of these matters at greater length.

But there is a matter which is graver than these, a special point which it is necessary that I should not pass over. I would they were even cut off that trouble you, and would reintroduce a second Judaism, and a second circumcision, and a second system of sacrifices. For if this be done, what hinders Christ also being born again to set them aside, and again being betrayed by Judas, and crucified and buried, and rising again, that all may be fulfilled in the same order, like the Greek system of cycles, in which the same revolutions of the stars bring round the same events? For what the method of selection is, in accordance with which some of the events are to occur and others to be omitted, let these wise men who glory in the multitude of their books shew us.

But since, puffed up by their theory of the Trinity, they falsely accuse us of being unsound in the Faith and entice the multitude, it is necessary that people should know that Apollinarius, while granting the Name of Godhead to the Holy Ghost, did not preserve the Power of the Godhead. For to make the Trinity consist of Great, Greater, and Greatest, as of Light, Ray, and Sun, the Spirit and the Son and the Father (as is clearly stated in his writings), is a ladder of Godhead not leading to Heaven, but down from Heaven. But we recognize God the Father and the Son and the Holy Ghost, and these not as bare titles, dividing inequalities of ranks or of power, but as there is one and the same title, so there is one nature and one substance in the Godhead.

But if anyone who thinks we have spoken rightly on this subject reproaches us with holding communion with heretics, let him prove that we are open to this charge, and we will either convince him or retire. But it is not safe to make any innovation before judgment is given, especially in a matter of such importance, and connected with so great issues. We have protested and continue to protest this before God and men. And not even now, be well assured, should we have written this, if we had not seen that the Church was being torn asunder and divided, among their other tricks, by their present synagogue of vanity. But if anyone when we say and protest this, either from some advantage they will thus gain, or through fear of men, or monstrous littleness of mind, or through some neglect of pastors and governors, or through love of novelty and proneness to innovations, rejects us as unworthy of credit, and attaches himself to such men, and divides the noble body of the Church, he shall bear his judgment, whoever he may be, and shall give account to God in the day of judgment. But if their long books, and their new Psalters, contrary to that of David, and the grace of their meters, are taken for a third Testament, we too will compose Psalms, and will write much in meter. For we also think we have the spirit of God, if indeed this is a gift of the Spirit, and not a human novelty. This I will that thou declare publicly, that we may not be held responsible, as overlooking such an evil, and as though this wicked doctrine received food and strength from our indifference.

Against Apollinarius: The 2nd Letter to Cledonius (Ep 102)

Forasmuch as many persons have come to your Reverence seeking confirmation of their faith, and therefore you have affectionately asked me to put forth a brief definition and rifle of my opinion, I therefore write to your Reverence, what indeed you knew before, that I never have and never can honor anything above the Nicene Faith, that of the Holy Fathers who met there to destroy the Arian heresy; but am, and by God's help ever will be, of that faith; completing in detail that which was incompletely said by them concerning the Holy Ghost; for that question had not then been mooted, namely, that we are to believe that the Father, Son, and Holy Ghost are of one Godhead, thus confessing the Spirit also to be God. Receive then to communion those who think and teach thus, as I also do; but those who are otherwise minded refuse, and hold them as strangers to God and the Catholic

Church. And since a question has also been mooted concerning the Divine Assumption of humanity, or Incarnation, state this also clearly to all concerning me, that I join in One the Son, who was begotten of the Father, and afterward of the Virgin Mary, and that I do not call Him two Sons, but worship Him as One and the same in undivided Godhead and honor. But if anyone does not assent to this statement, either now or hereafter, he shall give account to God at the day of judgment.

Now, what we object and oppose to their mindless opinion about His Mind is this, to put it shortly; for they are almost alone in the condition which they lay down, as it is through want of mind that they mutilate His mind. But, that they may not accuse us of having once accepted but of now repudiating the faith of their beloved Vitalius which he handed in writing at the request of the blessed Bishop Damasus of Rome, I will give a short explanation on this point also. For these men, when they are theologizing among their genuine disciples, and those who are initiated into their secrets, like the Manichaeans among those whom they call the "Elect," expose the full extent of their disease, and scarcely allow flesh at all to the Savior. But when they are refuted and pressed with the common answers about the Incarnation which the Scripture presents, they confess indeed the orthodox words, but they do violence to the sense; for they acknowledge the Manhood to be neither without soul nor without reason nor without mind, nor imperfect, but they bring in the Godhead to supply the soul and reason and mind, as though It had mingled Itself only with His flesh, and not with the other properties belonging to us men; although His sinlessness was far above us, and was the cleansing of our passions.

Thus, then, they interpret wrongly the words, But we have the Mind of Christ, and very absurdly, when they say that His Godhead is the mind of Christ, and not understanding the passage as we do, namely, that they who have purified their mind by the imitation of the mind which the Savior took of us, and, as far as may be, have attained conformity with it, are said to have the mind of Christ; just as they might be testified to have the flesh of Christ who have trained their flesh, and in this respect have become of the same body and partakers of Christ; and so he says "As we have borne the image of the earth we shall also bear the image of the heavenly." And so they declare that the Perfect Man is not He who was in all points tempted like as we are yet without sin; but the mixture of God and Flesh. For what, say they, can be more perfect than this?

They play the same trick with the word that describes the Incarnation, viz.: He was made Man, explaining it to mean, not, He was in the human nature with which He surrounded Himself, according to the Scripture, He knew what was in man; but teaching that it means, He consorted and conversed with men, and taking refuge in the expression which says that He was seen on Earth and conversed with Men. And what can anyone contend further? They who take away the Humanity and the Interior Image cleanse by their newly invented mask only our outside, and that which is seen; so far in conflict with themselves that at one time, for the sake of the flesh, they explain all the rest in a gross and carnal manner (for it is from hence that they have derived their second Judaism and their silly thousand years delight in paradise, and almost the idea that we shall resume again the same conditions after these same thousand years); and at another time they bring in His flesh as a phantom rather than a reality, as not having been subjected to any of our experiences, not even such as are free from sin; and use for this purpose the apostolic expression, understood and spoken in a sense which is not apostolic, that our Savior was made in the likeness of Men and found in fashion as a Man, as though by these words was expressed, not the human form, but some delusive phantom and appearance.

Since then these expressions, rightly understood, make for orthodoxy, but wrongly interpreted are heretical, what is there to be surprised at if we received the words of Vitalius in the more orthodox sense; our desire that they should be so meant persuading us, though others are angry at the intention of his writings? This is, I think, the reason why Damasus himself, having been subsequently better informed, and at the same time learning that they hold by their former explanations, excommunicated them and overturned their written confession of faith with an Anathema; as well as because he was vexed at the deceit which he had suffered from them through simplicity.

Since, then, they have been openly convicted of this, let them not be angry, but let them be ashamed of themselves; and let them not slander us, but abase themselves and wipe off from their portals that great and marvelous proclamation and boast of their orthodoxy, meeting all who go in at once with the question and distinction that we must worship, not a God-bearing Man, but a flesh-bearing God. What could be more unreasonable than this, though these new heralds of truth think a great deal of the title? For though it has a certain sophistical grace through the quickness of its antithesis, and a sort of juggling quackery grateful to the uninstructed, yet it is the most absurd of absurdities and the most foolish of follies. For if one were to change the word Man or Flesh into God (the first would please us, the second them), and then were to use this wonderful antithesis, so divinely recognized, what conclusion should we arrive at? That we must worship, not a God-bearing Flesh, but a Man-bearing God. O monstrous absurdity! They proclaim to us today a wisdom hidden ever since the time of Christ — a thing worthy of our tears. For if the faith began thirty years ago, when nearly four hundred years had passed since Christ was manifested, vain all that time will have been our Gospel, and vain our faith; in vain will the Martyrs have borne their witness, and in vain have so many and so great Prelates presided over the people; and Grace is a matter of meters and not of the faith.

And who will not marvel at their learning, in that on their own authority they divide the things of Christ, and assign to His Manhood such sayings as He was born, He was tempted, He was hungry, He was thirsty, He was wearied, He was asleep; but reckon to His Divinity such as these: He was glorified by Angels, He overcame the Tempter, He fed the people in the wilderness, and He fed them in such a manner, and He walked upon the sea; and say on the one hand that the "Where have ye laid Lazarus?" belongs to us, but the loud voice "Lazarus, Come Forth" and the raising him that had been four days dead, is above our nature; and that while the "He was in an Agony, He was crucified, He was buried," belongs to the Veil, on the other hand, "He was confident, He rose again, He ascended," belong to the Inner Treasure; and then they accuse us of introducing two natures, separate or conflicting, and of dividing the supernatural and wondrous Union. They ought, either not to do that of which they accuse us, or not to accuse us of that which they do; so at least if they are resolved to be consistent and not to propound at once their own and their opponents' principles. Such is their want of reason; it conflicts both with itself and with the truth to such an extent that they are neither conscious nor ashamed of it when they fall out with themselves. Now, if anyone thinks that we write all this willingly and not upon compulsion, and that we are dissuading from unity, and not doing our utmost to promote it, let him know that he is very much mistaken, and has not made at all a good guess at our desires, for nothing is or ever has been more valuable in our eyes than peace, as the facts themselves prove; though their actions and brawlings against us altogether exclude unanimity.

Letter 125 to Olympus

Even hoar hairs have something to learn; and old age, it would seem, cannot in all respects be trusted for wisdom. I at any rate, knowing better than anyone, as I did, the thoughts and the heresy of the Apollinarians, and seeing that their folly was intolerable; yet thinking that I could tame them by patience and soften them by degrees, I let my tropes make me eager to attain this object. But, as it seems, I overlooked the fact that I was making them worse, and injuring the Church by my untimely philosophy. For gentleness does not put bad men out of countenance. And now if it had been possible for me to teach you this myself, I should not have hesitated, you may be sure, even to undertake a journey beyond my strength to throw myself at the feet of your Excellency. But since my illness has brought me too far, and it has become necessary for me to try the hot baths of Xanxaris at the advice of my medical men, I send a letter to represent me. These wicked and utterly abandoned men have dared, in addition to all their other misdeeds, either to summon, or to make a bad use of the passage (I am not prepared to say precisely which) of certain Bishops, deprived by the whole Synod of the Eastern and Western Church; and, in violation of all Imperial Ordinances, and of your commands, to confer the name of Bishop on a certain individual of their own misbelieving and deceitful crew; encouraged to do so, as I believe, by nothing so much as my great infirmity; for I must mention this. If this is to be tolerated, your Excellency will tolerate it, and I too will bear it, as I have often before. But if it is serious, and not

to be endured by our most august Emperors, pray punish what has been done —
though more mildly than such madness merits.